ROUTLEDGE LIBRARY EDITIONS:
HEALTH, DISEASE & SOCIETY

I0028284

Volume 12

INDIA'S HISTORICAL DEMOGRAPHY

INDIA'S HISTORICAL DEMOGRAPHY

Studies in Famine, Disease and Society

Edited by
TIM DYSON

Routledge
Taylor & Francis Group

LONDON AND NEW YORK

First published in the United Kingdom in 1989 by Curzon Press Ltd.

This edition first published in 2022
by Routledge
4 Park Square, Milton Park, Abingdon, Oxon OX14 4RN

and by Routledge
605 Third Avenue, New York, NY 10158

Routledge is an imprint of the Taylor & Francis Group, an informa business

© 1989 Centre of South Asian Studies, SOAS

British Library Cataloguing in Publication Data
A catalogue record for this book is available from the British Library

ISBN: 978-0-367-52469-2 (Set)
ISBN: 978-1-032-24476-1 (Volume 12) (hbk)
ISBN: 978-1-032-24489-1 (Volume 12) (pbk)
ISBN: 978-1-003-27876-4 (Volume 12) (ebk)

DOI: 10.4324/9781003278764

Publisher's Note
The publisher has gone to great lengths to ensure the quality of this reprint but points out that some imperfections in the original copies may be apparent.

Disclaimer
The publisher has made every effort to trace copyright holders and would welcome correspondence from those they have been unable to trace.

INDIA'S HISTORICAL DEMOGRAPHY
Studies in Famine, Disease and Society

Edited by
TIM DYSON

CURZON PRESS
THE RIVERDALE COMPANY

First published 1989 in the United Kingdom by
Curzon Press Ltd., 42 Gray's Inn Road, London WC1
ISBN 0 7007 0206 7

First published 1989 in the United States of America by
The Riverdale Company, 5506 Kenilworth Avenue, Riverdale, MD 20737
ISBN 0 913215 43 0

British Library Cataloguing in Publication Data
India's historical demography: studies in famine, disease and society
(Collected papers on South Asia, ISSN 0141-0156; no. 8)
1. India. Population, history. Demographic aspects. Socioeconomic aspects
I. Dyson, T. (Tim) II Series
304.6'0954

Exclusively distributed in India by
Manohar Book Service
1 Ansari Road, Daryaganj
New Delhi-110002

Printed in Great Britain by
Billing & Sons Ltd, Worcester

CONTENTS

CONTRIBUTORS

David Arnold, Professor, Department of History, School of Oriental and African Studies, Malet Street, London, WC1E 7HP, U.K.

Alice W. Clark, Research Associate, Graduate Group in Demography, Program in Population Research, 2234 Piedmont Avenue, University of California, Berkeley, California, 94720, U.S.A.

Simon Commander, Research Fellow, Overseas Development Institute, Inner Circle, Regent's Park, London, NW1 4NS, U.K.

Nigel Crook, Lecturer, Department of Economics and Political Studies, School of Oriental and African Studies, Malet Street, London, WC1E 7HP, U.K.

Kingsley Davis, Senior Research Fellow, Hoover Institution, Stanford, California, 94305, U.S.A.

Tim Dyson, Reader, Department of Population Studies, London School of Economics, Houghton Street, London, WC2A 2AE, U.K.

Deborah Guz, Economics Officer, Commonwealth Secretariat, Marlborough House, Pall Mall, London, SW1 5HX, U.K.

Roland Lardinois, Chargé de Recherche, Centre D'Études De L'Inde Et De L'Asie Du Sud, 54 Boulevard Raspail, 75006 Paris, France.

P. N. Mari Bhat, Associate Fellow, Centre for Development Studies, Ulloor, Trivandrum 695 001, India.

Ian D. Mills, Government Statistician, Office of Population Censuses and Surveys, St. Catherine's House, Kingsway, London, WC2B 6JP, U.K.

EDITOR'S NOTE

The idea of assembling a volume of papers dealing with India's historical demography has been in my mind for several years. But its realization — in the form of this book — has only been possible with help and encouragement from a number of people. Nigel Crook provided me with the initial stimulus to translate thought into action, and begin the task of actually canvassing potential contributors. A period as Visiting Fellow in the Demography Department of the Australian National University, at the invitation of Jack Caldwell, was specifically devoted to editing duties. Others, either in London or Canberra, who have assisted the enterprise in various ways include Doreen Castle, Betty Cohen, Kae Mardus and Stella Wilks. At the LSE, especial thanks go to Marilyn Hynes for diligently typing so much of the manuscript, and to Jane Pugh and Gary Llewellyn for providing such excellent final versions of the diagrams. Perhaps most of all, I am indebted to Kingsley Davis for kindly agreeing to contribute a Foreword.

There is certainly sufficient demography here to justify the book's title. But, clearly, the volume can hardly claim to be comprehensive regarding such a huge subject. The reader will also discover that the papers herein illustrate different approaches to this field of study. Some reflect the mainly qualitative perspective of the historian. Others are demographic and technical. A third group reflect both historical and demographic methods. Given the formative stage of Indian historical demography this variety of approach is probably to be expected. But one of the main purposes behind the book is to enlarge the area of common ground, hopefully to the advantage of future research. We also hope that the volume will inspire greater interest and work in the field, perhaps particularly among India's own talented fellowship of demographers.

Tim Dyson

FOREWORD

Not only historical demographers but also historians of other kinds — economic, medical, political — will find a feast awaiting them in this symposium. Each chapter opens its own particular window on one of the world's oldest and most complex agrarian civilizations at the very moment in history (roughly the century from 1850 to 1950) when that civilization was gradually being transformed by the impact of European industrialism. One gets a glimpse of the evolutionary process — at bottom a demographic process — by which one stage of civilization replaces another.

In reading the chapters, I am struck again, as I have been in the past, by the complexity and tenacity of mature agrarian societies. As exemplified by India, and as classical Greece and Rome remind us, a remarkable superstructure can be built on rudimentary foundations — land, human and animal muscle, handicrafts, and communicative arts. It is this superstructure, its parts interdependent, that makes possible the tenacity of agrarian systems. Despite devastating droughts, famines, epidemics, wars, and civil strife, despite crowding and chronic poverty, illiteracy and superstition, life goes on. Most of the studies in the present book — six out of ten chapters — deal with calamities, but after each calamity the survivors regroup and rebuild, starting the cycle over again.

Impressed by this resilience, one is tempted to view Indian civilization as a long-enduring static system in which the centuries roll by monotonously with little or no change. The truth, however, is different, and demographic history provides an excellent basis for demonstrating it. In the first place, when viewed in evolutionary perspective, agriculture itself — starting some 10,000 years ago — is relatively new. The appearance of mature agrarian civilization is newer still — dating from some 6,000 years ago. Both periods are thus too short to have had much influence on man's genetic constitution. Agrarianism is therefore not a trait of *Homo sapiens*. It is a man-made institutional system to which, in many ways, human beings are poorly adapted. In the second place, the notion of stability in agrarian systems is an illusion created by distance. When one gets close to details, as the present volume does, one finds tremendous short-term fluctuations. Looked at demographically, these fluctuations are created fundamentally by the lack of control over mortality. Fertility can be controlled by such measures as regulating the age at marriage, prolonging lactation, and practising abstinence, abortion, and infanticide. Mortality, on the other hand, can suddenly explode due to one or another of the numerous calamities to which pre-industrial people are subject.

In the third place, the idea of fixity in agrarian demography tends to obscure the fascinating interplay between agriculturism and world population change. As noted several times in the present volume, there is no 'natural' fertility or mortality to be found in Indian history, nor any 'normal' rate of population growth. Instead, one finds data that can be interpreted in the light of the stage of development achieved and the moment in history when that stage was reached. In long-term perspective, the unprecedented world population growth during the last 10,000 years came from the invention and spread rather than the simple practice of farm technology. A purely agricultural regime cannot keep piling people on the land. To accommodate more people, it must add new land or improve cultivation. In pre-industrial history it was the addition of new land that mainly facilitated the global rise of population. In older farming areas such as India, however, saturation of the land seemingly led to increased mortality and, to some extent, lower fertility, with approximately zero long-run population growth. But in India, as elsewhere, industrialization began before agriculture had finished spreading. This created a double boost to subsistence, because the industrial system did not displace agriculture the way agriculture had displaced hunting and gathering. Instead, it marvellously improved the technology of cultivation and facilitated the rapid spread of agriculture to virgin regions. Until around 1955 the world's cultivated area kept expanding, but since then the doubling of the earth's population has depended on improved productivity rather than expansion. Simultaneously, the industrial system has developed a specialized medical technology capable of limiting mortality. The result is a massive population growth. Since the second world war India has added over 400 million people.

The present volume is thus a variegated case study. By concentrating on a given region at a given moment in history it throws rare light on world demographic history. It reveals in vivid detail the fascinating but sometimes painful demographic features of mature agrarianism and of the collision with industrialism — a collision often repeated around the world but seldom so well documented. The editor is to be congratulated on his selection of contributors, the contributors on the excellence of their analyses. The science of demography is permanently enriched by this volume.

Kingsley Davis

1

INDIAN HISTORICAL DEMOGRAPHY: DEVELOPMENTS AND PROSPECTS

Tim Dyson

It is probably fair to say that the historical demography of India is a field of academic inquiry which hardly exists. Yet, especially in the developing world, few countries can match India's wealth of historical demographic data. There has, too, certainly been no shortage of scholars who have proclaimed the prospects for such work.[1]

This is not to say that there are no major studies pertaining to India's past population. There are. We would mention in particular the Reports which accompanied the early Indian censuses, and Kingsley Davis' classic volume, *The Population of India and Pakistan*, published in 1951.[2] But in general these were not intended primarily as works in historical demography, being more concerned with developments contemporary to their times. And if we put these studies on one side, then the number of other works which have directly addressed historical demographic data for India is certainly small. Perhaps the only major study which falls unequivocally under the heading 'Indian historical demography' is Leela and Pravin Visaria's consideration of population trends during the period 1757 – 1947.[3]

However, the recent past has seen a growing interest in the field by scholars in a number of disciplines. Also, as several of the papers in this volume attest, technical advances have created new possibilities for analysing old data sets. Therefore the present book brings together work by researchers in demography, history and economics. It is a collective effort to help establish this field of inquiry, and provide both stimulus and focus for future research.

In our view, increased knowledge regarding India's population history not only has considerable intrinsic value, but may also have important implications for social and economic historians of India. Further, as Nigel Crook notes in his contribution here, the development of Indian historical demography can only augment the comparative dimension for similar work dealing with other regions of the world. In addition, an historical perspective can undoubtedly contribute to our

understanding of the contemporary characteristics of the population of
the country. In this introductory chapter we will briefly try to illustrate
some of these points. We will review the contributed papers to the
book, and provide some specific statements on the possibilities for
future research.

REVIEW OF CONTENTS

The volume contains two papers which focus primarily on the
precensus period, i.e. prior to 1872.[4] The first, by Roland Lardinois,
considers the population history of rural Tamil areas in the late
eighteenth and early nineteenth centuries.[5] Obviously the data for this
early period tends to be both less systematic and more questionable than
those available for later years. But, nevertheless, one cannot but be
impressed by the richness of the early records that survive. For
example, there exist rough district population counts from the 1790s.
Also important for Lardinois' purposes are lists of villages compiled for
revenue reasons, and the first detailed district maps drawn up very early
in the nineteenth century. He argues that these and other sources,
together with reports by East India Company officers, plus recorded
political and military history, provide a fairly consistent picture as
regards rural population trends. In short, there was widespread
desertion of villages, abandonment and decay of both irrigation systems
and cultivatable land, and general stagnation in the agricultural sector.
This rural disintegration was probably most intense in the 1780s and
1790s, and it is these decades especially that may have witnessed real
population decline in Tamil rural areas. But Lardinois contends that the
general negative effects persisted into the early decades of the
nineteenth century. Thus the undoubted faster Tamil population growth
which seems to have set in from around 1830 has to be seen in the
context of demographic stagnation, even decline, over the preceding
sixty or seventy years.[6]

   In the second contribution on early population trends, Simon
Commander addresses developments in the Doab region of north India
during the nineteenth century. Again, there is evidence of depopulation
in the late eighteenth century. But Commander argues that the rural
population of the period was sometimes quite mobile, and that therefore
migration probably constitutes a significant part of the explanation for
some declines in population. However, the first half of the nineteenth
century appears to have been characterized by both significant
population and economic growth. Conversely, the second half of the
century saw not only slower population growth, but also a probable

decline in agricultural incomes. In Commander's view infectious diseases came to play an increasingly prominent role in the causation of famines during the late nineteenth century. At the same time the impact of agricultural crises became significantly more differentiated in social terms.

This brings us to demographic trends during the period covered by modern Indian censuses. The volume contains three papers which attempt to estimate trends in mortality and fertility since 1881.[7]

The first, by P. N. Mari Bhat, applies the new 'variable r' methodology to all-India census age distributions. His is a formidable treatment which will undoubtedly inform future research. The author argues powerfully that the age pattern of mortality that prevailed in India during the early decades of the present century, and earlier, was probably substantially different from that which has held in more recent decades. India's past high mortality regime was characterized by extraordinarily heavy *adult* mortality, rather than by extraordinarily heavy mortality at young ages. As Mari Bhat notes, this feature is not well reflected by most modern demographic models which tend to be based upon more recent data which are associated with relatively high life expectations.[8]

A major implication of Mari Bhat's analysis is that Indian life expectation over the period 1881 – 1951 was probably somewhat higher than most previous research has suggested; relatedly, fertility levels were somewhat lower.[9] According to this analysis decadal average total fertility rates during 1881 – 1951 were fairly constant at around 5.7 to 5.9 live births per woman.[10] The mean age of maternity increased slightly during this period, partly because the age of females at first marriage tended to rise, and partly because mortality improvements led to declines in widowhood, which in turn produced higher fertility rates among older women of reproductive age.[11] In addition, mortality improvements in the present century also changed India's age structure in such a way as to contribute to the slight long-run decline in the country's crude birth rate up to around 1951. Mari Bhat maintains that it was not until the 1951 – 61 decade that male life expectation at birth in India exceeded that of females. He argues that other analysts have wrongly concluded that higher male than female life expectation was attained at an earlier time because they have failed to allow adequately for the greater propensity of males to overstate their age in the census.[12]

Nevertheless, there is no doubt that, in general, female life expectation this century improved more slowly than did that of males; Mari Bhat attributes this to slower female mortality improvement at adult ages, arguing that this may in part be because men benefited more than women from increased control of famine.

In her paper Alice Clark also uses 'variable r' methodology, together with the new United Nations 'South Asia' model life tables. She focuses

on developments in United Provinces, Bombay and Madras Presidencies during 1881 – 1931. She shows that there was undoubtedly
regional demographic variation in India during this period. For
example, life expectation was considerably lower in United Provinces
than in Madras.[13] In accounting for this regional mortality gradient
Clark notes that the former Presidency was probably more prone to
endemic malaria and harvest failure than was Madras. Her results
strongly suggest that higher male than female life expectation at birth
probably did characterize some major parts of India (e.g. Bombay
Presidency) during the late nineteenth and early twentieth centuries —
even if this was not the case at the national level. In her view the faster
male than female mortality gains of the present century have occurred
partly because patterns of discrimination against females could become
both more selective and refined as the overall level of mortality
improved.

Clark suggests that the age pattern of mortality that held in 'crisis
decades', such as 1891 – 1901, must have been very different from that
prevailing at other times. During periods of extreme crisis adult
mortality must have worsened to a much greater degree than did child
mortality — a point of some similarity to that made by Mari Bhat. To
reject this would mean accepting that really incredibly low life
expectations, and incredibly high levels of fertility, prevailed at such
times.[14]

Studies based on census age data are undoubtedly important to our
knowledge of India's historical demography. But the poor quality of
census age returns inevitably places limits on what can be achieved. In
this context the paper on Berar by the present writer argues that in some
districts of India vital registration data can provide a fruitful
complement to census-based research. Instead of providing average
estimates of fertility and mortality for intercensal decades such data
may be able to give *annual* estimates of the main demographic rates.
Also, annual time series can obviously provide a very informative
picture of demographic change. For example, the material on Berar
clearly shows that, historically, birth and death rates tended to vary
inversely; when death rates were relatively low, birth rates were
relatively high, and vice versa. Of course, registration data have their
own problems, so much of the paper essentially constitutes a defence of
the quality of the material we have been able to assemble for Berar.

The general neglect of vital registration data for India is a little
puzzling.[15] To some extent it may reflect what has come to be regarded
as an almost self-evident proposition, namely that such material would
inevitably prove a waste of time. But the far greater accessibility of
census data to researchers is also probably part of the explanation.
Certainly, the results derived from vital registration for Berar gain

strength if viewed against estimates from work using census data. For example, it is interesting to compare decadal averages of annual figures on life expectation at birth for Berar with the estimates for all-India derived by Mari Bhat using census age distributions. Table 1 shows that both the level and trend of life expectation indicated by the two studies over the period 1881 – 1951 are similar.

Each of the next three papers in the volume addresses some of the developments illustrated by the figures in Table 1. Deborah Guz studies the 1896 – 7 and 1899 – 1900 famines in Hissar district of Punjab, crises which together contributed to the very low life expectations of around 22 – 24 years for the decade 1891 – 1900; Ian Mills deals with the calamitous influenza of 1918 – 19 which also left its mark (see Table 1); lastly, David Arnold addresses the history of cholera in British India with particular reference to the general decline in cholera mortality after about 1900.

In some regions of India the famine of 1899 – 1900 was associated with the death of about ten per cent of the total population. So its detailed demographic consideration is long overdue. Guz argues persuasively that the famine of 1899 – 1900 cannot be considered apart from that of 1896 – 7. Both famines were precipitated by drought. But the later famine was much more severe, although prices actually rose less than in 1896 – 7. It should be emphasized that the British administration undoubtedly appreciated that the famine consequences of drought operated mainly through a loss of purchasing power among the poorest groups, rather than through simple shortage of food. This observation can hardly be considered modern.

Guz tells us that in March 1900 one fifth of Hissar's total population was on official public relief works, and the registered infant mortality rate in that year was nearly fifty per cent. In both crises maximum deaths occurred after the peak in food prices. Mortality from the second disaster exhibited an especially dreadful tail over time — lasting well into 1901, and even 1902. The author states that it is clear that relief measures cannot be relaxed — as they were in Hissar — as soon as normal diet is resumed. She argues that in many ways the authorities were remarkably knowledgeable about the mechanics of the phenomenon to which the population was subject. Eventually the Famine Code was implemented, and it certainly contained potentially useful components. But the administration was preoccupied with the cost of relief works, and Guz concludes that the severe attitude of the relief administration was one of the factors accounting for the greater mortality of the later famine.

The influenza of 1918 – 19 also had severe and long-lasting effects. Mills shows that the disease almost certainly radiated from Bombay, and that the mortality it caused was much less severe in eastern and

Table 1. Census Population Totals and Intercensal Population Growth Rates, India, 1881 – 1961, with Selected Estimates of Life Expectation at Birth.

Census Year	Population (000s)	Average Annual Rate of Growth (%)	Life Expectation at Birth			
			All-India		Berar	
			male	female	male	female
1881	193,609	—	—	—	—	—
1891	233,322	1.86	26.3	27.2	29.5	30.1
1901	237,515	0.18	22.2	23.4	23.8	24.9
1911	251,167	0.56	25.3	25.5	26.4	27.6
1921	250,432	-0.03	21.8	22.0	24.0	26.2
1931	278,051	1.05	29.6	30.1	28.5	30.7
1941	317,042	1.31	29.5	29.6	29.0	30.2
1951	356,787	1.18	31.0	31.8	30.1	31.2
1961	438,654	2.06	36.8	36.6	38.3	40.7

Notes: (1) The population totals and growth rates relate to the current territorial jurisdiction of India.
(2) The growth rates and life expectations refer to the decade preceding the census year shown.

Sources: The population totals are taken from S. B. Mukherjee, *The Age Distribution of the Indian Population*, East-West Center, Honolulu, 1976. The life expectation estimates are taken from the papers by Mari Bhat and Dyson in the present volume; those for Berar are derived from vital registration.

southern India than in the north and west. A particularly interesting feature of this paper is the use of influenza incidence and case mortality rates among jail populations. While *mortality* varied regionally, the jail information strongly suggests that influenza *prevalence* was fairly constant across the country. It is possible that the greater diurnal temperature range of northern and western India increased the chances of an infected person developing pneumonic complications, and thus dying. But Mills notes that these regions experienced major food shortages at about the same time, and this also may have contributed to their greater mortality. He estimates that in total about 17 – 18 million excess deaths occurred in a four or five month period because of the flu. Subjecting vital registration data for Bombay Presidency to 'growth balance' methods, Mills estimates that period life expectation at birth in 1918 may have fallen as low as six years.

Indian data also reflect some of the peculiar features of the 1918 – 19 influenza as they were recorded in western countries. Deaths tended to be concentrated in the middle adult years, and women were more likely to die than men (especially if pregnant). In addition, the fertility effects of the episode were complex. There was a reduction in the number of births occurring in the first half of 1919 and something of a recovery in the second half of that year. But this recovery was only partial. Mills' analysis suggests that in Bombay Presidency as much as nine per cent of the total female population died, and almost twenty per cent of marriages involving women aged 20 – 39 were dissolved by the death of one or both partners from flu. Hence the effects on the birth rate were of extended duration. Lastly, Mills' piece is a fine example of how to make use of the variety of data sets — such as army and ecclesiastical records, and data from jails — which can inform our understanding of India's population in the past. It may also provide clues as to how the 1918 – 19 pandemic affected other large agricultural populations for which comparable data are lacking.

This brings us to the paper on cholera by Arnold. The history of the decline of this disease — which presumably contributed to the long-run mortality gains shown in Table 1 — is certainly complex. Bacteriological change may have played a role, but can only be part of the answer. The same applies to the general reduction in the frequency of famine. In any event, Arnold considers that the link between cholera and famine may have been exaggerated due to misclassification of non-cholera deaths at times of severe food crisis. Also, improvements in specific cholera therapies probably made little if any contribution to the long-run decline in cholera mortality.

Yet Arnold argues that sanitary and medical interventions may have played a significant, even decisive role. This was due to developments in the basic epidemiological understanding of, and response to, the

8   TIM DYSON

disease. By themselves each development can be considered minor. But he argues that their *combined* impact may have been considerable. Thus the authorities increasingly tried to isolate points of origin of cholera, and improve procedures for its surveillance and notification. Since pilgrims and festivals were understood to play major parts in transmission, greater attention came to be given to the provision of basic toilet facilities and protected water supplies whenever large religious gatherings took place. While the benefits of cholera inoculation may indeed be partial and of short duration, Arnold considers that mass immunization campaigns for people attending religious fairs — events which also tend to be of short duration — may well have helped limit the frequency and growth of epidemics. In this context he mentions the recent decision of the Indian government to abandon compulsory inoculation for pilgrims attending festivals. Finally, in major urban areas such as Madras, where admittedly surveillance also tended to be better and remedial action could be more prompt, the introduction of piped water systems seems to have had an effect in reducing outbreaks of the disease.

DISCUSSION

Standing back, perhaps we can tentatively identify four broad phases to India's population growth during the period considered in this book (see Table 2).

Though Lardinois and Commander focus on different regions, they seem to agree that the period preceding the establishment of British rule — approximately 1760 to 1820 — was characterized by a very low, possibly negative, rate of population growth. It is certainly well established that when the British completed their hegemony of the country up to the Sutlej in 1818 they found a country in ruins, with widespread social breakdown, the results of lengthy wars.[16] This first phase seems to have been followed by a second in which generally positive population growth ensued. This second phase is only represented here by the work of Commander on the Doab region of Uttar Pradesh. But, for example, as previously mentioned, it appears that the population of Madras Presidency also grew at a comparatively fast rate after about 1830. It is interesting that Visaria and Visaria remark that India's population probably grew marginally faster in the early and middle decades of the nineteenth century than during the last half of the eighteenth century.[17]

Table 2. Tentative Schema of Broad Phases of Population Growth in India over the period 1760 – 1960.

Phase	Approximate Period	Population Growth	Social and Other Correlates
1	c.1760 – 1820	Near zero, possibly negative.	Wars; economic disruption, social breakdown.
2	c.1830 – 1891	Generally positive, but of unknown magnitude; mortality may have improved compared with Phase 1	Recovery from Phase 1; fewer wars; increased social and economic stability; economic growth (?)
3	1891 – 1920	A reduced rate of growth compared with Phase 2, possibly due to deterioration in mortality.	Increase in epidemics; famines; a period of significant change in the mix of causes determining the overall level of mortality.
4	1921 – 1960	Population growth positive and increasing, as mortality improves.	Increased control over disease and famines; political independence; economic development etc.

Note: (1) We should underscore the tentative, incomplete and highly simplified nature of the above schema. This is emphasized, for example, by the fact that the dates given for the first two phases neither meet nor overlap. As the text makes clear, we would expect to find substantial regional variation, and it may even prove impossible, or inappropriate, to distinguish between certain phases (e.g. 2 and 3). Clearly, phase 4 in particular could well be subdivided.

Clearly there is scope for research on other regions of India to ascertain whether they also experienced two such phases of population growth. To what extent was migration responsible for rural depopulation during the first phase, and to what degree was slower natural increase the likely cause? Relatedly, if the middle part of the nineteenth century indeed saw a period of relatively fast growth — and it must be said that the existence of such a distinct 'second phase' has yet to be generally established — to what extent did this reflect 'recovery' from the ravages of the first phase, as Lardinois tends to maintain, and to what degree did it mirror a period of comparative economic growth, as is argued by Commander?[18] No doubt the answer to these questions will vary between regions.

The third and fourth phases of growth are a little easier both to identify and chronicle (see Table 2). Table 1 shows that during the period 1891 – 1920 the population of India increased by only seventeen million. This implies a low average annual rate of growth of 0.24 per cent over thirty years. Indeed we cannot be sure that the preceding second phase itself exhibited a faster population growth rate than this. But after 1921 we enter a fourth phase; there is a definite quickening in the rate of growth as mortality begins to improve (see Table 1).

The comparatively slow population growth of what we have termed the 'third phase' has attracted much interest, yet comparatively little detailed empirical demographic research. Instead we sometimes confront rather naive interpretations of the economic implications that are thought to be deduced from the fact of comparatively slow population growth.[19] Yet it may well be that — to the extent that they can be separated — the economic consequences of demographic events during the period 1891 – 1920 were at least as great as the demographic consequences of economic change. Here we are referring to the increase, at various times, of diseases such as malaria, cholera and influenza.[20] Nor do variations in the prevalence of such diseases necessarily reflect policy measures in any straightforward way. Clearly there is also much scope for work on plague and tuberculosis in India during this and other periods. It is particularly important to appreciate that changes in the level of mortality are the net result of a variety of processes, some positive and some negative; thus changes in mortality level can rarely be taken simply as reflections of economic changes per se, though clearly such changes can play a role. More work is required on the various factors which together condition mortality in order to assess whether the period 1891 – 1920 really did witness a worsening of mortality, and if so, why.

According to Table 1, average life expectation during 1891 – 1920 was marginally lower than 25 years. This undoubtedly signifies conditions of very heavy mortality. But research on the historical demography of other world regions, including parts of nineteenth-century Europe, is increasingly finding populations with broadly comparable levels of mortality.[21]

This brings us to some of the comparative considerations raised by Crook in the final paper in this volume. He notes that though research has undeniably demonstrated that pre-transitional populations were often subject to dramatic short-run fluctuations in death rates, such populations could still experience periods of comparatively fast growth. Clearly the annual growth rate of 1.86 per cent between the 1881 and 1891 censuses shown in Table 1 supports this possibility in the case of India (though changes in the level of census coverage could also be relevant). Concerning fertility, Crook notes that the moderate levels that were for so long considered to be special to pre-transitional Europe in fact have counterparts elsewhere, for example, Japan. In his paper here Mari Bhat contends that neither in India nor China were pre-transitional fertility levels particularly high. Crook considers that it may well be incorrect to assume that fertility in Asian populations was universally uncontrolled. And we can add that some aspects of the time series on births provided by Guz for Hissar might be thought consistent with anticipatory fertility control by the population as a probable future crisis looms.[22]

Whether or not average mortality levels in the decades around 1900 represent a deterioration compared with some preceding decades, there can be no doubt that after 1921 we enter a fourth phase when population growth is consistently and strongly positive as mortality improves (see Tables 1 and 2). The vital registration data on Berar indicates that death rates fell especially sharply in the period 1948 – 52. If the contemporary Indian age pattern of mortality differs significantly from that which prevailed historically, as Mari Bhat maintains, then the years around 1948 – 52 may prove a fruitful location at which to begin consideration of the mechanics and causes of such a change. Coming to still more recent times, the material for Berar indicates that a small but significant component of the acceleration in population growth during the 1950s reflects a brief period of rising fertility. There exist similar signs for other areas of India.[23] It is for such reasons that we believe that historical research can throw light on contemporary conditions.

Finally in this section we should note that it appears that the acceleration in India's rate of population growth was halted in the 1970s, almost certainly because of fertility decline. This may be considered the beginning of a fifth broad phase of the country's demographic development, which will presumably be characterized by a long-run reduction in the rate of population growth.

FUTURE RESEARCH

The foregoing schema of phases of growth may prove much too simplistic — especially as regards more recent periods when it becomes feasible to address fertility and mortality trends separately. However it may be of use in marshalling future research, although clearly the schema stands to be elaborated or rejected. In these final paragraphs it seems worthwhile briefly offering some further suggestions regarding future research.

There are various traditional indigenous records which might conceivably be of use. Thus during Mughal and Maratha periods there sometimes occurred counts of households such as the *Khanna Shumari*.[24] It may still be possible to find old documents pertaining to these enumerations on the shelves of some archives. Dharma Kumar has drawn attention to other potential sources such as temple lists, genealogical scripts, and records kept by specific religious groups like Sikhs and Parsis.[25]

One set of records probably ripe for exploitation are Christian parish registers; for example, the data on baptisms, burials and marriages maintained by the Portuguese in Goa from the seventeenth century onwards. There must be a real chance that such material can be subjected to modern techniques of historical demography such as family reconstitution; investment of time and effort may pay rich dividends. Also, in Goa the registration of births, deaths and marriages for non-Christians dates from 1865.[26] Several studies in this volume make use of vital registration data. We believe that it is probably feasible to construct fairly good long-run time series of annual birth and death rates from vital registration for quite a few districts in India.

Of course, the census is, and will probably remain, the single most valuable source for work on the relatively recent historical demography of India. It provides structure to the overall endeavour. But — as the contents of this volume attest — increasingly research is going to have to go well beyond the census for its primary sources of data. Locations such as State Archives, the India Office Library in London, and the National Archives in New Delhi, are likely to prove especially fruitful. The papers in this book also show the gains that can be reaped by employing new methodologies. Much past work on India's population history has perhaps relied a little too much upon the excellent discussions found in official records such as the census reports. In the future, use of such discussions as sources must increasingly be complemented by analysis, or reanalysis, of the primary data themselves.

We hope that the papers in this volume demonstrate the promise offered by Indian historical demography and that they stimulate others to participate in such research.

NOTES TO CHAPTER 1

1 See, for example, Dharma Kumar, 'New Prospects for Historical Demography in India' in Ashish Bose, Devendra B. Gupta and Gaurisankar Raychaudhuri (eds.), *Population Statistics in India*, Vikas Publishing House Pvt. Ltd., New Delhi, 1976; P. Krishnan, 'Toward a historical demography of India: some preliminary findings', *Demography India*, Volume 8, nos. 1 and 2, 1979; also Morris D. Morris, 'Towards a Reinterpretation of Nineteenth-Century Indian Economic History', *The Indian Economic and Social History Review*, Volume V, No. 1, March 1968; and Morris D. Morris, 'Trends and Tendencies in Indian Economic History', *The Indian Economic and Social History Review*, Volume V, No. 4, December 1968.

2 An example of such a Report is Census of India, 1911, Part 1, *Report*, Superintendent of Government Printing, Calcutta, 1913; see also Kingsley Davis, *The Population of India and Pakistan*, Princeton University Press, Princeton, New Jersey, 1951.

3 L. Visaria and P. Visaria, 'Population (1757 – 1947)' in Dharma Kumar (ed.) *The Cambridge Economic History of India*, Orient Longman, Hyderabad, 1984. Work in Indian economic history which treats demographic material well is rare, but see Michelle B. McAlpin, *Subject to Famine: Food Crises and Economic Change in Western India, 1860 – 1920*, Princeton University Press, Princeton, New Jersey, 1983. The work of Klein on the history of disease in India during colonial rule, though not specifically demographic, is also worthy of mention, see, for example, I. Klein, 'Death in India, 1871 – 1921', *Journal of Asian Studies*, Volume XXXII, No. 4, August 1973.

4 The census of 1881 was the first in which the population was classified into conventional age groups.

5 For a notable piece of research by this author which also falls squarely under the heading 'Indian historical demography' see R. Lardinois, 'Une conjoncture de crise démographique en Inde du Sud au XIX siècle. La famine de 1876 – 1878', *Population*, Volume 37, No. 2, March – April, 1982.

6 On the comparatively fast population growth of Madras Presidency after about 1830 see Visaria and Visaria cited in note 3, pp. 465 – 9.

7 Because of the consideration of note 4 above, the decade 1881 – 91 is the first for which intercensal demographic estimates for India can be made.

8 For example, the new South Asia model life tables of the United Nations are based largely upon empirical life tables for the 1970s from Bangladesh, Iran, India and Sri Lanka; see United Nations, *Model Life Tables for Developing Countries*, United Nations, New York, 1982.

9   The lower fertility levels result from the conclusion that mortality at young ages historically was somewhat lower than has usually been previously entertained (because the age pattern of mortality in the past was different from that prevailing today).

10 However, in this context it must be noted that Mari Bhat assumes that marital fertility was constant until 1961.

11 'Mean age of maternity' here refers to the mean of the age specific fertility distribution.

12 Other things equal, age overstatement biases intercensal estimates of life expectation upwards.

13 This same regional variation in mortality and fertility still occurs today, see T. Dyson, 'India's Regional Demography', *World Health Statistics Quarterly*, Volume 27, No. 2, 1984.

14 For example, for the 1911 – 21 decade Clark's 'South Asia' estimates of male and female life expectation in Bombay Presidency are 12.38 and 11.39 years respectively, and the corresponding level of total fertility is about 8.6 live births per woman.

15 But for profitable use of such data see, for example, Davis cited in note 2, and McAlpin cited in note 3.

16 See, for example, P. Spear, *A History of India 2*, Penguin Books, Harmondsworth, 1970, pp. 116 – 18.

17 See Visaria and Visaria cited in note 3, pp. 465 – 9.

18 Of course, these two explanations for the faster growth rate of any 'second phase' are by no means mutually exclusive.

19 The papers by Morris, cited in note 1, show signs of this tendency.

20 For a review of how 'modernizing works' such as the growth of irrigation systems probably spread malaria, see I. Klein, 'Malaria and Mortality in Bengal, 1840 – 1921', *The Indian Economic and Social History Review*, Volume IX, No. 2, June 1972.

21 In Europe this is particularly true of Mediterranean regions (Richard Smith, personal communication). As late as 1875 – 80 areas of southern Germany experienced *average* levels of infant mortality in excess of 300 infant deaths per thousand live births, probably related to the practice of early weaning, see J. E. Knodel, *The Decline of Fertility in Germany, 1871 – 1939*, Princeton University Press, Princeton, New Jersey, 1974.

22 We are referring to the small downturns in births early in 1896 and 1899 for which Guz offers alternative possible explanations. For a parallel occurrence in the 1974 famine in Bangladesh see A. K. M. Alauddin Chowdhury and L. C. Chen, 'The Dynamics of Contemporary Famine' in *Proceedings of the International Population Conference, Mexico 1977*, published by the International Union for the Scientific Study of Population, Liege, 1977.

23 See, for example, the crude birth rate time series for the states of Tamil Nadu and Bombay contained in T. Dyson and M. Murphy, 'The Onset of Fertility Transition', *Population and Development Review*, Volume 11, No. 3, September 1985.

24 See D. Bhattacharya, 'Data Base of Historical Demography of India Since 1771' in Ashish Bose *et al*, cited in note 1.

25 See Dharma Kumar cited in note 1.
26 Preliminary work on data for Goa has been undertaken. See, for example, H. C. Srivastava, 'Registration of Vital Events in Goa — A Study of the Current System in Retrospect', *Artha Vijnana*, Volume 13, No. 4, December 1971. It is possible that parish records also exist for other areas such as Pondicherry.

2

DESERTED VILLAGES AND DEPOPULATION IN RURAL TAMIL NADU *c.* 1780 – *c.* 1830

Roland Lardinois

Historians have not entirely ignored reports concerning deserted villages in southern India in the late eighteenth and early nineteenth centuries. But they may well have minimized both the frequency of this phenomenon, and its social and economic correlates. The destruction of previously inhabited sites has often been blamed on the wars that occurred in the region from at least the middle of the seventeenth century. But prevailing opinion has held that the desertion of villages, resulting partly from these conflicts, was really rather limited both in time and space. For example, Dharma Kumar writes that, 'some writers based their accounts on hearsay or exaggerated the effects of wars'. She goes on to say that 'villagers were often left in peace, or they fled to the hills, to return when the shortlived battle was over. Even trade was often uninterrupted by war'.[1] Clearly we must not prejudge the issue. But such views are a little surprising when one considers that most of the evidence on which they are based is simply reports of visual observations, rather than careful reconstructions using available data. Further, deserted villages were actually the subject of fairly systematic censuses conducted by the East India Company from as early as the late eighteenth century.

In this paper we present results of research underway on the agrarian history of the Tamil region during the early colonial period, focusing on deserted villages. The aforementioned censuses are one of few sources which permit us to address the beginnings of the modern demographic history of the Tamil population around 1800. We will start by briefly reviewing available data sources. We then try to establish roughly the extent of such village desertions, their timing and geographical distribution. The resulting approximate quantitative assessment is linked to both first-hand reports of observers of the time, and a consideration of the agrarian crisis which affected the Tamil rural economy between about 1780 and 1830. In essence we are addressing the issue of *depopulation*. Did it occur? And if so, to what extent? At this stage of the work it is probably impossible even to attempt a complete explanation of this extremely complex phenomenon. But we can at least suggest some lines of inquiry for future research.

SOURCES AND METHODS

Probably the best sources for the identification of deserted villages are found in the archives of the Survey of India, especially the reports and registers of villages kept in the Topography Department and the Board of Revenue. The staff of the Survey compiled lists of villages in connection with their land revenue collection duties (through the *ryotwari* settlement) and also drew up the first district maps. These lists include both inhabited and uninhabited sites, and village location can usually be established using the accompanying co-ordinates. The second important data source is the archives of the Board of Revenue of Madras Presidency. Deserted villages were frequently recorded by Collectors in the early Settlement Reports. They also sometimes recorded such sites in connection with the annual *Jamabandi*, when the basis for taxation was established. These data are similar in nature to the records of the Survey of India. In both cases the initial register of sites was established through a combination of tours around districts and consultations of traditional local records.[2] Generally, inhabited sites are called *basti*, and are classified into two categories: *mazrā* (principal villages) and *majrā* (secondary villages). These sites can be contrasted with *be-chiragh* villages (literally, those without a lamp), meaning uninhabited villages or those in ruins. Sometimes *be-chiragh* villages are also differentiated according to their principal or secondary status.[3] The maps which accompany these various reports and registers are also important documents for research into deserted village sites.[4] When detailed maps were first drawn up for districts and taluks, deserted places were usually designated by a special sign. Thus in preparing instructions for the Survey of Mysore in 1800 – 05, Mackenzie writes:

> It will be necessary to notice villages contained in the official lists . . . or any alterations that may have occurred . . . to assist Revenue management. *Ruined or deserted villages may be considered by a star*; . . . new villages not in the list should also be distinguished; villages in jungles should be noted with as much accuracy as their situation can admit.[5]

These maps are the more precious because sometimes the corresponding reports and registers are either missing or incomplete. For example, in 1792, at the end of the third war against Tipu Sultan, the East India Company occupied Salem and the Baramahal, and required John Mather to conduct a survey of these districts for the Collector, Alexander Read. While we know that this survey took place, no statistical tables survive, although there do still exist records of Mather's memoirs of the undertaking.[6] However, the Tamil Nadu State Archives contain the corresponding maps, but without the necessary legends. These legends, which differentiate between 'principal village, subordinate village, village not in the Collector's register and ruined village' can be found in another map drawn by Mather in 1800 – 05; thus we can identify, count and locate abandoned sites.[7] In addition, in some instances statistics concerning villages, and occasionally population totals, are marked in the margins of such maps.[8]

Though both inhabited and uninhabited sites appear to be meticulously recorded in these maps, there is little comment upon their precise definition. To some extent the meaning of 'deserted village' has probably been governed by practical considerations related to the extension of the authority of the colonial administration, particularly as regards taxation. A strictly numerical demographic definition of a village has a meaning when an *inhabited* site has to be located on a given map. However, not all inhabited sites are necessarily villages, even though they may be related to villages in some way (e.g. as outlying hamlets). Thus to comprehend fully these various definitions would require a more detailed understanding of the settlement patterns prevailing in rural Tamil areas at the end of the eighteenth century. More generally, both the simple character of the definitions used, and their partly foreign (i.e. British) origin, further obscure their precise meaning. Again, what we really need is knowledge of the network of relationships holding between places, social groups and the landholding system.[9]

However we should also be careful in our interpretation of the term 'deserted village'. In European historiography this term does not usually encompass temporary absence from an inhabited site, whether a village or a hamlet. Rather, according to Roncayolo, it implies a complete break in the continuity of occupation, a fundamental discontinuity in human exploitation of the soil.[10] The question arises as to whether such a definition is relevant in the present case?

The Board of Revenue was primarily interested in recording villages which could pay land tax to the central administration. It was also concerned with the identification of groups within the villages who should pay this tax. In the crisis which prevailed in southern India in the late eighteenth and early nineteenth centuries, on which we elaborate below, it is probable that some villages contained only a few low-caste peasant groups upon whom no claim of tax could be made. And in some instances such villages — in which only a remnant of the population remained — might have been classified as 'deserted' by Collectors simply because no *taxable* inhabitants were left behind. On the other hand, though the logic of the definitions employed by the Survey Department is probably never completely independent of the tax administration, the categories used do obey consistent principles of their own. For example, the term 'deserted village' certainly was routinely employed for villages in a state of physical ruin. However even this might not preclude some habitation. Thus one can imagine that in many cases a few basic thatched cottages might have been occupied by one or two agricultural worker families.

To gain a better understanding of the extent to which deserted villages may have reflected complete breaks in the continuity of settlement, we would really have to increase the scope of the research. It would be particularly desirable to compare systematically the lists of deserted villages compiled at the beginning of the nineteenth century, with those drawn up around 1900, and indeed with more recent lists.[11] However this latter exercise lies beyond the present paper. Though the definitions are undoubtedly ambiguous, here we will use the early data on 'deserted villages' as this term was employed by the colonial administration of the time, though its use was certainly affected by considerations relating to tax. However, an examination of other data sources, together with a consideration of historical events, should improve our understanding of what was actually implied by village desertion.

THE GEOGRAPHY OF DESERTED VILLAGES

We have collected statistics on deserted villages between about 1790 and 1850. The detailed figures are contained in the Appendix. Most data pertain to the period 1800 – 25, except the material for Coimbatore district in Table A5 which relates to a more recent period (1846 – 7).[12]

Overall the data in the Appendix concerns 86 administrative units.[13] These contained 32,993 sites, of which 28,765 were classified as inhabited, and 4,228 (12.8 per cent) were considered as either deserted or in ruins. In the late eighteenth and early nineteenth centuries an important feature of Tamil population history seems to have been a movement towards village desertion that is striking in its extent. Approximately a fifth of taluks in the Appendix exhibit a desertion rate above 20 per cent, and slightly over half have more than 10 per cent of their village sites classified as either deserted or in ruins. The phenomenon is also impressive in the breadth of its geographical distribution: it is found from the north of Madras, to Cape Cormorin in the south; it occurs in the dry central tablelands, as well as in irrigated lowland areas of the coastal plain. Few regions appear to have been left unscathed.[14]

We can begin by considering Madurai, which is one of the districts most affected. As Table A8.2 of the Appendix shows, in Tirumbur taluk in 1813 – 14 nearly half of the sites were classified as deserted, and particularly high rates of desertion were implied for the taluks of Tenkari, Madakulam, Sholavandam, and Ramanathapuram zamindari. As a whole, over 30 per cent of sites in Madurai around 1815 were categorized as deserted. Moving south to Tirunelveli district, Table A9 shows especially high desertion rates in the taluks of Cheranmahadevi, Nellaiyambalam and Tenkasi. In Tiruchirapalli district the taluks of Lalgudi, Conaud, and Ariyalur all have desertion rates between 16 and 18 per cent (see Table A6). In the heart of the Cauvery delta, in Thanjavur district, taluks such as Tiruarur, Mannilam, Tiruvaiyaru and Kumbakonam exhibit desertion rates around or exceeding 20 per cent (see Table A7). Moving north, the phenomenon seems to be both less intense and more localized. For example, in North Arcot district 12 per cent of sites are classified as deserted, although this reaches 23 and 30 per cent respectively in Venkatagiri zamindari and Wandiwash taluk (see Table A2). In Salem around 1795 only 7.5 per cent of sites are described as deserted, and this proportion remains fairly stable until at least 1835 – 40.[15] However this average figure hides a marked contrast within the district between the north around Hosur, where nearly 39 per cent of sites were classed as deserted in 1800 – 02, and the south where the average desertion rate is only about 3 per cent (see Tables A4.1, A4.2 and A4.3).

From numerous visual testimonies which can be cited in support of these facts we will single out that of Collector G. Wynch. The following quotation comes from a report, dated 1791, concerning Dharapuram taluk (then in Dindigul, now in Coimbatore district). Its accuracy is based, so the author reminds us, upon 'local knowledge of the country'.[16]

All the villages in this district have suffered much, but none more severely than those immediately surrounding the fort where the devastation has been general. In the fort, every house is destroyed. West of the fort the pettah of Dharapuram stood, containing 297 houses built with teak and tiled, of these only 25 are now remaining and they have received much injury. Close adjoining was the village of Soondramiah Acharum which contained 22 good houses, not one of which is now left. On the south side remains the village of Naragavayen Acharum, here were formerly 20 houses all entirely destroyed, and of the adjoining village of Bumaroyen Acharum formerly consisting of 74 houses, only 7 remain. East of the fort stood the village of Collenjee Vady containing 226 houses, of these 46 only remain, the greatest part of which are now inhabited. Many small villages on the banks of the Ambraye are entirely destroyed. Great pains must have been taken to destroy this place so effectually. The houses were mostly built of teak and tiled; the walls are left standing, but of the wood and tiles scarcely any remain.[17]

The data for two districts which we have yet to review — namely Chinglepet and South Arcot — are a little perplexing (see Tables A1 and A3). This is because it was in precisely these areas that, from time to time, occurred the Carnatic wars. In his report on the *jagir* of Chinglepet around 1795, Place remarks on the destructive effect of these wars on the social and economic life of the region. However, he only identified a total of 52 deserted or ruined villages in the district. And when in 1843 – 4 the local Collector proceeds to undertake a new enumeration, only a dozen such villages remain.[18] In 1806 – 7 the Collector for South Arcot mentioned that of a total of 408 *inam* villages (i.e. those not subject to taxation) approximately 45 per cent were deserted; half these deserted villages were located in Tiruvannamalai taluk.[19] At the same time, no village paying full land tax to the East India Company was classified as either deserted or ruined. And if one relates the deserted *inam* villages to the total number of sites in South Arcot (i.e. those both subject and not subject to taxation) then an average desertion rate of only 3.6 per cent results. In a later count in 1821 – 2 only 45 sites in the district were categorized as deserted (no other details being given), and in combination with the recorded total number of sites this gives a desertion rate of 1 per cent (see Table A3). However, the fact that the survey of 1806 – 7 produced a total number of sites exceeding five thousand, while the total of the 1821 – 2 survey was only 3,961, underlines the approximate nature of the village categories employed by the early colonial administration.

For the most part, all administrative statistics on villages were defined to some degree with reference to principal villages, i.e. *revenue* villages, the linchpins of the ryotwari land revenue system. The status of revenue villages was further enhanced by the introduction of a cadastral survey and the regular taking of censuses. Secondary or subordinate villages — linked to the revenue village — could vary in size from simple small dependent hamlets to sites of comparable population to that of the principal village. So the distinction between principal and secondary villages was mainly administrative. But it could hide a complex social distinction. In particular, secondary villages might preponderantly reflect sites inhabited by service castes, while a revenue village was much more likely to be inhabited by landowning families. The question arises as to which kind of site and social grouping most often tended to be classified as deserted?[20]

To try to answer this question we must briefly outline the settlement patterns holding in the Tamil countryside at the end of the eighteenth century. The impression that emerges regarding the north of the region is of scattered rural settlements of small communities containing only a few families. This impression is probably stronger for tableland areas of the interior than for irrigated valleys and the coastal plain. Thus in Salem district the average number of people per site is less than 100 inhabitants: this figure attains 108 in Krishnagiri taluk in the north, but is higher still — 126 and 133, respectively — in the more fertile taluks of Sankagiri and Namakkal which are both situated along the Cauvery river.[21] However, in the coastal plain region of Chinglepet the average number of inhabitants per site is almost 250.[22] But these mean values hide considerable variation. For example, in interior areas of Salem the majority of sites are recorded as having very much less than 100 inhabitants. In contrast, on the Coromandel coast near Madras 36 per cent of inhabited sites exceed 250 persons in size. It is therefore clear that coastal and irrigated valley sites generally had significantly larger populations than villages located in interior dry zones. One can speculate that this was probably the case throughout rural Tamil areas at that time.[23]

This said, the available data do not really permit firm conclusions regarding the distribution of deserted villages by their principal or secondary status *within* interior or coastal areas. Thus in North Arcot district about 12 per cent of both principal and subordinate villages were classified as deserted. In Coimbatore in 1846 – 7 about 9 per cent of secondary villages were designated as deserted, compared with just over 2 per cent of principal sites. Also, in Tiruchirapalli district no principal villages were classified as deserted, whereas nearly 27 per cent of subordinate villages were so described. Yet in Madurai in 1813 – 14 about 32 and 28 per cent of principal and secondary villages, respectively, were classed as deserted (see Tables A2, A5, A6 and A8.2).

What can we learn from the data regarding the chronology of the desertion of villages? In 1802, when the East India Company first took control of the southern Tamil district of Tirunelveli, the Collector, S. Lushington, made an interesting observation in the first Settlement Report. He writes, 'A dreadful famine affected the province from a scarcity of grain, the effects of which are still to be traced in the ruins of villages then filled with a numerous population; this calamity happened in 1774'.[24] Other materials exist for Thanjavur district in 1788 – 9. This sketches the demographic landscape after the second war between Tipu Sultan and the British. It suggests that nearly 4 per cent of all villages in the district were destroyed in the early 1780s, and over 17 per cent in the Sirkali region.[25] Though it is impossible to confirm these figures, they roughly accord with what is known about developments in the rural economy during this time, and also with visual reports contained in other sources.[26] Forty years later nearly 19 per cent of all villages in the whole of the Cauvery delta were classed as deserted.[27] Also, in 1795, after the third British war with Tipu Sultan, nearly 37 per cent of villages in Dindigul district were classed as deserted. However, twenty years later this proportion seems to have declined significantly if we compare it with statistics for the whole of Madurai (see Tables A8.1 and A8.2). Lastly, in the case of Coimbatore, we can compare the foregoing description of events in Dharapuram, given by Wynch in 1791, with the statistics available for the same taluk in 1846 – 7 (see Table A5). The tentative suggestion is that the deserted villages of 1846 – 7 may have been merely those surviving from a much larger number earlier in the previous fifty years.

AGRARIAN CRISIS AND DEPOPULATION

Surely we have established that the desertion of previously inhabited village sites, both primary and secondary, was probably a real and major feature of rural Tamil society at the end of the eighteenth century. To this phenomenon there also corresponded a general reduction in cultivation of the soil. In short, there are obvious signs of both a demographic and an economic crisis in rural areas at this time. Thus in 1795 Wynch writes of Combu taluk in Madurai district:

> That these jungles were formerly cultivated can admit of no doubt, for in penetrating through thick jungle for a distance of nearly three miles, I observed the vestiges of garden, very fine topes [plantations] of mangoo and jack trees, which from their magnitude must have been of many years growth.[28]

However, it is very difficult to measure the extent of the probable reduction in cultivation that occurred. In 1800 in Vanyiambadi taluk of Salem, the Collector estimated areas under cultivation in 153 villages. According to these data, in 23 per cent of cases only a quarter of village land was being cultivated, and in a further 55 per cent of villages only half the land was under cultivation.[29] But, of course, the problem in interpreting such information is obvious. At a time when no village cadastral was being properly kept, what exactly constituted 'village land' in the mind of the Collector is certainly open to debate. It may have referred to the total area under present and past cultivation, including fallow fields. Alternatively, 'village land' may have included all land which the administration felt should be put into cultivation, thus including the category 'cultivatable waste land' as well. Note that this latter classification would tend to maximize the land area that would be subject to tax.

Nevertheless, there can be no doubt that at the end of the eighteenth century the British administration was genuinely amazed at the area of land which had apparently been deserted by the peasants, especially in dry interior regions. For example, in Salem around 1795 the distribution of land was recorded as follows: only 27 per cent was in cultivation, 5 per cent was fallow, and 36 per cent was classed as cultivatable waste land. Thus it was estimated that 68 per cent of total land was either being cultivated or could be cultivated, while as much as 32 per cent was considered genuine waste land.[30] These figures may well reflect confusion between fallow and waste land in the mind of the administration. It has also been argued recently by Murton and Stein that the land categories employed by the British demonstrated a fundamental misunderstanding of Tamil agriculture.[31] Nevertheless, the figures do suggest that very large areas of cultivatable land were not being used. And there are still more signs of a reduction in cultivation at this time.

There exist many reports for most parts of rural Tamil Nadu on major disruption of systems of irrigation. For example, in 1794 the Assistant Collector for Namakkal taluk in Salem writes that '. . . one tank has been repaired . . . which has been broken for the last 25 years at the expense of upwards of 3000 Rupees. In the same district the tank of Pudukotta, which has been broken for the last 10 years, has been repaired at nearly the same expense'.[32] To the east, near the Cauvery region, Wynch insists: 'I have been particular in this point to evince the utility of a strict attention to the repair of those nullah [drains] which I am sorry to say have been so totally neglected as scarcely to convey any water to the lands; many of the principal nullah were nearly filled up, and none of them had been cleaned or dug for the last five years'.[33]

As with villages, so with irrigation: the early colonial administration surveyed Tamil irrigation systems methodically in order to best assess their potential for taxation.[34] Undoubtedly the resulting statistics on tanks, drains and wells have limitations. But they do correspond with first-hand observations such as those cited above, and they also allow us to draw broad conclusions regarding the general situation. Thus in Salem in 1801 about 30 per cent of all tanks were classed as unusable, and in taluks such as Bellur, Virabadradrug and Paramathi the figure is approximately 60 per cent.[35] In Coimbatore in 1818 – 22 about 55 per cent of tanks, 42 per cent of drains, 31 per cent of canals (watercourses) and 23 per cent of wells were recorded as having deteriorated to such an extent that they were practically worthless.[36] In North Arcot in 1827 about 30 per cent of all tanks were classed in a similar way.[37] And in Madurai in 1827 approximately 13 per cent of reservoirs and 31 per cent of anicuts (dams) were classified as being in a bad state of repair.[38] These statistics, whether or not exact in detail, support a picture of general neglect in rural Tamil areas at the start of the nineteenth century. Once more we confront unmistakable signs of a major rural crisis affecting both the dry interior and the coastal plain.

Clearly the search for the basis of this crisis must begin with consideration of developments in the second half of the eighteenth century. Given the present state of research it is impossible to reconstruct in detail the economic developments of that time. But we have been able to assemble some relevant, if crude, time series. These relate to the districts of South Arcot, Chinglepet, Thanjavur and Tirunelveli, all in the Carnatic region, and then under the control of the Nabab of Arcot who received their land taxes.[39] The general picture these data convey is of stagnation in the quantities of land tax paid, interspersed with periods of decline. In both South Arcot and Chinglepet total land revenue fell between 1780 and 1790, and again in the late 1790s (see Fig. 1). In Thanjavur paddy production fell sharply in 1781 – 2 and only regained its pre-1780 level after a period of almost twenty years (see Fig. 2). Note that the rise in the price in 1781 was insufficient to compensate for the fall in production, since total land revenue fell in that year. Thanjavur then experienced stagnation in land revenue until the early 1790s. Much further south, in Tirunelveli district, we can detect an interesting cyclical pattern in land revenue which appears to have occurred roughly every ten years (see Fig. 3). The scant data available on paddy production in Tirunelveli in the late eighteenth century also suggest general stagnation and intermittent decline. Again, we cannot take these time series data as precise, but it is probably safe to infer broad trends.[40]

THE FORCES BEHIND THE AGRARIAN CRISIS

Let us briefly summarize the facts as we have tried to establish them. In the second half of the eighteenth century rural Tamil society appears to have experienced not only widespread desertion of villages, but also a collapse of irrigation, abandonment of land previously under cultivation, and general stagnation in both rice production and land revenue. The data are certainly patchy, but all point in the same direction. Most of the forces behind this crisis can probably be summarized in the trilogy: war, famine and epidemic. The facts are partly known, particularly as they relate to military history. We shall only briefly review them here.[41]

During the fifty years which preceded the imposition of colonial rule, southern India was torn by a succession of wars involving the native powers, and Britain and France. The main conflicts were as follows: the Maratha invasion of 1740 – 41, the Carnatic wars of 1746 – 48, 1749 – 54 and 1756 – 63; the wars against Tipu Sultan in 1767 – 69, 1780 – 84, 1790 – 92 and 1799 – 1800; and finally the repression of the *Poligar* uprising in 1800 – 01.[42] These conflicts affected the economy of the region in somewhat different ways. For example, the Carnatic wars were largely positional in nature: armies of thousands of cavalry and infantry fought around major fortified centres such as Madras, Pondicherry, Arcot and Ginji. Although the countryside undoubtedly suffered from the passage of troops and the looting of vanquished populations, there are reasons to consider that the ensuing destruction was comparatively confined. However, the conflicts involving Tipu Sultan, from the late 1760s onwards, seem to have affected the rural economy to a greater degree. Thus, according to a survey of Thanjavur district undertaken in 1788 – 89, the population declined by 38 per cent after the second Anglo-Mysore war; it fell from just over a million in 1779 – 80 to about six hundred and fifty thousand in 1788 – 89. The survey implies that about half this loss was due to deaths connected in some way with the fighting, while the remainder was due to subsequent population movement on the orders of Tipu Sultan.[43]

Whatever the validity of such statistics, all these conflicts probably led to the increasing orientation of the rural economy towards the dictates of war. An army not only entails the loss of economic production of the troops involved, but they also have to be fed and paid. In those days the transport of basic provisions such as grain and salt was achieved by means of caravans consisting of many thousand oxen.[44] As the struggle with Tipu Sultan intensified, the resulting social and political instability made delivery of any grain to the British army problematic. The British were thus compelled directly to acquire both grain, and the oxen to transport it, rather than relying upon the services of local chiefs. 'The ploughs stood still, ripe grains decayed on the ground, and much was lost for the want of cattle to water it, owing to the public service employing their bullocks' wrote the Collector of Coimbatore in 1791.[45]

Another important aspect of the economy of war relates to the increased monetary needs of both the colonial and indigenous powers in order to finance their military efforts. These enhanced financial requirements occurred at a time when looting and kidnapping for ransom were in any event generally disrupting monetary circulation.

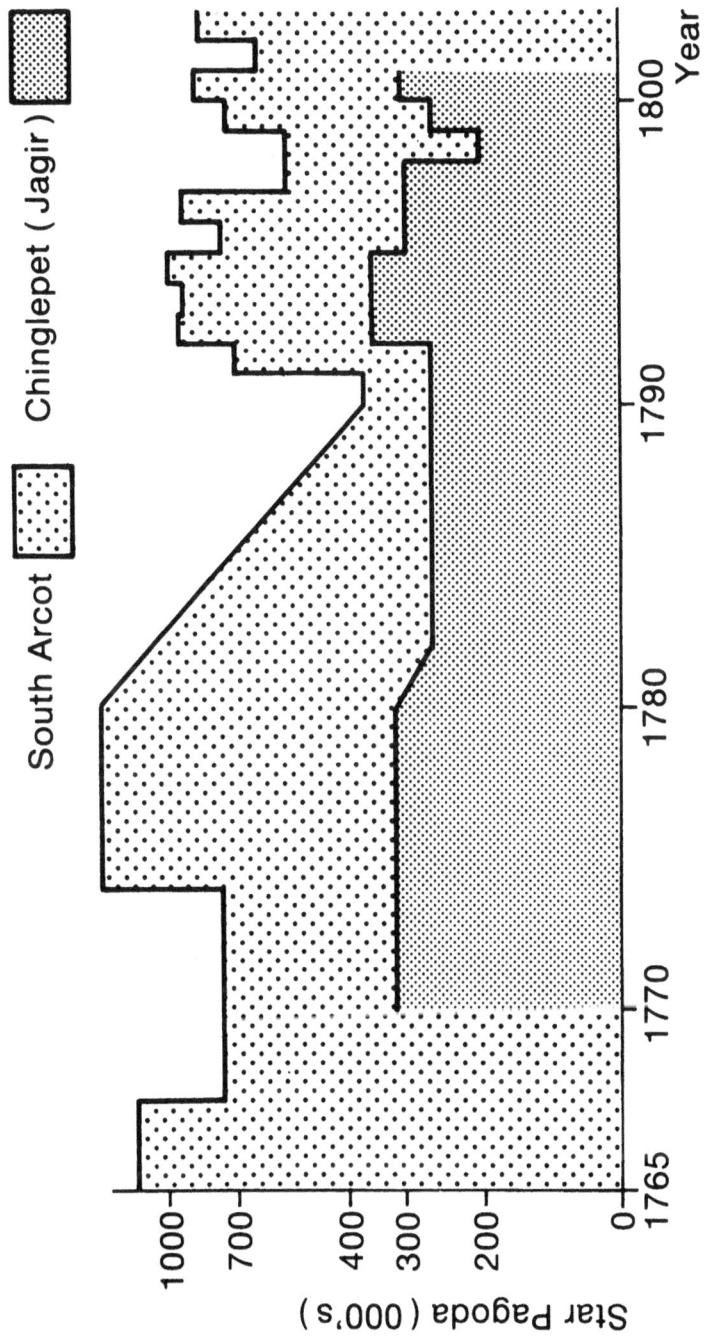

Fig.1 Land Revenue for South Arcot and Chinglepet Districts, 1765–1803

Sources: South Arcot: *Collectorate Records*, TNSA, volume 178; Chinglepet: *Madras Revenue Consultation*, TNSA, volume 116, 1802.

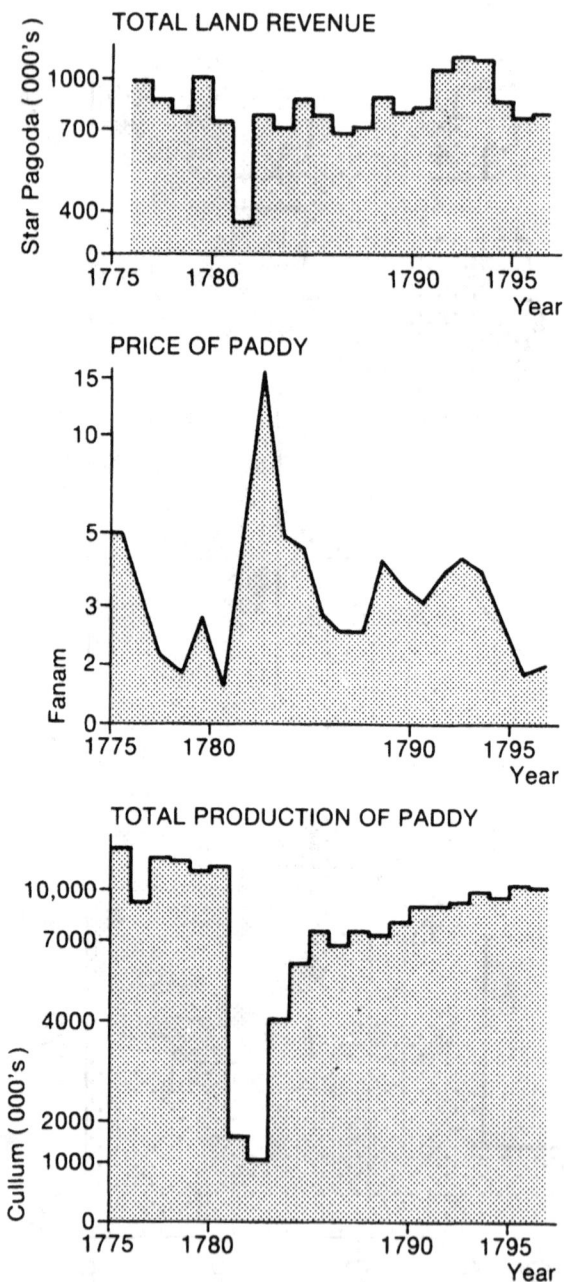

Fig.2 Land Revenue, and Paddy Price and Production for Thanjavur District, 1775–1797

Source: General Comparative Statement of the Tanjore Revenue, *The Tanjore Report*, Madurai Collectorate Records, TNSA, volume 1103.

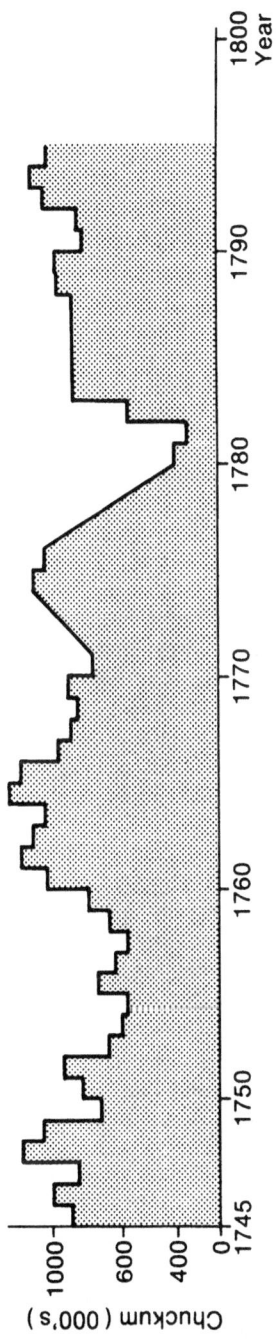

Fig.3 Land Revenue for Tirunelveli District, 1745 – 1801

Source: *Settlement Report of Mr Lushington, 1802, TNSA: ASO(D), 382.*

One visible manifestation of such processes was the indebtedness of the Nabab of Arcot.

We must also consider famines and epidemics. In 1774, 1780 – 82, 1790 – 93, 1802 – 03, and above all in 1833, major droughts occurred in southern India, leading to widespread food shortages and famines.[46] There is little reason to believe that the climate has changed greatly since the end of the eighteenth century. Then, as now, variation in monsoon rains could interject havoc into agricultural life, particularly in dry interior regions.[47] Obviously, the consequences of climatic variation were further aggravated by the frequency of war. We know that the forces fighting in Salem district in 1799 – 1801 had extreme difficulty in obtaining food supplies; and even when fighting ceased, serious food shortage continued until at least 1807.[48] The general disruption certainly favoured both endemic and epidemic disease. Cholera and smallpox outbreaks raged in the armies, and a serious outbreak of fever affected rural Tamil areas between 1809 and 1811.[49]

What can we say regarding the effect of all these developments on population growth? The data available on the issue have the same origin as the statistics on deserted villages. The earliest period for which we have systematic population totals for all Tamil districts is 1821 – 6.[50] Table 1 shows that, when combined, these put the total Tamil population, excluding the town of Madras, at approximately six and a quarter million.[51] The sex ratio of the population is 105 males per 100 females. Thus there are no very obvious signs of major differential female underenumeration. But we certainly cannot exclude the possibility that the figure of six and a quarter million itself represents an undercount of the total population.

The previously mentioned survey of Thanjavur in 1788 – 9 estimated the district's population ten years earlier at slightly over one million.[52] Thus Table 1 suggests that the population may not have regained this size even as late as 1821 – 6. A similar comparison can be made for Salem. In 1792 the district's population, excluding Hosur, was estimated to be six hundred thousand; to this must probably be added several thousand tribal people living in hilly tracts not covered by the survey. In 1800 – 02 we have a second count for the same areas; it estimated the population at six hundred and fourteen thousand, plus 60,600 in Hosur, giving a total for the entire district of 675,000.[53] Yet as Table 1 shows, twenty years later the Collector only enumerated 616,689 people in Salem.[54] The very high taxes imposed in the early 1800s, the failure of the zamindari system, and the general political instability of the times, all contributed to perpetuate the agrarian crisis until at least the 1820s.[55] Given these circumstances it is hard to believe that the population grew significantly, even if the figure of six and a quarter million around 1821 – 6 does indeed represent an undercount.

Table 1. Total Population of Tamil Districts *c.* 1821 – 5.

District	Males	Females	Total	Sex Ratio (m/f)
Chinglepet	190,243	172,886	363,129	1.100
North Arcot	462,410	429,882	892,292	1.076
South Arcot	234,946	219,574	454,520	1.070
Salem	315,990	300,699	616,689	1.051
Coimbatore	417,654	409,886	827,540	1.019
Tiruchirapalli	247,569	233,723	481,292	1.059
Thanjavur	464,874	436,479	901,353	1.065
Madurai	497,843	477,256	975,099	1.043
Tirunelveli	386,258	380,489	766,747	1.015
Total	3,217,787	3,060,874	6,278,661	1.051

Notes: (1) As mentioned in the text, the totals above exclude the population of the city of Madras.
(2) The figures for Madurai include Dindigul and Sivaganga.
(3) The figures for Tirunelveli refer to 1826 – 7.

Sources:
Chinglepet: BRP, 7 March 1822, TNSA, volume 907, pp. 2202 – 04
North Arcot: BRP, 23 September 1822, TNSA, volume 924, pp. 8694 – 96
South Arcot: BRP, 18 March 1822, TNSA, volume 908, pp. 2479 – 80
Salem: BRP, 18 July 1822, TNSA, volume 919, p. 6714
Coimbatore: BRP, 16 February 1824, TNSA, volume 975, pp. 1445 – 48
Tiruchirapalli: BRP, 10 June 1822, TNSA, volume 917, pp. 5712 – 13
Thanjavur: BRP, 4 November 1822, TNSA, volume 929, pp. 10248 – 53
Madurai: BRP, 24 June 1822, TNSA, volume 917, pp. 6020 – 24
Tirunelveli: BRP, 17 February 1831, TNSA, volume 1278, pp. 2053 – 56

However, we must briefly address one further point sometimes raised in connection with deserted villages. This is that they simply reflected *temporary migrations* of the rural population. Such an interpretation might seem particularly supported by the case of Chinglepet,[56] and perhaps even South Arcot, discussed earlier. But such an explanation is unlikely to have been applicable throughout rural Tamil areas as a whole. Moreover, even if desertion rates were relatively low in these two districts, we cannot conclude from this that they were unaffected by depopulation. If we are to consider the role of migration then we must distinguish between flows to the towns and movement within rural areas. We know that at the end of the eighteenth century landed castes in Chinglepet were experiencing severe difficulties in finding agricultural labourers to work their lands. The general social dislocation severed traditional links between landed and landless castes, and thus prompted migration of low-caste groups towards Madras. Several questions arise here. Was such migration permanent or temporary? Did it involve other Tamil cities? Were the colonial centres of Madras and Pondicherry representative or atypical in their experience of this migration? More generally, what impact did the crisis in the Tamil countryside have on *urban* centres of the time?

Given the current state of research these questions cannot be satisfactorily answered.[57] But the relevant documents I have seen suggest that Tamil cities were indeed affected by the general crisis. Also, with the possible exception of the colonial ports, it is unlikely that cities could provide much haven for migrants from rural areas. So, did the displaced Tamil population simply diffuse itself throughout other rural areas, away from the main zones of conflict? We know, for example, that in the 1790s many thousands migrated from areas under the control of Tipu Sultan to take refuge in Salem, then under the sway of the British.[58] It is also known that there were instances of temporary migration from villages — people returning after hostilities had ceased.[59] However, if migration constituted a major part of the answer to the question of deserted villages, then we might expect to find records of the establishment of *new* villages, particularly in areas of low population density where there nevertheless still existed reasonable amounts of land. Yet, with one or two isolated and rather special exceptions, I have been unable to find any reports of the foundation of new villages by migrants who came to clear new lands. It therefore seems likely that migration is only a part of the answer to the phenomenon of deserted villages in the late eighteenth and early nineteenth century Tamil countryside.

The population history of Thanjavur and Salem districts over the period 1780 – 1830 may well be broadly representative of trends afflicting the region as a whole at that time: a decline in population of perhaps 15 to 20 per cent in the last ten to fifteen years of the eighteenth century, followed by virtually no population growth in the first decade of the nineteenth century. The general crisis which eventually led to colonial rule in southern India was not only political and military in nature; it also had major economic and demographic dimensions, the consequences of which lasted into the middle of the nineteenth century. It seems likely that the positive population growth that we observe in the middle of the nineteenth century partly reflects demographic *recovery* from the open crisis of the second half of the eighteenth century. In this paper we have mainly been concerned with the external forces which shook southern India at this time. But it is reasonable to inquire whether these alone were responsible for the crisis. Should we not also address the fundamental contradictions inherent in earlier Tamil society, contradictions which also probably helped mould its historical development over the period with which we have been concerned?

APPENDIX TO CHAPTER 2

Inhabited and Deserted Villages by District and Taluk

Table A1: Deserted Villages in Chinglepet District, *c*. 1795

Total Villages:	2241
Deserted Villages:	52

Source: L. Place, Report on the Jagir of Chinglepet, Board of Revenue Miscellaneous Records (Chinglepet), TNSA, volume 48.

Table A2: Deserted Villages in North Arcot District, 1816 – 17

Taluk	Principal Villages				Subordinate Villages				Total Villages			
	Inhabited	Deserted	Total	% Deserted	Inhabited	Deserted	Total	% Deserted	Inhabited	Deserted	Total	% Deserted
Chittoor	91	0	91	0.0	285	37	322	11.5	376	37	413	9.0
Tirupati	52	0	52	0.0	41	4	45	8.9	93	4	97	4.1
Kaveripakkam	133	16	149	10.7	35	4	39	10.3	168	20	188	10.6
Sholingur	105	3	108	2.8	73	7	80	8.8	178	10	188	5.3
Thiruvalam	121	5	126	4.0	164	7	171	4.1	285	12	297	4.0
Satghur	146	21	167	12.6	89	7	96	7.3	235	28	263	10.6
Cuddapah	242	72	314	22.9	58	15	73	20.5	300	87	387	22.5
Arcot	122	17	139	12.2	39	0	39	0.0	161	17	178	9.6
Vellore	188	3	191	1.6	100	0	100	0.0	288	3	291	1.0
Tiruvathipuram	255	5	260	1.9	2	0	2	0.0	257	5	262	1.9
Polur	163	29	192	15.1	40	21	61	34.4	203	50	253	19.8
Wandiwash	176	50	226	22.1	3	3	6	50.0	179	53	232	22.8
Suttavaid	117	11	128	8.6	69	15	84	17.9	186	26	212	12.3
Bungauree	254	15	269	5.6	156	10	166	6.0	410	25	435	5.7
Mogaraul	218	35	253	13.8	228	44	272	16.2	446	79	525	15.0
Venkatagiri Zd	160	57	217	26.3	7	22	29	75.9	167	79	246	32.1
Assumed Jagirs	27	1	28	3.6	9	5	14	35.7	36	6	42	14.3
Total	2570	340	2910	11.7	1398	201	1599	12.6	3968	541	4509	12.0

Data are not available for some zamindaris such as Kalastri, Arni and Kangudi.

Source: Board of Revenue Proceedings, 15 October 1818, TNSA, volume 805, pp. 11402 – 72.

Table A3: Deserted Villages in South Arcot District, 1821 – 22

Taluk	Number of Villages			% Villages Deserted
	Inhabited	Deserted	Total	
Tindivanam	302	1	303	0.3
Thiruvahidhapuram	251	0	251	
Valavanur	198	0	198	
Villupuram	157	0	157	
Bhuvanagiri	272	0	272	
Tiruvannamalai	498	25	523	4.8
Uridhachalam	406	0	406	
Elavanasur	304	0	304	
Tirukoilur	345	6	351	1.7
Kallakurichi	225	1	226	0.4
Chetpet	452	12	464	2.6
Mannargudi	148	0	148	
Chidambaram	205	0	205	
Cuddalore	153	0	153	
Total	3916	45	3961	1.1

Source: Board of Revenue Proceedings, 29 August 1822, TNSA, volume 923, pp. 8182 – 99.

Table A4.1: Deserted Villages in Salem District, *c.* 1795

Taluk	Number of Villages Deserted	Number of Villages Total	% Villages Deserted
Kangudi	8	360	2.2
Vanyiambadi	2	136	1.5
Tiruppattur	2	220	0.9
Mallapadi	1	53	1.9
Kunnattur	16	211	7.6
Kambalnallur	58	386	15.0
Krishnagiri	56	370	15.1
Virabadradrug	149	467	31.9
Tenkaraikotta	20	281	7.1
Dharmapuri	36	305	11.8
Pennagaram	8	137	5.8
Nangavalli	5	96	5.2
Omalur	17	458	3.7
Idapadi	8	249	3.2
Sankagiri	16	491	3.3
Tiruchengode	4	251	1.6
Salem	3	187	1.6
Bellur	5	144	3.5
Attur	4	75	5.3
Viraganur	9	177	5.1
Sendamangalam	9	308	2.9
Namakkal	11	288	3.8
Paramathi	5	220	2.3
Rasipuram	0	67	0.0
Chennagiri	2	84	2.4
Total	454	6021	7.5

Source: The Baramahal Records, Section II, Geography, Board of Revenue Miscellaneous Records (Salem), TNSA, volume 151.

Table A4.2: Deserted Villages in Balaghat in Salem District, *c.* 1800 – 02

| Taluk | Number of Villages | | | % Villages Deserted |
	Inhabited	Deserted	Total	
Ankisgiri	171	75	246	30.5
Shoolagiri	120	62	182	34.1
Bagalur	75	17	92	18.5
Hosur	168	57	225	25.3
Denkanikotta and Ratnagiri	423	396	819	48.4
Total	957	607	1564	38.8

Source: Colin Mackenzie, Report on the Survey of Mysore, British Museum, London, Additional Manuscript 13660 (folio 94).

Table A4.3: Deserted Villages in Salem District, *c.* 1835 – 40

Taluk	Number of Villages			% Villages Deserted
	Inhabited	Deserted	Total	
Hosur	492	82	574	14.3
Denkanikotta	350	59	409	14.4
Krishnagiri	678	90	768	11.7
Tiruppattur	482	0	482	0.0
Dharmapuri	597	136	733	18.6
Tenkaraikotta	433	0	433	0.0
Omalur	277	11	288	3.8
Salem	231	5	236	2.1
Attur	144	6	150	4.0
Sankagiri	313	1	314	0.3
Rasipuram	158	0	158	0.0
Namakkal	282	15	297	5.1
Tiruchengode	274	1	275	0.4
Paramathi	279	0	279	0.0
Total	4990	406	5396	7.5

Note: Hosur includes Ankisgiri, Shoolagiri and Bagalur zamindaris.

Source: National Archives of India, Abstract register of villages of the Salem and Baramahal districts, in Descriptive Memoir and a register of villages, Baramahal and Salem, by C. R. MacMahon, 1 July 1844, Survey of India, Memoirs, volume 101M (folio 433).

Table A5: Deserted Villages in Coimbatore District, 1846 – 47

Taluk	Principal Villages				Subordinate Villages				Total Villages			
	Inhabited	Deserted	Total	%	Inhabited	Deserted	Total	%	Inhabited	Deserted	Total	%
Coimbatore	181	0	181	0.0	220	12	232	5.2	401	12	413	2.9
Sathyamangalam	139	2	141	1.4	354	81	435	18.6	493	83	576	14.4
Danayakkankottai	192	20	212	9.4	142	111	253	43.9	334	131	465	28.2
Kollegal	139	10	149	6.7	269	46	315	14.6	408	56	464	12.1
Pollachi	160	4	164	2.4	206	6	212	2.8	366	10	376	2.7
Perundari	147	0	147	0.0	392	8	400	2.0	539	8	547	1.5
Andhiyur	68	0	68	0.0	279	23	302	7.6	347	23	370	6.2
Erode	63	0	63	0.0	190	4	194	2.1	253	4	257	1.6
Dharapuram	41	0	41	0.0	301	24	325	7.4	342	24	366	6.6
Kangayam	42	0	42	0.0	269	29	298	9.7	311	29	340	8.5
Karur	90	1	91	1.1	648	14	662	2.1	738	15	753	2.0
Cheyur	105	0	105	0.0	284	33	317	10.4	389	33	422	7.8
Palladam	89	0	89	0.0	315	21	336	6.3	404	21	425	4.9
Chukkragiris	94	0	94	0.0	169	9	178	5.1	263	9	272	3.3
Nilgiris	5	1	6	16.7	47	0	47	0.0	52	1	53	1.9
Total	1555	38	1593	2.4	4085	421	4506	9.3	5640	459	6099	7.5

Source: Board of Revenue Proceedings, 29 May 1848, TNSA, volume 2139, pp. 8259 – 63.

Table A6: Deserted Villages in Tiruchirapalli District, c. 1803 – 10

Taluk	Principal Villages Inhabited	Subordinate Villages				Total Villages			
		Inhabited	Deserted	Total	% Deserted	Inhabited	Deserted	Total	% Deserted
Conaud	155	109	52	161	32.3	264	52	316	16.5
Vetticutty	82	285	33	318	10.4	367	33	400	8.3
Ayilur	52	101	7	108	6.5	153	7	160	4.4
Lalgudi	183	54	46	100	46.0	237	46	283	16.3
Thuraiyur	173	134	38	172	22.1	307	38	345	11.0
Udayarpalayam	299	81	49	130	37.7	380	49	429	11.4
Ariyalur	222	14	53	67	79.1	236	53	289	18.3
Valikandapuram	105	49	22	71	31.0	154	22	176	12.5
Total	1271	827	300	1127	26.6	2098	300	2398	12.5

Source: India Office Records, London, A Khanashumari and Dehazada Table of the Eight Taluks of the Province of Trichinipoly, Record Department, Manuscript 3.

Table A7: Deserted Villages in Thanjavur District, 1821 – 22

Taluk	Number of Villages			% Villages Deserted
	Inhabited	Deserted	Total	
Tiruvaiyaru	410	114	524	21.8
Papanasam	307	68	375	18.1
Tiruarur	483	120	603	19.9
Mannargudi	480	82	562	14.6
Keevalur	607	82	689	11.9
Pattukottai	880	267	1147	23.3
Kumbakonam	553	154	707	21.8
Mayuram	815	139	954	14.6
Mannilam	369	98	467	21.0
Total	4904	1124	6028	18.6

Source: Board of Revenue Proceedings, 4 November 1822, TNSA, volume 929, pp. 10248 – 53.

Table A8.1: Deserted Villages in Dindigul, Madurai District, *c*. 1795

Taluk	Number of Villages			% Villages Deserted
	Inhabited	Deserted	Total	
Combu	4	0	4	0.0
Uthamapalayam	11	6	17	35.3
Percakulam	16	7	23	30.4
Andipatti	24	65	89	73.0
Vadakulam	19	6	25	24.0
Dindigul	109	36	145	24.8
Sandaiyur	24	0	24	0.0
Total	207	120	327	36.7

Source: Report on Dindigul by G. Wynch, 24 November 1795, Madurai Collectorate Records, TNSA, volume 5160.

Table A8.2: Deserted Villages in Madurai District, 1813 – 14

Taluk	Principal Villages				Subordinate Villages				Total Villages			
	Inhabited	Deserted	Total	% Deserted	Inhabited	Deserted	Total	% Deserted	Inhabited	Deserted	Total	% Deserted
Madakulam	49	23	72	31.9	20	24	44	54.5	69	47	116	40.5
Sholavandam	24	6	30	20.0	15	19	34	55.9	39	25	64	39.1
Tirumangalam	57	5	62	8.1	99	36	135	26.7	156	41	197	20.8
Tirumbur	52	49	101	48.5	11	6	17	35.3	63	55	118	46.6
Melur	26	0	26	0.0	84	2	86	2.3	110	2	112	1.8
Anaiyur	59	7	66	10.6	138	76	214	35.5	197	83	280	29.6
Natham	32	1	33	3.0	119	78	197	39.6	151	79	230	34.3
Thadicombu	47	0	47	0.0	203	41	244	16.8	250	41	291	14.1
Aiyampalayam	59	5	64	7.8	148	8	156	5.1	207	13	220	5.9
Tenkari	13	0	13	0.0	60	54	114	47.4	73	54	127	42.5
Uthamapalayam	13	0	13	0.0	8	7	15	46.7	21	7	28	25.0
Total	431	96	527	18.2	905	351	1256	27.9	1336	447	1783	25.1
Ramanathapuram	1391	757	2148	35.2	249	102	351	29.1	1640	859	2499	34.4
Grand Total	1822	853	2675	31.9	1154	453	1607	28.2	2976	1306	4282	30.5

Sources: Board of Revenue Proceedings, 21 November 1814, TNSA, volume 660, pp. 14076 – 84. Geographical and Statistical Memoir of the Ramnad Zamindari, by J. Turnbull, Madurai Collectorate Records, volume 9085.

Table A9: Deserted Villages in Tirunelveli District, 1821 – 22

| Taluk | Number of Villages | | | % Villages |
	Inhabited	Deserted	Total	Deserted
Nadumandalem	521	113	634	17.8
Sankaranayanarkoil	184	16	200	8.0
Tenkasi	135	36	171	21.1
Srivaikuntam	358	20	378	5.3
Bramadesam	130	19	149	12.8
Nellaiyambalam	185	60	245	24.5
Cheranmahadevi	120	60	180	33.3
Vidugranam	86	12	98	12.2
Alwar Tirunagari	129	11	140	7.9
Nanguneri	521	93	614	15.1
Panchmahal	398	16	414	3.9
Total	2767	456	3223	14.1

Source: Geographical and Statistical Memoir of Tirunelveli and its Zamindaris, British Museum, London, Additional Manuscript 14380 (folios 227 – 41).

NOTES TO CHAPTER 2

This research was conducted mainly in Madras in 1981 – 5 while a Fellow of the French Institute of Pondicherry, with financial assistance from the French Ministry of Foreign Relations. I am grateful to Tim Dyson for assistance in translation.

1 See Dharma Kumar, 'Regional Economy (1757 – 1857)' in Dharma Kumar (ed.), *The Cambridge Economic History of India*, Volume 2, Cambridge University Press, Cambridge, 1983, pp. 352 – 3. For an identical view see B. Murton, 'Land and Class: Cultural, Social and Biophysical Integration in Interior Tamil Nadu in the Late Eighteenth Century', in R. E. Frykenberg (ed.) *Land Tenure and Peasants in South Asia*, Manohar Publications, New Delhi, 1984, pp. 81 – 99. However, such an interpretation is not shared by Richards, who writes: 'The mythical picture of the unconcerned peasant peacefully tilling his field while armies clash in the distance is far from accurate for early eighteenth century Hyderabad', see J. F. Richards, *Mughal Administration in Golconda*, Clarendon Press, Oxford, 1975, p. 263.

2   The records of the Survey of India are kept with the National Archives of
    India (Delhi). The specific documents with which we are concerned
    belong to the series 'Memoirs and Field Books', see D. A. Low, J. C. Iltis
    and M. D. Wainwright, *Government Archives in South Asia, A Guide to
    National and State Archives in Ceylon, India and Pakistan*, Cambridge
    University Press, Cambridge, 1969, pp. 194 – 5. For a summary
    presentation of these documents see D. Battacharya and R. D. Roy,
    'Khanasumari Records and the Statistical System of India', in *Forty-Fifth
    Session of the Indian Historical Records Commission*, Mysore, 1977, pp.
    29 – 39; see also, P. L. Madan, 'Field Books and Memoirs: Untapped
    Source for Historical Research' in *Indian History Congress Proceedings*,
    Bombay, 1980, pp. 446 – 52; and R. H. Phillimore, *Historical Records of
    the Survey of India*, (4 volumes), Survey of India, Dehra Dun, 1945 – 58.

3   In the documents consulted in the present research I have never met the
    Persian term, *wiran*, which Shireen Moosvi informs me, is often used to
    describe ruined villages in Mughal sources. In what follows our use of
    'deserted' incorporates ruined villages.

4   See R. H. Phillimore, 'Historical Maps of the Survey of India' in *The
    Indian Archives*, Volume 1, No. 3, July 1947, pp. 198 – 205. See also
    S. N. Prasadd (ed.), *Catalogue of the Historical Maps of the Survey of
    India (1700 – 1900)*, National Archives of India, New Delhi, undated.

5   See Phillimore cited in note 2, Volume 2, p. 211. We have added the
    italics in this quotation.

6   See *General Descriptive Catalogue of Memoirs, Maps and Geographical
    Materials of the Southern Provinces of the Peninsular of India, 1827*,
    National Archives of India, Delhi, SGO, Manuscript 565, p. 17.

7   See *The Baramahal Records* (Manuscript), Section II, Geography, Board
    of Revenue Miscellaneous Records (hereafter BRMR), Tamil Nadu State
    Archives (hereafter TNSA), volume 151, undated; also *The Baramahal
    Records* (Manuscript) Section XXI, Miscellany, volume 1, BRMR,
    TNSA, volume 178, undated: and *Map of the Salem Collectorate
    Compiled Chiefly from a Survey of the Baramahal and Salem District,
    Executed by Mr Mather under the Direction of Colonel Read and from the
    Original Materials of the Mysore Survey Executed under the Direction of
    Colonel Mackenzie*, National Archives of India, Map F 147/56, undated.

8   See, for example, *Statistical and Geographical Maps of the Mysore
    Survey*, National Archives of India, Maps F 132/13, F 132/16 and F 134/
    6, all undated.

9   See, for example, Dharma Kumar, *Land and Caste in South India*,
    Cambridge University Press, Cambridge, 1965

10 See M. Roncayolo, 'Géographie et villages désertés' in *Villages Désertés
    et Histoire Économique XIe – XVIIIe siècle*, SEVPEN, Paris, 1965, p. 26.

11 An important data source on deserted villages at the end of the nineteenth
    century is mentioned in D. Rothermund, 'A Survey of Rural Migration
    and Land Reclamation in India, 1885' in *Journal of Peasant Studies*,
    Volume 1, No. 4, April 1977, pp. 230 – 42. I have been unable to locate in
    the National Archives of India a relevant document mentioned by
    Rothermund, namely W. W. Hunter, *Movements of the People and Land*

Reclamation Schemes, undated. For data on deserted villages in more recent years, see Census of India, *Uninhabited Villages of Mysore*, Occasional Paper – 1, Karnataka, 1981.

12 Coimbatore fell under the authority of the East India Company in 1800. It was therefore included in the Survey of Mysore directed by Mackenzie. But in 1807 the regular district survey still did not take place, see Madras Public Consultation, 13 March 1807, TNSA, volume 323, pp. 1470 – 5. Further, we know that at the end of the eighteenth century some areas of Coimbatore were particularly affected by depopulation. This was the case, for example, in Dharapuram and Dindigul-Madurai (see the testimony of G. Wynch that we cite in the text below).

13 The more recent data for Coimbatore district are not included in this total of 86. Generally, the administrative units employed in this paper correspond to taluks and zamindaris in their geographical boundaries. Sometimes it was necessary to regroup data so that valid comparisons could be made.

14 Approximately 15 per cent of administrative units had no deserted sites.

15 Sometimes it is not clear whether the statistics on deserted villages in Salem in 1835 – 40 are completely independent of the figures compiled earlier by Mather.

16 See G. Wynch, Collector of Dindigul, to J. Huddleston, Dharapuram, 30 April and 1 June 1791, Board of Revenue Proceedings, Conquered Countries, (hereafter BRPCC), TNSA, volume 2, p. 252 and pp. 280 – 9.

17 See G. Wynch, cited in note 16, pp. 280 – 9.

18 See Board of Revenue Proceedings (hereafter BRP), 21 October 1844, TNSA, volume 1934, p. 13807.

19 See BRP, 7 September 1807, TNSA, volume 452, p. 7123.

20 For a study of settlement patterns by land tenure status see M. L. Reiniche, 'Statut, fonctions et droits. Relations agraires au Tamilnadu' in *L'Homme*, Volume XVIII, January – June 1978, pp. 135 – 66.

21 See *The Baramahal Records* (Manuscript), Section X, Village Register, volumes 2, 4 and 5, BRMR, TNSA, volumes 166, 168 and 169. I thank Brian Murton for providing me with a copy of these documents.

22 See L. Place, *Report on the Jagir of Chinglepet* (Enclosures and Statements), BRMR, TNSA, (Chinglepet), volume 48A.

23 In this connection we know that the Brahmadeya villages of the coastal plains were particularly important centres of Tamil culture during the medieval period, see B. Stein, *Peasant State and Society in Medieval South India*, Oxford University Press, Delhi, 1980, pp. 141 – 72.

24 See S. Lushington, *Settlement Report*, Tirunelveli, 28 May 1802, TNSA, ASO (D) 382, p. 4.

25 See Census of Thanjavur, Papers of The Walkers of Bowland, Manuscript 13615 B, National Library of Scotland, Edinburgh.

26 See, for example, *Report of the Tanjore Commissioners, A.D. 1799*, District Press, Tanjore, 1904; also T. V. Row, *A Manual of the District of Tanjore in the Madras Presidency*, Government Press, Madras, 1883. For a relevant overview see K. Gough, *Rural Society in South East Asia*, Cambridge University Press, Cambridge, 1981, especially chapter 6.

27   In this context we should note that the wars of the second half of the
     eighteenth century appear to have affected both the valleys and interior
     areas. So it is difficult to take for granted that 'the warfare took place
     mostly on the plains and seems, except for occasional tribute raids, to have
     avoided the valleys' as Baker writes; see C. J. Baker, *An Indian Rural
     Economy, 1880–1955*, Oxford University Press, Delhi, 1984, p. 49.
28   See Wynch cited in note 16, pp. 280–9.
29   See J. G. Graham, *Second Report on the Settlement of the Estates
     Composing the Vanyambadi District of Krishnagiri Division of Barama-
     hal*, BRMR, TNSA, volume 142, folio 18.
30   See *The Baramahal Records* (Manuscript), Section II, cited in note 7.
31   See Murton cited in note 1; and B. Stein, 'Idiom and Ideology in Early
     Nineteenth Century South India' in P. Robb (ed.), *Rural India: Land,
     Power and Society Under British Rule*, Curzon Press, London, 1983, pp.
     23–58 and 46–7.
32   See W. MacLeod, Assistant Collector, to Captain A. Read, Rasipuram, 1
     November 1794, *The Baramahal Records*, Section I, Management, The
     Government Press, Madras, 1907, p. 234.
33   See G. Wynch, to the Board of Revenue, BRCC, TNSA, volume 2, pp.
     409–12.
34   For a history of the administration's interest in irrigation see Phillimore
     cited in note 2.
35   See BRP, 13 August 1802, TNSA, volume 323, pp. 8825–86. Twenty
     years later, the cost of renovating the irrigation system of Salem was
     estimated at more than 86,000 rupees, see BRP, 28 January 1822, TNSA,
     volume 904, p. 891.
36   See BRP, 20 August 1818, TNSA, volume 799, p. 9094; BRP 13 May
     1822, TNSA, volume 912, p. 4368; and BRP, 15 May 1823, TNSA,
     volume 948, p. 4104.
37   See BRP, 5 December 1827, TNSA, volume 1125, p. 13308.
38   See BRP, 22 November 1827, TNSA, volume 1122, p. 12287.
39   On the history of Muslims in South India see S. Bayly, *Islam and State
     Power in Pre-colonial South India*, Centre d'Études de L'Inde et de l'Asie
     du Sud, Paris, May 1986.
40   In using conventional economic categories here — such as price, production
     and land revenue — we are implicitly assuming that they are at least partly
     appropriate to an understanding of the economic history of pre-colonial India.
     However, we know that such categories can fail to reflect other transactions
     which may be important, such as reciprocal forms of exchange.
41   The present writer is currently undertaking a wider study of the crisis in
     south India in the eighteenth century.
42   See H. Dodwell, *Dupleix and Clive, The Beginning of Empire*, Frank
     Cass, London, 1967. On the Poligar uprising see K. Rajayyan, *South
     Indian Rebellion, The First War of Independence, 1800–1801*, Rao and
     Raghavan, Mysore, 1971.
43   To be precise, the population totals are 1,058,424 and 655,271 for
     1779–80 and 1788–89 respectively. The source for these statistics is
     Census of Thanjavur, cited in note 25.

44 See J. Deloche, *La circulation en Inde avant la révolution des transports, Tome 1, La voie de terre*, Ecole Française d'Extrème Orient, Paris, 1980, especially pp. 250 – 6.

45 See W. Corbett, Collector of Coimbatore, to the Board of Revenue, 30 March 1791, BRCC, TNSA, volume 2, p. 141.

46 For an overview see B. Murton, 'Spatial and Temporal Patterns of Famine in Southern India before the Famine Codes' in B. Currey and Graeme Hugo (eds.), *Famine as a Geographical Phenomenon*, Reidel Publishing Company, Dordrecht, 1984, pp. 71 – 89.

47 This is based on a study of the ecology of the Salem region undertaken by the French Institute in Pondicherry.

48 See the data compiled on this by the Grain Committee, in Madras Public Consultation, 1807, TNSA, volumes 321 – 5.

49 On this fever epidemic, see Madras Revenue Department Consultation, 18 October 1811, TNSA, volume 185, pp. 3320 – 541.

50 For a really complete demographic study of this period it would be necessary to present in detail all the available pre-census statistics, see R. Lardinois 'Les statistique pre-censitaires de la population Tamoule 1792 – 1871' mimeo, in preparation. See also Kumar cited in note 9, pp. 120 – 4.

51 The census of 1871 gave a population of 397,552 for Madras, thus casting some doubt on the 1822 census total for the town of 462,051. See *Census of the Town of Madras, 1871*, Government Press, Madras, 1873.

52 See note 43.

53 For the statistics relating to Hosur see C. Mackenzie, *Report of the Survey of Mysore*, British Museum, Additional Manuscript 13660, folio 94; for the other districts in Salem see BRP, 13 August 1802, TNSA, volume 323, pp. 8825 – 86.

54 This number is less than two other contemporary estimates of the population calculated on the basis of assuming mean household sizes of 4.5 and 5.0 persons. These produce respective totals of 966,000 and 1,056,000 people, see BRP, 29 August 1822, TNSA, volume 923, pp. 8157 – 60.

55 See J. W. B. Dykes, *Salem, an Indian Collectorate*, W. H. Allen, London, 1853.

56 See *Chinglepet District Records, Report of Mr. Place dated 6th October 1795*, ASO (D), TNSA, volume 85, p. 2.

57 There is no detailed study of the urban sector in south India in the eighteenth century. For some preliminary views see N. Gupta, *Towers, Tanks and Temples: Some Aspects of Urbanism in South India in the Eighteenth and Nineteenth Centuries*, Urban History Association of India, Occasional Papers, Series 5, 1983. On the growth of colonial ports in an earlier period, see, for example, S. Arasaratnam, 'Factors in the Rise, Growth and Decline of Coromandel Ports Circa 1550 – 1720', in *South Asia, Journal of South Asian Studies*, Volume 7, No. 2, December 1984, pp. 19 – 30.

58 See D. Cockburn, Collector of Salem, to the Board of Revenue, BRP, 30 August 1802, TNSA, volume 323, p. 9897.

59 See G. Wynch, Collector of Dindigul, to J. Huddleston, Dharapuram, 30
    May 1791, BRPCC, TNSA, p. 252.

3

THE MECHANICS OF DEMOGRAPHIC AND ECONOMIC GROWTH IN UTTAR PRADESH; 1800 – 1900

Simon Commander

Surprisingly little is known about the economic and demographic dynamics of the Indian subcontinent in the period prior to the organized collection of official statistics towards the end of the nineteenth century. This paper attempts to piece together available data dealing with the overall development of a part of the north Indian economy. The paper is particularly concerned with the Doab, the alluvial plain between the Jumna and the Ganges that stretches down from Saharanpur — at the foothills of the Sewaliks — to the confluence of the rivers at Allahabad.[1] Located in the modern Indian state of Uttar Pradesh, the Doab was, at various times, administratively a part of the North Western Provinces and subsequently the United Provinces.

Lack of basic information on the development of the region prior to 1870 – 80 is most striking with regard to demographic details. In general, little attempt has been made to estimate the population of the region prior to 1872. When such estimates have been made then simple backward extrapolation has yielded the figures.[2] But if backward extrapolation was a suitable mechanism for estimating the population of pre-1872 Uttar Pradesh, then an immediate problem would arise. Would it be sensible to take the relatively slack growth rates that prevailed between 1872 and 1921 as the underlying trend, or the more rapid growth rates that resulted in the doubling of population in the fifty years after 1921? Equally, might not the low growth rates that prevailed between 1872 and 1921 merely reflect the operation of Malthusian checks, the surpassing of which was determined by medical advances or advances in production technology? In short, the problems, are significant, and in the absence of reliable regional and national data it is necessary to pull together some of the data available from primary and other sources.

There is little doubt that the economy of late eighteenth century and early nineteenth century north India was overwhelmingly rural. For sure, there were developed centres of handloom production and a range of small-scale rural processing industries. But these accounted for a relatively small share of the labour force when measured in terms of the aggregate potential supply of labour in the economy. At the same time, the fluidity of the economy needs to be emphasized. In the face of military and economic disturbances, communities proved to be highly mobile. Indication of this can be seen in both eastern Uttar Pradesh in the Gorakhpur region, and also in some of the districts, such as Hissar, that now fall in Haryana. In Gorakhpur, for example, widespread depopulation occurred, probably in the period 1762 – 70.[3] High revenue rates and climatic disturbance combined to stimulate external migration, mostly into neighbouring Nepal or Champaran in Bihar. From a level of around 19,600 villages in Asaf-ud-daula's time, this had fallen to under 6,700 by 1801 with a mere third of the district falling under cultivation. Nevertheless, twenty years later it was estimated that at least two-thirds of the district was cultivated and the population had reached over one and a half million. Thereafter, the trend in population was consistently upwards.

Mobility in the late eighteenth or early nineteenth century context was not merely a function of fiscal or military pressures. In most parts of the region labour scarcity was the primary constraint on production and in the absence of effective and generalized institutional constraints on mobility, this implied that economic hardship or pressure could be responded to by means of desertion or migration.[4] This included migration from countryside to towns, though the scale of such movements, let alone the timing, is almost impossible to estimate. Nevertheless, there are indications that such mobility was made more limited through the operation of guild or guild-like restrictions on employment in urban trades.[5] Given what is known about the production structures and consumption patterns that guided urban output, this would have placed a major barrier to the growth of a rural-urban migratory process, on account of the limited unskilled, casual labour market.

The fact that for the greater part of northern India labour scarcity was the principal feature of the agricultural labour market was undoubtedly enhanced by the impact of the Chalisa famine of 1783. However, there can be little doubt that the degree of scarcity was differentially distributed, and that this was a function not only of relative tax burdens, but also of the tenurial status of the cultivator and the level of fixed capital formation. In the absence of irrigation canals and with masonry wells incurring substantial construction costs, irrigated, better quality soils would obviously generate a higher supply price in terms of potential migration or desertion than the more precarious, rainfed lands that remained predominant. To that extent, population mobility cannot be dissociated from other indices of economic welfare. In parts of eighteenth century Rajasthan, for example, it appears that even with scarce labour, foreclosure on prime irrigated land proximate to market centres was actively pursued by wealthier, capital-advancing cultivators and traders.[6]

If the populations of north India were highly mobile, then this means that close attention has to be paid, particularly at the start of the nineteenth century, to the possibility that major redistributions of population had occurred in the latter part of the eighteenth century. The Gorakhpur example is a particularly clear case. Thus the earliest available estimates of population for the region may represent somewhat abnormal distributions that tend to be subject to a reversion to past distributions over the first twenty years of colonial rule. This appears to be almost certainly the case in those districts of the Upper Doab — Meerut, Muzaffarnagar and Saharanpur — about which the earliest non-census population data are available.

A detailed report compiled in 1807 on the economic condition of the Upper Doab concluded that cultivation was at a lower level than a hundred years earlier.[7] Other sources also suggest that low cultivation levels and population were still common in the second decade of the nineteenth century.[8] However, it is also interesting to note that, where elementary military protection against Sikh raids had been provided, cultivation was far more advanced. The large estate of Raja Ramdayal Singh, around Landhaura in Saharanpur, was widely noted for its prosperity and, by implication, its availability of cultivators. Political and military instability was further reflected in the pattern of settlement, with large and often fortified villages predominating.

Table 1 indicates the apparent evolution of population in the Upper Doab for the period 1807 – 81 with aggregate numbers being deflated by both area terms and in relation to the cultivated area. From these figures it appears that in the case of the Upper Doab, the most rapid acceleration in population occurred in the first fifty years of colonial rule and was accompanied, as would be expected, by an extensive growth in agricultural production, the result of a larger cropped area. For Farrukhabad, a district situated lower down in the Doab, the available evidence points to the most major increases in population occurring prior to the mid-1840s. There, however, extensive growth was less feasible given the already high levels of land occupancy that had been attained by the end of the eighteenth century.

The hypothesis that the first seventy years of the nineteenth century saw major growth in population in the region is partly supported by other available data. In the mid-1830s a systematic survey carried out in the *pargannas* of Mat, Jalesar and Noh Jhil in Mathura district estimated the level of cultivation as well as the number of inhabitants. Between 1834 and 1872 it appears that in these areas the total

Table 1. Population Density: Upper Doab and Farrukhabad, 1807 – 1881.

	Upper Doab		Farrukhabad	
Year	Density per sq. mile	Density per cultivated sq. mile	Density per sq. mile	Density per cultivated sq. mile
1807	119	331	–	–
1814	–	–	203	375
1840	329	566	329	655
1845	–	–	424	786
1850	–	–	473	892
1853	432	701	501	910
1865	437	707	541	953
1872	452	707	527	856
1881	483	744	527	888

Note: (1)   Upper Doab includes the districts of Saharanpur, Meerut and Muzaffarnagar.

Sources:
Upper Doab — Coll. Saharanpur, 22 December 1807 (BRCC, 91, Vol. 18); R. M. Bird, P.P. 1852/53, p. 142 – 5; Census of 1853 (1854), pp. 98 – 9, 110 – 111, 120 – 21; Census of 1865 (1867), General Statement No. 1; Census of N.W.P., 1872, Volume 1, pp. viii – ix; Census of N.W.P., 1881, Volume 1, Forms I, II and XXI.

Farrukhabad — Home Misc. Volume 776: Report on Farrukhabad District by W. Wright, 27 October 1814; K. M. Bird, P.P. 1852/53, pp. 142 – 5; District Gazeteer of U.P., Volume IX, Chapter III, p. 62 (1911); Statistics of Farrukhabad, Report, dated 22 September 1851, from W. H. D'Gruyther, Deputy Collector to Secretary of Govt, N.W.P. regarding a Census taken on the 31 December 1849, in Selections from Records of Govt., N.W.P., No. LIX, pp. 279 – 85 (1855); Census of 1853, pp. 252 – 3; Census of 1865, Table No. 1, pp. 16 – 17; Census of N.W.P., 1872, Volume I, p. ix; Census of N.W.P., 1881, Volume I, Forms I, II and XXI.

population increased by between 42 and 48 per cent.[9] In Bareilly, in neighbouring Rohilkhand, another sample census taken in 1828 suggests that between that year and 1872 the population density of the district almost doubled.[10] Other evidence from parts of Punjab and from the Bombay Deccan appears to demonstrate high population growth rates through the pre-census period of the nineteenth century.[11] This process is likely to have stretched back into part of the eighteenth century, and the rate of increment, at least in areas of the Doab, may have been given a marked upward bias by the migration of populations in the earliest decades of the nineteenth century. Nevertheless, it was widely noted that by the 1850s, if not earlier, land-labour ratios were being radically modified. One consequence was that the *pahikasht* (non-resident cultivators) that were plentiful at the start of the nineteenth century had become altogether rarer by the middle of the century.

The data fragments that have been presented above relate to the overall distribution of population within particular districts of the Doab. To get an occupational or locational breakdown is yet more difficult. The 1881 census report estimated that around 71 per cent of the population of Uttar Pradesh was agricultural.[12] But the conventional census classification of the urban population was simply based on the fact of residence in a settlement with over five thousand inhabitants. In the Upper Doab, as has already been mentioned, villages tended to be large and hence, for example, in Meerut over 15 per cent of the population was classified as urban.[13] This is clearly an overestimate, particularly if this distribution is taken to be representative of the earlier part of the nineteenth century. However, it is important to note that it was precisely the later transformation of large villages into a range of small towns, market and service centres that was a critical ingredient in the superior growth path achieved by that part of the region.

For the greater part of the Doab it is clear that the vast majority of the population lived in settlements of less than one thousand inhabitants. Of the larger settlements — those with more than five thousand inhabitants — the level of concentration was quite high. By 1880 eight large towns — Saharanpur, Meerut, Koil (Aligarh), Agra, Mathura, Farrukhabad, Kanpur and Allahabad — accounted for just under 6 per cent of the total Doab population and over half the estimated urban population. Piecing together a number of population estimates for five major towns, it can be seen that population growth was substantial through the early part of the nineteenth century (see Table 2). Although old centres, like Agra, grew less rapidly both as a function of its decline as an administrative centre and because of the weak agricultural performance of the surrounding area, there was considerable growth in intermediate size market towns, like Hatrass, Khurja, Jalesar or Firozabad.[14] Kanpur — its growth stimulated by its role as a military and commercial centre[15]

Table 2. Population of Principal Towns, 1815 – 1881.

Agra		Allahabad		Kanpur	
Year		Year		Year	
1815	92,658	1814 – 15	43,000 – 49,494	1803	33,390
1829	96,500	1824	38,231	1830	c. 50,000
1839	75,250	1831	64,785	1847	108,796
1846	103,572	1838	52,000	1853	118,000
1853	125,000	1853	72,093	1865	113,601
1865	142,000	1865	105,926	1872	122,770
1872	149,000	1872	143,693	1881	151,444
1881	160,203	1881	148,547		

Meerut		Koil	
Year		Year	
1830	c. 40,000	1847	36,181
1853	41,759	1853	55,001
1865	79,378	1865	48,403
1872	90,808	1872	58,539
1881	99,565	1881	62,443

Sources:

Agra — UPSA, Agra Judicial 13, cited by C. Bayly — 'Town Building in North India, 1790 – 1830', *Modern Asian Studies*, 9, 4 (1975), p. 489; *Bengal and Agra Annual Guide and Gazeteer*, 1841, Volume 1, Part 1, p. 121; Bayly (1975), loc. cit.; Census of 1853, p. 233; Census of 1865, Volume 2, Table 8; Census of 1872, p. 202; Census of 1881, Volume 2, Table 7. The Census passages noted here also apply, for those years, to the figures for Allahabad, Kanpur, Meerut and Koil.

Allahabad — Home Misc. Volume 776, Allahabad District by T. Fortescue, 1 September 1814, p. 771; Bayly (1975), loc. cit.; *Journal of Asiatic Society of Bengal*, Volume 1, January 1832, pp. 34 – 5, and Volume 3, May 1834, p. 244; Census of 1853, p. 343.

Kanpur — C. E. Trevelyan, 'Report upon the Town Duties of the Bengal Presidency', Calcutta, 1835 (Calcutta, 1976), p. 471; R. Montgomery, *Statistical Report of the District of Kanpur* (Agra, 1849), Appendix XXVII, Census of 1853, p. 301.

Meerut — Trevelyan, loc. cit.; Census of 1853, p. 131.

Koil — District Gazeteer of U.P., Volume VI, Aligarh (Allahabad, 1909), p. 197.

— was exceptional in that a significant demand for labour originated by the 1880s from a developing cotton mills sector, that later provided a major base for the city's transformation into an industrial centre. Elsewhere within the region, the most striking feature of the nineteenth century was the very limited growth of a non-agricultural sector where production was not small-scale and predominantly artisan. For the most part, it is evident that agricultural processing and services generated the most significant demand for labour outside of agriculture proper. Indeed, possibly the largest and most widespread 'proto-industrial' activity was that of *khandsari*, a local sugar manufacturing process. Although widespread through eastern Uttar Pradesh and in the Upper Doab, khandsari was principally concentrated in Rohilkhand. Advances were paid to cultivators, thereby effectively hypothecating the crop. Manufacture of sugar was conducted using very simple techniques of production with output being marketed in the local towns. Production was mainly carried out between December and June and clearly generated a demand for labour. Seasonal work for these local sugar manufacturers complemented and, to a certain extent, stabilized the incomes of small farm households, so that as the pressure on land resources grew greater, so equally there was some growth in off-farm employment opportunities.[16]

Information regarding the occupational breakdown of the population is very sparse and mostly unreliable.[17] An interesting twenty-three mouza sample survey, done in Haveli Palam in the vicinity of Delhi in 1827, gives some indication of the occupational composition of the villages. Of a total sample of around 11,500, about 62.5 per cent were classified as cultivators, either as pahikasht tenants, as *zamindars* or as hereditary cultivators. A further 20.5 per cent were classed as manufacturers or traders, 6 per cent as agricultural labourers and a further 11 per cent with a range of professions.[18] In the Doab proper it seems likely that the share of agricultural labourers would have been higher than in the more sparsely populated area near Delhi. Some indication of the number of agricultural labourers can be derived from the caste breakdown for the region. In most official calculations, for instance, *Chamars* were generally assumed to be agricultural labourers or service sector workers. By 1880 Chamars comprised around 15 per cent of the population, the same share attributed by the 1881 census to agricultural labourers.[19] However, it is important to note that agricultural labouring did not necessarily imply lack of access to land, but rather was often associated with access to small parcels of largely unirrigated and relatively unproductive land. A vivid description of the conditions of this group in Aligarh in 1880 exists:

> Though very many of them [Chamars] hold land of their own . . . yet the
> majority are little more than serfs; they are the hired labourers who follow
> the plough, drive the bullocks and sow the seed of both the tenant and
> landlord; they perform most of the menial offices of a village and
> landowners are so jealous of their services that no partition is complete until
> an adequate number of Chamars have been apportioned off to each co-sharer
> in proportion to his interests in the estate.[20]

The strong association between caste status, relative lack of access to
land and employment as agricultural labourers, preceded the period of
land scarcity that emerged towards the end of the nineteenth century.
To that extent, inequalities in land endowments were drawn from a
more complex range of factors than mere labour availability relative to
land.

This can be further seen in the case of the *jajmani* system, where
cultivators were linked to service castes through obligations and grain-
based transactions. Such service groups — carpenters, potters,
ironsmiths, barbers and so on — were clearly a critical component of
any reasonable sized village. Where labour scarcity was the primary
feature of the labour market, as in the sparsely populated region around
Karnal, the number of *kamins*, or service castes, working in a village
was a distinct sign of its prosperity. Although it is clear that in most
villages the working of the jajmani system was far removed from later
models of its functioning, scattered estimates of the share of kamin
population in a village are available.[21] In general, between 15 and 20
per cent of a village's population may have been of service castes.
However, the latter commonly owned small plots of land, and
particularly in the second half of the nineteenth century, a smaller
proportion were actively incorporated in a regular *jajman-kamin*
relationship. This was partly a function of the growing availability of
labour and the fall in the real wage rate, but it was also linked to the
growing preference by employers for payments in cash rather than
through the traditional allocation of wages in kind. In areas where
public works or non-farm employment became available, this also acted
as a factor for breaking apart a more traditional patron-client
relationship.[22]

Summarizing the paper so far, it can be seen that, contrary to earlier
presumptions about the rate of demographic increase, the first seventy
years of the nineteenth century saw a very significant upward shift in
the population of the Doab. There was some urban growth, but it seems
likely that the distribution of the labour force remained roughly
constant. By 1880 it was estimated that over 70 per cent of the
population were employed in agriculture with a further 15-20 per cent
absorbed by the service sector. Manufacturing accounted for less than

10 per cent of the total labour force. However, with the service and manufacturing sector labour forces it is evident that links to agriculture often remained strong, with seasonal participation in family farm or agricultural employment being relatively common. Textile manufacturers in Kanpur, for example, found that imposing labour discipline on the work-force was hardest with regard to mobility restrictions. Employees left the mills to work on their own farms at the peak harvest seasons and these practices remained widespread into this century.[23]

The relative lack of change in the sectoral composition of output through the nineteenth century, when coupled to fairly sharp rates of demographic growth in the Doab, resulted in high-population land densities by the later part of the century. For the Doab as a whole the average density of people per square mile approached 800 by 1880. At the same time, by way of comparison, the population density of Spain's most populated region — Catalonia — was no higher than 280 per square mile.[24] In short, this part of India was already heavily populated with a strong, rather undifferentiated dependence on agriculture.

This high level of population density can be attributed to a number of factors. The Doab — and, in particular, the Agra region — was the former centre of the Mughal state system. High levels of cultivation and human occupation had been attained by the end of the sixteenth century. Moreland estimated that for the Mughal provinces of Agra and Delhi (broadly coterminous with the Doab) the area cultivated in Akbar's time was about three-fourths of that attained by 1920.[25] An alternative estimate by Moosvi, using figures from the Ain-i-Akbari, suggests that gross cultivation in the Doab in 1595 had attained over 70 per cent of the level existing in 1909 – 10.[26] Cultivation, due principally to lower population levels, was maintained at much lower intensity levels, with fallow land being included in the 1595 calculation of cropping coverage. Cultivation intensity was, of course, greatest in areas watered by the major irrigation canals, particularly the eastern Jumna and Delhi Canals. Elsewhere in the Doab, masonry well construction was reasonably advanced by the seventeenth century, with further widespread use of seasonal and temporary *kucha* wells.

Apart from being at the core of the Mughal system, the Doab — a mostly fertile plain — had sustained high rates of demographic growth precisely on account of the capacity to augment production, both — at least in the earlier part of the nineteenth century — through extensive growth and later through intensification, a consequence of enhanced public and private investment in irrigation.

A third factor relates to the demographic system itself. Fertility rates appear to have been high, in that the population age structure tended to be fairly young with a concentration of women in the early child-bearing years. The age at marriage remained very young. 'Effective' marriage most frequently occurred when the bride was around fifteen years old. In the 1880s it appears that in the 15 – 19 age group just under 90 per cent of females in Uttar Pradesh as a whole were married, with that share rising to around 93 per cent for the age bracket 20 – 29 years.[27] Though life expectancy may have been no higher than 30 years through most of the nineteenth century, the birth rate remained high on account of the absence of contraception and the predominance of early marriage. Sharp peaks in the death rate, associated with the presence of dearth and subsistence crises, acted as a temporary break on the rate of population growth. However, the population statistics addressed in this section suggest that even major mortality crises, such as the famine of 1837 – 8, may not have acted as a long-run brake on population growth and may actually have served as demographic 'accelerators' when viewed in a longer term perspective (see below).

THE EVOLUTION OF THE AGRICULTURAL GROSS PRODUCT

The sectoral composition of aggregate output for the region was characterized throughout the nineteenth century by the predominance of agriculture. This much is clear. Yet output trends remain as elusive as those for population. Even post-1880, considerable debate rages concerning the reliability or otherwise of the official statistics.[28] What is clear is that in an economy where, pre-1880, intensification of production through double-cropping was weakly developed, there would be a strong positive correlation between output and population, albeit with falling marginal returns to labour, given constant technology. Diminishing returns would obviously have an impact on the price level for wage goods, and hence for the general price level. Thus, output and productivity trends can, at least in part, be inferred from the cropped area and from the evolution of prices.

As has already been mentioned, the gross cropped area was already high in Mughal times. While military and other disruptions at the end of the eighteenth century resulted in population movements, and in some areas in dislocation of the production process, it would appear that in general the degree of dislocation was not that significant. By 1815 roughly 51 per cent of the total Doab land area was cultivated. There was, however, considerable intra-regional variation. In Etawah as much as 60 per cent of the total area was under the plough, while in the Upper Doab — far more affected by political and military disturbances — around 30 per cent of the total area was cultivated. What emerges consistently from the available records is that between 1815 and 1860 – 70 there was a significant expansion of cultivation in the Upper, and in parts of the Middle Doab.

Thus, from 51 per cent of the total area being cultivated in 1815, this had risen to 56 per cent by 1840 and to just under 62 per cent by 1875 – 80.[29] This share remained broadly constant for the remaining decades of the nineteenth century. In other words, the most pronounced period of extensive growth fell in the half century between 1815 and 1865, and was particularly concentrated in the Upper Doab. There, the growth path was consolidated by the expansion of the canal irrigation system and by the consequent boost to agricultural productivity. Intensification of production also grew particularly rapidly in that part of the Doab. But as elsewhere, this was mostly in the period after 1870. Around 1870 – 5 the proportion of the gross cropped area that was subject to double-cropping was under 5 per cent for the whole Doab. A decade later this share had risen to about 15 per cent, and for the period 1895 – 1920 about a third of the total cultivated area was double-cropped, and over 37 per cent in the Upper Doab.[30]

Despite the fact that the net cropped area increased through the nineteenth century, population growth experienced a far sharper upward trajectory. In the Upper Doab the population may have quadrupled between 1807 and 1880, so that despite the growth in the cultivated area the density of humans per cultivated square mile more than doubled in this same period. For Meerut one of the Settlement Reports noted that:

> the average size of the *abadi* is in fact a good indication in this district of fertility and always varies with the density of population. This density is again adjusted with remarkable exactness to the means of subsistence. Not only is it high in the better parganas — it is nearly 700 per square mile in the North West and about 550 in the East — . . . but . . . the density also follows improvement or deterioration.[31]

In neighbouring Muzaffarnagar it was also reported that by the end of the nineteenth century subdivisioning of holdings had become so minute that the provision of an adequate agricultural base for the growing population was thought to be contingent on improvements in production techniques. The evidence from districts such as these that per capita food output was consistently falling, led many observers to believe that in the absence of population controls, the result would be a form of immiserizing growth.[32]

The rate of growth in the agricultural gross product for the region is difficult to quantify and the measures cited below need to be treated with caution. There is no available evidence on the value of aggregate output in agriculture. Output figures are thus crude physical magnitudes that do not take account of cropping shifts in the intervening periods.

However, it appears that despite the introduction of the Ganges Canal and the rehabilitation of the Eastern Jumna Canal, the scale of cropping shift was not substantial. The cropped area under so-called cash crops — indigo, cotton, sugar-cane — did not expand in the later part of the nineteenth century, but it is important to note that it was in the period 1800 – 30 that the area under cash and export crops was highest relative to the cropped area.[33] With the revenue system and the need for cash payments, output maximization was in relation to relative crop output prices and costs, rather than in relation to some hypothetical satisfaction of consumption needs.

Assuming that cropping shifts did not overly distort the composition of aggregate agricultural output, it seems that in the Upper Doab between 1807 and 1880 output of all crops increased by around eight times, with the net cropped area nearly trebling and population quadrupling in the same period.[34] In Agra district, food grain output may have increased by around 80 or 85 per cent between 1811 and 1880, but in the same period the population of the district doubled.[35] In Kanpur between the late 1830s and 1870 there was a small increase in the cultivated acreage — of around 4 per cent — but total agricultural output may have remained roughly constant with little shift in crop composition.[36]

An attempt to draw up some crude input-output statistics for food production was undertaken as part of the Famine Commission Report published in 1881. Apart from the Upper Doab area — the Meerut Division — all other parts of the Doab were marked by significant consumption gaps that required the importation of grain from other regions of the country.[37] This was at a time when non-foodcrops accounted on average for between 15 and 16 per cent of the total cropped area. It is clear that the region was inscribed in a far larger trading circuit that makes estimating production capacity in relation to endogenously derived consumption needs an inapposite calculation.

What is rather more relevant, however, is the fact that despite major extensive growth at the start of the nineteenth century, coupled later to accelerated intensification of production, productivity trends may not in general have been strongly positive. Waterlogging and salination of land fed by canals, as well as over-cropping, soil degradation and the absence of yield-enhancing inputs had negative implications for productivity in the nineteenth century. In Muzaffarnagar — a district where output growth was more pronounced than in most of the Doab-crop-cutting experiments demonstrated that both for irrigated and unirrigated similar soils wheat yields remained almost constant between 1840 and 1978. In that district, average physical yields for crops other than sugar-cane may have declined by around 10 per cent between 1840 and 1924.[38] For the Doab as a whole, it is very unlikely that average physical productivity for most major crops increased. There is no evidence that the quality of husbandry or the technical production function saw a major positive shift, while there are convincing general indications that irrigation and climatic constraints served to hold back substantive productivity increments. Per capita output of all agricultural commodities undoubtedly fell over the nineteenth century, though this was not the case in the more dynamic parts of the region, such as Meerut.

Food crop and productivity trends could be expected in a largely agricultural economy, marked by a low general development of productive forces, to be strongly reflected in the rate of inflation, given likely consumption weights. Yet, it ought to be borne in mind that despite a tendency for prices to converge around a mean with the advent of the railways and more developed commercial flows of information[39], for much of the nineteenth century there was no such thing as a unified price level. This was not only because of unequal trade relationships and interlinked markets, but also because of substantial informational constraints and bordered markets. Nevertheless, it can be hypothesized that the price level for domestic food items would be negatively associated with the trend in agricultural sector productivity.

Analysis of the available price series for the Doab demonstrates that agricultural prices underwent very sharp short-run output determined fluctuations. This was because stocks were implicitly excluded from affecting aggregate available production over the short run. With often dramatic fluctuations in the gross product across season — particularly in the semi-arid and unirrigated tracts — the price level showed similar fluctuations with an obvious inverse relationship. However, using five-year moving averages for five places in the Doab — Jalalabad (Muzaffarnagar), Agra, Aligarh, Farrukhabad and Kanpur — it appears that gram, barley and wheat prices were subject to a weak underlying upward trend between the first and second decades of the nineteenth century and 1857, the year of the so-called Mutiny. Post-1857 there was a very clear upward shift in the food price level. In the short and medium run this was attributed not only to the Mutiny but also to the famines of 1860 – 1 and 1868 – 9. During the 1870s prices fell back under the impact of good harvests, but continued to display a strong underlying upward movement over the next half-century. Between 1861 and 1890 the retail price index for all-India for foodgrains rose by 24 per cent and by 23 per cent for all agricultural commodities. The increase was roughly comparable in the Doab.[40]

At this stage it is appropriate to summarize and extend some of the points of the argument. In the first place, the paper has demonstrated that significant demographic and productive growth was achieved in the north Indian economy through the nineteenth century. The strongest rates of growth fell in the period prior to 1860 – 70. However, despite the fact that the land-labour balance fell in favour of labour, state taxation of cultivators was high. Land revenue demand ranged between 91 and 67 per cent of average anticipated assets between 1812 and 1844, being reduced post-1855 to 50 per cent, and subsequently in 1875 to 50 per cent of actual existing assets.[41] The burden of state taxation was undoubtedly at its peak in the first forty years of colonial rule. As prices remained broadly constant between the first decade of the nineteenth century and the late 1850s, trends in the nominal incidence of taxation would tend to approximate trends in the real rate of fiscality. For the Doab it can be calculated that the effective rate of taxation by the State per unit of land rose, in index terms, from the base year of 1803 – 4 to 132 in 1810 – 11. Subsequently it reached 148 in 1817 – 18, 158 in 1824 – 25, 175 in 1838 – 40 and peaked at 180 in 1840 – 42. Between 1840 – 42 and 1880 – 81 the taxation rate remained broadly constant in nominal terms, declining in real terms.[42] Thus, the highest taxation levels were registered in the first three decades of colonial rule and were evidenced in the relatively high levels of revenue default and auction sales that were a marked feature of districts such as Mathura and Aligarh.[43] It was partly on account of the burden of state taxation and difficulties in meeting arrears that landholders or zamindars deserted their holdings at times of severe production shortfalls in the early colonial period. However, the longer-run trend for state taxation was downwards. So given farm-gate price increments post-1860 and, on account of an increasingly larger supply of labour, a tendency for real agricultural wages to fall, landholders unencumbered with debt and interest payments would have seen possibly significant income gains from farm activity. More marginal farmers, landless labourers and debt-encumbered cultivators would have, in contrast, either faced harder times, or else have realized a far smaller share of potential income gains from this combined movement of basic economic indices. Tenant farmers — an increasingly larger share of the total cultivating population in the Doab — would, in the face of a strongly competitive land market and not wholly effective rent laws, have also faced higher costs for access to land.[44] Despite the fact that in irrigated areas of the Doab yields may have increased for certain crops, or at least remained constant, there are indications that where assured irrigation was not available, productivity levels were subject to a long-run declining trend. The failure to raise land and labour productivities in the core productive sector — agriculture — naturally had major and largely deleterious implications for the welfare of farmers, tenants and labourers in the region. The decline in per capita incomes in the sector was accelerated by these factors in the second half of the nineteenth century.

OUTPUT VARIANCE, SUBSISTENCE CRISES AND MORTALITY

Although it is just about possible to estimate the production trend for the region through the greater part of the nineteenth century, agricultural output was subject to very substantial seasonal and annual fluctuations. These fluctuations were of great significance in determining the distribution of income over a short and medium term, both within the agricultural classes and between parts of the region. In the latter regard, those areas that gained access to canal irrigation and where the constancy of water supply was the main positive feature — such as parts of Meerut, Bulandshahr or Kanpur — were also characterized by more stable and probably higher farm income levels. The inequality of harvests was obviously strongly determined not only by the initial distribution of entitlements at the household level, but also by relative levels of fixed capital investment and social infrastructure. Where the latter was higher, the income stabilization effect, when ironing out windfalls or slump years, was almost invariably associated with a dynamic, superior growth path.

Output fluctuations were largely a function of climatic variance and of rainfall in particular. In much of Uttar Pradesh the average coefficient of variation for rainfall across the year exceeded 30 per cent. In the central Gangetic plain where average rainfall varied between 14 and 50 inches, areas with between 30 and 50 inches could expect ten dry years in fifty, and in Kanpur it was estimated that one in five years was marked by dearth or severe natural disorder.[45] While regional famine periods are easy to identify — examples include 1813 – 14, 1833, 1837 – 38, 1860 – 61, 1868 – 69, 1877 – 78, and 1896 — almost every year was characterized by often severe intra-regional, often very localized shortages. After 1860 when official data make it easier to monitor output fluctuations, it can be calculated that between 1860 and 1880 the risk of harvest failure was of the order of 8 or 9 harvests out of a total of 20 harvests.[46] The scale of crop loss could be substantial. In Agra in 1812 a lack of timely rain severely depleted the output of the *kharif* crop. For the major food crops — jowar, bajra, rice, maize as well as oil seeds and pulses — output was a mere 15 per cent of the previous year, and that previous year's output was in turn some 20 per cent smaller than the kharif crop of 1810. In other words, the 1812 crop was barely 12.5 per cent of the output level of 1810.[47]

When faced with large shortfalls in production over a series of years and, in the first decades of colonial rule, inflexibility in the collection of land revenue, desertion to other parts of the region was relatively commonplace. But by the 1850s, as demographic growth restricted the availability of land, this option was not as feasible, at least for zamindars. However, less constrained mobility was not necessarily a correlate of a better ability to cope with drought or dearth. Famines in the pre-1840 period were marked by very severe rates of human and animal mortality. The famine of 1837 – 8 is probably the most extreme case in point.

In that year famine covered as large an area as 25,000 square miles in which normally lived a population of around 8 million. Auckland's report of February 1838 gives some idea of the scale and gravity of the situation:

> From Kanpur to Farrukhabad the agricultural distress and destitution of the people was the most important issue and harrowing accounts pour in from Kalpi, Agra, Etawah and Mainpuri. This is the part of the country that has suffered most and where the largest expenditure is required in order to palliate the evil and prevent a total depopulation of the country by starvation and emigration. The fall in the usual season of rains was unusually late and scanty and an absolute drought has followed up to the present time — half the kharif crop in these districts has entirely failed and grass and fodder also lost. There is extensive mortality among the cattle . . . and in some districts those that have not died have been driven off to other parts of the country in order that they might be saved. There is great difficulty in irrigating the land for the rabi crops — much land is not cultivated as a consequence and is lying waste. There is every reason to suppose that there is still a large quantity of grain in store in these provinces and this is shown by the comparatively reasonable price of grain, viz. 10 – 16 seers per Re. But, still the fields are thrown out of cultivation, cultivators are unemployed and merchants can no longer support them, when there is no coming crop to make good the advance. Even if the price of grain were lower it would do little to alleviate the distress.[48]

The quotation brings out very clearly the main features of Indian famines — sharp falls in current output with comparable decline in the sown area for the next harvest, and a severe contraction in the level of employment generated both within family farms and through the labour market. Apart from the obvious short-run inverse association between prices and output, the fall in the sown area structured future price expectations, driving food prices further upwards. For those with stocks or sufficient grain, this price rise effectively deflated the real weight of state taxation. For those without stocks and with declining access to the labour market, and hence to off-farm generated entitlements, years of dearth tended to coincide with years of heavy revenue default and, particularly in the first three decades of the nineteenth century, high levels of distress sales of landholding (*malguzari*) rights. In the earlier part of the century when migration or desertion remained one possible strategy in the face of famine, this naturally raised the level of risk associated with money-lending or grain advances. With inefficient collateral — a function of potential mobility — this normally resulted in a very thin capital market. While loans could not normally be called in, new lending tended to be suspended. However, as the mobility option faded in the later part of the century, the credit constraint became less binding and this may have been an important factor in evening out liquidity or food variance over the production cycle. At the same time, it ensured that debt linkages — and hence service payments — became more entrenched.[49]

Yet the feature of Indian famines and production variance that is of most concern in this paper was the impact on human mortality. In 1837 – 8 it is possible to put together some broad indicators. For Agra, the worst affected district, it appears that as much as 20 per cent of the population of the district either perished or migrated in the famine year.[50] In Sukrawa — a pargana of Farrukhabad — between 22 and 25 per cent of the population died,[51] while in Etawah district it was estimated that as much as 15 per cent of the total population died.[52] If it is remembered that in the 1860 – 1 famine, where mortality was at much lower levels than in 1837 – 8, deaths from famine in Bulandshahr — an area not that badly affected — approached 4 per cent of the total population,[53] then an overall mortality rate of between 15 and 20 per cent for large parts of the Doab in 1837 – 8 does not seem improbable. In Agra town alone, it is clear that the total population declined substantially on account of famine (see Table 2). Through the year 1838 daily burials by the police exceeded 400 and this continued for over 7 months.

If the famine of 1837 – 8 was the most serious of the century in north India and was accompanied by the highest level of excess mortality, the rate of recovery was remarkably fast. In Agra where excess mortality may have been in the region of 20 per cent, the population fifteen years after the famine year was about 50 per cent higher than in the pre-famine period. In neighbouring Mathura, it was noted that '1838 is invariably given as the date when the land began to be largely reclaimed'. This was in part attributed to 'the number of new roads then opened up for the purpose of affording employment to the starving population'.[54] Apart from anything else, such infrastructural investment encouraged new settlers into the region.

The relatively rapid rate of recovery from famine was evident through most of the Doab and was evidenced in the high level of revenue recovery achieved by the State in the years immediately following the famine. In Kanpur, where excess mortality had been reported to be high, by 1840 conditions were being reversed, as the following quotation shows:

The district is now in a flourishing condition which is amazing considering the ruin of 1837 – 8. With the exception of Bhognipur and southern parts of Derapur and Ghatampur, scarcely any perceptible decrease of cultivation has taken place, and it is from the number of unroofed and ruined houses alone that a stranger could suppose that the country had so recently been visited by one of the most awful calamities on record. However, there is still a general reduction of rent rates and cultivation is below the earlier standard, although from the land abandoned being at a distance from the villages, the eye of a casual observer is not struck by the change. The cultivators of the out-field, who were thrust out, as it were, by a dense population, now finding room, have returned to the better lands of the in-field, leaving the poor soils in the exterior to lie waste, or be cultivated by non-resident cultivators at rates two-thirds below what the same land formerly yielded, and in several parganas, the hamlets or off-shoots of the old village, which owed their existence to a superabundant population have entirely disappeared.[55]

The demographic and economic impact of famine was thus far weaker than appears, say, to have been the case in the *ancien regime* economies of Europe.[56] Rather than providing the effective ceiling for population growth within a demographic system characterized by dynamical stability, Indian nineteenth century famines may have acted more as demographic accelerators. Coupled with low life expectancy levels, such famines ensured that the age structure of the population remained very young.[57] Over the medium term, this had a strong positive impact on the fertility rate and it was generally noted that years of heavy mortality and high prices were commonly followed by sharp upswings in the number of marriages and births.

The impact and incidence of famine on the population underwent a major change through the course of the nineteenth century. With the introduction of a Famine Code and a more organized system of food and work distribution, excess mortality rates were distinctly lowered in the period post-1840. In the major famine year of 1860 – 1 excess mortality in the worst affected tracts did not exceed 10 per cent.[58] At the same time, the impact of dearth was more differentiated in social terms. A report on the 1868 – 9 famine noted that agricultural labourers, weavers, artisans and the urban poor were the hardest hit.[59] With limited access to credit and the collapse of the market for non-food items, urban petty producers and other artisans were a major casualty of famine years. Where assured supplies of irrigation were not forth-coming, the major issue was the lack of work, rather than simple foodgrain availability. The collapsed demand for labour was a principle spur to the movement of agricultural labourers and marginal farmers towards either relief works or else to areas where irrigation had maintained the demand for labour. However, as a consequence of improved transportation of grains, an elaborate system of famine relief, and growth in the share of total cultivated area that was irrigated, wide fluctuations in mortality attributable to output trends and food prices were significantly abated. Instead, excess mortality and relatively low demographic growth rates were, post-1880, increasingly associated with the outbreak of several powerful epidemic-induced crises that culminated in the extraordinary influenza outbreak of 1918 – 19. This outbreak resulted in at least two million deaths in Uttar Pradesh alone.[60]

Disease-induced mortality was by no means dissociated from famine or periods of dearth. In 1878 – 9 excess mortality levels in the Doab were largely the combined result of famine and the spread of 'fever' and general illness that followed the food shortages of 1878.[61] This pattern of famine being followed by disease can be traced throughout the nineteenth century. In 1856, for example, cholera outbreaks started in Agra town and followed a period of high food prices. The passage of the disease can be quite closely studied.[62] Two weeks after its first appearance in Agra, cholera outbreaks were reported in Aligarh and Mathura, and within a month it had spread further to Meerut, Muzaffarnagar and Saharanpur.

Nevertheless, the virulence of the epidemic outbreaks that occurred in the latter decades of the century and the first two decades of the twentieth century went beyond the customary, relatively short-run linkages between shortages, high prices and disease. Rather the nature of these later epidemics has to be explained not merely by their exotic, non-endogenized properties — as with plague — but also with regard to the material environment in which such maladies were nurtured. Firstly, the mortality effect of these epidemics was strongest in the more backward and highly populated parts of the Doab. Secondly, as in famine periods, the incidence of mortality was highest among the poorer classes in both town and countryside. This was obviously related to nutritional status and general living conditions. To that extent, the mortality focus of later periods of dearth and disease was more socially discriminatory.

From what has been said in this section, it is clear that a simple distinction can be drawn between the character of mortality — and, in particular, mortality peaks — in the earlier part of the nineteenth century and that which developed in the forty years post-1880. In the first period, roughly 1800 – 80, output variance was commonly expressed in a classical subsistence-cum-demographic crisis. Sometimes this was the result of outright production shortfalls in effectively closed small-scale economies. Mostly, however, it resulted from lack of purchasing power and liquidity, which was largely a function of the withdrawal of borrowing rights and employment. In the second phase, 1880 – 1920, high mortality in Uttar Pradesh tended to become more a function of disease which, though periodically associated with food shortages, was not invariably synonymous with dearth.

CONCLUSION

The paper has attempted to present a broad overview of the main economic and demographic developments in the Doab region of Uttar Pradesh. Because of the very close association between population and output trends, and hence with the level of cultivation, a range of indicators have been used to provide a broad picture of the pre-1870 production and demographic regime.

While the data that have been presented for population are subject to a high level of error, there is a very general concordance from all sources regarding the strong upward movement in population and output in the first half of the nineteenth century. If the exact measures of change will continue to remain debatable, it nevertheless appears quite clear that the demographic developments that prevailed in Uttar Pradesh, and indeed throughout the subcontinent, between 1880 and 1920, were strongly discontinuous from those of the previous fifty years. In that earlier period, despite a series of major famines culminating in the high mortality of 1837 – 8, the population of the region had grown substantially, and with this growth there was a notable increase in the cultivated area. Indeed, until the 1870s the main characteristics of output growth from the core sector of the economy — agriculture — was its extensive nature. After 1870, the declining availability of land, and falling productivity, accelerated the development of double-cropping. Where irrigation was secure, intensive growth — particularly in the Upper Doab — was accompanied in the longer run by significant advances in productivity.

The failure to shift the technology frontier outwards while, at the same time, conserving a high fertility demographic regime, had serious implications for the welfare of the region's inhabitants. It seems likely that for the bulk of agricultural landholders, tenants and labourers, per capita income levels fell. This was not simply due to severe short-run disequilibria introduced by massive climatic and hence output variance, but also to the emerging distribution of rights to land, capital and employment. If the Doab economy largely failed to achieve major productivity advances in the period under study, this did not imply that the lower level of aggregate welfare that resulted was the type of 'shared poverty' that Geertz argues emerged in colonial Java.[63]

Inequalities in land endowments and, increasingly, in access to labour markets became more pronounced. For if much of nineteenth century growth was of the 'old style' — through extensive means — this was closely linked to the highly skewed distribution of assets and income that has subsequently come to be a hallmark of the Indian agrarian economy.

NOTES TO CHAPTER 3

1   The paper draws extensively upon the author's Ph.D. thesis: *The Agrarian Economy of Northern India, 1800 – 1900*, Cambridge University, 1980.
2   See, for example, M. D. Morris, 'The Population of All-India, 1800 – 1951', *Indian Economic and Social History Review*, Volume 11, 1974, pp. 309 – 13.
3   Mufti Ghulam Hazrat, *History of Gorakhpur, c. 1810*, India Office Library (henceforth IOL), Mss 4540; Memorial Relative to Gorakhpur District by P. W. Grant, Surveyor and Joint Commissioner on the Frontier, Lucknow, 10 March 1821, Allahabad, Uttar Pradesh State Archives (henceforth UPSA), Gorakhpur Commissioner's Pre-Mutiny Records, Volume 15, File 17, part 1. See also, R. Balfour, Collector, Gorakhpur to Bd (12 June) 16 July 1810, IOL, Board of Revenue, Coded and Conquered Provinces, (henceforth BRCC) Range 91, Volume 44.
4   See, for example, J. R. Hutchinson, *Allygurh Statistics*, Tehsil Koil, Roorkee, 1856; W. Tyler, Mathura to T. J. Turner, 10 April 1835, UPSA, Mathura Revenue, Volume 138; R. H. Tulloh, Meerut to H. H. Thomas, 16 June 1823, UPSA, Meerut Collectorate Book 18; H. G. Christian, Agra to M. Moore (10 April 1818) 5 January 1819, IOL, BRCC, Range 93, Volume 43; A. Wright, Agra to M. Moore (7 May) 4 June 1816, BRCC, Range 92, Volume 58; H. Mackenzie to A. Ross, 18 July 1822, UPSA, Saharanpur Revenue, Volume 8; *Notes on Tenant-Rights and on the rights of Jagirdars*, Allahabad, 1869, pp. 31ff.
5   C. A. Bayly, *Rulers, Townsmen and Bazaars: North Indian Society in the Age of British Expansion, 1770 – 1870*, Cambridge, 1983.
6   I am indebted to Madhavi Bajekal for this information.
7   H. Wilkinson, Magistrate, Zillah Saharanpur to G. Dowdeswell (8 December 1805) 2 January 1806, Bengal Criminal and Judicial, Range 129, Volume 8: National Archives of India (henceforth NAI), Survey of India Memoir 381, 1814 – 1817, Saharanpur.
8   R. W. Gillan, *Final Settlement Report of Meerut District*, Allahabad 1901; A. Cadell, *Report on the Settlement of the Ganges Canal Tract in Muzaffarnagar District*, Allahabad 1878; J. Powell to Captain Armstrong, Fort William, 3 March 1804, No. 75, NAI, Foreign Secretariat, 3 March 1884, Volume 3.
9   Calculated from, Report on the Settlement of the District of Mathura, in *Reports on the Revenue Settlement of the NWP under Reg IX, 1833*,

Volume 2, Part 1, 1863, pp. 51 – 7; R. S. Whiteway, *Settlement Report of Mathura District*, Allahabad, 1879, pp. 25 – 6.

10 H. S. Boulderson, Abstract Statement of 412 villages in Zillah Bareilly, *Journal of Asiatic Society of Bengal*, Volume 3, September 1834, p. 1475; Census of NWP, 1881, Volume 1, Appendix 9, p. xxxiv.

11 See, for example, T. Kessinger, *Vilyatpur*, Berkeley, 1974, p. 86; Sumit Guha, *The Agrarian Economy of the Bombay Deccan, 1818 – 1941*, Oxford, 1985; Dharma Kumar, *Land and Caste in South India*, Cambridge, 1965.

12 Census of NWP, 1872, No. VII, p. 201.

13 Census of NWP and Awadh, 1881, Volume I, pp. 2 – 7.

14 J. Marjoribanks, Aligarh District, Home Misc. Volume 776, February, 1815, p. 1445; W. H. Smith, *Final Report on the Revision of Settlement of Aligarh District*, Allahabad, 1882, p. 819.

15 R. Montgomery, *Statistical Report on District of Kanpur*, Agra, 1849.

16 For a fuller discussion, see, S. J. Commander, 'Proto-Industrial Production as a Barrier to Industrialisation? The Case of the North Indian Sugar Industry, 1850 – 1980', *Economic and Political Weekly*, Volume 20 (12), March 23, 1985, pp. 505 – 16.

17 J. Krishnamurthy, 'The Occupational Structure', in Dharma Kumar (ed.), *Cambridge Economic History of India*, Volume 2, Cambridge, 1982, pp. 533 – 50.

18 Boards Collections, IOL, Volume 1213, No. 30953.

19 Census of NWP, 1881.

20 W. H. Smith, *Final Report on the Settlement of Aligarh*, Allahabad, 1882, p. 35.

21 S. J. Commander, 'The Jajmani System in North India; An Examination of its Logic and Status across Two Centuries', *Modern Asian Studies*, Volume 17 (2), 1983, pp. 283 – 311.

22 T. Kessinger, cited in note 11, p. 156.

23 Chitra Joshi, 'Kanpur Textile Labour — Some Structural Features of Formative Years', *Economic and Political Weekly*, Special Number, 1981, pp. 1823 – 38.

24 P. Romero de Solis, *La poblacion española en los siglos XVIII y XIX*, Madrid, 1973, pp. 262.

25 W. H. Moreland, *India at the Death of Akbar*, Delhi, 1962, p. 113.

26 S. Moosvi, 'The Magnitude of the Land Revenue Demand and the Income of the Mughal Ruling Class under Akbar', *Medieval India*, Volume 4, Delhi, 1977, pp. 91 – 121.

27 Census of NWP, 1881, Volume 1, pp. 78 – 83.

28 See, for example, A. Heston, 'Official Yields per Acre in India, 1886 – 1947', *Indian Economic and Social History Review*, Volume 10, 1973; C. Dewey, 'Patwari and Chaukidar', in C. Dewey and A. G. Hopkins (eds), *The Imperial Impact*, London 1978; G. Blyn, *Agricultural Trends in India, 1891 – 1947: Output, Availability and Productivity*, Philadelphia, 1966; Satish Misra, *Patterns of Long-run Agrarian Change in Bombay and Punjab 1881 – 1972*, Cambridge University Ph.D., 1981.

29 For a more detailed discussion, see Commander, 1980, cited in note 1, pp. 60ff.
30 *Returns of Agricultural Statistics for British India, 1884/85*, pp. 24 – 5; T. Matsui, *Agricultural Prices in North India*, Tokyo, 1977, Volume 2, Table B2.
31 S. Gillan, *Report on the Settlement of Meerut District*, Allahabad, 1981, p. 9.
32 See, for example, W. W. Hunter, *The India of the Queen and Other Essays*, London, 1903, p. 147.
33 See Commander, 1980, cited in note 1, pp. 86ff.
34 Calculated from, Collector, Saharanpur to BD, (22 December 1807) 8 January 1808, IOL, BRCC, Range 91, Vol 18; E. A. Atkinson, *Statistical, descriptive and historical account of the NWP*, Allahabad, 1875, Volume 2; Census of NWP, 1881.
35 A. Wright, Collector, Agra to M. Moore (20 February) 18 March 1813, IOL, BRCC, Range 92, Volume 13; Atkinson, op. cit, Volume 7, p. 495.
36 R. Montgomery, *A Statistical Report of Kanpur District*, Allahabad, 1849, Appendix 5; W. S. Halsey, *A Report on the Question of Temporary and Permanent Settlements in Kanpur*, Allahabad, 1872; F. N. Wright, *Final Report on Settlement of Kanpur*, Allahabad, 1878, p. 50.
37 *Parliamentary Papers*, 1881, Volume 71, (2), pp. 69 – 72.
38 E. Thornton, *Report on Settlement of Muzaffarnayar*, Agra, 1842; A. Cadell, *Report on Settlement of Ganges Canal Tract of Muzaffarnayar*, Allahabad, 1878, pp. 21 – 3; A. Saith, *Agrarian Structure, Technology and Marketed Surplus*, Cambridge University Ph.D., 1978, Appendix A, pp. 342 – 61.
39 J. Hurd, 'Railways and the Expansion of Markets in India, 1861 – 1921', *Explorations in Economic History*, Volume 3, 1975.
40 The discussion is based on, Commander, 1980, cited in note 1, pp. 137 – 66.
41 W. H. Moreland, *The Revenue Administration of the United Provinces*, Allahabad, 1911, p. 49.
42 Commander, 1980, cited in note 1, pp. 169 – 70.
43 J. G. Deedes, *Report on the Settlement of Mathura*, Agra, 1842; J. Thornton, *Report on Settlement of Aligarh*, Agra, 1842.
44 D. Rothermund, *Government, Landlord and Peasant in India: Agrarian Relations under British Rule, 1865 – 1935*, Wiesbaden, 1978.
45 S. A. Hill, *Report on the Rainfall of the NWP*, Allahabad, 1879; *District Gazeteer of the UP*, Kanpur, Volume 19, Allahabad, 1909, p. 22.
46 E. Whitcombe, *Agrarian Conditions in Northern India*, Berkeley, 1971, Fig. 1.
47 A. Wright, Collector, Agra to M. Moore, Sec. to Board, 5 January 1813, 18 March 1813 and 2 April 1813, IOL, BRCC, Range 91, Volume 32 and Range 92, Volumes 13 and 16.
48 S. J. Auckland Camp Meerut to Court of Directors, 13 February 1838. NAI, Home Misc Volume 487, 1838 – 9.
49 Commander, 1980, cited in note 1, pp. 250 – 308.

50 Douglas Dewar, *A Handbook to the English Pre-Mutiny Records*, Allahabad, 1920; C. G. Mansel, *Report on the Settlement of Agra District*, Agra, 1842.
51 Settlement of Pargana Sukrawa, Zillah Farrukhabad, 3 April 1847, in Selections from *Records of Government*, NWP, No. 22, Agra, 1855, pp. 84 – 5.
52 M. R. Gubbins, *Report on the Settlement of Zillah Etawah*, 1841, Agra, 1842, pp. 4, 46 and 61.
53 R. Baird Smith, 'Report on the Famine of 1860/61 in Upper India', *Parliamentary Papers*, 1862, Volume 40.
54 F. S. Growse, Mathura District, *Indian Antiquary*, Volume 1 (1) March, Bombay 1872, p. 66.
55 H. Rose, *Report on the Settlement of Kanpur District, 1841*, Agra, 1842, p. 12.
56 For Europe, see: J. Meuvret, 'Les Crises de Subsistence et la Demographie de la France d'Ancien Régime', *Population*, Volume 1, (4) 1946, pp. 643 – 50; E. Le Roi Ladurie, *Les Paysans de Languedoc*, Volume 1, Paris 1966; P. Goubert, *Beauvais et le Beauvaisis de 1600 à 1730*, Paris, 1960.
57 For a fuller discussion, see S. J. Commander, 'Malthus and the Theory of Unequal Powers: Population and Food Production in India, 1800 – 1947', *Modern Asian Studies*, Volume 20, (4), 1986, pp. 661 – 701.
58 Baird Smith, 1862, cited in note 53, p. 342 and pp. 374 – 5.
59 F. Henvey, *Narrative of the Drought and Famine which prevailed in the NWP, 1868, 1869 and 1870*, Allahabad, 1871.
60 Commander, 1986, cited in note 57, pp. 695 – 8. Also see chapter 8 of the present volume.
61 *Parliamentary Papers*, 1881, Volume 71, C3086, part one, p. 211.
62 J. Murray, *Report on the Outbreak of Cholera in the Central Prison at Agra*, Allahabad, 1856, pp. 12 – 14.
63 C. Geertz, *Agricultural Involution: The Processes of Ecological Change in Indonesia*, Berkeley, 1963.

4

MORTALITY AND FERTILITY IN INDIA, 1881 – 1961: A REASSESSMENT

P. N. Mari Bhat

Ever since the seminal work of Hardy at the end of the last century, there have been numerous attempts to estimate fertility and mortality levels in India from census age returns.[1] But some recent developments seem to call for a reconsideration of the issue.

First, in the last decade or so, significant progress has been made in the craft of demographic estimation. In particular, the recent discovery of generalized stable population relationships has vastly advanced our knowledge on how a population's past and present levels of fertility and mortality are reflected in its age distribution and patterns of age-specific growth. This has led to the formulation of more robust estimation techniques for the measurement of basic demographic measures from intercensal analyses.[2] Perhaps nowhere are these techniques more relevant than in India, which has had a very deficient vital registration system, but fortunately a long history of census taking.

Secondly, for the period since 1961, the multiplicity of data sources, and availability of reliable information on child mortality, has helped considerably in revealing the true levels of fertility and mortality in India for more recent periods.[3] As we will soon discover, this newly-gained knowledge can open up new avenues for historical demographic estimation. Finally, an emerging controversy about the level of fertility in pre-revolutionary China has revived interest in the fertility levels of peasantries of the past.[4] At the heart of this debate is the issue of whether every traditional society that managed to survive for long kept its fertility at a moderate level, thus avoiding risks of both high and low rates of reproduction. A question that arises almost instantaneously is how did Indian fertility at the beginning of this century compare with that of the Chinese?

Below we develop procedures that take advantage of the recent advances in both data and theory, and apply them to Indian censuses, starting with 1881. The discussion is primarily focused on the pre-1961 era where existing estimates seem to require significant revision. The

new results suggest that earlier studies have overstated the pre-
transitional levels of fertility and mortality in India, and consequently
exaggerated subsequent declines. The new estimates reveal an
astonishing amount of similarity in the vital rates of India and China at
the beginning of this century. Insights are also obtained on the sex
differential of mortality in India, and on the probable age pattern of
mortality at very low levels of life expectancy.

METHOD OF ESTIMATION

Everyone interested in estimating fertility and mortality levels for India
from census age distributions faces two difficult problems: (i) gross age
distortions in the recorded distributions, and (ii) the paucity of reliable
information on infant and child mortality. It is mainly the suggested
solutions to these problems, or the lack of them, that distinguish the
methodologies of previous efforts to estimate Indian vital rates.

Indian census actuaries, concerned mainly with the construction of a
life table from census age data, handled the first problem by subjecting
the reported distributions to heavy smoothing. This has the disadvantage of removing some real irregularities in the population's age
structure, and may also produce biased estimates of trends in vital rates
if smoothing procedures are varied from census to census.

Among demographers it is customary to use the age distributions as
reported. However, demographers sometimes choose an estimate based
on a cumulated age segment that is believed to be least affected by age
misstatements, or an average over several age intervals. Elsewhere we
have shown that when certain systematic distortions are present in
reported ages, such rules of thumb perform less than adequately.[5] A
continuous overstatement or understatement of age often creates a
situation wherein the slope of the reported age distribution is erroneous,
and the estimated survival probabilities are biased in the same direction
at most ages. In such instances, a mean based on several ages would
still be in error. Nor is it possible to identify an age segment that is least
affected by age misstatements, as very little is known about the true
levels of vital rates. Below we propose some new methods to handle
this thorny issue that simultaneously take advantage of some independent information available for the 1970s.

Most age distribution-based methods need reliable information on
infant and child mortality for an accurate measurement of fertility and
mortality. This information is now usually supplied by the 'Brass'
questions on children ever-born and children surviving. While such
information is available for the 1960s onwards, for earlier periods it is
either non-existent or too localized to be of value for our purposes.

Early Indian life tables constructed by Hardy employed childhood mortality rates of 'Proclaimed Clans' — certain Rajput communities of the former North-Western Province (largely the contemporary Uttar Pradesh) — among whom female infanticide was suspected, and vital events were recorded under strict vigilance.[6] However, the question remains as to how well their mortality represented that of the country as a whole.

Later attempts to estimate vital rates for the same period made heavy use of age patterns of mortality contained in the Coale and Demeny system of model life tables.[7] But the relevance of these tables to India, especially to the levels of mortality prevailing in early parts of this century there, is seriously in doubt. We will return to this topic at a later point in this chapter. Suffice it to note here that a one parameter system of model life tables is quite inadequate to represent the age structure of mortality during the period under consideration.

The solution we offer to the foregoing problem is somewhat involved. We will first describe a procedure of estimating the product of the crude birth rate (b) and the probability of survival to age five (l_5) from a population's age distribution and age-specific growth rates. The method is essentially Preston's, except for a modification to take into account the effects of age misreporting.[8] This procedure can be readily applied to data from Indian censuses to estimate the product, $b \times l_5$. The crude birth rate for the beginning of the 1960s can be estimated from this by using a survey estimate of child mortality. Since no such information exists for earlier periods, we are obliged to assume that there was no change in marital fertility during 1881 – 1961. Under this assumption, indirect standardization techniques can be employed to ascertain the trend in the crude birth rate during the above period from changes in the population's age and marital status composition. Once the trend in the crude birth rate and its level at the beginning of the 1960s are known, the child survival factor can be easily extracted from the product, $b \times l_5$ for any other period.

Estimation of $b \times l_5$

From a generalization of stable population relations it has been shown that the following identity pertains to any closed population:[9]

$$c(x,t) = b(t)e^{-\int_0^x r(a,t)da} l(x,t), \qquad (1)$$

where,

$c(x,t)$ = proportion of population aged x at time t

$b(t)$ = crude birth rate at time t
$r(a,t)$ = annual growth rate of persons aged a at time t
$l(x,t)$ = probability of survival from birth to age x according to the mortality conditions at time t

By dropping the time identifier, t, and rewriting equation (1) in terms of $l(x)$, we get:

$$l(x) = \frac{c(x)}{b} e^{\int_0^x r(a)da} \tag{2}$$

In principle, equation (2) can be directly used to calculate a period life table from the age distribution of a population at two enumerations if an independent estimate of the crude birth rate is available. But when no such estimate exists, and age distributions are severely distorted by age misstatements, some further assumptions and manipulations are necessary.

Brass has shown that a two parameter, linear logit transformation of a judiciously selected standard survivorship function provides a fair representation of the age curve of mortality among human populations.[10] The Brass logit transformation can be written as:

$$\ln \frac{1 - l(x)}{l(x)} = \alpha + \beta \ln \frac{1 - l_s(x)}{l_s(x)}, \; x > 0, \tag{3}$$

where $l_s(x)$ denotes the survivorship function of the standard life table.[11] The constants, α and β, represent respectively the level and pattern of mortality in the population, relative to the standard. An increase in α lowers the proportion surviving to every age above zero. On the other hand, an increase in β raises all $l(x)$ values under an age to which only half of the births survive in the chosen standard, but lowers them at all higher ages. In most human populations, variations in the age pattern of mortality result mainly from differences in relative levels of adult and child mortality. For ages above five, adequate representation can be obtained from a single parameter logit transformation. In any event, when reported ages become particularly unreliable at older ages, as in India, little improvement can be expected from the use of an additional parameter to describe adult mortality patterns. Therefore, we shall assume that:

$$\ln \frac{1 - l^*(x)}{l^*(x)} = \alpha + \ln \frac{1 - l^*_s(x)}{l^*_s(x)}, \; x \geq 5,$$

where $l^*(x)$ and $l^*_s(x)$ are probabilities of survival to age x for someone who has survived to age five in the respective populations. By setting $e^\alpha = k$, we may write the above as:

$$\frac{1 - l^*(x)}{l^*(x)} = k \frac{1 - l^*_s(x)}{l^*_s(x)}, \quad x \geq 5. \tag{4}$$

We may also note that by definition $l(x) = l_s l^*(x)$, where l_s is the probability of survival from birth to age 5. Substituting this in equation (4) and rearranging the terms yields:

$$\frac{1}{l(x)} = \frac{1}{l_s} + \frac{k}{l_s} \times \frac{1 - l^*_s(x)}{l^*_s(x)}, \quad x > 5. \tag{5}$$

From equations (2) and (5) we get:

$$\frac{e^{-\int_0^x r(a)da}}{c(x)} = \frac{1}{bl_s} + \frac{k}{bl_s} \times \frac{1 - l^*_s(x)}{l^*_s(x)}, \quad x \geq 5. \tag{6}$$

It may be noted that equation (6) is essentially a reformulation of Preston's 'integrated' formula.[12] It shows that if a line is fitted to the elements of both sides of equation (6), the reciprocal of the intercept provides an estimate of the product $b \times l_s$, and dividing the slope by the intercept gives an estimate of the 'level' of adult mortality, k.

The elements of the left side of equation (6) are derivable from enumerations of a population at two points in time. The values of $c(x)$ can be approximated by the mean intercensal age distribution of the population,[13] while intercensal growth rates at each age provide the schedule of $r(a)$'s. In developing countries, however, age misstatement can severely distort their values, especially those of $c(x)$'s, in a non-random fashion, i.e. the expected mean of the errors may not be zero, or may have a non-zero covariance with the X-values (i.e., right-hand side values). To remedy the situation, we need to model the pattern of errors.

We may write the proportionate errors in the recorded age distribution from age misstatements or age-selective under-enumeration as:

$$v(x) = \frac{c^\circ(x) - c(x)}{c(x)} = \sigma v_s(x) + u(x) \tag{7}$$

where
$c(x)$ = true proportion of the population aged x
$c^\circ(x)$ = observed proportion of the population aged x
$v_s(x)$ = standard pattern of systematic or nonstochastic errors in $c(x)$
$u(x)$ = random or stochastic errors in $c(x)$
σ = 'level' of systematic errors in $c(x)$.
 From equation (7) it follows that:

$$c(x) = c^\circ(x) / (1 + \sigma v_s(x) + u(x)). \qquad (8)$$

It also follows that if the errors in $c(x)$ were as shown in equation (7), and if they were to remain unchanged in two consecutive censuses, the schedule of age-specific growth rates would be unaffected from age misreporting. Therefore, by substituting equation (8), in equation (6), and rearranging terms, we have:

$$\frac{e^{-\int_0^x r^\circ(a)da}}{c^\circ(x)} = \frac{1}{bl_s} + \frac{k}{bl_s} \times \frac{1 - 1*_s(x)}{1*_s(x)}$$

$$- \sigma v_s(x) \frac{e^{-\int_0^x r^\circ(a)da}}{c^\circ(x)} - u(x) \frac{e^{-\int_0^x r^\circ(a)da}}{c^\circ(x)}, \; x \geq 5. \qquad (9)$$

Equation (9) provides a multiple regression format for the estimation of model parameters. Using the subscript i to denote age-specific values, and setting:

$$Y_i = \frac{e^{-\int_0^x r^\circ(a)da}}{c^\circ(x)}, \text{ and } X_i = \frac{1 - 1*_s(x)}{1*_s(x)},$$

we may rewrite equation (9) as:

$$Y_i = \beta_0 + \beta_1 X_i + \beta_2 v_{s,i} Y_i - u_i Y_i \qquad (10)$$

where $\beta_0 = 1/bl_s$, $\beta_1 = k/bl_s$, and $\beta_2 = -\sigma$.
 The above suggests that in the presence of age misstatements the estimating equation for the integrated procedure should involve an additional interaction term between Y-values and the nonstochastic age errors. Also suggested is that the residuals of the equation would be

heteroskedastic as the stochastic component of the errors is attached to a non-random variable. Therefore, the parameter estimates from the ordinary least-squares (OLS) regression would be inefficient (i.e., they will have high variance). Fortunately, since the source of the heteroskedasticity is known, the situation can be easily remedied by weighting the regression by the reciprocal of Y_i^2. Since Y_i increases with age (because it is the reciprocal of $b.1(x)$) such a procedure would give more weight to observations at younger ages where reported ages are usually more accurate.

Estimation of b

From its definition, the crude birth rate of any closed population at a moment in time can be written as:

$$b(t) = c(x,t) \, g(x,t) \, m(x,t) \, dx \qquad (11)$$

where $g(x,t)$ is the proportion currently married of population aged x at time t, and $m(x,t)$ is its marital fertility rate at age x at time t.

We assume that during the period 1881 – 1961, Indian fertility was characterized by:

$$m(x,t) = M \, n(x)$$

where $n(x)$ is the marital fertility at age x in an appropriate standard population, and M is the level factor assumed to be invariant with respect to both time and age. From the substitution of this in equation (11) we have:

$$b(t) = M \int_0^\infty c(x,t) \, g(x,t) \, n(x) \, dx,$$

or, for any two time periods, j and k,

$$b(j) = b(k) \frac{\int_0^\infty c(x,j) \, g(x,j) \, n(x) \, dx}{\int_0^\infty c(x,k) \, g(x,k) \, n(x) \, dx} \qquad (12)$$

Equation 12 essentially describes an indirect standardization format for the estimation of the crude birth rate if its level is known for any

moment in time, j, of a broader time span when a constant marital
fertility regime prevailed.

IMPLEMENTATION TO INDIA, 1881 – 1961

The basic data for the implementation of the method are the
population's age-sex distribution from every census since 1881.[14] A
useful source is Mukherjee's compendium on Indian age distributions,
which incorporates elaborate adjustments for massive territorial
changes during 1881 – 1961.[15] The analysis below is based on his
painstaking work. There are, however, three minor problems in using
these data. First, age distributions were not available for Kerala and
Rajasthan for 1881, and Jammu and Kashmir for 1951. Therefore, the
all-India analysis below omits them for the decades involving these
dates. We also discovered that for some unknown reason, the all-India
distributions given by Mukherjee exclude Chandigarh from all
censuses. However, the effect of this omission should be trivial.

Secondly, Mukherjee employed a uniform open interval of 60+ to
present the age distributions. Because of sensitivity to mortality level, it
would have been desirable to have further age breakdowns of the
population aged over 60 years. Third, serious gaps exist in the 1931 and
1941 censuses. The age distributions from the 1931 census were
smoothed by the census office before publication. For the 1941 census,
age tabulations are available only from a two per cent sample for the
majority of territories; where they are available for the total population,
they are believed to be smoothed; and for large portions of Punjab,
Madhya Pradesh, Andhra Pradesh and Karnataka, none are available.
Mukherjee made a valiant attempt to remedy these problems, but our
analysis suggests that a few still remain.

Also needed for our purposes were the marital distributions of
women by age from every census. For India and its major zones,
Mukherjee provides these for the censuses of 1901 to 1961. For the
remaining censuses we gathered them directly from the relevant census
publications, and made our own adjustments for territorial changes.

Before using the above data for the estimation of fertility and
mortality, it would be nice to adjust them for migration and changes in
enumeration completeness of censuses. Historically, international
migration has played an insignificant role in India's population growth.
Although data on these movements are exceedingly rough, we opted to
use them because they appear to provide the true directions of net
transfers.

Table 1 shows the decadal estimates of net migration to India from
1881 to 1981, compiled from various sources. Most of these estimates

Table 1. Estimates of Net International Migration, in Thousands, 1881 – 1981

Decade	Males	Females	Sources
1881 – 1891	– 415	– 178	A
1891 – 1901	– 1039	– 445	A
1901 – 1911	– 598	– 256	A
1911 – 1921	– 585	– 250	A
1921 – 1931	– 692	– 296	A
1931 – 1941	330	220	B
1941 – 1951	420	280	C
1951 – 1961	1756	1340	D
1961 – 1971	123	316	E
1971 – 1981	– 642	81	E

Sources:

A: See Davis, op. cit. in note 1, p. 99. A male to female ratio of 7/3 among migrants has been assumed.

B: Writer's estimate based on the information on overseas movements published periodically in the *Statistical Abstract of British India.*

C: India, Registrar General, *Appendices to the Report, 1951*, Census of India, 1951, Vol. I, Part I – B, (Delhi: Manager of Publications, 1955): 111 – 113, with an assumed sex ratio of 6/4.

D: K. C. Zachariah and K. S. Seetharem, 'Inter-state migration in India, 1951 – 1961', *Indian Journal of Public Health*, 12, no. 1 (1968): 47 – 63.

E: Writer's estimate. See Bhat, op. cit. in note 3, Appendix A.

simply provide the balance of transfers across the borders, and thus are not adjusted for the births and deaths that occurred to migrants during the interval. But we have used them as if they were so adjusted because neither the quality of the data, nor the size of the adjustment, justified a more sophisticated treatment. The migration corrections were made by adjusting the population totals age-wise. Such a correction needs an age distribution of migrants at the end of a ten year migration period. For this purpose, an age distribution of interstate migrants derived from 1971 census data on duration and residence was used.[16]

Estimates of the completeness of census enumerations are even less reliable. It is believed that levels of under-enumeration in the 1881 and 1891 censuses were larger than in more recent censuses. The Census Commissioners of the period made some rough estimates of these, and we have borrowed them directly.[17] It has also been stated that in some parts of India the enumeration in 1931 was affected by Gandhi's non-co-operation movement.[18] There are also indications that there may have been some over-enumeration of the population in Punjab and West Bengal in the 1941 census. Since the age data from these two censuses have other problems as well, we did not consider it worthwhile to make allowance for these errors in census totals. The post-enumeration checks of more recent censuses do not suggest any significant change in census enumeration completeness; however there is some indirect evidence that the 1971 census may have had a greater undercount, especially among females.[19] On the basis of trends in the population's sex ratio, and some independent evidence, we raised the female population of the 1971 census by 0.8 per cent to make it comparable to the totals of the 1961 and 1981 censuses.[20]

With the above data and adjustments, two fundamental inputs to the procedure, namely, the age-specific growth rates, and the mean intercensal age distribution of the population, can be derived for each intercensal period. Since ages were tabulated in discrete five-year intervals, we proceeded as follows. The age-specific growth rates for the population aged x to $x + 5$ during the interval t to $t + h$ were computed as:

$$_5r_x = \frac{\ln \, _5N_x \, (t+h) - \ln \, _5N_x \, (t)}{h}$$

where $_5N_x$ is the number of persons reported as aged x at time t, and h is the length of the intercensal period. The cumulated growth rates from birth to age x were approximated by:

$$_0\!\int^x r°(a)da = 5 \sum_{x=0}^{x-5} {}_5r_a.$$

For a discrete time interval, $c°(x)$ can be conceived of as the ratio of persons attaining their x'th birthday to the total person-years lived during the interval. The most satisfactory procedure for computing this is a 'cohort' interpolation procedure developed elsewhere.[21] However, since the method requires a $priori$ knowledge on the number of births during an intercensal period, it was not considered suitable to the problem at hand. Therefore, a more conventional approach was used.

The total person-years lived between ages x to $x + 5$ during the period t to $t + h$ was estimated as:

$$_5N_x \text{ (t to t+h)} = \frac{_5N_x\,(t+h) - {_5N_x}(t)}{h \cdot {_5r_x}}.$$

From this $c°(x)$ was derived as:

$$c°(x) = \frac{_5N_x\,(t \text{ to } t+h) + {_5N_{x-5}}\,(t \text{ to } t+h)}{D \sum\limits_{a=0}^{\infty} {_5N_a}\,(t \text{ to } t+h)}$$

For $x \geq 10$, the value of D, a constant that helps to maintain the above equality, was assumed to be 10. But for $x = 5$, to account for nonlinearities in the underlying survival function, D was assumed to be 10.2. This corresponds roughly to the value of $_{10}L_0/l_{15}$ in the 'Indian' standard life table discussed below.

Standard Schedules

In addition to age distributions of the population, the methodology also employs several 'standard' schedules. Since results can be sensitive to their choice, we proceeded with care. One such standard needed was to represent the age pattern of marital fertility during 1881 – 1961. Perhaps a reasonable choice for this is the 'natural' fertility schedule developed by Coale and Trussell.[22] But in this instance a schedule of observed rates seemed preferable as the object was to use it for the estimation of changes in the crude birth rate from observed distributions of currently married women by age. Such a combination is likely to produce crude birth rate estimates that are less sensitive to age misreporting. After some searching, we selected a marital fertility schedule for rural India from a 1972 survey.[23] The choice of a rural schedule was deliberate because a substantial number of urban women had probably begun using contraception by the time of this survey.

There were, however, two problems besetting this schedule. First, because it was based on 'births-last-year' reports, a half-year displacement was present in the age reports of women. Second, the marital distribution of women in the survey deviated significantly from that recorded in the 1971 census.[24]. Therefore, the age-specific fertility rates from the survey were first adjusted for the half-year age displacement, and then converted into marital fertility rates by employing the 1971 census marital distribution.[25] Their corresponding total marital fertility rate is 6.56 births. For the estimates presented here, however, it is the age pattern of this standard schedule that is critical, and not its level.

Table 2. Standard Schedules of Mortality and Age Distortions

Age (x)	Standard l(x)		Standard v(x)	
	Males	Females	Males	Females
5	.8095	.7854	−.0490	−.0189
10	.7932	.7666	.0626	.0571
15	.7851	.7581	−.0012	−.0324
20	.7762	.7460	−.0788	−.0660
25	.7657	.7303	−.0410	.0239
30	.7552	.7148	−.0129	.0331
35	.7413	.6979	.0046	.0182
40	.7213	.6791	.0388	.0164
45	.6933	.6578	.0462	−.0043
50	.6524	.6288	.0947	.0123
55	.5958	.5867	.0441	−.0465
60	.5203	.5276	.0779	.0173
65	.4248	.4484	.1694	.1072
70	.3137	.3493	.1200	.0488
75	.1994	.2383	.2908	.1569
80	.1013	.1325	.4490	.2580
85	.0368	.0539		

A standard schedule was also required to represent the shape of the survivorship function at ages above five years. For this we selected a life table constructed from the age distribution of deaths from India's Sample Registration System (SRS), and age-specific growth rates derived from the 1971 and 1981 censuses. Elsewhere we have shown that this combination provides quite acceptable levels of completeness of death reports in the SRS at adult ages if SRS age distributions are employed.[26] Like any life table based on Sample Registration System age-specific death rates, this life table has unusually low mortality at ages 10 – 50 years, and unusually high mortality at ages beyond this span. We have also been able to show that such deviations from the age patterns of mortality contained in the Coale and Demeny model life table system cannot solely be due to typical patterns of age misstatement.[27] The l_x values for the new standard life table are shown in Table 2. For convenience, we will call this the 'Indian' standard. Although for 1971 – 81 the above standard may be nearer to the true conditions than any of the Coale and Demeny families, this may not be so for earlier decades. In order to investigate the sensitivity of the estimates to the choice of standard mortality pattern, we also used a life table from the South model family (level 13) as a standard. The life tables of this family provide a middle ground between those of Coale and Demeny's West model and the 'Indian' standard.

A novelty of the present methodology is the use of a standard pattern of age distortions. For this we made use of a distortion pattern derived from comparison of a constructed age distribution for 1971 – 81 with the recorded mean distribution for the same period from the 1971 and 1981 censuses. The 'true' age distribution was constructed from a life table estimated for the decade (which in fact is the above designated 'Indian' standard), and the age-specific growth rates from the censuses.[28] Comparison of cumulative age distributions shows that the proportion of the population reported below a given age is usually smaller than the 'true' proportion below that age. This indicates a strong tendency to exaggerate age, and this is strongest for males. An important implication is that conventional intercensal techniques that employ reported age distributions may understate the true level of adult mortality. Elsewhere we have shown that only when such age exaggerations are assumed do adult mortality levels implied by the SRS become consistent with levels implied by census age distributions.[29]

As the proposed estimation methodology is to be implemented by averaging the recorded population in two consecutive five-year age intervals, what we really need are the distortions in such averages. These have been computed for 1971 – 81 and are shown in Table 2. They form the schedule, $v_s(x)$, to be employed in the estimation of demographic parameters for earlier decades.

RESULTS

Table 3 shows the parameter estimates of equation (10) derived by the weighted least-squares procedure. Owing to data limitations, for decades up to 1951 – 61 regressions were fitted to values for ages 5 – 55, while for more recent decades those of ages 60 and 65 were also employed. From Table 3 we observe that with time, the model R^2 increases while standard errors of parameter estimates diminish, suggesting that the model fits more recent decades better. It is also observed that, except for males in 1961 – 71, the use of the Indian

Table 3. Parameter Estimates and Standard Errors for the 'Age-Error Parameterized Integrated Model' from Weighted Least-Squares Regression

	Male							
	Indian standard life table				South model level 13			
Decade	β_0	β_1	β_2	Model R^2	β_0	β_1	β_2	Model R^2
1881 – 1891	33.056 (1.463)	222.703 (18.414)	– 1.092 (.499)	.962	33.212 (2.269)	157.856 (20.169)	– 743 (.748)	.911
1891 – 1901	37.137 (1.415)	314.203 (18.985)	– .909 (.407)	.979	37.641 (2.568)	213.524 (24.159)	– .489 (.718)	.931
1901 – 1911	34.193 (1.234)	243.574 (15.590)	– 1.278 (.404)	.975	34.410 (2.193)	167.675 (19.556)	– .915 (.695)	.922
1911 – 1921	35.518 (1.168)	380.311 (16.658)	– 1.242 (.333)	.988	36.146 (2.230)	259.548 (22.303)	– .790 (.621)	.957
1921 – 1931	33.320 (1.113)	157.231 (12.625)	– 1.275 (.409)	.960	33.243 (1.841)	110.632 (14.902)	– 1.029 (.647)	.896
1931 – 1941	33.591 (.867)	153.692 (9.663)	– 1.462 (.326)	.974	33.099 (1.041)	113.690 (8.383)	– 1.360 (.376)	.965
1941 – 1951	35.732 (.766)	117.357 (8.085)	– .904 (.281)	.971	35.424 (1.308)	85.485 (9.978)	– .785 (.459)	.922
1951 – 1961	29.532 (.485)	99.731 (5.096)	– 1.165 (.215)	.983	29.185 (.860)	73.685 (6.551)	– 1.076 (.365)	.950
1961 – 1971	31.757 (.531)	50.071 (3.948)	– .941 (.276)	.971	30.317 (.327)	48.992 (2.051)	– .932 (.147)	.991
1971 – 1981	33.296 (.123)	36.971 (.827)	– 1.041 (.064)	.997	32.270 (.583)	35.109 (3.367)	– .942 (.262)	.949

Note: Standard errors of the estimates are shown in parentheses.

	\multicolumn{4}{Female Indian standard life table}				Female South model level 13			

Decade	β_0	β_1	β_2	Model R^2	β_0	β_1	β_2	Model R^2
1881 – 1891	33.998	183.527	– 2.089	.937	34.188	165.229	– 2.296	.923
	(1.832)	(17.603)	(.734)		(2.024)	(17.706)	(.813)	
1891 – 1901	38.370	237.695	– 1.718	.958	38.622	214.064	– 1.938	.945
	(1.817)	(18.097)	(.631)		(2.069)	(18.764)	(.721)	
1901 – 1911	35.000	216.226	– 2.145	.965	35.278	194.055	– 2.357	.950
	(1.527)	(15.219)	(.581)		(1.801)	(16.328)	(.688)	
1911 – 1921	35.651	334.958	– 1.984	.980	36.137	300.284	– 2.219	.970
	(1.531)	(17.268)	(.528)		(1.849)	(18.953)	(.643)	
1921 – 1931	33.344	139.947	– 2.118	.948	33.486	126.104	– 2.303	.933
	(1.365)	(12.376)	(.576)		(1.551)	(12.813)	(.656)	
1931 – 1941	34.127	136.334	– 1.529	.989	34.163	124.380	– 1.714	.987
	(.590)	(5.241)	(.253)		(.659)	(5.357)	(.282)	
1941 – 1951	34.400	113.221	– 1.384	.963	34.449	102.902	– 1.555	.951
	(.956)	(8.195)	(.408)		(1.103)	(8.643)	(.470)	
1951 – 1961	29.401	97.399	– 1.517	.991	29.427	88.816	– 1.686	.985
	(.405)	(3.468)	(.204)		(.517)	(4.050)	(.260)	
1961 – 1971	31.066	55.740	– 1.172	.994	30.322	59.127	– .892	.988
	(.254)	(1.405)	(.128)		(.376)	(2.107)	(.175)	
1971 – 1981	33.852	37.293	– 1.105	.997	33.260	40.116	– .903	.984
	(.135)	(.670)	(.066)		(.328)	(1.663)	(.148)	

standard provides a substantially better fit than the South model life table, giving us one reason for relying on estimates based on the former.

The parameter β_2 underscores the value of the present approach. The coefficient of the age-error interaction term (i.e. β_2) is generally found to pass the five per cent significance criterion, even with only eleven or thirteen observation points. A few exceptions occur among males with the South model variant. It was also observed that the inclusion of this term significantly reduces the standard errors of the two remaining coefficients.[30]

Since the absolute value of β_2 is a measure of σ, the relative level of age distortions, its trend can be a useful indicator of changes in the level of age distortions. A value of σ greater than unity suggests that the extent of age distortions in the population is larger than in the chosen standard, while the contrary is true if it is less than unity. The results in Table 3 suggest a strong possibility of improvement in age reporting among females, while for males the trend is somewhat ambiguous. Mukherjee came to a similar conclusion using the more conventional measures of age ratio and sex ratio scores.[31]

With these general remarks, we now turn to more substantive results based upon the estimates of the two remaining coefficients.

Estimates of the Crude Birth Rate and Child Mortality

As shown above, the reciprocal of the intercept provides the estimate of $b \times l_5$. Table 4 shows the estimates so derived. For the total population, separate estimates for males and females were combined by employing their respective population sizes as weights. Needless to say, the observed trend in the estimates of $b \times l_5$ reflects changes in both fertility and child mortality. Nevertheless, for the period before 1961, one can safely assume that it is mainly a reflection of the latter. Estimates presented in Table 4 indicate that after fluctuating around a mean value, $b \times l_5$ abruptly increased by about fifteen per cent during 1951 – 61. Since then it has shown a tendency to fall, suggesting a possible drop in fertility. Both the 'Indian' and South model standard life tables provide very similar estimates of $b \times l_5$ for decades up to 1951 – 61. After this period, estimates based on the South model standard are somewhat higher.

By what factor might the decadal level of the crude birth rate have changed from 1881 to 1961? The major sources of the instability in the crude birth rate during this period are changes in the population's age and marital distributions. Of course, birth rate levels were known to fall significantly during periods of famine or epidemic, and rise to higher

Table 4. Estimates of Crude Birth Rates and Child Mortality

Decade	b×l₅ Male	b×l₅ Female	b×l₅ Both sexes	Population's Sex ratio	b(t)/b(61)	Crude birth rate (both sexes)	l₅ estimates Both sexes	l₅ estimates Male	l₅ estimates Female
	(1)	(2)	(3)	(4)	(5)	(6)	(7)	(8)	(9)
				Indian Standard					
1881 – 1891	.0303	.0294	.0298	103.8	1.045	.0470	.635	.637	.632
1891 – 1901	.0269	.0261	.0265	103.7	1.036	.0466	.568	.571	.565
1901 – 1911	.0292	.0286	.0289	103.5	1.041	.0468	.617	.617	.617
1911 – 1921	.0282	.0280	.0281	104.4	1.023	.0460	.610	.607	.614
1921 – 1931	.0300	.0300	.0300	105.2	1.030	.0464	.647	.645	.650
1931 – 1941	.0298	.0293	.0295	105.5	1.035	.0466	.634	.638	.631
1941 – 1951	.0280	.0291	.0285	105.6	1.008	.0454	.629	.616	.642
1951 – 1961	.0339	.0340	.0339	105.9	1.016	.0457	.742	.740	.744
1961 – 1971	.0315	.0322	.0318	106.6	.984				
				South Model Level 13					
1881 – 1891	.0301	.0292	.0297	103.8	1.045	.0470	.631	.634	.629
1891 – 1901	.0266	.0259	.0262	103.7	1.036	.0466	.563	.564	.562
1901 – 1911	.0291	.0283	.0287	103.5	1.041	.0468	.613	.613	.613
1911 – 1921	.0277	.0277	.0277	104.4	1.023	.0460	.601	.597	.606
1921 – 1931	.0301	.0299	.0300	105.2	1.030	.0464	.647	.647	.647
1931 – 1941	.0302	.0293	.0298	105.5	1.035	.0466	.639	.647	.630
1941 – 1951	.0282	.0290	.0286	105.6	1.008	.0454	.631	.621	.641
1951 – 1961	.0343	.0340	.0341	105.9	1.016	.0457	.746	.749	.744
1961 – 1971	.0330	.0330	.0330	106.6	.984				

levels following such catastrophic events. The impact of such probable
fluctuations in marital fertility can be regarded as minimal in the
decadal averages we deal with.[32]

The effects of changes in age and marital distributions of the
population were assessed by the standardization procedure described
above. By employing our standard marital fertility schedule, crude
birth rates standardized for age and marital composition were
calculated for each period. Their ratios to the mean of the values for
1951 – 61 and 1961 – 71 are shown in column 5 of Table 4. They
describe the probable trend in crude birth rate as a result of changes in
the population's age and marital composition. We see that the crude
birth rate might have been about 4 per cent higher at the start of this
century than it was at the beginning of the 1960s.

In order to derive the actual levels of the crude birth rate, we need
independent information on its level for at least one period.
Fortunately, such an estimate can be made for the beginning of the
1960s. From retrospective questions on children ever-born and children
surviving contained in the National Sample Survey of 1965 – 66, it is
possible to arrive at an estimate of q_5, the probability of dying before
the fifth birthday. Elsewhere we have derived this for the two sexes
combined as 0.256 during the early 1960s.[33] For the same period, the
estimate of $b \times l_5$, assumed to be the average of the 1951 – 61 and
1961 – 71 figures, is 0.0329 with the Indian standard life table, and
0.0336 with the South model standard (see Table 4). These figures give
the crude birth rate at the beginning of the 1960s as 44.2 – 45.1 per
thousand. In order to make some allowance for a possible decline in
marital fertility during the late 1960s, we have adopted 45 per
thousand, a level near the upper limit, as the true estimate of the crude
birth rate in 1961. Combining this birth rate estimate with the trend
estimated from standardization, the birth rates can be estimated for each
decade between 1881 and 1961. These are shown in column 6 of Table
4. They suggest that the crude birth rate was in the neighbourhood of 47
per thousand during the early part of this century. The level of the total
marital fertility rate for 1881 – 1961 implied by these estimates is 7.13
births per woman, which was derived by raising the rate of the standard
schedule by 8.7 per cent. Such an upward revision to the level of the
standard marital fertility schedule (6.56 births) is needed to produce the
crude birth rate estimates from reported age and marital distributions.

Once levels of crude birth rates are known, estimates of l_5 can be
derived from the product, $b \times l_5$. They can be made separately for the
sexes, since sex-specific estimates of the birth rate can be derived from
the population's sex ratio and the sex ratio at birth.[34] The estimates of l_5
so derived are shown in Table 4. We observe that the estimates of child

mortality are insensitive to the choice of standard mortality pattern. Before the dawn of the second half of this century, nearly 40 per cent of babies born were dying before attaining their fifth birthday. But during the 1950s this toll suddenly reduced to 26 per cent.

Estimates of Adult Mortality and Life Expectancy

As suggested above, the adult mortality parameter, k, can be inferred by dividing the slope coefficient, β_1, by the intercept, β_0. This estimate of k can be used to construct a life table beginning at age five from the inversion of equation (4). Since we also have an estimate of l_5, the origin of this life table can easily be shifted to zero, and an estimate of expectation of life at birth can be made.[35]

Table 5 shows the estimates of life expectancy at age five, e_5, and life expectancy at birth, e_0, so derived. It can be observed that the South model consistently provides somewhat higher estimates of life expectancy than the Indian standard. Generally, estimates of e_5 from the South model are higher by slightly over a year; however, differences in the estimates of e_0 tend to be smaller because both standards provide similar levels of child mortality. Apparently, use of the South model results in lower estimates of adult mortality because we have few observation points above age 55, and the method implicitly extrapolates the inferred mortality at younger ages to older ages according to the standard pattern chosen. Since within the observed range mortality accelerates less slowly with age in the South model life table than in the Indian standard, the former produces lower estimates of overall adult mortality.

As the choice of standard pattern appears to be of some importance to the estimates of adult mortality, we applied another of the 'variable-r' procedures, developed by Preston and Bennett.[36] An advantage of their approach is that no assumption regarding the age pattern of mortality at adult ages is needed. Additionally, it makes use of information on the open-ended age interval, which the above procedure ignores. The method was applied as outlined by Preston and Bennett, with one significant exception: the person-years lived at each age interval during the intercensal period was computed using a cohort interpolation procedure rather than using the originally suggested 'period' interpolation. It is not only that such a procedure is theoretically more sound;[37] it was also found to dampen the effects of age misstatements on the estimated survival function, and thus estimates of e_x are less distorted.[38] A drawback of the procedure, however, is that life expectancy estimates cannot be made at younger ages without

Table 5. Estimates of Average Years of Life Expectancy at Age 5 and at Birth from the 'Age-Error Parameterized Integrated Model'.

Decade	Life expectancy at age 5		Life expectancy at birth	
	Male	Female	Male	Female
Indian Standard				
1881 – 1891	35.7	37.5	26.3	27.2
1891 – 1901	33.2	35.6	22.2	23.4
1901 – 1911	35.3	35.7	25.3	25.5
1911 – 1921	30.3	30.2	21.8	22.0
1921 – 1931	40.3	40.8	29.6	30.1
1931 – 1941	40.7	41.4	29.5	29.6
1941 – 1951	44.6	43.9	31.0	31.8
1951 – 1961	44.3	43.9	36.8	36.6
South Model, Level 13				
1881 – 1891	37.0	38.6	27.0	27.8
1891 – 1901	34.8	36.7	22.8	23.9
1901 – 1911	36.7	36.8	26.0	26.0
1911 – 1921	31.7	31.3	22.3	22.4
1921 – 1931	41.7	42.0	30.5	30.7
1931 – 1941	41.3	42.4	30.3	30.2
1941 – 1951	45.8	45.1	31.9	32.5
1951 – 1961	45.2	44.9	37.9	37.4

independent information on intercensal births. Fortunately in our case this was not a problem, as they are derivable from the above estimated crude birth rates.

The life expectancy estimates for ages 0 to 50 from this procedure are shown in Table 6. Their ratios to those of the Indian standard life table are plotted for a few selected decades in Fig. 1. The Figure shows that distortions in life expectancy estimates from age misreporting, though less than normal, still remain. Nevertheless, the graphs disclose a significant feature of the mortality change in India: the equidistance of the lines suggests that expectation of life rose nearly proportionately in every age group above five.

Table 6. Estimates of Average Life Expectancies at Various Ages from the Preston-Bennett Procedure, using Cohort Interpolation.

Age	1881 – 91	1891 – 1901	1901 – 11	1911 – 21	1921 – 31	1931 – 41	1941 – 51	1951 – 61
				Male				
0	26.1	21.9	25.0	21.5	29.4	30.1	31.0	37.4
5	36.9	33.9	36.8	32.2	41.6	41.6	44.5	46.7
10	35.2	32.6	34.8	30.5	38.9	39.1	42.0	42.9
15	34.9	32.0	34.2	30.0	38.2	38.8	40.7	41.3
20	34.0	31.3	33.5	29.7	37.2	38.4	39.1	39.5
25	29.5	27.3	29.4	26.6	32.4	34.3	34.3	35.2
30	24.3	22.8	24.5	22.6	26.9	29.3	28.9	30.2
35	20.9	19.6	21.0	19.7	22.9	25.6	25.0	26.2
40	18.6	17.3	18.4	17.5	20.0	22.5	21.7	22.9
45	16.4	15.2	16.2	15.6	17.4	19.6	18.7	19.8
50	14.4	13.4	14.2	13.8	15.0	17.0	15.8	17.0
				Female				
0	26.9	22.9	25.0	21.5	30.0	29.9	31.4	36.7
5	38.3	35.6	36.5	31.8	41.5	41.5	44.4	45.5
10	38.5	36.0	36.0	31.3	40.1	40.4	42.5	42.8
15	38.4	35.6	35.5	31.1	39.3	40.1	40.8	41.1
20	35.1	32.8	33.0	29.4	36.0	37.8	37.5	38.1
25	28.9	27.5	27.8	25.1	30.0	32.6	32.0	33.1
30	24.1	23.2	23.4	21.6	25.2	28.3	27.5	28.8
35	21.6	20.8	20.8	19.5	22.3	25.6	24.5	25.8
40	19.9	19.0	18.8	17.9	20.1	23.2	22.1	23.3
45	18.0	17.0	16.8	16.2	17.9	20.6	19.6	20.6
50	16.3	15.1	15.1	14.6	15.7	18.2	17.0	18.1

We have shown elsewhere that estimates of e_0 and e_5 from this procedure are fairly robust to the typical patterns of age misstatement found in India. However, estimates at older ages are often biased upward by age exaggeration. Therefore, taking the mean or median of values of several adult ages should not automatically be considered as an ideal solution. Comparing the estimates of e_0 and e_5 presented in Table 6 with those of Table 5, we find that the estimates of e_0 derived from the Preston-Bennett method are very close to those based on the Indian standard, but the estimates of e_5 are closer to those based on the South model life table. Thus, probably because the differences we are dealing with are small, the results of the Preston and Bennett method are not very helpful in resolving the issue. Nevertheless, certain consistency checks described below do indicate that the adult mortality pattern contained in the South model life tables may be inappropriate for India in the early twentieth century. Once the life table is constructed from the above described 'age-error parameterized integrated' technique, it is also possible to estimate the 'true' age distribution of the population from the following relation:[39]

$$c(x) = \frac{e^{-\int_0^x r(a)\, da}\, l(x)}{\int_0^\omega e^{-\int_0^x r(a)\, da}\, l(x)\, dx}.$$

Note that its computation provides an implicit estimate of the crude birth rate, as $b = c(0)$. In practice, this estimate is an approximate one, as the input data needed are usually available only in discrete age intervals. However, it is worth noting that the estimating equation suggests that biases in the birth rate estimate may be inversely related to errors in the estimated person-years lived in the stationary population. This sensitivity to errors in life expectancy measures can be of value in selecting one set of figures over another.

In Table 7 we compare the input estimates of the crude birth rate (i.e., those used for inferring the child mortality level from the product, $b \times l_5$), with those derived in the above described procedure. We may denote the latter as 'slope-based' because of their sensitivity to the slope coefficient, β_1, used in inferring the adult mortality level. It can be observed that the slope-based estimates are always lower than the input crude birth rates, but the differences are much smaller for those based on the Indian standard life table. This raises the possibility that the use of the South model pattern tends to overstate the survival probabilities; if so, this bias must have come from the underestimation of adult mortality, because the estimates of l_5 used were approximately the same (see Table 4).

Table 7 also shows a comparison of the recorded mean proportion of the population aged 60 years and over in each intercensal period with

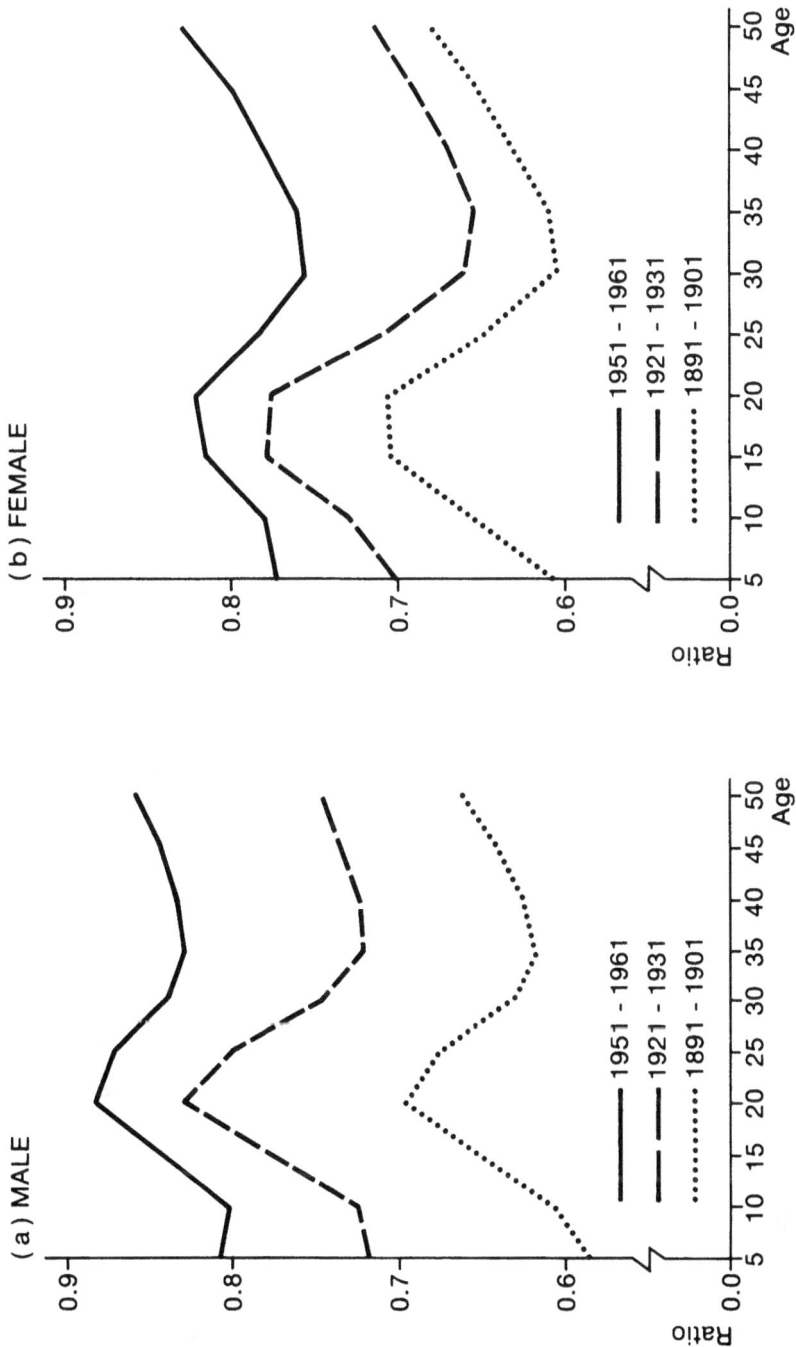

Fig.1 Ratios of Estimated e(x) Values to those of the Indian standard.

Table 7. Estimated Values of the Crude Birth Rate and the Proportion of the Population over Age Sixty, compared with their Input/Observed Values.

Decade	Input/observed values		Estimated using:			
			Indian standard		South model, level 13	
	Crude birth rate (CBR)	Prop. over age 60 (C60+)	CBR	C60+	CBR	C60+
Male						
1881 – 1891	47.5	.0463	46.9	.0328	45.9	.0469
1891 – 1901	47.1	.0459	46.3	.0365	45.2	.0533
1901 – 1911	47.4	.0469	46.6	.0346	45.6	.0494
1911 – 1921	46.4	.0494	45.6	.0347	44.7	.0509
1921 – 1931	46.5	.0496	45.8	.0360	44.8	.0498
1931 – 1941	46.7	.0517	46.6	.0317	45.9	.0421
1941 – 1951	45.4	.0537	45.2	.0427	44.3	.0566
1951 – 1961	45.8	.0539	45.6	.0385	44.8	.0504
Female						
1881 – 1891	46.5	.0590	45.9	.0492	45.3	.0602
1891 – 1901	46.1	.0573	45.2	.0524	44.5	.0645
1901 – 1911	46.3	.0563	45.2	.0526	44.5	.0647
1911 – 1921	45.7	.0570	44.7	.0513	44.0	.0640
1921 – 1931	46.2	.0554	45.1	.0504	44.5	.0613
1931 – 1941	46.5	.0566	46.4	.0428	45.9	.0514
1941 – 1951	45.3	.0584	44.7	.0516	44.1	.0617
1951 – 1961	45.7	.0579	45.3	.0485	44.8	.0578

the 'true' values computed according to the above formula. The estimated proportions are always lower than the observed values if the Indian standard is used, but the contrary is generally the case if the South model is employed. Thus use of the Indian standard suggests inflation of the population aged 60 and over by age exaggeration, while use of the South model pattern suggests the possibility of population depletion from age understatement. But the latter is against the spirit of the standard pattern of age distortions we employ, which assumes heavy age overstatement among the elderly. It seems more likely that the South model pattern exaggerates the over 60 population because it underestimates the mortality of the elderly population, relative to that of the young.

Therefore, we conclude that the estimates based on the Indian standard are nearest to the true values. The key to the unsuitability of the South model may lie in the divergent role tuberculosis played in shaping the mortality patterns of early twentieth century India and nineteenth century Europe.

DISCUSSION

In this section we compare our estimates with those of others for the same periods, and explain why the current estimates may be more reliable. The discussion will also shed new light on the age and sex-specific nature of mortality changes in India, and raise questions about the relevance of model age patterns of mortality to extreme conditions.

Fertility Estimates

The most frequently quoted estimates of the crude birth rate for pre-Independence India are those made by Davis.[40] His estimates for the beginning of this century fall in the neighbourhood of 48 per thousand. Two equally eminent demographers, Coale and Demeny, estimated its level to be 49 per thousand.[41] Compared to these, our estimate of about 47 per thousand shown in Table 4 is somewhat low. What may explain this deviation?

Davis's estimates are based on the back projection of the recorded population aged 0 – 9 in the census using the child mortality figures from the actuarial life tables. There are serious doubts about the accuracy of the reported numbers aged 0 – 9, and the validity of the mortality levels of this age interval in the official life tables. The fact that the mortality estimates were based on the experience of some remote communities is only part of the problem; also to be noted is that rates for females were derived by accepting sex ratios of the population of only selected regions of the country, and, more seriously, that mortality trends were distorted by the then prevailing actuarial practice of eliminating the effects of catastrophes in an attempt to arrive at the 'normal' level of mortality.[42]

Coale and Demeny, and several later researchers, employed tabulations of model stable populations to estimate demographic measures.[43] This procedure implicitly accepts the age pattern of mortality contained in a given model life table, and presupposes the accuracy of the population reported in a certain cumulated age range. But for the levels of mortality we are dealing with, the relevance of model patterns is open to question, and certain anomalies in their construction — discussion of which is postponed till later — make their use even more open to question.

In contrast to the above, the precision of our estimates hinges on the accuracy of the constant marital fertility assumption and on the trustworthiness of the estimated child mortality levels for the early 1960s. Of these, we are more certain of the latter. The child mortality estimates were based on the usually reliable Brass technique,[44] and were significantly higher than both direct and indirect information available from the SRS for the late 1960s. The assumption of constant marital fertility during the period 1881 to 1961 is, of course, not so easily defended. But whatever changes occurred, they were probably in a direction that would bias our estimates of the crude birth rate upward, and not downward as the above comparisons suggest. It is likely that during the late nineteenth century and in the early part of this century, fecundity was held in check by the frequent occurrence of famines and epidemics, endemic malaria, and general ill-health of the population. An increase in marital fertility during 1881 – 1961 can also be postulated from the weakening of traditional customs relating to breast-feeding, delayed cohabitation and post-partum abstinence.

Several studies have suggested a possible rise in fertility during the initial phase of the demographic transition. Newman reported a significant increase in the crude birth rate in Sri Lanka following the island's highly successful malaria eradication campaign.[45] In an analysis at a more global level, Dyson and Murphy found evidence that fertility rose in a number of developing countries after the post-war reductions in mortality.[46] Srinivasan and Jejeebhoy, comparing data from a 1959 and a 1972 survey, observed that marital fertility increased in several Indian states.[47] However, one cannot rule out the possibility that this rise may have been a spurious result of changes in the completeness of survey birth-reports.[48]

The bottom line, however, is that if an increase in marital fertility indeed took place during 1881 – 1961, its effect on the birth rate would be counter to the effects of the changes in the age and marital distributions of the population. Thus the true level of the crude birth rate at the beginning of this century would be about the same as, or lower than, that we have derived for the beginning of the 1960s (45 per thousand).

Though there appear to be reasons for assuming that marital fertility actually rose, we should not loose sight of the fact that it might have also fallen from the so-called 'interval effect' of declining mortality. When mortality is very heavy during infancy, a common cause for the termination of breast-feeding is the infant's death itself. Therefore, an improvement in child survival, by prolonging breast-feeding, might lengthen average intervals between births. Since a sizeable reduction in child mortality seems to have occurred during 1951 – 61, this factor cannot be ignored. Thus, because of the likely presence of offsetting errors, we consider our estimates of the birth rate for the beginning of this century as neither too high nor too low.

Having discounted the possibility of a significant change in marital fertility during the period 1881 to 1961, we may examine the age-specific fertility rates presented in Table 8 for the effects of changes in the marital composition of the population. These rates were derived by multiplying the standard marital fertility rates by the proportions of currently married females by age, in respective periods, and raising the resulting fertility rates by 8.7 per cent so that, when combined with the population's age distributions, they produced the crude birth-rate estimates shown in Table 4.

The rates presented in Table 8 suggest that there may have been significant changes in the age structure of fertility during 1881 – 1961, even though the level remained more or less the same. While the fertility of teenage women was falling from the postponement of marriage, older women were witnessing a steady rise in their fertility from decreases in widowhood. Both of these trends contributed to a year's increase in the mean age of child-bearing during 1881 – 1961. However, these factors had a mutually offsetting influence on total fertility. Still, the total fertility rate may have increased by about 0.3 births, because the effect of widowhood changes probably outweighed the impact of postponement of first marriage. Even so, the crude birth rate estimates shown in Table 4 suggest a drop of about 4 per cent between 1881 and 1961. There are two reasons for this apparent contradiction: first, a moderate increase in longevity was making the age structure of the population younger; second, as noted above, the mean age of child-bearing was rising owing to the postponement of marriage and a decreased incidence of widowhood. Both of these processes acted to suppress the crude birth rates of more recent periods.

Table 8. Estimates of Age-specific Fertility Rates, Total Fertility Rates, and Mean Ages at Maternity.

Decade	Age Interval							TFR	Mean age
	15 – 19	20 – 24	25 – 29	30 – 34	35 – 39	40 – 44	45 – 49		
1881 – 1891	.178	.302	.279	.202	.125	.057	.019	5.81	27.7
1891 – 1901	.174	.301	.278	.202	.125	.057	.019	5.78	27.7
1901 – 1911	.170	.300	.278	.203	.126	.058	.019	5.77	27.8
1911 – 1921	.167	.298	.277	.203	.126	.058	.019	5.75	27.8
1921 – 1931	.173	.300	.279	.208	.128	.064	.020	5.86	27.9
1931 – 1941	.167	.306	.287	.217	.131	.068	.020	5.98	28.0
1941 – 1951	.148	.306	.288	.220	.138	.069	.022	5.96	28.3
1951 – 1961	.146	.308	.295	.227	.147	.074	.025	6.11	28.5

Mortality Estimates

Though fertility levels were reasonably steady during the period under review, this cannot be said of mortality. But considerable disagreement exists as to its precise level and trend. Table 9 shows some previous estimates of life expectancy and child mortality. These may be compared with our estimates presented in Table 4 and Table 5. As we have more confidence in the estimates based on the Indian standard, they are used in this comparison. A number of points arise.

First, our estimates of life expectancy at birth around the turn of the century are about one to two years higher than the previous estimates. But as the years progress, differences diminish, and for 1951 – 61 our estimates are actually lower.

Second, our estimates of e_0 for the beginning of this century are greater precisely because our estimates of child survival levels are noticeably higher than either those contained in the actuarial tables, or those derived from model life tables. For example, our pre-1921 estimates of chances of survival to age five are approximately 8 per cent higher than the actuarial estimates, and 20 per cent higher than the estimates derived from stable population analyses using West model tables. As in the case of e_0, the differences diminish with the passage of time.

Third, in direct contrast to the differences in the child mortality estimates, our estimates of e_5 are generally lower than those derived from actuarial methods, and are especially low compared to those based on the forward survival procedure. In other words, our estimates imply an age pattern of mortality that is quite different from those contained in the actuarial tables or those observed in the Coale and Demeny models.

In our view, previous studies overestimated the level of e_5 because they did not adequately adjust for the effects of age exaggeration. This is reflected in the fact that upward biases are seen, particularly in the estimates for males, who are more prone to such exaggeration. Age over-statement, by giving an appearance of greater survival at older ages, produces downward biases in estimated mortality levels. The smoothing techniques employed by actuaries, though helping to even out age-to-age fluctuations, do little to correct for possible distortions in the recorded age distribution's slope. In the intercensal techniques devised by demographers, such as the forward survival procedure, considerable arbitrariness exists in selecting the estimates of what ages to average. It is not inconceivable, indeed it is quite likely, that in the presence of age exaggeration life expectancy estimates at most ages are biased upwards, and so might be their mean. These arguments derive support from simulation exercises.[49]

Table 9. Selected Estimates of Life Expectancy and Child Mortality from other Sources.

Decade	Life Expectancy at Birth				Life Expectancy at Age 5				Probability of Survival to Age 5			
	Actuarial estimates[1]		Stable population analysis[2]		Actuarial estimates[1]		Forward Survival analysis[3]		Actuarial estimates[1]		Stable population analysis[4]	
	Male	Female	Male	Female	Male	Female	Male	Female	Male	Female	Male	Female
1881 – 1891	24.6	25.5	—	—	37.1	36.1	40.0	40.3	.574	.612	—	—
1891 – 1901	23.6	24.0	20.5	22.5	36.3	35.2	37.1	37.5	.561	.586	.471	.508
1901 – 1911	22.6	23.3	24.4	23.9	35.0	35.4	39.0	37.5	.553	.566	.532	.529
1911 – 1921	19.4	20.9	20.5	21.7	31.8	31.4	36.5	32.9	.515	.557	.471	.495
1921 – 1931	26.9	26.6	28.8	28.5	39.0	36.6	41.3	39.2	.601	.643	.594	.593
1931 – 1941	32.1	31.4	34.0	31.9	44.0	41.7	46.7	44.7	.647	.664	.660	.635
1941 – 1951	32.5	31.7	35.8	33.3	40.9	40.9	44.8	43.2	.700	.681	.682	.652
1951 – 1961	41.9	40.5	38.9	38.6	48.7	47.0	47.4	45.6	.756	.789	.716	.711

Notes:
(1) Actuarial reports were not prepared for the 1911 – 1921 and 1931 – 1941 decades; instead, two unofficial life tables constructed by Davis (Davis, op. cit. in note 1) have been used. Also, estimates for decades prior to 1941 – 1951 refer to pre-partition India.
(2) From Mukherjee, op. cit. in note 1; only the larger of the two sets of estimates made by Mukherjee are shown.
(3) From Mukherjee, op. cit. in note 1; only estimates based on a West model life table are shown.
(4) These figures were derived from West model life tables corresponding to the estimates of life expectancy at birth.

On the other hand, for several reasons, previous efforts have overstated the true levels of child mortality. As noted earlier, their levels in the official life tables of the late nineteenth and early twentieth centuries were based upon communities that were simply not representative of the whole of India. It is worth noting that Uttar Pradesh, wherein the 'Proclaimed Clans' lived, still has one of the highest levels of infant and child mortality in India. Other studies have implicitly assumed the age patterns of mortality in the Coale and Demeny life tables. The reason that these tables may provide too high a level of child mortality at extremely low levels of life expectancy is more complex.

It is well known that the life tables of the Coale and Demeny family were based on regressions of the probability of dying in an age interval ($_nq_x$) on life expectancy at age 10 (e_{10}). But none of the input life tables employed in the construction of these models had levels of life expectancy near those prevailing in India at the beginning of this century. Thus the child mortality rates provided by the models at low levels of life expectancy essentially constitute extrapolations.

What makes them even less attractive is the way this extrapolation was carried out. One might suppose that the relationship between child and adult mortality found in model life tables of low life expectancy closely resembles that contained in the estimated regression equations. This, unfortunately, is not true. The explanation lies in the fact that there are two e_{10} values associated with each Coale and Demeny model life table: (i) the e_{10} that served in the generation of $_nq_x$'s from the regression equations, and (ii) the e_{10} implied by the predicted $_nq_x$'s, and shown in the model life table. For the West model male life tables, their values are as shown in Table 10.[50]

Table 10. Values of e_{10} Associated with West Model Male Life Tables

e_{10}	Life Expectancy Level					
	1	3	5	7	9	11
Seed value	21.9	28.7	34.3	39.1	41.2	46.8
Calculated value	33.2	36.2	39.0	41.8	44.5	47.2
Difference	11.3	7.4	4.7	2.7	1.3	0.4

Similar differences are also found for females. The fact that the difference between the two e_{10} values increases as the mortality 'level'

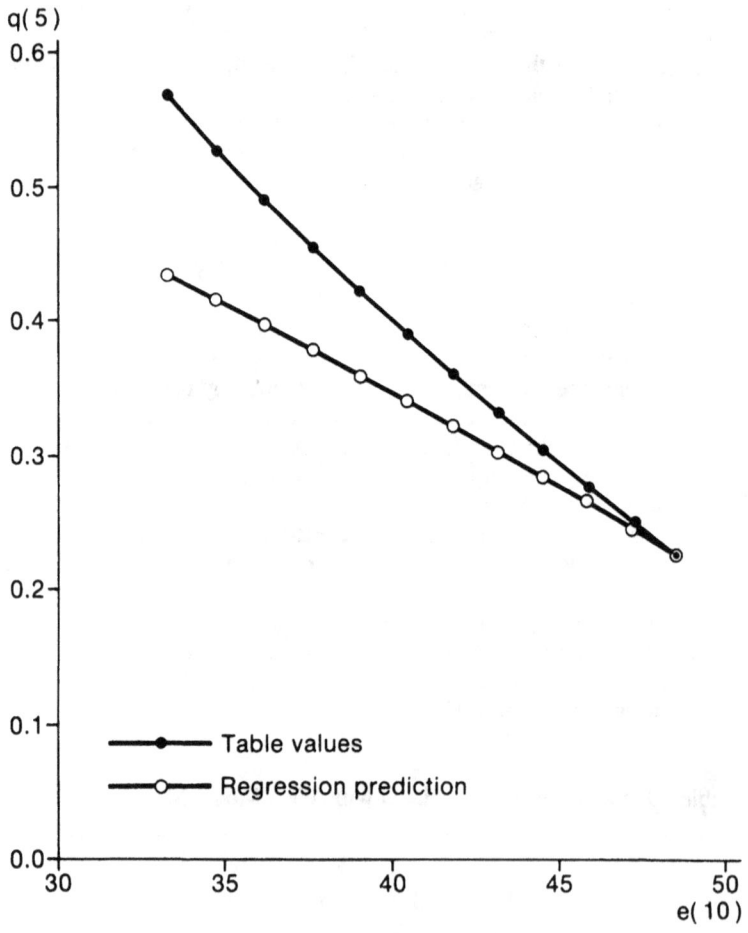

Fig.2 Two Divergent Paths of Child Mortality in the West Model
Life Tables.

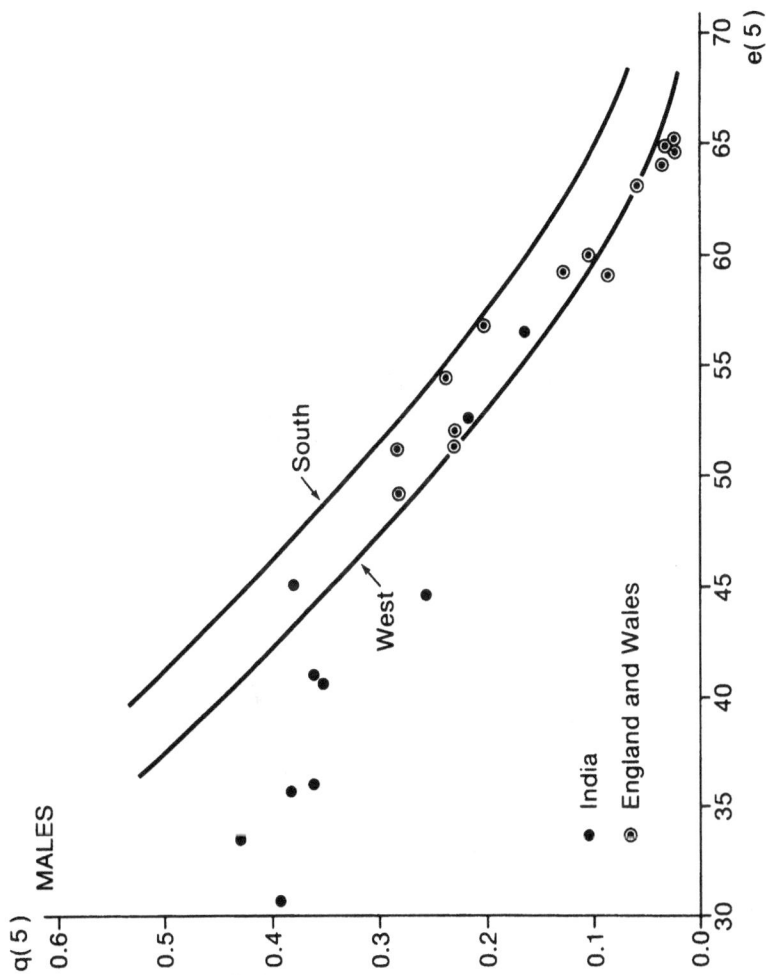

Fig.3 Estimated and Model Relationships between q(5) and e(5).

decreases shows how poorly the extrapolation performs at low levels of life expectancy. A little-known fact is that this difference played a crucial role in shaping the age pattern of mortality found in the model tables of extremely high mortality. This can be demonstrated by comparing the q_5 value provided in a given model life table with the q_5 value predicted from the regression equations by employing the e_{10} value shown in the same table. Fig. 2 makes such a comparison for West model male life tables. It can be observed that at low levels of life expectancy, the values of q_5 shown in the model life tables are noticeably higher than those predicted from the regression equations by employing the table values of e_{10} as the seed values. This difference occurs simply because the table values of $_nq_x$'s were generated by employing e_{10} values much lower than the values shown in the tables.[51] Also, the model life tables show substantially sharper reductions in child mortality as life expectancy rises, precisely because the difference between the two e_{10} values diminishes.

The reason why the model life tables of the Coale and Demeny family provide unusually high estimates of child mortality at very low levels of life expectancy may have to do with the assumed functional form of its relationship with an index of adult mortality, such as e_{10}. This point is illustrated in Fig. 3 where we have plotted estimates of q_5 against those of e_5, for England and Wales as derived by Keyfitz and Flieger,[52] and for India as we have estimated them. To strengthen the comparison, for India we have also included estimates for more recent periods which have been discussed elsewhere.[53] Also graphed are the continuous relationships found in the West and the South model families. As one would expect, the fit of the model to the life tables of England and Wales is reasonably precise. But the model patterns diverge noticeably from the estimates for India at lower levels of life expectancy.

Sex Differentials in Mortality

One of the major revisions the present set of estimates offers is with respect to sex differentials in mortality. Contrary to indications from previous studies, our estimates suggest that male life expectancy at birth did not exceed that of females in India until 1951–61. Nevertheless, they do suggest that the female advantage has been disappearing since the beginning of the century, a trend consistent with the recorded rise in the sex ratio of the population. The reason that earlier estimates suggested the appearance of greater male advantage quite early on is probably that the estimates for this sex are affected to a greater extent by age exaggeration. Few previous authors attempted to correct for the effects of such sex-selective biases in reported age distributions. It may be noted that the sex ratio of India's population did not exceed the sex ratio at birth (approximately 106) until 1961. Only when such a cross-over occurs, can one be sure that males enjoy greater longevity than females.

On the other hand, from an in-depth study of registration and survey data on sex differences in mortality, Visaria seems to conclude that higher female mortality was a characteristic of India even before the 1960s.[54] But the evidence presented by him is compelling only in two cases, Punjab and Rajasthan, which accounted for less than ten per cent of India's population in 1961. The bulk of the data presented for south India suggest excess male mortality, and the evidence examined for the rest of the country is inconclusive. In this context, it is of interest to note that mortality data collected for rural India in the National Sample Survey of 1958 – 59 produced an expectation of life at birth for females about one year higher than for males.[55] This evidence is, of course, open to the criticism that deaths could have been subject to differential completeness by sex, but so is the evidence presented by Visaria.

The present study also sheds new light on the sex differential in child mortality. It is important to note that our estimates are not sensitive to the fertility assumptions of the methodology. Indeed, they can be computed without knowing the levels of the crude birth rate. The average differences between the male and female death rates in the age interval 0 – 4 (per thousand) implied by our sex-specific estimates of $b \times l_5$ (see Table 4) are as shown in Table 11.

Table 11. Average Differences between Male and Female Death Rates in Age Interval 0 – 4 (per thousand)

Decade	Indian Standard	South, Level 13
1881 – 1891	– 1.43	– 1.61
1891 – 1901	– 2.11	– 0.72
1901 – 1911	0.10	– 0.22
1911 – 1921	2.29	3.09
1921 – 1931	1.42	0.10
1931 – 1941	– 2.22	– 5.38
1941 – 1951	8.30	6.28
1951 – 1961	1.15	– 1.38
1961 – 1971	3.34	– 1.10
1971 – 1981	– 5.12	– 7.85

Only minor variations result from the choice of standard mortality pattern. Both series indicate an excess of mortality among female children at the end of the nineteenth century, and a gradual reduction since then, with a re-emergence during 1971 – 81. Some unevenness in the trend during the period 1921 to 1951 may be attributed to the problems of the 1931 and 1941 age distributions. An independent check on these estimates is possible for 1971 – 81, for which period rates from the SRS become available. The average death rates from this source suggest an excess mortality of 6.4 per thousand among females in the 0 – 4 age interval. This matches remarkably well with the estimates shown above.

The finding that excess mortality of female children did not worsen, or perhaps even improved, during the first half of this century — a period when the sex ratio of the population was increasing — calls for a fresh examination of the causes and consequences of early mortality decline in India. We wish to draw particular attention to the fact that observers of the Bangladesh famines in the early 1970s have noted that girls died in unusual numbers.[56] There is also some supporting evidence for this from earlier famines of the subcontinent.[57] A likely explanation is that differential allocation of family resources by sex of child becomes acute and life threatening only under extreme conditions. Therefore, female children may have benefited to a greater extent from the decreased incidence of famines since the beginning of this century. An alternate explanation for the trend is that female infanticide was still prevalent in some communities during the late nineteenth and early twentieth centuries, but gradually disappeared with time because of legislation and modernization.

If male children did not benefit differentially from the decline in mortality, then the rise in the sex ratio of the population must have been caused by what was happening to adults. The estimates of e_5 presented in Table 5 do show that the female advantage at ages above five found at the beginning of this century gradually disappeared by 1951 – 61.

More convincing evidence for this, however, comes from the comparison of age-specific survival ratios derived from the Preston-Bennett method. Though our new procedure of computing person-years lived during each age interval provides a built-in smoothing of reported ages, one can still observe the effects of age misreporting in computed five-year survival rates. Nevertheless, it is perhaps reasonable to suppose that implicit trends in the ratios are reliable. To minimize the errors from age misreporting, we shall consider only the survival chances in three broad age intervals: (i) from birth to ages 10 – 14, (ii) from 10 – 14 to 30 – 34, and (iii) from 30 – 34 to 50 – 54. In Table 12 the trends specific to these intervals are examined by dividing the survival rates of each intercensal period by a set of base period rates. The base period rates are taken to be the average values for 1891 – 1901

Table 12. Trends in Age-specific Survival Ratios, 1881–91 to 1951–61.

Survival ratios	Base period values (1891–1911)	Ratios to base period values					
		1881–1891	1891–1901	1901–1911	1911–1921	1921–1951	1951–1961
Male							
5L10/5L0	.494	1.077	.953	1.050	.982	1.154	1.376
5L30/5L15	.761	1.054	.978	1.022	.891	1.099	1.125
5L50/5L30	.497	1.030	.961	1.041	.942	1.275	1.360
Female							
5L10/5L0	.470	1.063	.955	1.048	.985	1.184	1.405
5L30/5L15	.828	1.082	.999	1.001	.866	1.057	1.049
5L50/5L30	.492	1.020	1.010	.990	.905	1.198	1.277

and 1901 – 11; the first was a decade of relatively slow population growth, and the second was a decade of relatively rapid growth.

The observed trends are consistent with U-shaped changes in age-specific mortality. By 1951 – 61, chances of survival appear to have gone up by nearly 40 per cent under age 15, and by about 30 per cent at ages 30 to 55. For the intervening ages, however, the change was less than 10 per cent. The reliability of these figures gets support from the observed changes during 1911 – 21. This was the decade of the great influenza epidemic. This epidemic had a very unusual age pattern, mortality being heavy among adults, and pregnant women in particular.[58] Such a pattern is also discernible from the indices presented in Table 12. This illustrates the utility of the recorded age data, so long as census authorities did not complicate such data by trying to 'discipline' them.[59]

Some interesting facts emerge when the indices are examined by sex. As observed above, these indices also show that mortality improvements at childhood ages were about the same for the two sexes. But in adult years, especially between ages 10 – 14 and 30 – 34, gains were noticeably smaller among females (see Table 12). There are at least two plausible explanations for such a trend. First, the incidence of tuberculosis was probably rising during the period, and it took a greater toll among women because of the burdens of rapid child-bearing, prolonged lactation, the *purdah* system, and general neglect.[60] Second, as Visaria has speculated, men probably benefited more from the control of famines than did women.[61] The vast literature on Indian famines suggests that, though perhaps female children died more frequently during periods of famine, at older ages males were more susceptible.[62]

Comparison with China

Our estimates of fertility and mortality for India at the turn of this century make a striking comparison with those made by Barclay and colleagues for China in the pre-revolutionary era.[63] These are shown in Table 13.

The estimated level of Indian fertility is somewhat higher than the Chinese, while the estimated mortality levels in the two populations are nearly equal. Thus, during the period of comparison, the population of India was exhibiting a slight tendency to grow, while China's population was estimated to be nearly stationary.

There are some significant variations in the fertility measures of the two nations. Indian marital fertility was about 13 per cent higher than the Chinese, but the estimated difference in the total fertility rate was

Table 13. Estimates of Fertility and Mortality for India and China

		India 1891 – 1911	Chinese farmers 1929 – 31
Fertility measures			
Crude birth rate		46.7	41.2
Total fertility rate		5.8	5.5
Total marital fertility rate		7.1	6.2
Mortality measures			
Crude death rate		42.7	41.5
Life expectancy at	male	23.7	24.6
birth (e_0)	female	24.4	23.7
Life expectancy at	male	34.2	33.5
age five (e_5)	female	35.7	33.2
Proportion surviving	male	.594	.633
to age five (l_5)	female	.591	.611

only 5 per cent. Since both populations were marrying early, the discrepancy arose primarily because of the taboo on widow remarriage among higher castes in India. Still, the crude birth rate in India was about 13 per cent higher, which suggests the compensatory role played by India's younger age distribution and its lower average age at maternity.

Even though overall levels of mortality were similar in the two regions, their distributions by age and sex were not identical. Curiously, mortality estimates show greater female disadvantage in China. As to the age pattern of mortality, the estimates of e_5 and l_5 suggest that though adult mortality was lower in India, child mortality was lower in China. In other words, the age pattern of mortality implied by the estimates for China diverges even more from model age patterns than does India's. Thus the evidence from the world's two largest nations indicates that at low life expectancy levels, child mortality levels are not nearly as high as those suggested by models.[64]

CONCLUSION

In this chapter 'variable-r' procedures have been employed to estimate levels of fertility and mortality in India during 1881 – 1961 from census age distributions. Particular attention has been paid to problems of age misstatement and the paucity of reliable information on child mortality, and some new techniques have been proposed to handle them. The only restrictive assumption imposed in the methodology is that of constant marital fertility. Though this may amount to introducing an assumption of stability through the back door, it is considered worthwhile because no other satisfactory solution exists for the lack of independent information on child mortality levels.

The analysis suggests that previous estimates have exaggerated the true levels of fertility and mortality at the beginning of this century. Our estimates of the crude birth rate for this period are about 2 – 5 per cent lower than existing estimates, while our estimates of expectation of life at birth are generally one or two years higher. The new figures, particularly those of mortality, compare well with those made by Barclay and his colleagues for traditional rural China. This suggests that the world's two largest peasant cultures began their descent towards a new demographic equilibrium from similar levels of mortality and fertility.

During 1881 – 1961, India's crude birth rate is estimated to have decreased by two per thousand from changes in age and marital composition of the population. In the same period, total fertility may have increased by 0.3 births from a reduction in the risk of widowhood. Nevertheless, the crude birth rate fell because of the rejuvenation of the population's age structure, and upwards shifts in the age of maternity.

Significant revisions are proposed with respect to mortality differentials in India by sex and age. Though the female advantage in life expectancy was diminishing from the beginning of this century, our estimates indicate that male life expectancy at birth did not exceed that of females until the 1950s. It appears that previous studies showed lower mortality among males because they made no allowance for the effects of greater age exaggeration among members of this sex. The current reappraisal also suggests that the sex ratio of India's population rose because of relatively modest improvements in the death rates of adult women compared to men. No evidence is found to substantiate the claim that discrimination against female children precipitated the rising trend of the sex ratio.

The age pattern of mortality implied by our estimates is significantly different from those contained in model life tables or the actuarial tables. We derive levels of child mortality for the beginning of this century that are substantially lower than those previous studies have shown. But our estimates of adult mortality are generally higher. The reason that we arrive at higher levels of adult mortality has mostly to do with the correction we incorporated for the effects of age misstatement. The estimates of child mortality are different because, while previous estimates rested on uncertain ground, we derive ours from census age distributions employing independent estimates of the crude birth rate. Our estimates of the birth rate are less open to question because they are derived from more reliable estimates of child mortality for recent periods, and rest on the relatively defensible assumption of constant marital fertility during 1881 – 1961.

The comparison of estimated age structures of mortality in India and China during the pre-transitional period suggests that Coale and Demeny model life tables may give an erroneous picture of the age pattern of mortality at very low levels of life expectancy. From this it is tempting to conclude that high mortality regimes are characterized not so much by high child mortality, as model life tables indicate, but by extraordinarily high adult mortality.

NOTES TO CHAPTER 4

This is a part of my doctoral dissertation written at the University of Pennsylvania. I am deeply indebted to Professor Samuel H. Preston who supervised the thesis. Comments of Ansley Coale, and the editorial assistance received from Tim Dyson and Meg Greene were instrumental in improving the manuscript. My graduate study at the University of Pennsylvania was made possible by generous grants from the Population Council and the Hewlett Foundation.

1 Actuarial reports authorised by Hardy were published as parts of the census reports of 1881 and 1891, while that of the 1901 census was published independently as: George F. Hardy, *Memorandum on the Age Tables and Rates of Mortality of the Indian Census of 1901*, (Calcutta: Superintendent of Government Printing, 1905). Some notable later attempts are: Kingsley Davis, *The Population of India and Pakistan*, (Princeton, N.J.: Princeton University Press, 1951); Ansley J. Coale and Paul Demeny, *Manual IV: Methods of Estimating Basic Demographic Measures from Incomplete Data*, (New York: United Nations, 1967); Pravin M. Visaria, 'Mortality and fertility in India: 1951 – 1961', *The Milbank Memorial Fund Quarterly*, 47, no. 1 (January 1969): 91 – 116; Prithwis Das Gupta, 'Estimation of demographic measures for India, 1881 – 1961, based on census age distributions', *Population Studies*, 25, no. 3 (November 1971): 395 – 414; Sudhansu B. Mukherjee, *The Age Distribution of the Indian Population: A Reconstruction for the States and Territories, 1881 – 1961*, (Honolulu: University Press of Hawaii, 1976).

2 For a thorough discussion on the theory underlying these methods, see Samuel H. Preston and Ansley J. Coale, 'Age structure, growth, attrition and accession: a new synthesis', *Population Studies*, 48, no. 2 (Summer 1982): 217 – 59. For the procedures see: Samuel H. Preston and Neil G. Bennett, 'A census-based method for estimating adult mortality', *Population Studies*, 37, no. 1 (April 1983): 91 – 104; Samuel H. Preston, 'An integrated system for demographic estimation from two censuses',

Demography, 20, no. 2 (May 1983): 213 – 26; Neil G. Bennett and Shiro Horiuchi, 'Mortality estimation from registered deaths in less developed countries', *Demography*, 21, no. 2 (May 1984): 217 – 33.

3   See P. N. Mari Bhat, Samuel H. Preston and Tim Dyson, *Vital Rates in India, 1961 – 1981*, (Washington D.C.: National Academy Press, 1984). Also see P. N. Mari Bhat, *Mortality in India: Levels, Trends and Patterns*, Unpublished Ph.D. Dissertation, University of Pennsylvania, 1987.

4   See, Arthur P. Wolf, 'Fertility in pre-revolutionary China', *Population and Development Review*, 10, no. 3 (September 1984): 444 – 470, and Ansley J. Coale, 'Fertility in pre-revolutionary China: Defense of a reassessment', *Population and Development Review*, 10, no. 3 (September 1984): 471 – 80.

5   P. N. Mari Bhat, op. cit. in note 3, Chapter 2.

6   For obvious reasons, the 'Proclaimed Clan' statistics were made use of only in the construction of male life tables. Female tables were derived from sex ratios of the population recorded in certain eastern and southern provinces where the enumeration of females was thought to be more complete.

7   Ansley J. Coale and Paul Demeny, *Regional Model Life Tables and Stable Populations*, (Princeton, N.J.: Princeton University Press, 1966); also see Ansley J. Coale, Paul Demeny and Barbara Vaughan, *Regional Model Life Tables and Stable Populations*, Second edition, (New York, Academic Press, 1983).

8   See Preston, loc. cit. in note 2.

9   See Preston and Coale, loc. cit. in note 2.

10 William Brass, 'On the scale of mortality', in William Brass (ed.) *Biological Aspects of Demography*, (London, Taylor and Francis, 1971): 60 – 110.

11 In its more traditional form the logit transformation is written as:

$$\text{logit } l(x) = \frac{1}{2} \ln \frac{1 - l(x)}{l(x)}.$$

However, since the constant, ½, does not alter the functional form of the relationship, it is often dropped.

12 Preston, loc. cit. in note 2.

13 Ideally, one would like to use the 'cohort' interpolation technique discussed elsewhere (see Bhat, op. cit. in note 3, Chapter 2). However, because the requisite estimates of intercensal births are not usually known beforehand, it is difficult to apply in this case.

14 Although India is credited with having taken its first census during the early 1870s, it was not synchronous, and underenumeration was believed to be quite substantial.

15 Mukherjee, op. cit. in note 1.

16 This is largely unpublished data, but it was kindly made available to the National Academy of Sciences' Panel on India by the Registrar General, see Bhat, Preston and Dyson, op. cit. in note 3. The age distribution

employed was that of gross interstate migrants as, at the all-India level, age distributions of in-migrants and out-migrants were not exactly identical.

17 See E. A. Gait, *Report*, Census of India, 1911, Vol. I, Part I (Calcutta: Superintendent, Government Printing, 1913): 56.

18 See J. H. Hutton, *Report*, Census of India, 1931, Vol. I, Part I (Delhi: Manager of Publications, 1933).

19 See for example, Pravin M. Visaria, 'Provisional population totals of the 1971 census: Some questions and research issues', *Economic and Political Weekly*, 6, no. 29, (July 17, 1971): 1459 – 65.

20 For more on this see Bhat, op. cit. in note 3, Chapter 4.

21 For details see Bhat, op. cit. in note 3, Chapter 3.

22 Ansley J. Coale and T. James Trussell, 'Model fertility schedules: Variations in the age structure of child-bearing in human populations', *Population Index*, 40, no. 2 (April 1974): 185 – 258.

23 See India, Registrar General, *Fertility Differentials in India 1972*, (New Delhi: Office of the Registrar General, 1976).

24 See Bhat, Preston and Dyson, op. cit. in note 3, pp. 83 – 5.

25 Fertility rates were adjusted for the half-year displacement using a procedure described in Kenneth Hill, Hania Zlotnik, and T. James Trussell, *Manual X: Indirect Techniques for Demographic Estimation*, (New York, United Nations, 1983): 34. The standard marital fertility rates so derived are as follows:

Age Interval

15-19	20-24	25-29	30-34	35-39	40-44	45-49	TMFR
.193	.309	.294	.233	.159	.090	.034	6.56

26 See Bhat, op. cit. in note 3, Appendix C.

27 See ibid., Appendix D.

28 See ibid., Appendix C.

29 See ibid., Appendix C.

30 See ibid., Chapter 3.

31 See Mukherjee, op. cit. in note 1, pp. 51 – 61.

32 For example, during 1881 – 1891 many parts of India experienced severe famines, and population growth was negligible. But our estimate of $b \times l_s$ for this decade is only 10 per cent lower than the average of the estimates for the previous and succeeding decades. Since most of the change was certainly due to mortality, very little is left to be explained by means of a fertility decline.

33 The initial set of estimates from this survey is given in Bhat, Preston and Dyson, op. cit. in note 3. Some further analyses of the same data appear in Bhat, op. cit. in note 3, Chapter 4, from which the above estimate of q_s is taken.

34 We have assumed a sex ratio at birth of 106. The basis for this is an inquiry on births in hospitals during 1949 – 58. See K. V. Ramachandran and

Vinayak A. Deshpande, 'The sex ratio at birth in India by regions', *The Milbank Memorial Fund Quarterly*, 42, no. 2 (April 1964): 84 – 95.

35   The following approximations were used in the construction of the life table $_rL_x$ column:

$$_5L_0 = l_0 + 4l_5$$
$$_5L_x = 2.5l_x + 2.5l_{x+5}, 5 \leqslant x < 80$$
$$_\infty L_{80} = l_{80} (3.725 + 6.25l_{80}).$$

36   See Preston and Bennett, op. cit. in note 2.

37   See Ansley J. Coale, 'Life table construction on the basis of two enumerations of a closed population', *Population Index*, 50, no. 2 (Summer, 1984): 193 – 213.

38   The reason is self-evident in the cohort interpolation formula employed in the calculation of person-years lived during a 10-year intercensal period; see Bhat, op. cit. in note 3, Chapter 3.

39   In implementing the equation, one needs an estimate of the average length of the open-ended interval, $w+$. This may be computed using an empirical relation developed by Preston and Bennett:
$$y = e(w)[0.802 - 0.0106e(w) - 1.34r(w+)].$$
See Preston and Bennett, op. cit. in note 2.

40   See Davis, op. cit. in note 1.

41   See Coale and Demeny, op. cit. in note 1.

42   This is precisely the reason that the actuarial life table for 1891 – 1901 does not show appreciable change in mortality, even though the decade recorded one of the lowest population growth rates in the modern era.

43   See, for example, Visaria, loc. cit. in note 1, or Mukherjee, op. cit. in note 1.

44   See Hill, Zlotnik, and Trussell, op. cit. in note 25, pp. 73 – 85.

45   See Peter Newman, *Malaria Eradication and Population Growth: With Special Reference to Ceylon and British Guiana*, (Ann Arbor, Michigan: School of Public Health, The University of Michigan, 1965).

46   See Tim Dyson and Mike Murphy, 'The onset of fertility transition', *Population and Development Review*, 11, no. 3 (September 1985): 399 – 440.

47   See K. Srinivasan and Shireen Jejeebhoy, 'Changes in natural fertility in India, 1959 – 1972', in K. Srinivasan and S. Mukerji (eds), *Dynamics of Population and Family Welfare, 1981*, (Bombay: Himalaya Publishing House, 1981): 91 – 117.

48   Indeed, we believe so strongly in this possibility that we refrained from using the 1959 survey's estimate to represent the pre-transitional level of marital fertility.

49   See Bhat, op. cit. in note 3, Chapter 2.

50   Although the seed values of e_{10} were not provided by the authors, they can be derived from the regression equations using the predicted values of $_nq_x$ shown in the tables as inputs. Of the two functional forms used in the construction of the model tables, the linear specification appears to apply to the West model life tables of below level 13.

51 In a private communication to the author, Ansley J. Coale points out that since all $_nq_x$ values of a given model life table were derived from using the same index value of e_{10}, their levels at all ages would be biased approximately in the same proportion, thus the age pattern of mortality implied by them would still be reliable. Nevertheless, we maintain that since the estimated values of $_nq_x$ do not imply the same level of e_{10} as the one used in their generation, and this difference is not trivial, the age pattern of mortality implied by them is unreliable at low levels of life expectancy. Coale correctly surmises that the discrepancy between the index e_{10} and the calculated e_{10} was caused by 'the regression towards the mean' of $_nq_x$ estimates when a very low value of the index e_{10} is selected. But he considers that this has no direct bearing on the appropriateness of the model age pattern of mortality at low levels. On the other hand, we interpret the regression towards the mean of predicted values as showing that functional forms of the relationships between $_nq_x$'s and an overall index of mortality were misspecified in the original regressions. Unfortunately, in the procedure of model life table construction adopted by Coale and Demeny, their *a priori* specification was unavoidable.

52 See Nathan Keyfitz and Wilhelm Flieger, *World Population: An Analysis of Vital Data*, (Chicago & London: The University of Chicago Press, 1968).

53 These are Brass-type estimates derived from surveys. See Bhat, op. cit. in note 3, Chapter 4.

54 See Pravin M. Visaria, *The Sex Ratio of the Population of India*, Census of India 1961, Monograph No. 10 (Delhi: Manager of Publications, 1971).

55 See Ajoy Kumar De and Ranjan Kumar Som, 'Abridged life tables for rural India, 1957 – 1958', *The Milbank Memorial Fund Quarterly*, 42, no. 2 (April 1964): 96 – 106; also see Visaria, op. cit. in note 54, p. 43.

56 See, for example, Radheshyam Bairagi, 'Food crisis, nutrition and female children in rural Bangladesh', *Population and Development Review*, 12, no. 2 (June 1986): 307 – 15.

57 See E. A. H. Blunt, *Report*, Census of India, 1911, United Provinces of Agra and Oudh, Vol. XV, Part I, (Allahabad: Superintendent, Government Press, 1912): 195; Paul R. Greenough, *Prosperity and Misery in Modern Bengal: The Famine of 1943 – 1944*, (New York, Oxford University Press, 1982): 309 – 15.

58 See, for example, Macfarlane Brunet and David O. White, *Natural History of Infectious Disease*, Fourth edition (Cambridge: Cambridge University Press, 1972): 204 – 7.

59 Because the census authorities resorted to such practices in 1931 and 1941, it becomes impossible to rely on the estimated changes in the age pattern of mortality during 1921 – 1951. Therefore, in Table 12 only the combined figures for this period are shown.

60 See A. C. Ukil, 'Tuberculosis in India', *Proceedings of the Fourth International Congress on Tropical Medicine and Malaria*, Vol. II, (Washington D.C.: Government Printing Office, 1948): 1509; Davis, op. cit. in note 1, pp. 55 – 7; Visaria, op. cit. in note 54, pp. 62 – 3.

61 See Visaria, op. cit. in note 54, p. 61.

62   Extracts of various views on this issue appear in Gait, op. cit. in note 17
     pp. 220 – 22.
63   See George W. Barclay, Ansley J. Coale, Michael A. Stoto, and T. James
     Trussell, 'A reassessment of the demography of traditional rural China',
     Population Index, 42, no. 4 (October 1976): 606 – 35.
64   However, Ansley J. Coale informs the author that life tables of the West
     model provide a good fit to age-specific death rates from Taiwan for 1905,
     with an e_0 of about 25 years, and from Netherlands for 1816 – 25, with an
     e_0 of about 29 years, even though neither were used in the construction of
     the models.

5

MORTALITY, FERTILITY, AND THE STATUS OF
WOMEN IN INDIA, 1881 – 1931

Alice W. Clark

This chapter speaks to a set of issues in the study of Indian society and history which are being discussed in the framework of several disciplinary and interdisciplinary approaches: Indian social and economic history, the study of women in society, and Indian demographic history. It does so using a conceptually very simple stratagem, the production of new life tables for several regions of India using new methods. Because the history of mortality is central to the quality of life, whether gauged economically or culturally, new statements about mortality history can inform discussion in a range of areas even wider than those selected for attention here.[1]

There is a current and long-standing debate on the social and economic effects of the British period in Indian history, which for our purposes can be somewhat crudely characterized as the 'immiserization versus progress' debate. This debate did not, of course, begin with the influential paper which infused new life into it, Morris David Morris's 'Towards a Reinterpretation of Indian Economic History', but reaches back at least as far as R. C. Dutt's classic indictment of British imperialism.[2] The reinterpretationists have become a new classical school in themselves, however, for they have given recent expression to their views in the new *Cambridge Economic History of India*;[3] and those views speak for progress in many spheres of the economy during the British era. To dispute this has now become the diehard position. Of recent contributions to the debate, the titles alone suggest its flavour: Irfan Habib's critique entitled 'Studying a Colonial Economy — without Perceiving Colonialism' is countered by Dharma Kumar's 'The Dangers of Manichaeism'.[4]

Population is one of the inherent parameters in the debate, but is, for the most part, inadequately discussed within that context. For example, while the new Cambridge history contains an article by the Visarias on what is known of India's demography since 1757, its findings are not integrated into the rest of the volume.[5] In his critique, Habib argues that mortality history suggests rather less favourable conclusions about economic performance than the contributors acknowledge (and this is also Klein's often repeated view).[6] The present study suggests an even harsher picture of the history of Indian mortality than did those of the Visarias and earlier authorities such as Davis and Mukherjee.[7] While its full implications for economic analysis are not pursued here, this picture challenges some parts of the interpretation of the period as one of steady economic development. For the development of the infrastructure which would later bring economic advancement, it appears that human beings may have paid a heavier price than we realized.

Within the study of women in Indian society, there is a much newer debate which has at least a common starting point. There is agreement that the traditional status and autonomy of women in India is low compared to some other parts of the world, and is lower in the northern part of India than in the south. The causes of the phenomenon are debated, with those leaning towards a labour-market explanation being countered by those urging that causation lies (not solely, but primarily) in cultural differences expressed in kinship patterns that have existed almost from time immemorial.[8] Miller's 1981 study embraces both perspectives.[9]

The present study, utilizing an historical perspective, takes issue with some of the assumptions of this debate. Differences in women's position between north and south are reflected in population sex ratios resulting in large part from differential survival by sex. But, as we will see here, these sex differentials in mortality (whatever their origins) have not had nearly so large an effect for female mortality or fertility as have differences between the overall levels of mortality by region. This study finds mortality differences by region large enough to make it necessary to take issue with Dyson and Moore (and with Asok Mitra, whom they cite) for their idea that 'female social status is probably the single most important element in comprehending India's demographic situation.'[10] Agreeing in part with Davis, the Visarias, Klein, and also McAlpin, this study gives greater primacy to the economic and epidemiological (and, by implication, to the historical) context.[11] The role of crisis mortality is sharply etched in our results. It is also very clear that the different regions have had underlying differences in mortality levels, reflecting different historical experiences; some (but not all) of these continue to be reflected in contemporary experience.

This study demonstrates that as measured by mortality differentials, the relative status of women worsened in both northern and southern India in the early part of the twentieth century, supporting what studies based on sex ratios have also suggested. The mortality sex differential increased progressively throughout the period, even when (and arguably *especially* when) the level of mortality was improving.

In terms of issues in Indian demographic history, this chapter is an essay in the historical use of new methodology and new model life tables. In every systematic study of India's demography in the past, a crucial issue for the estimation of fertility as well as mortality has been the identification or creation of the right life tables. Kingsley Davis, working at the level of all-India, relied upon some modifications of the life tables computed by actuaries working for the Census of India, and on two he constructed for decades in which official tables were missing, using census survival methods on modified data.[12] Sudhansu Mukherjee devised many tests for fitting Indian census age distributions to those attached to model stable life tables, using all four model families of Coale and Demeny;[13] he calculated a set of estimates of mortality and fertility directly from these. Leela and Pravin Visaria also utilized stable age distributions, relying primarily on the West family of models from Coale and Demeny, and likewise provided mortality and fertility estimates directly from them.[14]

The present study uses intercensal analysis procedures developed by Preston and Bennett that require no fitting or smoothing.[15] We construct life tables based on three different sets of models, the preferred in most cases being from the new United Nations model tables, South Asia pattern.[16] The chapter discusses why these methods and models may be more appropriate to India than previous ones, and shows that mortality history looks rather different from what it has in earlier studies when viewed through these newer instruments. It does not claim that these recent tools are indubitably the right ones. Methodologists scrutinizing the results may find information in them which is useful for an evaluation of the methodology of Preston and Bennett — especially for conditions of very high levels of mortality. Our principal use of the results here will focus on directions in which our view of Indian mortality history may need to be revised, rather than claiming authority for a fixed set of numbers.

CASES SELECTED, AND THE DATA

The study takes as its specific subject matter the mortality and fertility experience of three of the largest presidencies of British India, along with their associated princely states: the United Provinces, in the north, now Uttar Pradesh; Bombay, in the west, now Maharashtra and Gujarat; and, in the far south, Madras, now Andhra Pradesh and Tamil Nadu. Bombay Presidency, for the purposes of this paper, includes the large princely state of Baroda, now a major part of Gujarat. United Provinces and Madras are selected in order to present the comparison between north and south, so much a part of the recent discussion of women's status. Bombay is included to represent western Indian experience, the main subject of the author's research in history. It would be desirable to extend the study to other major units of British India, particularly the Punjab and Bengal.

Presidencies have been selected as units of analysis because of the availability at that level of data on lifetime migration. For the mortality estimation methodology used here, the prior estimation of intercensal migration is crucial, because the census age distributions must be cleared of the effects of migration before they can be used for the estimation of mortality. Methods were devised for transforming data on migration by place of birth into intercensal migration estimates, using in part the work of K. C. Zachariah.[17]

The years of the census that have been chosen partly reflect the availability of migration data. No such data were collected in the 1941 census, which was greatly abbreviated due to the exigencies of the war; this made it impossible to estimate net intercensal migration for either 1931–41 or 1941–51. The 1872 census was avoided because different parts of it were taken in different years, necessitating considerable adjustment before it could be used for anything approximating decadal mortality estimation. In addition, considerable recent work has appeared on the more contemporary decades, so we need not duplicate it here.

The input data for this study are the age distributions from the census of India for the census years 1881 to 1931, as compiled into comparable format by S. B. Mukherjee.[18] There was considerable district swapping, boundary changing, and territorial acquisition among the Indian presidencies during the decades we are concerned with; Mukherjee, by regularizing the data so that they uniformly pertain to modern state boundaries, has offered a very useful aid to historical demographers. The Mukherjee data on Uttar Pradesh provide estimates for the United Provinces, and thereby for the north of India; those on Maharashtra and Gujarat do so for Bombay Presidency plus Baroda (the west); and data on Andhra Pradesh and Tamil Nadu provide estimates for Madras in the south. Because we are using the boundaries of modern states or pairs of states for estimation of presidency-wide mortality and fertility, the migration data based on presidency boundaries are adjusted so as to be applicable to the population totals being used.

The supplementary sets of data used are the statistics on migration by birthplace from the original census volumes.

METHODOLOGY AND RESULTS

Establishing the Level of Mortality

Indian age distributions, as reflected in the censuses, are very irregular, due to age misreporting and underenumeration. This poses a problem for mortality estimation. One solution to this problem in the past has been to fit faulty census age distributions to selected points along model age distributions, thereby smoothing the data. But such models, based on model life tables, reflect patterns of mortality and fertility that may not apply to Indian experience. Data smoothed according to models, when used to estimate vital rates, then carry assumptions about vital rates.

The mortality estimation method used in this paper is based on the new adaptation of stable population theory by Preston and Coale known as the 'variable r' version, by way of the methodology based on it that has been devised by Preston and Bennett.[19] With 'variable r' procedures, we begin with unsmoothed data, based on the presumption that characteristic patterns of error in the Indian census remain much the same over time within age groups. That is, we assume that particular age groups are underenumerated to about the same extent over time, and that age misreporting also follows predictable patterns.

The initial input data are the raw census age distributions of each sex for each census year, paired with migration-adjusted distributions for each subsequent census year. The technique of Preston and Bennett is to compare age groups to their equivalents across census years, and to compute intercensal growth rates for each age group. Life-table functions are then computed using (i) the sum of these rates to each age, and (ii) the mid-decade population of each age. The most important output is the life expectancy column, showing the number of years of expected remaining life for persons surviving to ages from five to fifty-five (at five-year intervals). This column gives us the basic outline of the level of adult mortality for the decade.

Adjustment for Migration

Before actually estimating mortality levels in this way, it was necessary to clear the populations for the second year of each pair of the effects of migration. This required its own methodology which is outlined only briefly here.[20] There are three sets of inputs into the migration estimation procedure: the data given in the census on the population of each presidency broken down by place of birth; the age structure of interstate migration as found in the 1971 census, which was the first census to provide us with such information; and the model migration schedules devised by Rogers and Castro.[21]

Zachariah's work in estimating *total* net intercensal migration from birthplace data in the census was useful for this study, though we cannot agree with his age-distribution estimates.[22] Using Rogers and Castro's ideas, the age structure of migration streams can be modelled without reference to age-specific mortality; Zachariah's age distributions, by contrast, depend on compromising assumptions about mortality. Of course it is important for our study to avoid prior assumptions about mortality to the greatest extent possible.

Certain conditions are important for the application of model migration schedules. It turns out that the age structure of net migration closely follows that of the dominant gross migration stream in those cases where (i) the ratio of inmigrants to outmigrants is not too close to one, and (ii) the two streams are small relative to the population. Both these conditions are met in the Indian regional cases.

Starting with the age distribution of interstate migration from the 1971 census (which was presented mostly in fifteen-year age groups, but with two central five-year groups), we utilized the migration models of Rogers and Castro, adjusting their parameters by successive approximations in order to create a model migration schedule specifically applicable to each sex and region. The new model was made both to agree with the 1971 schedule, and to provide migration rates for five-year age groups. These rates were then applied to the age-specific populations for each decade under study, and the estimated migrants for each age were added up to get a total. The proportion of this artificial migration total contributed by each age group was computed. These age-specific proportions of total migration gave us estimated age structures of migration, which conformed very well with the shapes of the model schedules seen in terms of rates. These proportions were then ready to be applied to the actual net migration totals for each region, sex and decade; once these were computed, this would provide the method of age-distributing the migration totals.[23]

In a separate procedure, the birthplace migration data from the census were adjusted to provide estimates of total net intercensal migration. This required two correction factors. First, it required applying the ten-year survival ratio from an appropriate life table to the migrants who were enumerated in the earlier of each pair of censuses. The necessary survival ratios were taken from all-India life tables computed by the Preston-Bennett method for each sex and decade.[24] Second, the net migration totals thus estimated were adjusted for the difference in size between the population of the presidency as recorded in the census, and the populations from the Mukherjee data. These adjustments were very small.

Using the age structures of migration estimated via the adaptation of Rogers and Castro's models, as described above, these net migration totals were then distributed by age, and used for adjusting each census age distribution for the effects of migration. The pairs of age distributions used for making intercensal estimates of mortality, then, were in each case, the initial unadjusted one paired with the subsequent adjusted one.

Life Table Construction

The basic output data produced by the Preston-Bennett procedure are the expected values of remaining life for each age between five and fifty-five (i.e., part of the $e(x)$ column of a life table). This column cannot very well be used as a life table in itself, as the $e(x)$'s fluctuate widely and have peaks and valleys like those caused by age misreporting in the age distributions themselves. Figs. 1 and 2 show the Preston-Bennett life expectancies for Indian females and males plotted against the corresponding expectancies of Coale and Demeny's South model (level 2). The age-specific fluctuations of the plots have characteristic sex-specific patterns across India. Further procedures are needed to produce life tables which are more plausible.

Preston and Bennett suggest using the mean ratio of the first ten $e(x)$ values to the corresponding ten values in a model life table as a level indicator, expressing the prevailing level of adult mortality for each sex, region and decade.[25] This can be done without assuming that the model life table chosen is applicable. We computed the mean ratios of the Preston-Bennett life expectancies to those of model South life tables with a life expectancy at birth of 25.5 years.[26] Each other level in the same family has its own mean ratio to this level, so that each mean ratio implies a particular level of mortality.

New model South life tables were generated to match precisely each computed mean ratio. This involved generating several with life expectancies at birth well below the lowest published level of twenty years. These are presented as the first pairs of estimates in Table 1.

From each new table the survival value l_{20} was then used so as to provide the level parameter to anchor another set of life tables, generated according to the Brass logit transformation procedure. These were made so that the shapes of the age distribution of deaths would correspond to those found in the new United Nations South Asia model tables.[27]

This second estimating procedure was chosen for the following reasons. Since we have no historical life tables for India that we can

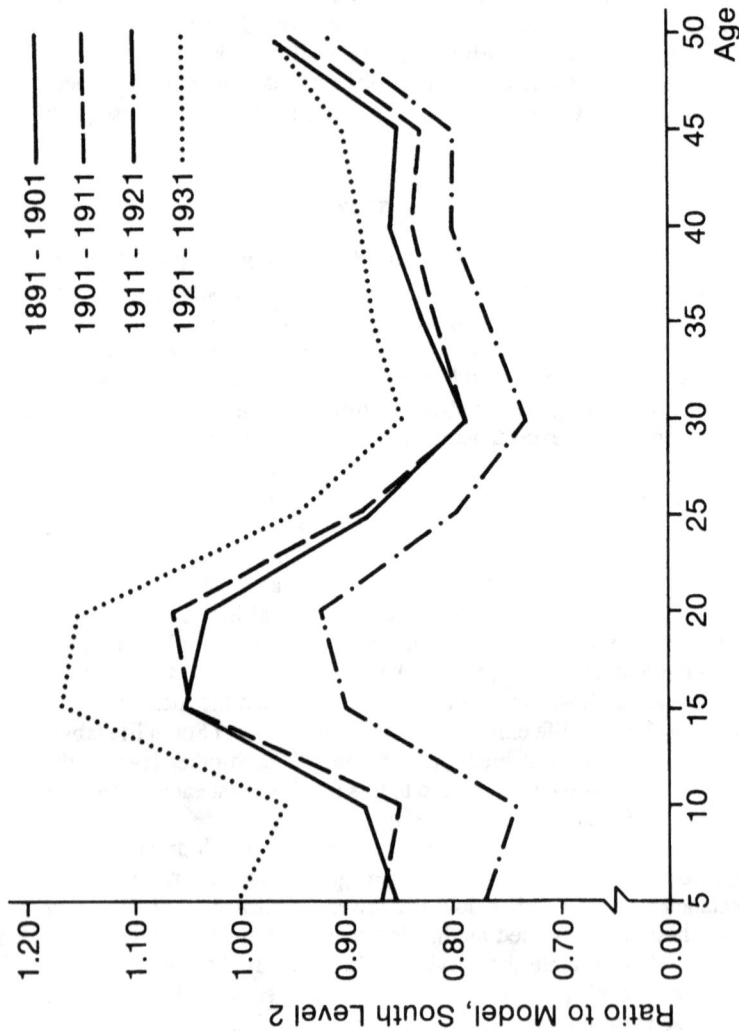

Fig.1 Ratios of Preston-Bennett Life Expectancies to Model South Life Expectancies by Age, India, Females.

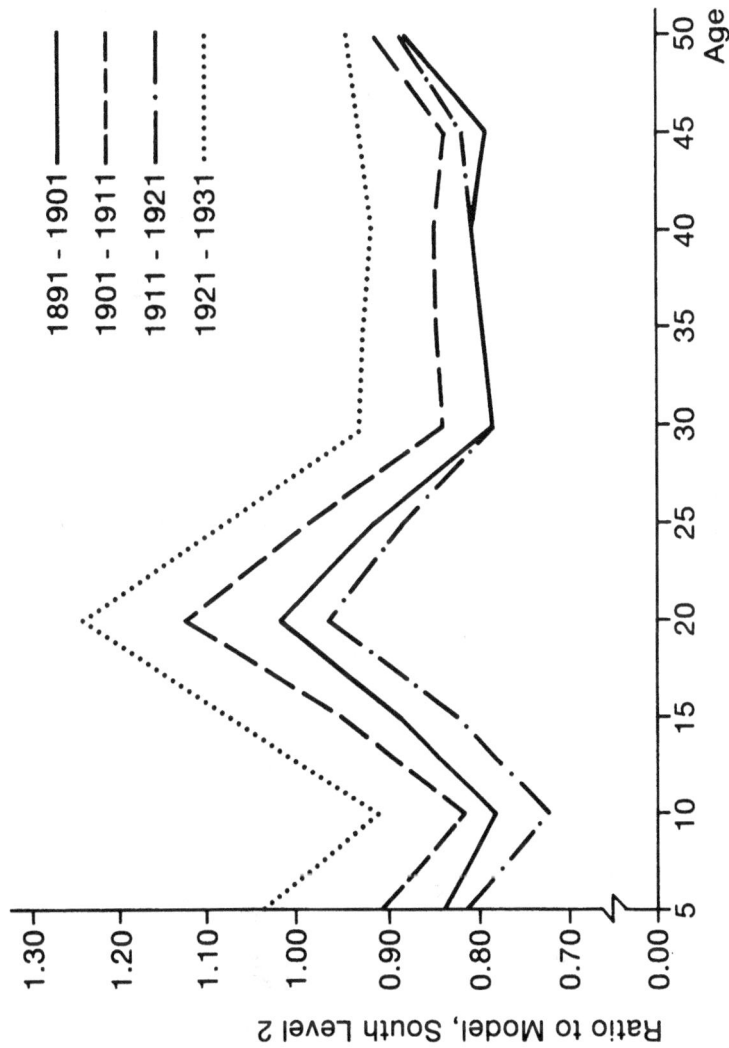

Fig.2 Ratios of Preston-Bennett Life Expectancies to Model South Life Expectancies by Age, India, Males.

Table 1. Alternative Sets of Life Table and Fertility Estimates for Three Indian Presidencies, 1881 – 1931

| Decade/Index | BOMBAY | | | | | |
| | Model South | | South Asia | | Crisis Model | |
	Male	Female	Male	Female	Male	Female
1881 – 91						
e(0)	25.67	24.94	27.27	25.98		
e(5)	43.30	42.50	48.02	45.96		
l(5)	0.520	0.512	0.505	0.499		
l(30)	0.390	0.372	0.420	0.386		
GRR		3.235		3.045		
1891 – 01						
e(0)	10.62	14.90	11.93	16.12	20.92	21.54
e(5)	32.46	35.09	42.70	42.11	34.90	36.34
l(5)	0.263	0.353	0.238	0.329	0.512	0.509
l(30)	0.154	0.218	0.182	0.237	0.340	0.334
GRR		3.748		3.328		3.103
1901 – 11						
e(0)	18.91	17.63	20.63	18.99		
e(5)	38.75	37.21	45.61	43.16		
l(5)	0.418	0.401	0.397	0.380		
l(30)	0.287	0.261	0.318	0.279		
GRR		3.343		3.014		
1911 – 21						
e(0)	11.04	10.42	12.38	11.39	21.12	20.08
e(5)	32.81	31.34	42.85	40.40	35.31	33.29
l(5)	0.272	0.264	0.247	0.237	0.511	0.510
l(30)	0.161	0.147	0.189	0.165	0.343	0.311
GRR		4.867		4.201		3.559
1921 – 31						
e(0)	25.44	22.92	27.05	24.06		
e(5)	43.15	41.08	47.93	45.18		
l(5)	0.517	0.484	0.502	0.468		
l(30)	0.387	0.342	0.417	0.358		
GRR		3.417		3.189		

| Decade/Index | UNITED PROVINCES | | | | | |
| | Model South | | South Asia | | Crisis Model | |
	Male	Female	Male	Female	Male	Female
1881 – 91						
e(0)	19.88	22.42	21.60	23.58		
e(5)	39.42	40.73	45.95	44.99		
l(5)	0.433	0.438	0.413	0.460		
l(30)	0.302	0.335	0.333	0.350		
GRR		3.081		2.853		
1891 – 01						
e(0)	14.69	18.29	16.29	19.55	18.56	20.64
e(5)	35.68	37.71	44.12	43.41	37.18	38.32
l(5)	0.344	0.412	0.320	0.329	0.429	0.465
l(30)	0.220	0.272	0.250	0.237	0.295	0.316
GRR		3.414		3.086		3.110

Decade/Index	Model South		South Asia		Crisis Model	
	Male	Female	Male	Female	Male	Female
1901 – 11						
e(0)	13.44	12.70	14.97	13.83	18.09	19.55
e(5)	34.72	33.30	43.69	41.27	36.33	34.70
l(5)	0.320	0.302	0.296	0.286	0.426	0.479
l(30)	0.200	0.183	0.230	0.202	0.288	0.302
GRR		3.885		3.385		3.110
1911 – 21						
e(0)	11.27	11.06	12.63	12.07	17.19	17.56
e(5)	32.99	31.90	42.92	40.64	34.80	31.03
l(5)	0.277	0.277	0.252	0.251	0.419	0.471
l(30)	0.164	0.157	0.193	0.175	0.273	0.267
GRR		4.206		3.629		3.369
1921 – 31						
e(0)	21.82	20.23	23.53	21.46		
e(5)	40.75	39.15	46.64	44.15		
l(5)	0.464	0.443	0.445	0.425		
l(30)	0.332	0.301	0.363	0.318		
GRR		3.235		2.962		

MADRAS

Decade/Index	Model South		South Asia		Crisis Model	
	Male	Female	Male	Female	Male	Female
1881 – 91						
e(0)	32.68	32.07	33.90	32.58		
e(5)	47.71	47.32	50.60	48.75		
l(5)	0.612	0.604	0.602	0.597		
l(30)	0.492	0.474	0.518	0.484		
GRR		2.719		2.640		
1891 – 01						
e(0)	28.42	27.91	29.90	28.76		
e(5)	45.06	44.55	49.02	47.11		
l(5)	0.558	0.552	0.545	0.542		
l(30)	0.431	0.415	0.459	0.428		
GRR		3.051		2.912		
1901 – 11						
e(0)	27.50	25.69	29.03	26.69		
e(5)	44.48	43.03	48.68	46.25		
l(5)	0.546	0.523	0.532	0.510		
l(30)	0.417	0.383	0.446	0.397		
GRR		3.057		2.889		
1911 – 21						
e(0)	18.09	15.76	19.80	17.00	25.07	22.48
e(5)	38.17	35.77	45.32	42.44	40.29	37.42
l(5)	0.404	0.368	0.382	0.345	0.544	0.518
l(30)	0.274	0.232	0.305	0.250	0.403	0.349
GRR		3.673		3.289		3.059
1921 – 31						
e(0)	26.25	22.28	27.83	23.45		
e(5)	43.67	40.63	48.22	44.94		
l(5)	0.528	0.474	0.513	0.458		
l(30)	0.399	0.333	0.428	0.348		
GRR		3.055		2.841		

Notes: (1) Clearly, 'Crisis Model' estimates are only given for crisis decades.
(2) The indices shown are: life expectation from age zero, e(0); life expectation from age five, e(5); life table survivorship to age five, l(5); life table survivorship to age thirty, l(30); and the gross reproduction rate, GRR.

trust, there is no way of creating life tables for extremely low levels of life expectancy which is not both artificial and mechanical. From the Preston-Bennett output data, we can ascertain the adult level, but not the shape at the youngest and oldest ages, of the total survival curve. We do not know exactly how much of the mortality up to some adult age took place in infancy and early childhood, or how fast or slowly the subsequent survival curve dropped with age.

We can produce an approximation to the total curve, however, if we have some model schedule of survival rates which we believe reflects the mortality experience of this region, at some time. Until recently, models based on western experience, diversified into different families, were the only model schedules we had. But in 1982 the United Nations produced a series of new model schedules which included a 'South Asia' pattern for each sex; and the data used in computing these new schedules include fairly accurate data on recent Indian experience. The models have been found in practical application to fit parts of India well.

The South Asia model tables only have life expectancies at birth of thirty-five years and over. They have been constructed recently, and do not reflect the high levels of mortality known to have prevailed in the region historically. Therefore some method is required to transform the lowest South Asia model for each sex to the even lower levels appropriate to each region and decade. The method chosen carries an explicit assumption, that at least as high a proportion of overall mortality was borne by children in the past as in the contemporary period.[28] In other words, the shape of the historical survival curve is initially assumed to be at least as steep at the earliest ages as that of the lowest recent one, which is now used as the standard.

A single value from each of the model South tables generated earlier was needed to anchor the new life tables, and the value chosen was that representing survival from birth to age twenty, or l_{20}. Experiments were made using survival to several different ages. It was clear that none of the age-specific survival values being considered would create a table unreasonably different from that of the model South family, but that the higher the age chosen as an anchor, the lower would be the resulting survival probabilities. The model South estimates made using the Preston-Bennett output already suggested extraordinarily high mortality. Survival to twenty seemed to be the youngest possible value which it was reasonable to use, since for logit life tables it is considered desirable to use an adult mortality value as anchor.

When one changes the shape of a mortality curve to reflect a higher proportion of child relative to adult mortality while a single indicator of its adult level remains constant, life expectancy changes, not (as one might expect) for the worse, but for the better. This is because more of the mortality cuts off very short spans of life, so that the total number of person-years lived in the life table increases, reflecting more long stretches. The new survival curve, in tilting down at its left end, rises on the right, relative to the old one (see Fig.3).

While the South Asia transform, by construction, implies higher child mortality relative to adult mortality than any western model, the difference between it and model South in this respect is about the same as the difference between model South and model West (the model life table family most often relied upon by earlier researchers). Thus, to consider the South Asia transform appears reasonable. The results are presented as the second pair of estimates in Table 1.

The South Asia estimates in one respect seem to fit the data better than those from model South. When the life expectancies derived from the South Asia transform for United Provinces females for the decade 1881 – 91 are plotted against those of the appropriate model South table and those of the Preston-Bennett output, the South Asia transform picks up the height of the peak of the Preston-Bennett series, though at an earlier age, while the model South does not (see Fig. 4).

However, for some decades, and especially for some provinces, both these new estimates and those generated from model South are unbelievable. The assumption which they both carry about the relative share of mortality borne by children produces unlikely life tables for the worst decades, wherever these occur. Table 1 shows this effect for United Provinces in the three middle decades of the period, for Bombay in 1891 – 1901 and 1911 – 21, and for Madras in 1911 – 21. In all these cases, the values of survival to age five suggest that 65 to 75 per cent, or more, of all children born died by that age.

These turn out to have been crisis decades for these provinces. It is well known that this fifty-year period contained decades of severe crisis mortality. In Bombay Presidency, 1891 – 1901 was a decade of plague followed by famine. United Provinces suffered from famine and from a prolonged string of epidemics between 1891 and 1911; in addition, it experienced endemic malaria. Then all across India, the 1918 world pandemic of influenza took hold, killing many millions and reducing 1911 – 21 life expectancies to the lowest levels of all. The mortality estimates produced so far suggest that these crises took their most immense toll on infants and small children. But we must question such a finding.

Either the model South tables generated, or straightforward transformations of the contemporary South Asia life table — both of which display somewhat higher than previously estimated child relative to adult mortality — appear quite reasonable for the non-crisis decades. But to produce better tables for *crisis* decades, a different procedure seemed necessary. In either set of life tables thus far discussed, we see

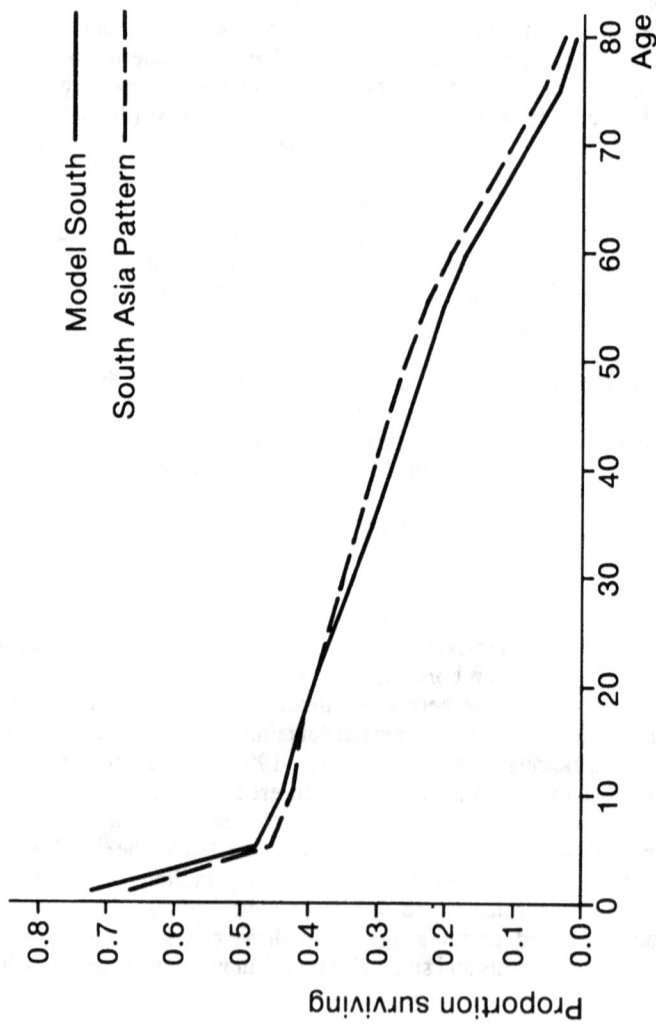

Fig.3 Life Table Proportion Surviving by Age, United Provinces, Females, 1881−91.

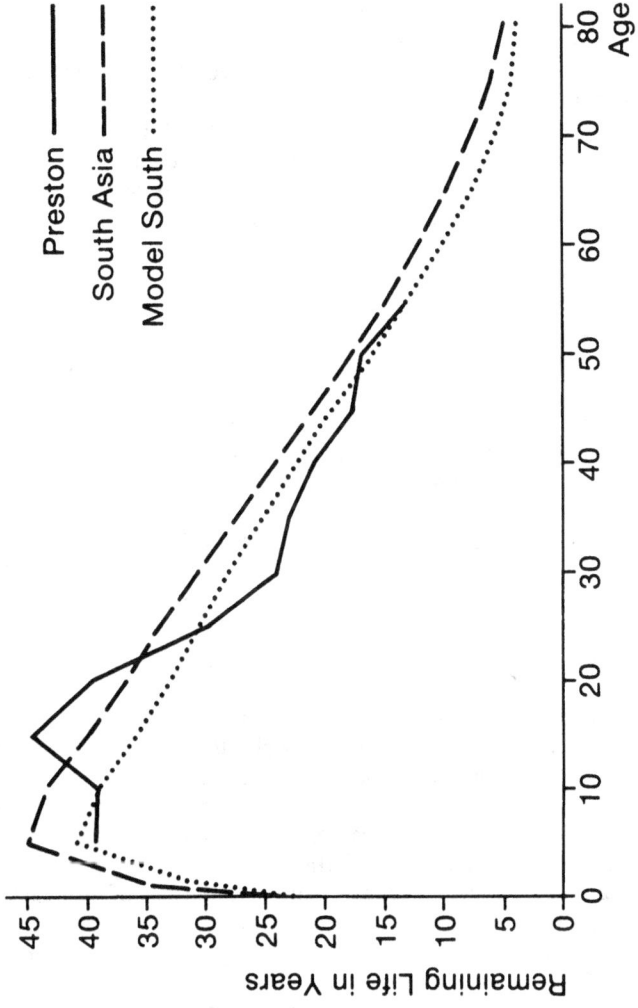

Fig.4 Age-Specific Life Expectancies, United Provinces, Females, 1881–91.

from Table 1 that life expectation at age five varied more moderately across decades than life expectancy at birth. The fluctuations in life expectancy at birth are extreme in these two sets, while those at age five are milder, particularly in the South Asia life tables with their high child mortality assumptions. They are, in fact, too mild for what we know about crisis mortality and its age effects.

The age structure of mortality is likely to have been quite different in bad years than in good years. In times of crisis, adult mortality worsens to a much greater extent than does early childhood mortality. Young children are protected to some degree by breast-feeding. Age-specific mortality rates for children under two, the persons with among the highest death rates already in most life tables, therefore probably rise very little, if at all, at the very time that age-specific rates for adults are rising catastrophically.

To obtain a third set of life tables, therefore, the logit transformation procedure was used in a different way. Child mortality was set at a level which remained close to that of one of the periods of 'good years': 1881 – 91 for United Provinces and Bombay, and 1901 – 11 for Madras. A range of child mortality values between the estimates from the two previously estimated models was accepted. Then the level parameter that would maintain this level of *child* mortality was set, and the appropriate shape parameter was searched for using two other criteria. First, the original output of the Preston-Bennett method was used for fitting. Other parameters were varied so as to produce a life table the life expectancies of which had a mean ratio to those of the Preston-Bennett output that was close to one. The second criterion was that fertility estimates should be minimized (the fertility estimates are discussed below).

Neither model South nor the South Asia pattern worked well for this 'crisis' set of estimates. With these models, the logit transformation procedure, once both its parameters were varied, reduced infant mortality to unbelievable levels when the other requirements were met. Since model West of the Coale-Demeny set of families had high infant relative to child mortality, transforming it via the logit procedure (which changed its shape) produced more credible sets of estimates of infant as well as adult mortality for crisis decades. In these crisis tables, adult survival slopes downwards more steeply than in the non-crisis tables (see Fig. 5).

Basic mortality and survival indicators from the newly-produced, 'crisis model' life tables are shown as the third pair of estimates in Table 1, for crisis decades only. Corresponding model West transforms for years that were less bad, and for good years, were also made. They produced life tables very close to, but not better than, those resulting from earlier procedures.

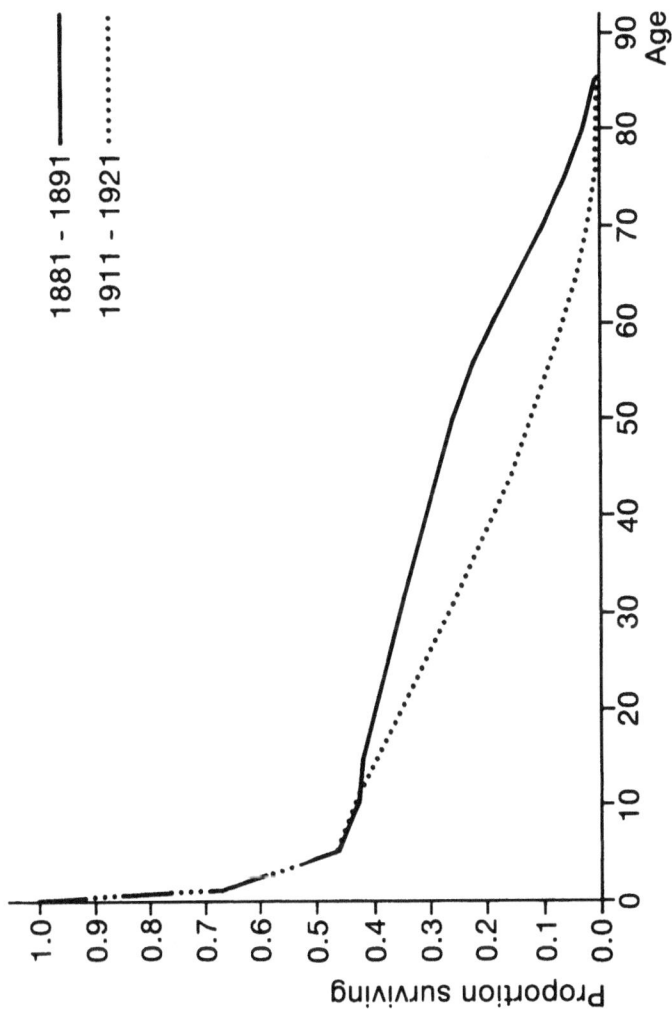

Fig.5 Comparison of Proportions Surviving by Age in Good and Bad Decades, United Provinces, Females, 1881−91 and 1911−21.

Fertility Estimates

Fertility was estimated by regression, using a procedure devised by Gunasekaran and Palmore.[29] This methodology uses census age distributions, coupled with estimates of life expectancy at birth. Both of these data sets are available as products of the present study. Since population age structures are determined by fertility and mortality regimes, a statistical analysis of the characteristics of the age distribution, coupled with a mortality measure, can provide an estimate of the level of fertility implied by the system as a whole.

The measure of fertility used is the gross reproduction rate (GRR), which is the number of female births per reproductive-age woman in the population. This measure is estimated by regression, in three sets, for each region and decade. These are the GRR estimates that are implied by each of the three sets of life tables, each having its own life expectancy and age structure effects. The estimated female GRRs are presented in Table 1 along with each life table. (Male GRRs were also estimated for each life table, but are not presented here. They were useful, as were the female GRRs, in the computation of the crisis life tables, for which the criterion of minimizing fertility results was employed.)

It must be said that these estimates of the level of fertility track the level of mortality more than is credible. One does not expect fertility to rise in crisis years; instead it may fall, due to greater maternal morbidity and debilitation than in better years. That the estimates do track mortality to such an extent is probably an artefact of the regression estimation method. It is clear, however, that without the special crisis life tables, fertility estimates for crisis decades are even less believable, due to overestimation of childhood mortality for these years. Model South produces the most extreme GRRs; those of the South Asia pattern are more moderate; while for crisis years, only the crisis models come even close to any prevailing trend which can be hypothesized from examining the estimates for better years.

MORTALITY AND FERTILITY IN INDIA

The Historical Context for Regional Mortality Levels

The difference in levels of mortality by region is quite pronounced (see Table 1). That between Madras and the other two provinces is particularly strong, with Madras showing far better survival probabilities than United Provinces and Bombay. This difference in mortality level continues until 1921 – 31, when Bombay begins to converge with Madras. Madras pursues a somewhat downward trend in life expectancy, while Bombay recovers almost to its 1881 – 91 level after the decade of the influenza epidemic. United Provinces' life expectancies remain extremely low, although they demonstrate a recovery after the three decades of crisis.

When we compare levels of life expectancy at age five over time, from whatever combination of models we choose, we see clear differences in underlying levels of adult mortality between the north and south of India (see Table 1). What can account for this? It is likely to be explained, in large part, by two things: differential levels of malaria, and the regularity of good harvests. Davis has shown that malaria outweighed all other major diseases combined as a cause of death.[30] It seems clear that malaria's incidence was greatly increased by the expansion of irrigation works concentrated in United Provinces, causing water-logging and drainage problems.[31] In addition, insufficient rain and harvest failures were a common feature of the economic life of semi-arid Bombay, causing regular food shortages.[32]

While Madras was spared neither dearth nor epidemic during this period, the underlying causes of extremely high mortality in northern and western India, namely endemic malaria and regularly occurring harvest failures, did not hold Madras in so tight a grip. Malaria tended to be epidemic and seasonal there, and the ratio of good to bad harvests was higher. Yet a slight general worsening of mortality conditions over time is suggested by our estimates.

Even taking account of the fact that we undertook adjustments to moderate extreme estimates of mortality patterns, our estimates of life expectancy at birth for the critical decades are still much lower than those of earlier researchers such as the Visarias and Mukherjee.[33] Yet they appear reasonable, for reasons that can be sketched briefly here.

Across India, particularly in the major presidencies, increasing densities had resulted from the uneven course of population growth over the whole of the nineteenth century, a period which was marked by fluctuations similar to those we observe here. Even though we cannot usually quantify either densities or growth fluctuations at the presidency level until the time of the census, these are evident in a consideration of the data available at both district and subdistrict levels.[34] Agricultural settlement increased over the century to an extent that sometimes overburdened the resources of the environments, particularly those of the north and west. During some parts of the period we are focusing on here, the carrying capacities of these systems, as then organized, were strained to their limits.

Towards the end of this period, however, these limits began to be extended by technological change, more effective intensification, and

changing relations of production. Some of these phenomena will be
accessible to closer analysis in the future, when land use and
environmental impact data, currently being generated, become available for all the regions dealt with here.[35] In addition, methods of
mortality control became far more effective.

Levels of Fertility

Immense fluctuations in fertility over time in any one region are highly
unlikely in this fifty-year period. This has been one factor which has
made necessary the estimation of crisis life tables for the worst decades.
Therefore, in making an estimate of average fertility levels over time,
we include the crisis tables for crisis decades, although these still
probably overstate fertility to some extent. For non-crisis decades, we
consider a range of fertility estimates between those derived from the
model South and those of the South Asia pattern tables.

These combined sets of tables for each region produce *average*
fertility estimates that are fairly consistent with those found in earlier
studies, though somewhat higher for the south of India. The Visarias
estimate gross reproduction rates averaging 3.1 for the north of India,
3.4 for the west, and 2.6 for the south.[36] The tables selected here
suggest average GRRs of between 3.1 and 3.2 for United Provinces,
between 3.2 and 3.3 for Bombay, and between 2.9 and 3.0 for Madras.
Depending on the proportions of women unmarried or widowed by age
in each region, these estimates suggest total marital fertility rates of
somewhat more than eight children in northern and western India, and
more than seven in the south.

Excess Female Mortality

What is most striking about all these new life tables is that in so many
there is greater female than male mortality. And the gap in life
expectancy becomes greater than ever in the most recent decade of our
study period (see Table 1). Suppose that we accept, as before, either the
model South or the South Asia pattern for non-crisis years, and the
crisis pattern for the worst decades. Then it appears that in United
Provinces males start out with lower life expectancies than females, but
the gap narrows during the decade of the flu epidemic; by the better
decade that follows, males have attained higher life expectancies than
females. In Bombay, the crisis decade 1891 – 1901 is the only one in
which females outstrip males in expectation of life at birth. In Madras,
male life expectancy outstrips that of females in every decade, and the

gap grows wider in 1921 – 31. These findings challenge the notion that
female status, relative to male, was materially better in the south than in
the north.

But do we have the right life tables for females in relation to males,
and is there not some criterion for judging this? Let us consider a
comparison of population sex ratios, as computed from census totals,
with the sex ratios implied by our life tables.

Each possible pair of life tables for males and females has its own
overall sex ratio, as has been pointed out by Visaria.[37] Life expectancy
at birth is a summary indicator of the length of all the lives lived in a
particular mortality regime, given an assumption of stability. So the
ratio of male to female life expectancy at birth, inflated by the sex ratio
at birth, should be equal to the sex ratio of a population within a stable
system.

To help gauge what *pairs* of life tables it may be best to accept for
each region, the population sex ratios based on census data, found in
Table 2, may be contrasted with the sex ratios generated from different
pairs of life tables, as presented in Table 3. Although we face the
problem that life expectancy during the period of this study was not
stable, but clearly varied over time, plus problems associated with the
census sex ratios themselves, this exercise is nevertheless suggestive.

Bombay's census sex ratios are approximated in most decades — with
the exception of the crisis decade 1891 – 1901 — by sex ratios based on
'mixed' life tables. The mixture which approximates most closely the
census sex ratios is the male model South table coupled with the female
South Asia table.

Pairing these life tables carries the implication that female mortality
in Bombay must have been more heavily weighted towards childhood
ages than was male. The absolute levels of mortality, as indicated by
the expectation of life at birth, would have been, in that case, almost
equal until 1921 – 31, when the male level began to outstrip the female.

Many of the life table-based sex ratios for United Provinces are too
low by comparison with the census sex ratios (see Tables 2 and 3). This
means that they do not reflect *enough* excess female mortality. It is
straightforward to compute what female life expectancies at birth
'should' be, given those of males and the sex ratio of the population.
Using model South and crisis model male levels (and again, clearly
begging the question of changing levels of mortality over time), these
computations suggest that in United Provinces female expectancies
should be about two years lower than shown in Table 1 for the first
three decades, about one year lower for 1911 – 21, and about one year
higher for 1921 – 31.

A mixture which moves in the right direction, however, is one
consisting of the male South Asia model and the female model South for

Table 2. Census-based Sex Ratios (m/f) for the Total Population, and Age Groups 0 – 4 and 5 – 14, of Three Indian Presidencies, 1881 – 1931.

			Decade		
	1881 – 1891	1891 – 1901	1901 – 1911	1911 – 1921	1921 – 1931
Bombay	1.0559	1.0294	1.0322	1.0474	1.0556
0 – 4	0.9398	0.9491	0.9540	0.9464	0.9627
5 – 14	1.1349	1.0975	1.1159	1.0954	1.0844
U.P.	1.0819	1.0680	1.0965	1.1030	1.1119
0 – 4	0.9844	1.0002	1.0039	0.9878	0.9755
5 – 14	1.2052	1.1663	1.1931	1.1935	1.1893
Madras	0.9892	0.9906	0.9874	0.9909	0.9989
0 – 4	0.9473	0.9433	0.9553	0.9508	0.9502
5 – 14	1.0772	1.0570	1.0410	1.0269	1.0461

Table 3. Sex Ratios (m/f) from Paired Life Tables.

	Model	Decade				
		1881 – 1891	1891 – 1901	1901 – 1911	1911 – 1921	1921 – 1931
Bombay	South	1.086	0.752	1.132	1.118	1.171
	S. Asia	1.107	0.781	1.146	1.147	1.186
	Crisis	–	1.025	–	1.110	–
	Mixed	1.042	–	1.051	1.023	1.116
U.P.	South	0.935	0.847	1.116	1.075	1.138
	S. Asia	0.966	0.879	1.142	1.104	1.157
	Crisis	–	0.949	0.976	1.033	–
	Mixed	1.016	0.936	–	–	1.073
Madras	South	1.075	1.074	1.129	1.211	1.243
	S. Asia	1.098	1.097	1.151	1.229	1.252
	Crisis	–	–	–	1.117	–
	Mixed	1.017	1.043	1.087	1.123	1.181

1881 – 91. The sex ratios produced by the pair from model South for 1901 – 11 and 1921 – 31, and by that of the South Asia pattern for 1911 – 21, are close to those of the census.

What seems to be suggested is that male mortality in childhood was even heavier before about 1900 than would be expected on the basis of model patterns, and that male survival was very much lower relative to female. It appears that male and female mortality followed more similar age patterns, or shapes, thereafter. In that case, an absolute difference in level becomes a distinguishing feature of United Provinces mortality, a difference which is to the disadvantage of males in 1881 – 91, and of females later. This suggests that lower survival rates for females after 1891 were widely distributed by age, rather than concentrated at certain ages.

For Madras, all the life table sex ratios are far too high by comparison with those from the census. This means that they reflect too much excess female mortality. For every decade, life table sex ratios closer to those of the census can only be produced by a male model South table combined with a female South Asia pattern table; but even these mixtures are too high. In addition, the extreme level differences between our estimated male and female life tables, which are the cause of such high life table sex ratios, are difficult to believe.

In order to remedy this situation, we need to consider the age patterns of differential mortality. One additional life table has therefore been generated for Madras based on these considerations. The result suggests that, for Madras we need life tables which are extremely close in level between males and females, but which differ in their shape.

DIFFERENCES BETWEEN AGE PATTERNS
OF DIFFERENTIAL MORTALITY

There were clearly very different patterns of excess female mortality by age among the various regions of India in the past. This is strongly suggested by an examination of the sex ratios of various age groups in the census data — even when we admit all the problems these data present with regard to differential underenumeration and age misreporting by sex. Table 2 presents the male to female sex ratios of the total populations of each region, and of persons aged 0 – 4 and 5 – 14, after the allocation of migrants back to their places of origin. For both Bombay and United Provinces, the overall sex ratios, and those of persons aged 5 – 14, are very much higher than those for Madras.

The ratios for persons of ages 0 – 4 are unrevealing, and in fact misleading. We have considerable reason to believe that in the north and west of India, many 'extra' female deaths took place in infancy and early childhood. Both United Provinces and Bombay contain groups that have been known to practise female infanticide, particularly in certain districts. The custom was outlawed in the Infanticide Act of 1872, but its incidence was at the same time recorded in considerable detail in official reports required under the Act.[38] We believe that a decrease in infanticide was followed by an increase in excess female mortality at early ages, due to neglect of female children.[39] The life tables constructed for this study do not reveal this, for neither do the census data on which they are based (as seen in Table 2 in the population sex ratios for persons aged 0 – 4). Let us consider a strategy that may more clearly shape the life tables to reflect this possibility.

The curve of age-specific sex ratios at a point in time can be seen, theoretically, as a cumulative measure of mortality at all earlier ages. In a population with stable rates over time, the ratios of male to female age-specific survival probabilities, inflated by the sex ratio at birth, should be close to the age-specific sex ratios of the population.

However, the actual census data produce ratios full of anomalies. Like the female age distributions themselves, the curves of these ratios zigzag because of age heaping. In addition, they suggest considerable under-representation of the population at younger ages. (The data were adjusted for age-specific migration before computing these ratios.) The Bombay and United Provinces sex ratio 'curves' have their highest peaks at ages 10 – 14; they then dip down, rising to another peak somewhere between ages forty and fifty. For Madras, the highest peak falls between ages forty and fifty, although a minor peak is found for ages 10 – 14. Some portion of these early peaks, large or small, have to be accounted for by the pattern of female age misreporting and underenumeration that has been found to characterize Indian censuses; 'valleys' occurring at ages 20 – 24 are a function of the same phenomenon, because many women under twenty are typically counted as having already reached that age.

But given what we believe we know about Indian female mortality, at least part of the sex ratio age patterns ought to be accounted for by age-specific patterns of excess female mortality. To approximate this better, the age-specific sex ratio curves for each presidency were smoothed by amalgamating several age groups together and locating their joint ratios on central ages. This procedure gets rid of the insistent peaks and valleys, and suggests where each real curve might have its single high point. It appears from this exercise that for most decades, United Provinces' sex ratio peak falls at around twenty, Bombay's at around thirty, and Madras's at around age forty-five. This suggests different age patterns of excess female mortality by region, including the likelihood that people in United Provinces and Bombay experienced some of their excess female mortality in childhood.

Having established in this way some estimate of where the single peak of the age-specific sex ratios occurs, a new female life table was created entirely by inflating or deflating a male table's survival column (adjusted for the sex ratio at birth) by a smoothed series of sex ratios leading to, and then descending from such a peak. This procedure, because it was rather arduous, highly speculative, and somewhat inelegant, was undertaken only for Madras for the decade 1901 – 11; the male model South table for that decade was used as its basis. The new, 'sex ratio-based' female life table was then put to the test of fitting the Preston-Bennett series for the decade; having gained as close a fit as seemed possible, its implied fertility was computed via the regression method. The result is a female life table for Madras which crosses the male life table at two age points (see Table 4).

The outcome of this exercise (like the overall census sex ratio) leads us to question whether the difference between Madras male and female life expectancies at *birth* could have been in the direction our earlier estimates suggested. But it also leads us to the conclusion that excess female mortality, at ages where it is not found in western models, certainly did occur in Madras. Moreover, nothing in this exercise leads us to suspect that the decline in female level relative to male, indicated by the model South or South Asia pairs, is incorrect (only that the absolute levels are different).

In addition, the absolute difference in mortality levels between the south and the other regions remains after considering these modifications in female life table estimates. Madras females had far better life chances than females from northern and western India. But they still had higher mortality rates than Madras males; and this was most probably concentrated within the ages between early childhood and old age.

In India generally, as mortality conditions improved for everyone, they improved more for males than females. We see in this study only the first decade of the historic improvement in life expectancy, in which it barely began to recover from crisis levels. Census sex ratios have continued to rise in the twentieth century until recently, during a period of unprecedented mortality decline. One way of summarizing this is to say that as mortality began to decline, it simply declined less fast for females than for males, as patterns of discrimination between the value of male and female life continued. With increased overall opportunity to survive, these patterns of discrimination could become even more refined, more selective.

Table 4. Summary Life Tables for Madras Presidency, 1901 – 11: Female Life Table created from Male, using Sex Ratio Curve.

Age x	Male Survival l(x)	Sex Ratio	Female Survival l(x)
0	1.00000	1.055	1.00000
1	0.73484	0.970	0.79923
5	0.54556	0.990	0.58138
10	0.51332	1.010	0.53619
15	0.49856	1.025	0.51315
20	0.47707	1.037	0.48535
25	0.44613	1.055	0.44613
30	0.41720	1.070	0.41135
35	0.39014	1.080	0.38111
40	0.36234	1.090	0.35071
45	0.33170	1.095	0.31958
50	0.29880	1.082	0.29134
55	0.26129	1.070	0.25763
60	0.21829	1.040	0.22144
65	0.16686	1.000	0.17604
70	0.11179	0.930	0.12682
75	0.05925	0.800	0.07354
80	0.02159	0.700	0.03254

	Male	Female
e(0)	27.50	28.11
e(5)	44.48	42.35
l(5)	0.546	0.581
l(30)	0.417	0.411
GRR		2.878
Mean Ratio to P-B series		1.02
Sex Ratio		1.032

Notes: (1) For the indices used in this Table see the notes to Table 1.
(2) The mean ratio to the Preston-Bennett (P-B) series given above relates to the values of e(x) from e(5) to e(50).

NOTES TO CHAPTER 5

1 The research on which this paper is based was conducted while the author was a postdoctoral fellow in the Graduate Group in Demography at the University of California, on a fellowship from the Social Science Research Council, New York; both the Council and the Group are gratefully acknowledged for their support. Thanks go to Carl Boe for programming, research assistance, and advice; to Neil Bennett for making available the Preston-Bennett programme; and to Li Li-Ying for data entry. For assistance at the project design stage we thank Alberto Palloni, Susan De Vos, Oleh Wolowyna, and Paul Frenzen. An earlier version of this paper was presented in 1986 at meetings of the Stanford-Berkeley Colloquium in Population in San Francisco, and the Association for Asian Studies in Chicago. Robert Chung, Andrew Foster, Ken Wachter, Ronald Lee, Sheila Johansson and Paul David offered helpful comments.

2 See Morris D. Morris, 'Towards a Reinterpretation of Nineteenth-Century Indian Economic History'. *The Indian Economic and Social History Review*, Volume 5, No. 1, 1968; also R. C. Dutt, *Economic History of India*, London, 1901.

3 See Dharma Kumar, (ed.), *The Cambridge Economic History of India*, Volume 2, Cambridge: Cambridge University Press, 1983.

4 See Irfan Habib, 'Studying a Colonial Economy — Without Perceiving Colonialism', *Modern Asian Studies*, Volume 19, No. 3, 1985; and Dharma Kumar, 'The Dangers of Manichaeism', *Modern Asian Studies*, Volume 19, No. 3, 1985.

5 See Leela Visaria and Pravin Visaria, 'Population (1757 – 1947)', in Dharma Kumar (ed.) cited in note 3.

6 See Irfan Habib cited in note 4, and Ira Klein, 'Population and Agriculture in Northern India, 1872 – 1921', *Modern Asian Studies*, Volume 8, No. 2, 1974.

7 See Kingsley Davis, *The Population of India and Pakistan*, Princeton: Princeton University Press, 1951; also Sudhansu Bhusan Mukherjee, *The Age Distribution of the Indian Population: A Reconstruction for the States and Territories, 1881 – 1961*, Honolulu: East-West Population Institute, 1976.

8 Those leaning towards the former explanation include Rosenweig and Schultz, and Bardhan; see Mark R. Rosenweig and T. Paul Schultz, 'Market Opportunities, Genetic Endowments, and Intrafamily Resource Distribution: Child Survival in Rural India', *American Economic Review*, Volume 72, No. 4, 1982; and Pranab K. Bardhan, 'On Life and Death Questions', *Economic and Political Weekly*, Volume 10, Nos 32 – 34, 1974. For studies stressing culture and kinship see D. E. Sopher (ed.), *An Exploration of India*, London: Longmans, 1980; and Tim Dyson and Mick Moore, 'On Kinship Structure, Female Autonomy, and Demographic Behavior in India', *Population and Development Review*, Volume 9, No. 1, 1983.

9 See Barbara D. Miller, *The Endangered Sex: Neglect of Female Children in Rural North India*, Ithaca: Cornell University Press, 1981.

10 See Dyson and Moore cited in note 8, p. 54.
11 See Davis cited in note 7, Visaria and Visaria cited in note 5, and Klein cited in note 6. For the last-mentioned study see Michelle Burge McAlpin, *Subject to Famine: Food Crises and Economic Change in Western India, 1860 – 1920*, Princeton: Princeton University Press, 1983.
12 See Davis cited in note 7.
13 See Mukherjee cited in note 7. For the Coale and Demeny models see Ansley J. Coale and Paul Demeny, *Regional Model Life Tables and Stable Populations*, Princeton: Princeton University Press, 1966.
14 See Visaria and Visaria cited in note 5.
15 See S. H. Preston and N. G. Bennett, 'A Census-based Method for Estimating Adult Mortality', *Population Studies*, Volume 37, No. 1, 1983.
16 For these new models see United Nations, *Model Life Tables for Developing Countries*, New York: United Nations, 1982.
17 See K. C. Zachariah, *A Historical Study of Internal Migration in The Indian Sub-Continent, 1901 – 1931*, Bombay: Asia Publishing House, 1964.
18 See Mukherjee cited in note 7.
19 See S. H. Preston and A. J. Coale, 'A Generalization of Stable Population Relations', *Population Index*, Volume 48, No. 2, 1982; also Preston and Bennett cited in note 15.
20 For more on this methodology see Alice W. Clark and Carl Boe, 'Estimating Internal Migration in India', paper presented at the weekly seminar of the Graduate Group in Demography, University of California, Berkeley, 1986.
21 See Andrei Rogers and Luis Castro, *Model Migration Schedules*, Laxenberg, Austria: The International Institute for Applied Systems Analysis, 1980.
22 See Zachariah cited in note 17.
23 The assumption was made that inmigration and outmigration shared a common age structure. No Indian data were available to test this assumption, but experiments were made combining different age structures of inmigration and outmigration. At the absolute levels of gross migration apparently prevailing in the relevant decades, none of these experiments changed the ultimate mortality estimates significantly.
24 The all-India life tables were constructed from the level parameter, alpha, supplied by the Preston-Bennett output, using the United Nations South Asia pattern as a model. The amount of international migration to and from India is considered negligible, so the all-India age data at least did not require migration-adjustment before the Preston-Bennett method was applied. These survival ratios prove not to be very sensitive either to model or level; they turn out to be fairly close to those used by Zachariah, (cited in note 17), who tried to take into account some return migration at older ages. In addition, the volume of net migration for these decades is so very small that adjusting it one way or the other by a few per cent does not appreciably change the regional life tables which emerge from the migration-adjusted age distributions. Adjusting by five per cent (equal to a

change in survival ratio of five levels of mortality) in fact changes the resulting life expectancy at birth only by a fraction of a year. Thus these all-India survival ratios have been judged adequate for the present purpose. These values are as follows:

Ten-Year Survival Ratios, India

	Male	Female
1881 – 91	.793	.788
1891 – 01	.787	.783
1901 – 11	.791	.782
1911 – 21	.785	.776
1921 – 31	.798	.789

25 See Preston and Bennett cited in note 15.
26 A male table with $e(0)$ of 22.5 years was constructed for this purpose, rather than using the published male level 2, with its slightly lower $e(0)$.
27 The difference between the logit of the selected $l(x)$, and the logit of the corresponding $l(x)$ of the South Asia life table with an $e(0)$ of 35, provided the level parameter, alpha. Beta was set at unity. For the logit transformation procedure see, for example, W. Brass, 'On the scale of mortality' in W. Brass (ed.), *Biological Aspects of Demography*, (Symposia of the Society for the Study of Human Biology), London: Taylor and Francis, 1971.
28 Utilizing the parameters which create new United Nations life tables would have somewhat reduced the share of mortality borne by children, see United Nations cited in note 16.
29 See Subbiah Gunasekaran and James A. Palmore, 'Regression Estimates of the Gross Reproduction Rate Using Moments of the Female Age Distribution', *Asian and Pacific Census Forum*, Volume 10, No. 4, 1984.
30 See Davis cited in note 7.
31 On this see Klein cited in note 6, and Visaria and Visaria cited in note 5.
32 See McAlpin cited in note 11.
33 See Visaria and Visaria cited in note 5, and Mukherjee cited in note 7.
34 See Alice W. Clark, 'Central Gujarat in the Nineteenth Century: The Integration of an Agrarian System', Ph.D. dissertation, Department of History, University of Wisconsin-Madison, Ann Arbor: University Microfilms, 1979.
35 See J. F. Richards, James R. Hagen and Edward S. Haynes, 'Changing Land Use in Bihar, Punjab and Haryana, 1850 – 1970', *Modern Asian Studies*, Volume 19, No. 3, 1985.
36 See Visaria and Visaria cited in note 5.
37 See Pravin Visaria, 'The Sex Ratio of the Population of India and Pakistan, and Regional Variations During 1901 – 61', in Ashish Bose (ed.), *Patterns of Population Change in India, 1951 – 61*, New Delhi: Institute of Economic Growth, 1964.

38 See Alice W. Clark, 'Limitations on Female Life Chances in Rural Central Gujarat', *Indian Economic and Social History Review*, Volume 20, No. 1, 1983.
39 See Miller cited in note 9.

6

THE HISTORICAL DEMOGRAPHY OF BERAR
1881 – 1980

Tim Dyson

In eastern Maharashtra, at the very heart of India, nestled to the south of the Satpura hill range, lie Akola, Amraoti, Buldana and Yeomatal districts, which together comprise the territory of the former British India province of Berar. 'Very few persons outside the province know where Berar is or what it is' wrote the province's Census Commissioner in 1892.[1] But the present paper intends to show that because of the quality of its demographic data, particularly its vital registration, Berar certainly merits the attention of scholars interested in unravelling India's population history.

The usual approach to estimating past demographic rates for India has been to employ the decennial census age distributions available since about 1881. By analysing the survivorship of the population between one census and the next these allow estimation of the death rate. Since the intercensal population growth rate is known, an estimate of the birth rate can be obtained by adding death rate and growth rate. Alternatively the birth rate can be estimated by 'reverse survival' procedures. Such techniques, together with stable and quasi-stable methods that also rely upon census age distributions, provide valuable estimates of past vital rates. But they have limitations. In particular, the resulting estimates are ten-year averages; they lack the detail often required to study interrelations between demographic and socio-economic variables. Moreover, with rare exceptions, analysts ignore the other major demographic data source operating since the second half of the nineteenth century — vital registration. Registration, we are told, is highly deficient, and resulting birth and death rates are much lower than those estimated by census-based procedures. Further, the degree of underregistration probably varies over time. As a result of these and other problems, it is almost routine for demographers to contend that vital registration is virtually useless in investigating past demographic levels and trends in India.[2]

Our position stands in contrast to this view. While denying neither the value of census-based approaches, nor the limitations that can attend registration material, we believe that Indian vital registration can be an extremely informative source on the country's demographic history. Indeed it probably provides the single most fruitful avenue for research. Rather than argue this position point by point, we decided to undertake a specific demographic case study using registration data. In what follows we have deliberately tried to avoid going beyond the indications of the raw material. Aside from the necessary adoption of model demographic age patterns, the levels of fertility and mortality produced below derive almost entirely from the numbers of births and deaths registered each year by the population of Berar themselves. Moreover we will show that our registration-based figures compare favourably with estimates derived using conventional census-based approaches.

BERAR

The existence of Berar as a separate province dates from 1853 when it was leased to the British 'in perpetuity' by the Nizam of Hyderabad. At its first census in 1867 slightly more than two million people were enumerated — a little under one per cent of then British India. By 1981 the population of the four districts of the former province was almost seven million — slightly over one per cent of contemporary India (see Table 1). The main language is Marathi, and the population is mostly Hindu (e.g. 86.7 per cent in 1901). From the middle of the nineteenth century the region's livelihood stemmed from the production of cotton from its rich alluvial soils. By the turn of the century 35.8 per cent of land under crop was sown with cotton and 42.4 per cent with *jowari* (great millet), the staple crop. By 1921 cotton covered 48 per cent of cultivated land. This dependence upon cotton made the area comparatively wealthy, and at times attracted seasonal, semi-permanent and permanent migrants. But it has also meant that in some periods local food production has been insufficient for local needs, and grain has had to be imported. Thus the population was particularly vulnerable in periods of general agricultural scarcity, or when there was a slump in the world price of cotton such as at the outbreak of World War I. Dependence upon cotton also meant that the wages of labourers could fluctuate greatly from year to year. Partly as a result of the commercialization of agriculture, good communications were established from fairly early on. By the end of the nineteenth century metalled roads criss-crossed most of the region, and a section of the Great Indian Peninsula Railway bisected Berar from east to west — a distance of 150 miles.[3]

Census data for the province are summarized in Table 1. In many
ways — for example as regards changes in intercensal growth rates,
proportions urban, or the female age at marriage — these data mirror
broad trends exhibited by all-India material. Some early intercensal
decades were characterized by low and even negative rates of
population growth; the modern acceleration of population growth really
began during the 1951 – 61 decade; in 1971 – 81 the rate of growth
declined. An interesting feature is the high annual growth rate of 1.8
per cent for 1867 – 81. In part this may reflect improvements in the
level of census enumeration. But there is little doubt that immigration
played a major role. To quote the Census Commissioner for 1881:

> The influx, beginning from the year 1868, of immigrants . . . attracted to
> Berar, partly by the high wages of labour, and partly by the favourable land
> tenure, is noticed in the Administration Reports from this year onwards . . .
> Although there has been a certain natural increment in the population, a
> small part of which has been counterbalanced by emigration, still the greater
> part of the increase must have been caused by immigration.[4]

Migration into Berar seems to have been particularly pronounced
prior to 1881, and probably helps explain the fairly masculine sex ratios
recorded by the first three censuses (see Table 1). It was facilitated by
increasing road and rail links, and the quotation implies, an improved
system of land revenue settlement. The effect of the American Civil
War in raising the world price of cotton also played a significant role.
By the end of the nineteenth century Berar was a major cotton exporter
to the mills of Lancashire, Germany and Japan.

VITAL REGISTRATION IN BERAR

Our choice of Berar for the present study stems from two main
considerations. First, for the century reviewed here (1881 – 1980),
there are no significant boundary changes to complicate analysis. Until
1903 registration statistics for the province were tabulated for its then
six constituent districts. But in that year these were exactly collapsed
into the four districts that have survived to the present day. The year
1903 was also that in which Berar was amalgamated with Central
Provinces to become 'Central Provinces and Berar'. For a short period
after Independence the territory fell under the jurisdiction of Madhya
Pradesh, before in 1956 being finally transferred to Maharashtra. These
changes make the compilation of long-run series of birth and death rates
an arduous affair, involving the extraction of data from reports
published by several provincial or state authorities. Moreover,

Table 1. Census Statistics, Berar, 1867 – 1981.

Census Year	Population	Average Annual Rate of Growth(%)	Sex Ratio (m/f)	Per Cent Urban	Per Cent of Females 15 – 19 Never-Married
1867	2,227,654	—	1.071	12.9	n.a.
1881	2,672,673	1.82	1.068	11.6	3.9
1891	2,897,491	0.81	1.061	12.4	3.8
1901	2,754,016	– 0.51	1.025	15.2	6.4
1911	3,057,162	1.04	1.029	12.1	3.1
1921	3,075,316	0.06	1.037	14.7	3.1
1031	3,441,838	1.13	1.046	15.2	3.9
1941	3,604,866	0.46	1.039	17.0	16.3
1951	3,784,304	0.49	1.029	19.8	n.a.
1961	4,580,302	1.91	1.053	19.6	20.0
1971	5,729,342	2.24	1.057	20.8	43.3
1981	6,934,562	1.91	1.053	22.2	n.a.

Notes: (1) In early censuses we have interpreted 'unmarried' to mean 'never-married', since 'widows' were specified separately; we have also taken 'towns' to mean 'urban areas'.

(2) For reasons of data availability we give proportions of females never married at ages 15 – 19. However these have been found to be highly correlated with estimates of the singulate mean age at marriage; see P. C. Smith, 'Indexes of nuptiality: Asia and the Pacific', *Asian and Pacific Census Forum*, Volume 5, No. 2, November 1978.

Sources: The principal sources used in compiling this table were as follows: (i) Census of India, 1881, *Report on the Census of Berar, 1881*, Bombay, 1882 (ii) Census of India, 1891, Volume VI, *Berar or the Hyderabad Assigned Districts*, Calcutta, 1892 (iii) Census of India, 1901, *Berar*, Part II, Imperial Tables, Allahabad, 1902 (iv) Census of India, 1911, Volume X, *Central Provinces and Berar*, Part II — Tables, Allahabad, 1912 (v) Census of India, 1921, Volume XI, *Central Provinces and Berar*, Part II — Tables, Allahabad, 1923 (vi) Census of India, 1931, Volume XII, *Central Provinces and Berar*, Part II — Tables, Nagpur 1932 (vii) Census of India, 1961, Volume X, *Maharashtra*, Part II-C(i), Social and Cultural Tables, Delhi, 1965 (viii) Census of India 1971, *Maharashtra*, Series 11, Part II-A, General Population Tables, New Delhi, 1976, and (ix) Census of India, 1981, *Maharashtra*, Series 12, Part II-A, General Population Tables, Bombay, 1983.

particularly after its amalgamation with Central Provinces, the amount of attention Berar receives in official publications is reduced. However the contemporary combined jurisdiction of Akola, Amraoti, Buldana and Yeomatal districts exactly conforms to the boundaries of Berar in 1881. Therefore we have been able to compile annual demographic time-series for the territory as a whole for virtually an entire century.[5]

The second reason for selecting Berar stems from the high quality of its vital registration data. The statistics themselves are examined in later sections. Here we focus chiefly upon the history of the registration system and its administrative structure.

Vital registration of deaths in India dates from the mid-1860s, and that of births from about a decade later. The development of the system owed much to the work of J. M. Cunningham M.D., the Sanitary Commissioner with the Government of India during most of the 1870s. He developed recommendations on procedure (e.g. forms, personnel etc.) and pressed for the implementation of a uniform system throughout British India. The following quotation illustrates the main rationale for introducing registration, and also the *laissez-faire* philosophy that underlay so many actions of the British:

> The object of registration is to localize disease, so that the causes which produce it may be sought out, and, if possible, removed; and to bring to the notice of the people any excessive mortality occurring, so that they may be impressed with the importance of bestirring themselves in sanitary reform. The Government can never cleanse India by any legislative enactments, or remove the many defects which more or less affect the inhabitants of every town and village . . . This must be the work of the people themselves. It is therefore of the first importance to make them realise the importance of such things, and for this purpose there is no more valuable means than teaching them to record all the births and all the deaths that occur amongst them. This cannot be accomplished all at once . . . but the progress already made in those parts of the country where it has received most attention is very encouraging.[6]

The regions Cunningham had in mind at the end of this quotation certainly included Berar. During the 1870s there are often favourable references to the quality of registration in the province in the Annual Indian Sanitary Reports. For example, in the fifteenth Annual Report for the year 1878 the Sanitary Commissioner writes that '. . . again Central Provinces and Berar takes the first place'; in the Report for 1883 he writes that 'In Central Provinces and Berar registration has for some years been general, and the system has become established on a fair footing'.[7] These judgements of Cunningham and later Commissioners as to the virtues of registration in Berar were reached in several ways. They included (i) comparison of registered vital rates with levels known to hold in Europe, (ii) basic tests of internal consistency, such as whether the registered sex ratio at birth fell within acceptable limits (see below), and (iii) first-hand inspection of registration procedures in the countryside.

The census of 1891 provided an independent test of the registration system. Unfortunately the tabulations on place of birth contained major errors, and the Census Commissioner for Berar could only conclude from the migration data itself that 'Roughly . . . the number of immigrants since 1881 has been 100,000 and the number of emigrants about 20,000' (i.e. a net inflow of approximately 80,000). The province's census totals for 1881 and 1891, combined with the registered excess of births over deaths for 1881 – 90, implied a decadal inflow of 82,126. Thus the Commissioner was able to conclude that 'the vital statistics are fairly accurate'.[8] Fortunately with the census of 1901 the migration tables were not so compromised, and the Census Commissioner was able to employ quite objectively the demographic balancing equation to assess registration coverage. In this case place of birth data indicated a small intercensal gain due to migration of 14,215, whereas the census totals, combined with the registered excess of deaths over births for 1891 – 1900, implied a decadal inflow of 17,689. Expressed another way: the actual population enumerated in 1901 differed from the 1891 population 'brought forward' by registration statistics, and adjusted for net migration, by only 3,474 persons. These results certainly confirm the 1901 Census Commissioner's statement that 'on the whole vital statistics in Berar are now recorded with a very fair approach to accuracy'.[9] After amalgamation with Central Provinces in 1903 census tabulations no longer give migration data for Berar alone, so similar consistency tests cannot be applied for later periods.

Finally it is worth noting the stringent arrangements established to register births and deaths in Berar. Registration was first introduced in the province in 1868, and modified in 1876, 1883 and 1894. An idea of the rigour of the system is conveyed by the Sanitary Commissioner with the Government of India for 1895:

In Berar . . . the village officials collect and register vital statistics, and the police compile and classify them. The village records are tested by the Superintendents of Vaccination. Whilst inspecting the results of vaccination in a village, they examine the registers. If the number of entries is suspiciously low, a house to house visitation is made, until the names of a considerable number of infants are obtained . . . The lists of names are then compared with the registers, and omissions are reported . . . During the year 1,793 village registers were thus examined, against 2,293 in 1894, and

6 per cent were found to be defective. Besides these inspections, many officers including Deputy Commissioners, Civil Surgeons, officers of the Police and Tahsildars examined, in all, 6,200 registers, of which 6 per cent were found defective. [10]

It is clear from this that in any year most of Berar's village registers must have been checked. The figure of 6 per cent seems to relate to registers that were defective in one way or another; it does not appear to be an estimate of underregistration. The village officials (*patwaris*) upon whom responsibility for reporting in rural areas devolved, sent their returns weekly to the police. The District Superintendent compiled a monthly statement, and this was scrutinized by the Civil Surgeon. In urban areas responsibility for reporting — within 72 hours of occurrence — rested with the public. Individuals were sometimes prosecuted in the event of non-registration. In addition, each urban area 'appointed its jamadar or ward peons for collecting the information regarding births and deaths within each division of the town, and one of the Municipal members personally checks the returns by house to house visitation'. [11] In both rural and urban areas still births were recorded separately from live births.

To sum up, it seems clear that from very soon after its inception, vital registration in Berar can be regarded in the words of the 1911 Census Report as 'specially accurate'. After its amalgamation with Central Provinces there are few statements specifically relating to the quality of registration in what then became only a fraction of the total province. But there are no reasons to believe that the system deteriorated in any significant way. Fortunately, in amalgamating with Central Provinces, Berar joined an administration that also ran a fairly rigorous system of vital statistics. But the integrity of the rules and administrative procedures operating in Berar was maintained with amalgamation. And even with the formation of Madhya Pradesh in 1950, the distinctive registration procedures operating in Berar were specifically left untouched. [12]

THE COMPILATION OF ADJUSTED SERIES OF VITAL RATES

Our main purpose is to produce annual demographic estimates for the period 1881 – 1980. An important preliminary step towards this objective is the compilation of series of annual crude birth rates (CBRs), crude death rates (CDRs) and infant mortality rates (IMRs). We will first consider CBRs and CDRs.

For years from 1881 to 1940 the Annual Public Health Reports published by the Government of India, and the Government of Central

Provinces and Berar, routinely included total numbers of births in Berar, plus corresponding vital rates. With simple adjustments these official rates can be marginally improved to produce 'adjusted' series. Until 1941 published CBRs and CDRs used the last census count as their denominator, with no allowance for intercensal population change. Therefore we calculated new denominators for each year of the six decades up to 1940 assuming the corresponding average annual rate of intercensal population growth (see Table 1). For 1891 – 1900 and 1911 – 20 this procedure was amended slightly. In 1900 and 1918 Berar suffered exceptional mortality crises which produced negative and near zero average decadal population growth rates if census counts at each end of these decades are compared (see Table 1). Yet population growth rates were almost certainly much higher during both of these decades up until the year of the crisis. To allow for this an estimate of the population size in 1899 and 1917 was made by working back from the 1901 and 1921 census counts using registered vital events for 1900 and 1918 – 20. New denominators for each year during 1891 – 99 and 1911 – 17 were then calculated assuming the indicated average annual population growth rates for these periods.

World War II and the interstate jurisdictional transfer of the four districts in the early 1950s, make reconstruction during 1940 – 57 especially difficult. Registration continued, but the publication of data and vital rates was sporadic and less comprehensive. After 1940 we can usually no longer deal with raw numbers and recalculate rates directly employing routine adjustments; instead we have to work with the published official rates themselves. For both 1946 and 1948 it remains possible to calculate Berar's rates directly from the raw data. But for other years during 1941 – 7 Annual Public Health Reports were not published. Therefore we can only obtain rates for 1941 – 5 and 1947 using the 'mean of the previous five years' rates published in the Annual Reports for 1946 and 1948. Using these we can solve for the average level of CBRs and CDRs for 1941 – 2, 1943 – 5 and 1947. But it must be borne in mind that these figures are derived from averages. For 1948 – 52 annual district-level rates were published, and these were weighted on 1951 district census population totals to give figures for the former province as a whole. Unfortunately it has not been possible to obtain rates for the four years 1953 – 6, and we have had to resort to interpolation (see below). Finally, district-level CBRs and CDRs are available for years after and including 1957. These were weighted by 1961, 1971 and 1981 district census totals to complete our series.[13]

Turning to infant mortality, the measure we would prefer to use is the infant mortality rate (IMR) i.e. the probability of dying before the first birthday. Until early in this century, the published official death rates were the year's infant deaths divided by an estimate (in fact the last census count) of the population aged under one. Sanitary Commissioners were quick to see that such a rate could be highly misleading.[14] In more recent times, including the post-Independence period, the infant death rate (IDR) has been the published index i.e. the year's infant deaths divided by the same year's births. This too can misrepresent levels of infant mortality, since some of a year's infant deaths derive from births in the previous year. Therefore for years prior to 1941 we estimated annual IMRs using data on the annual numbers of births and infant deaths, and the simple but reasonable assumption that 30 per cent of infant deaths in a year stem from births of the previous year. For 1948 – 52 only annual district-level IDRs are available, hence we have employed corresponding weighted-averages. For most years after 1957 annual data on numbers of births and infant deaths are again available, and IMRs can be estimated using the assumption mentioned above. Again, no rates can be obtained for 1953 – 6. Also, for infant mortality there are no published five-year averages to bridge 1941 – 5, so interpolation is required for two periods.[15]

In considering the issue of interpolation it is appropriate to examine the adjusted series as compiled so far. These are given in the Appendix and graphed in Figs. 1 and 2. The simulation methodology used below to estimate annual life expectancy and total fertility depends mostly on the CBR and CDR. Clearly the most difficult period is 1953 – 6 for which we have no data at all. Crude birth and death rates for this period were obtained by linear interpolation between the adjusted rates for 1952 and 1957. In the case of the CDR Fig. 1 lends support to this procedure, since the period bridged appears to be one when the death rate is experiencing a steady decline. However Fig. 2 shows that it is difficult to speculate about likely movements in the CBR during these years. Turning to infant mortality, linear interpolation between 1952 and 1957 would produce a rise in IMR because the registered rate for 1952 of 123 infant deaths per thousand live births is suspiciously low. Consequently an alternative procedure was used. The average rate for the three year period before 1953 – 6 is 145, and this is also the average rate for the three year period following 1953 – 6. Therefore we arbitrarily assumed that the IMR in each year 1953 – 6 was 145. Linear interpolation was employed for the war years when the infant mortality rate derived directly from registration data fell from 212 in 1940 to 200 in 1946.[16] This latter interpolation is less critical since we have registration CBRs and CDRs for the war period — although admittedly derived from averages. In what follows the particular difficulties relating to 1941 – 5, and more especially 1953 – 6, must be remembered. But of the total 420 observations (i.e. CBRs, CDRs and IMRs) on which the present exercise is based, only 12 pertain to years in which there is a complete absence of registration data.

A final point concerning the compilation of the adjusted series relates to sex differentials in mortality. For years before 1941 we were able to derive adjusted crude death rates and infant mortality rates separately for each sex. But data published for later years preclude this. Yet to assume no difference between male and female mortality for later years would interject a significant discontinuity. This is because registered death rates for males were higher than those for females for virtually all years before 1941. Indeed, for the period 1881 – 1940 the average registered male CDR exceeded that of females by 2.03 deaths per thousand. Accordingly, for years after 1940 we maintained a similar differential (a decision that may marginally exaggerate the scale of the female mortality advantage in very recent years). This was accomplished by adding one point to the adjusted population crude death rate to produce the rate for males, and subtracting one point to produce the rate for females. The indication of heavier male than female mortality in Berar is an interesting feature to which we will return.

THE ADJUSTED SERIES REVIEWED

At this stage it is appropriate to review briefly the adjusted series in the light of other data. Table 2 compares decadal averages of our adjusted CBRs and CDRs with corresponding averages of the official rates for 1881 – 1940. Since the denominators of the adjusted rates allow for population growth it is to be expected that they are slightly lower than the official rates originally published. Nevertheless, the general level of our adjusted series remains high. For the same six decades the Table also gives the average registered sex ratio at birth. As previously intimated, this falls within acceptable limits — although it is perhaps very marginally higher (i.e. more masculine) than we might anticipate, possibly reflecting a slight tendency to underregister female births. Together with Figs. 1 and 2, the coefficients of variation in Table 2 underscore the tremendous annual variability of vital rates — especially death rates — until around 1940. Indeed, CDRs fluctuate so much in Fig. 1 that much of the overall trend is obscured. Perhaps a better impression of average movements is conveyed if we plot a five-year moving average of the adjusted rates, as in Fig. 3.

A particularly encouraging feature of Table 2 is the close correspondence between the crude rates of natural increase (CRNI) as implied by registration, and the intercensal growth rates, as indicated

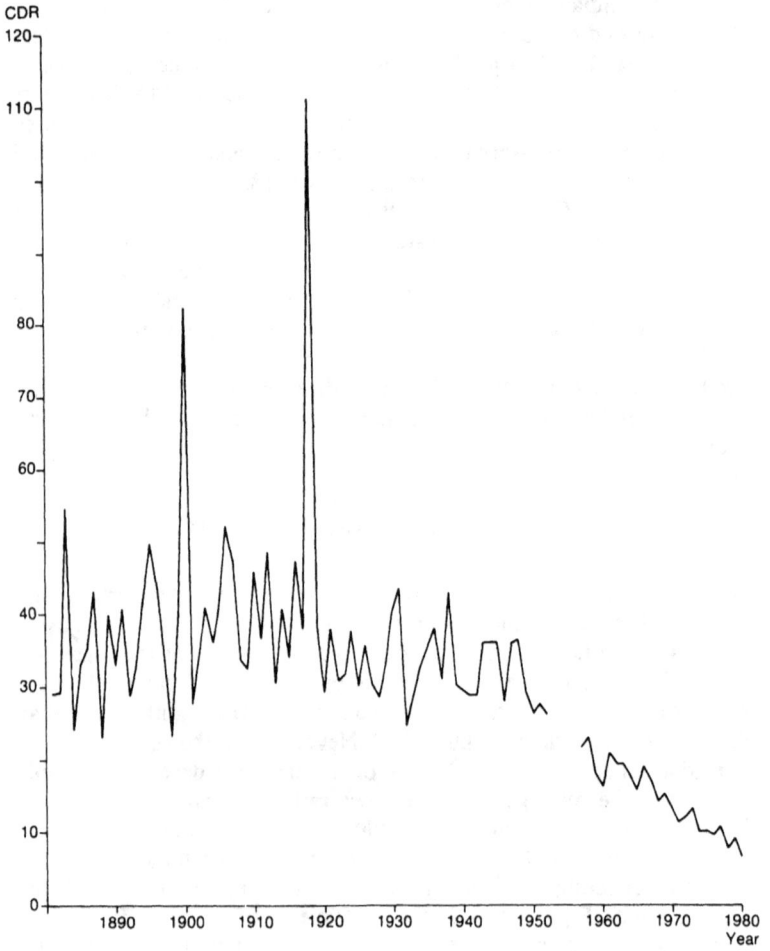

Fig.1 Adjusted Crude Death Rates, 1881–1980

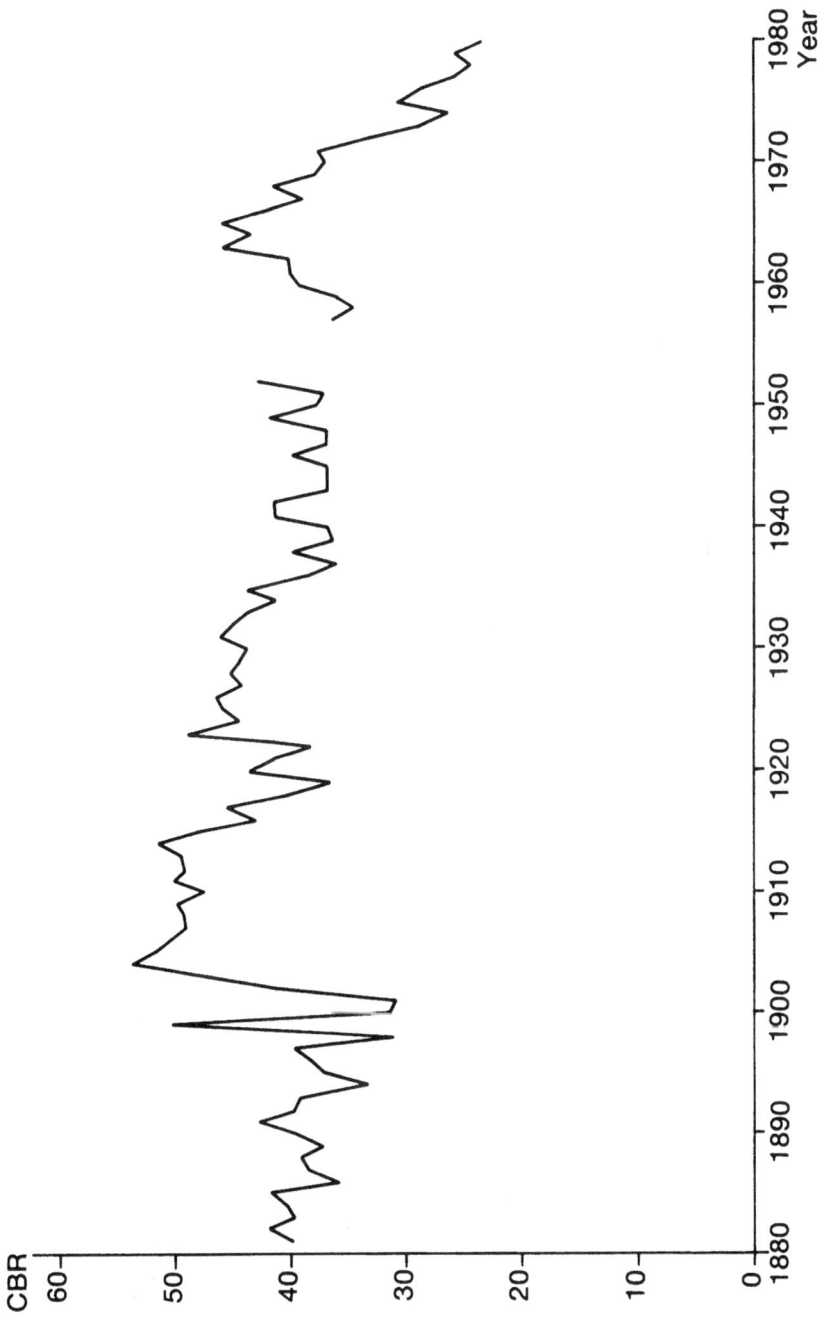

Fig.2 Adjusted Crude Birth Rates, 1881–1980

Table 2. Summary of the Adjusted Rates and Associated Statistics, 1881 – 1980.

Decade	Adjusted CBR	Coefficient of Variation	Registered Sex Ratio at Birth (m/f)	Adjusted CDR	Coefficient of Variation	Crude Rate of Natural Increase (CRNI)	Intercensal Rate of Growth (%)
1881 – 1890	39.37 (40.76)	4	1.062	34.44 (35.69)	26	0.49	0.81
1891 – 1900	38.30 (38.36)	14	1.058	43.60 (43.63)	35	– 0.53	– 0.51
1901 – 1910	47.08 (49.27)	13	1.053	38.94 (40.91)	19	0.81	1.04
1911 – 1920	45.62 (46.80)	10	1.059	45.50 (47.05)	50	0.01	0.06
1921 – 1930	44.13 (46.47)	6	1.061	33.72 (35.50)	11	1.04	1.13
1931 – 1940	40.66 (41.04)	9	1.064	33.69 (34.02)	17	0.70	0.46
1941 – 1950	38.60	5	n.a.	32.28	12	0.63	0.49
1951 – 1960	38.39	6	n.a.	22.97	14	1.54	1.91
1961 – 1970	41.09	7	n.a.	17.22	14	2.39	2.24
1971 – 1980	28.40	14	n.a.	10.18	17	1.82	1.91

Notes: (1) Adjusted CBRs and CDRs are decadal means of the annual rates in the Appendix. Figures in brackets are corresponding averages of the published official rates. For decades after 1941 adjusted and official rates are identical for practical purposes.
(2) The coefficient of variation is the standard deviation divided by the mean. The comparatively high coefficient of the CBR for 1971 – 80 reflects a downward trend in fertility rather than annual fluctuation.
(3) The Crude Rate of Natural Increase (CRNI) = CBR – CDR. Here the figure has been expressed in percentage terms.
(4) Data relating to the sex ratio at birth are generally not available for years after 1940.

Sources: For the denominators used in compiling the adjusted series of vital rates (see Appendix for full series) the sources are listed in Table 1. The numerators were obtained mainly from the following publications: (i) for years prior to 1903, *Annual Report of the Sanitary Commissioner with the Government of India*, Calcutta (various years), (ii) for years 1903 – 40 inclusive, and 1946 and 1948, *Annual Public Health Report of the Central Provinces and Berar*, Nagpur (various years), (iii) for years 1948 – 52, *Social Statistics of Madhya Pradesh, 1954 – 55*, published by the Directorate of Economics and Statistics, Madhya Pradesh, Nagpur, 1956, (iv) for years 1957 – 1979, *Vital Statistics of India*, Ministry of Home Affairs, New Delhi (various years) and (v) for 1980, *Handbook of Basic Statistics of Maharashtra State*, published by the Directorate of Economics and Statistics, Maharashtra, Bombay, 1983

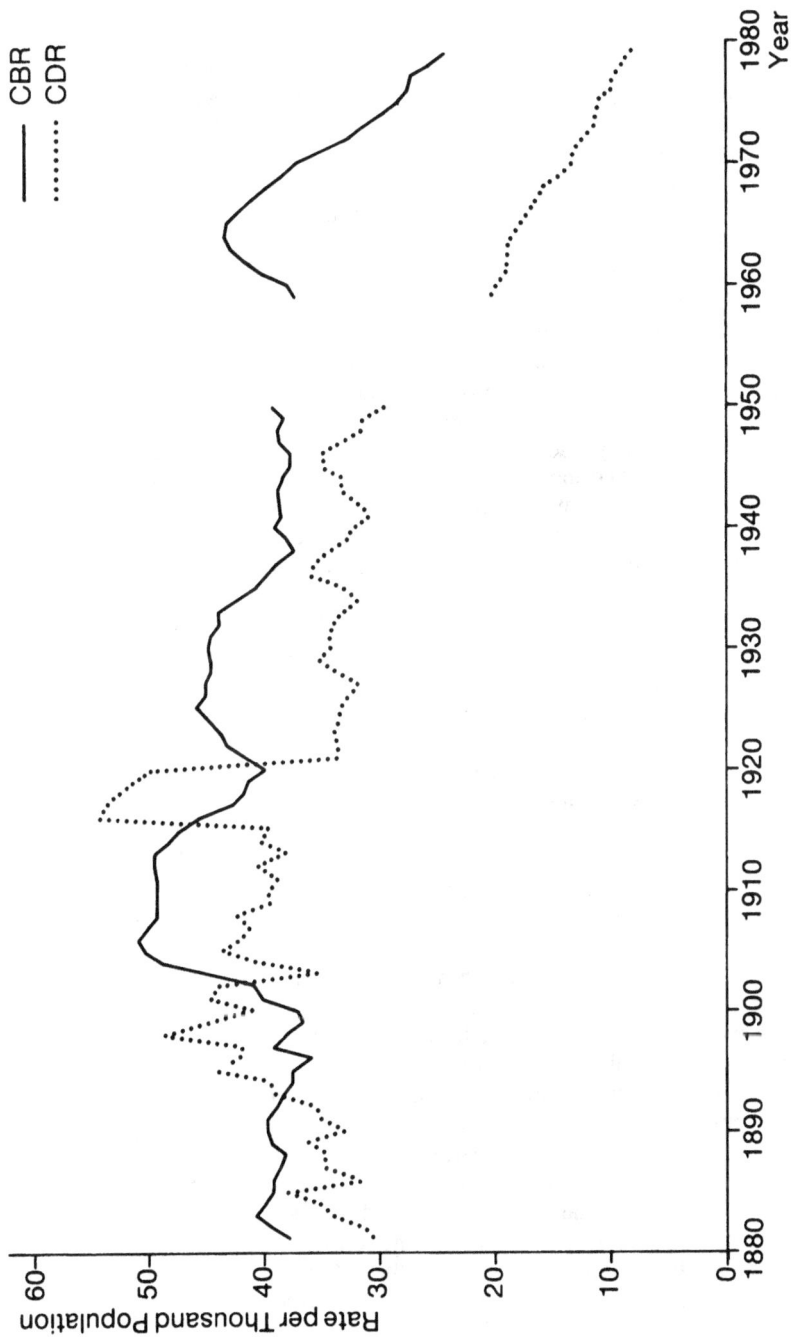

Fig.3 Five Year Moving Average of Adjusted Crude Birth and Death Rates, 1881–1980

by the censuses. Given the low level of precision common in estimating growth rates in such populations, the general degree of agreement over the ten decades is good. Of course, if registration CBRs and CDRs were both deficient, but to the same degree, they could still produce the correct CRNI, yet understate the true level of vital rates. But in this case the scope for underregistration is restricted given the general high level of both crude birth and death rates.[17] The correspondence between the rates of natural increase and intercensal growth rates is the more remarkable because the latter can be significantly affected by variation in census coverage level. For example, it has been argued that due to relatively poor census coverage in 1971 the intercensal growth rate for 1961 – 70 probably significantly understated the true rate of population growth in India, with the reverse implication for 1971 – 80. Such considerations may also be relevant in accounting for the differences in Table 2 for the two most recent decades.[18] Finally, intercensal growth rates reflect net migration in addition to natural increase. The fact that intercensal growth rates are marginally higher than crude rates of natural increase for the first five decades may result partly from immigration.

Of course we cannot maintain that our adjusted series are entirely without blemish. Indeed we can be specific in charting some of their probable limitations. If general experience elsewhere is relevant then the registration system probably tended towards underregistration rather than the reverse; we have already remarked on a possible indication of slight underreporting of female births. Also, the quality of registration-based rates for a few individual years may have been adversely affected by various administrative changes; thus in passing we questioned the registered infant mortality rate for 1952. Additionally, vital rates for years of acute crisis must be approached with particular caution. For example, writing in connection with the influenza pandemic of 1918 the Census Commissioner stated that 'deaths were undoubtedly much more numerous than reported, as the reporting agency broke down in places under the stress of the disease'. Yet even in the presence of such administrative dislocation the number of registered deaths in Berar in 1918 amounted to more than one person in ten. Death rates in famine years could be affected by deaths of people who migrated in search of food. In 1897 part of the high registered death rate was attributed to 'a large number of half-starved immigrants from the Central Provinces, most of whom were "too far gone from the effects of chronic starvation to be saved by food" '.[19] Clearly, such migration could bias death rates in either direction, and usually there is no quantitative information to assess the net balance of such migration flows. Distress migration did not occur with every famine, and administrators seem to have been more ready to mention the adverse influence of immigrants than to give corresponding consideration to possible outmigration from their areas.

We will return to some of these issues below. But before we can simulate Berar's demographic history using our adjusted series, we must examine the age-sex distribution; in particular that for the starting year of our simulation (1881).

THE AGE DISTRIBUTION

The census of 1881 is the first for which an age-sex distribution is available. Not surprisingly, the quality of age reporting was very poor, and the results exhibiṭ age errors in extreme form. Comparison with model age distributions, as in Table 3, strongly suggests net age shifting into the 5 – 9 and 20 – 34 age groups, and age overstatement at older ages (60+). There is also a marked deficit of people aged 15 – 19. Variation in age misreporting between males and females probably accounts for much of the irregular progression of the sex ratio by age. Extreme preference for the digit 0 helps to explain the obvious excess of people at 40 – 44 and 50 – 54.[20]

Certain features of Table 3 are especially noteworthy: for example, the overrepresentation at 20 – 34. There are two main explanations for this. The first is the tendency, particularly pronounced for women, systematically to misstate their ages towards the prime reproductive years — a phenomenon sometimes termed 'female age shifting into the reproductive span'. This type of age misstatement is often found in data for India. It accounts for some of the deficit at 15 – 19, and also, perhaps, the comparatively low sex ratios at 20 – 29. The second explanation is immigration for agricultural employment, which we have already had cause to mention. This usually involved more men than women. Nevertheless 46 per cent of life-time immigrants enumerated in Berar in the 1881 census were female. This comparatively high representation may have partly stemmed from the immigration of whole households in earlier times when cotton cultivation was expanding and some virgin land was still available. In addition the District Gazetteers stress that large and important areas of agricultural work were mainly the preserve of women — especially weeding, harvesting jowari, and picking cotton. Unfortunately the consideration of migration is complicated because the census coincided with the spring harvest which attracted seasonal migrants into Berar.[21]

A second interesting feature of Table 3 is that less than 38 per cent of the population was classified as aged under 15. In other words, compared with many developing country populations, Berar's age structure was *not* very young. Table 4 contains summary age

Table 3. The Age-Sex Distribution of Berar, 1881, compared with a Model.

Age Group	Male Numbers	Male %	Female Numbers	Female %	Sex Ratio (m/f)	Model %	Distributions Smoothed on Model Male	Female
0 – 4	191,950	13.91	202,598	15.68	0.95	14.99	206,936	193,698
5 – 9	171,443	12.42	172,778	13.37	0.99	12.08	166,763	156,095
10 – 14	149,989	10.86	122,120	9.45	1.23	10.94	151,026	141,365
15 – 19	86,180	6.24	91,258	7.06	0.94	10.09	139,292	130,381
20 – 24	98,270	7.12	120,776	9.35	0.81	9.07	125,211	117,201
25 – 29	133,832	9.69	122,104	9.45	1.10	8.05	111,130	104,021
30 – 34	138,960	10.07	116,288	9.00	1.19	7.12	98,291	92,003
35 – 39	89,056	6.45	63,434	4.91	1.40	6.25	86,281	80,761
40 – 44	101,999	7.39	86,981	6.73	1.17	5.42	74,823	70,036
45 – 49	44,036	3.19	34,023	2.63	1.29	4.59	63,365	59,311
50 – 54	74,697	5.41	66,185	5.12	1.13	3.75	51,768	48,457
55 – 59	19,576	1.42	15,393	1.19	1.27	2.91	40,172	37,602
60 +	80,504	5.83	78,243	6.06	1.03	4.74	65,434	61,250
Total	1,380,492	100.00	1,292,181	100.00	1.07	100.00	1,380,492	1,292,181

Note: (1) For details of the model employed see text and note 22.

Source: The data are taken from Census of India, 1881, cited in Table 1.

Table 4. Summary Age-Sex Distributions for Berar, 1881 – 1971

	1881				
	males			females	
	no.	%		no.	%
0 – 14	513,382	37.1		497,496	38.5
15 – 44	648,297	47.0		600,841	46.5
45 +	218,813	15.9		193,844	15.0
Total	1,380,492	100.0		1,292,181	100.0

	1891				
	males			females	
	no.	%		no.	%
0 – 14	557,001	37.3		545,968	38.8
15 – 44	688,369	46.2		645,468	45.9
45 +	246,456	16.5		214,229	15.2
Total	1,491,826	100.0		1,405,665	100.0

	1901				
	males			females	
	no.	%		no.	%
0 – 14	489,907	35.8		495,611	36.4
15 – 44	688,136	49.4		669,877	49.3
45 +	207,257	14.9		194,228	14.3
Total	1,394,300	100.0		1,359,716	100.0

	1911				
	males			females	
	no.	%		no.	%
0 – 14	569,271	36.7		562,353	37.3
15 – 44	701,120	45.2		694,786	46.1
45 +	280,223	18.1		249,409	16.6
Total	1,550,614	100.0		1,506,548	100.0

	1921				
	males			females	
	no.	%		no.	%
0 – 14	617,489	39.4		605,161	40.1
15 – 44	654,564	41.8		638,602	42.3
45 +	293,821	18.8		265,679	17.6
Total	1,565,874	100.0		1,509,442	100.0

	1931			
	males		females	
	no.	%	no.	%
0 – 14	675,742	38.4	679,736	40.4
15 – 44	797,618	45.3	756,645	45.0
45 +	286,219	16.3	245,878	14.6
Total	1,759,579	100.0	1,682,259	100.0

	1941			
	males		females	
	no.	%	no.	%
0 – 14	690,427	37.6	683,346	38.7
15 – 44	850,011	46.3	807,436	45.7
45 +	296,468	16.1	277,178	15.6
Total	1,836,906	100.0	1,767,960	100.0

	1951			
	males		females	
	no.	%	no.	%
0 – 14	740,922	38.6	733,630	39.3
15 – 44	861,875	44.9	814,551	43.7
45 +	316,707	16.5	316,619	17.0
Total	1,919,504	100.0	1,864,800	100.0

	1961			
	males		females	
	no.	%	no.	%
0 – 14	942,386	40.1	910,485	40.8
15 – 44	1,018,211	43.3	968,658	43.4
45 +	389,133	16.6	351,430	15.8
Total	2,349,730	100.0	2,230,573	100.0

	1971			
	males		females	
	no.	%	no.	%
0 – 14	1,256,640	42.7	1,212,917	43.5
15 – 44	1,169,851	39.7	1,119,645	40.2
45 +	517,526	17.6	452,763	16.3
Total	2,994,017	100.0	2,785,325	100.0

Notes: (1) Where necessary age-splitting coefficients were used in order to obtain numbers for the age groups used above.

(2) Persons classified as 'age not stated' (always less than one per cent of the population) were pro-rated on the distribution of the population for whom age was reported.

Sources: As for Table 1. The 1941 age data used are derived from the 'Y' (Yeatts) sample tabulations. They appear in Census of India 1951, *Madhya Pradesh*, Paper No. 9, Age Tables, 1941 on Y-Sample, New Delhi, 1954.

distributions for subsequent censuses. It shows that relatively low proportions at younger ages was a feature of most age distributions until 1961. Again, part of the explanation may relate to immigration, in which adults were probably preponderant. But even allowing for immigration (and age errors) it is difficult to conclude other than that Berar's population was not particularly young. This is significant because, *ceteris paribus*, it implies that we are dealing with a population with only a 'moderate' — as opposed to a 'high' — level of fertility. This is another issue to which we will return.

In view of the multitude of irregularities in the 1881 data — many of which are undoubtedly purely spurious outcomes of chronic age errors — we decided to employ a model in order to obtain a smooth age distribution for the starting year of our simulation. Accordingly a three parameter stable population age distribution was fitted to the proportion of the population aged under 15, and the proportion aged over 45. The particular model used is given in Table 3 in percentage terms, as well as pro-rated on the 1881 male and female census totals. It almost certainly gives a better representation of the broad features of the actual age distribution although, inevitably, it must also fail to reflect some genuine features.[22] It is worth emphasizing that we are using a stable population model simply as a convenient device to smooth the data; no assumption of stability has been made. Moreover, provided we restrict our choice to model populations that share the broad features of the 1881 census age distribution (i.e. 38 per cent aged under 15, and 16 per cent aged over 45) the demographic estimates we derive below are almost entirely independent of the selection of a particular model. We will elaborate this point below.

SIMULATION METHODOLOGY

We are now in a position to simulate the demography of Berar over 1881 – 1980. The method used involved projecting the 1881 age distribution forward one year at a time. In any year of the projection, and given the age-sex distribution holding in that year, a search was then conducted for the period total fertility rate (TFR) and model life table (with its associated characteristics) that would exactly produce the year's demographic parameters as specified by the adjusted series in the Appendix.

To be more specific, the following steps, illustrated with reference to the first projection year, 1881, were involved. First, a single year version of the smoothed age-sex distribution in Table 3 was obtained using standard interpolation coefficients. This gives us the population at the start of 1881.[23] Together the adjusted birth and death rates for 1881 allow us to compute the size of the population (as resulting from natural increase) at the end and midpoint of the year, and hence the number of births and deaths actually occurring in the year. We next require male and female life tables that, given the age and sex distribution at the start of the year, and the size of the year's birth cohort (i.e. the number of births occurring in the year), will exactly satisfy the adjusted sex-specific CDRs and IMRs specified for the year. To meet these requirements we employed the two parameter logit life table system devised by Brass. An advantage of this is its ability to generate a multitude of life tables at different levels of mortality, and with different overall relationships between early age and adult mortality, from a single standard life table. If mortality is constrained in some way — for example, if, as in the present case, the level of infant mortality holding in the year is fixed — then variation of the system's beta parameter will produce model life table variants over a wide range of mortality levels (i.e. life expectations at birth).[24] The standard life tables used in the present exercise were single year of age West models (level 5). The West model was selected mainly because it represents a fairly neutral choice. We have very little information regarding the age pattern of mortality prevailing in India in earlier times. Other scholars have also used the West. In any event the methodology employed here — in which life expectation at birth is fixed with reference to a specific CDR *and* IMR — is fairly robust to selection of a particular model as standard (see below).[25] For any year of the projection — in this case 1881 — use of the logit system enables us to generate an array of single-year-of-age life tables, all derived from the same standard, and all incorporating the IMR specified for the year, yet varying in their mortality at all ages other than infancy, and thus in their life expectation at birth. This is accomplished by varying beta. The array of life tables so produced — one array for each sex — can then be applied to the age-sex distribution at the start of the year (1881) and the size of the year's birth cohort.[26] Each application produces a corresponding projected number of male and female deaths for the year, depending upon the value of beta (i.e. the level of mortality). Since the number of deaths actually occurring has been determined, interpolation allows us to isolate life tables that will exactly give the required numbers of deaths to produce the year's CDR. Thus we can estimate male and female life expectation. The life tables obtained by interpolation are also used to project the age-sex distribution to the start of the next year (1882). All that remains is to determine the TFR required to generate the number of births that occurred in 1881. This is achieved by indirect standardization. Since age of mother was not recorded at birth, we have no guidelines as to the age pattern of fertility in Berar. Accordingly, a standard single year age-specific model fertility distribution appropriate for developing country populations was used.[27] The total fertility rate of this standard was 1.0. It was applied to the mid-year single year of age distribution of females aged 15 – 49 to give a projected number of births. The ratio of the size of the year's birth cohort (already determined) to this projected number gives the estimate of the TFR. This measure is the average number of live births a woman could expect to have in her lifetime, given prevailing age-specific fertility rates.

In this way male and female life expectation and period total fertility are estimated, and the age distribution is projected to the start of the next year. The procedure can then be repeated for 1882, and all subsequent years. The population's trajectory for the entire century is governed by the adjusted series of CBRs, IMRs and CDRs. One minor amendment was made in order to address the issue of migration. As described so far, the procedure simply projects the population enumerated in 1881, not subsequent immigrants or their descendants. Yet we have seen that, certainly in early decades, there probably was some continued immigration. Consequently every ten years projected and enumerated (i.e. census) population totals were compared in order to gain a rough idea of the direction and volume of net decadal migration. Also the projected male and female populations were pro-rated on the sex-specific population totals recorded in the census. We emphasize that this adjustment was restricted solely to totals. No account was taken of the age structure found by each census — this remains the product of the adjusted series of vital rates. Moreover the amendment was found to have no major effect upon the annual estimates of life expectation or TFR (see below).

The principal results of the full analysis, together with a complete listing of our annual vital rates (i.e. the adjusted series) are contained in the Appendix. But before discussing their substantive implications we must first address the technical issue of the extent to which we can validate our results.

ANALYSIS OF RESULTS

In this section we address three questions. First, how sensitive are our simulation results to the main assumptions we have had to make? Second, how well do our vital registration and simulation estimates compare with figures obtained using conventional census-based procedures? Third, how do the results tally with other work on India's demography?

Table 5. Summary Results from the Sensitivity Analysis.

Decade	Main Run		Initial Age Distribution Variant		South Model Life Table Variant		No Adjustment of Projected Population Variant	
	Life Expectation	Total Fertility	Life Expectation	Total Fertility	Life Expectation	Total Fertility	Life Expectation	Total Fertility
1881 – 1890	29.80	5.10	30.17	5.24	28.62	5.03	29.82	5.10
1891 – 1900	24.36	4.78	23.98	4.60	23.27	4.73	24.35	4.76
1901 – 1910	26.95	5.65	26.56	5.43	26.54	5.87	26.96	5.63
1911 – 1920	25.10	6.02	24.87	6.00	25.44	6.50	25.12	5.95
1921 – 1930	29.62	5.79	29.53	5.84	30.47	6.22	29.67	5.59
1931 – 1940	29.59	5.12	29.63	5.21	30.74	5.57	29.63	4.89
1941 – 1950	30.68	4.75	30.78	4.76	31.46	4.98	30.68	4.47
1951 – 1960	39.49	4.75	39.53	4.75	40.93	4.96	39.53	4.48
1961 – 1970	47.27	5.66	47.25	5.65	49.17	5.95	47.37	5.23
1971 – 1980	57.46	4.04	57.48	4.04	59.80	4.23	57.72	3.68

Notes: (1) The life expectations refer to both sexes combined; male and female figures have been weighted according to decadal population composition. 'Total Fertility' refers to the Total Fertility Rate (TFR).
(2) The variant initial age distribution had 41 per cent under 15 and 16 per cent aged 45 and over, with a growth rate of 2 per cent per annum. It was selected from the stable population models in Carrier and Hobcraft cited in note 22.
(3) The South model life table used as standard was level 5; see note 25.

Sensitivity Analysis

The sensitivity of the results to our principal assumptions is explored in Table 5. It compares decadal life expectation and total fertility rates from our main simulation run with figures obtained if variant assumptions are employed.

To examine the robustness of the present estimates to selection of initial age-sex distribution we ran the simulation with significantly different starting age data. Table 4 shows that 1961 is the first census when Berar's age distribution began a clear move away from its earlier approximately constant proportional configuration. Hence we arbitrarily selected an alternative initial age distribution based on the census of 1961. This was considerably younger, having 41 per cent aged under 15, and 43 per cent aged 15 – 44 (compared with figures of 38 and 46 per cent in the main run). Table 5 shows minor differences in the first few decades. Thus, given indirect standardization, the variant TFR for 1881 – 1890 is marginally higher than in the main run because of a lower proportion of females aged 15 – 44 (although Table 3 implies that, if anything, the age distribution used in the main run has overly reduced the proportion in the prime reproductive ages, thus leading to an overstatement of the TFR). As we might anticipate, Table 5 shows that the small differences introduced by a different starting age distribution disappear in later decades as convergence proceeds.

The sensitivity of results to use of a West model life table was also examined. For part of the post-Independence period there are indications that a pattern closer to the South model has probably prevailed in India. Table 5 shows that use of a South pattern as standard leads to slightly lower life expectations for the first three decades of the simulation, and slightly higher life expectations for the remaining decades. Differences in total fertility are generally minor. But in the variant run the period 1911 – 40 is one of significantly higher fertility — about half a live birth. The comparison illustrates the kind of variation that could derive from the operation of a markedly different age pattern of mortality. Our use of the West model in the main simulation seems justified by the requirement of adopting a single mortality pattern which, *with beta variation*, has to hold for a period of a hundred years. Recent research has cast doubt as to whether the South pattern could have prevailed in India in earlier decades.[28] Of course, in reality the age pattern of mortality in Berar has probably varied over time, switching from approximating different patterns as socio-economic and health conditions have changed. But modelling such alterations would pose problems, and more importantly, we have very little information regarding such changes.

The last issue addressed as part of the sensitivity analysis relates to the pro-ration of the projected populations on the numbers of males and females enumerated in the censuses. Table 5 contains results from a simulation in which only the initial 1881 population was projected, i.e. without any adjustment for subsequent immigration. As can be seen the differences introduced by omitting the pro-ration are generally small. They stem mainly from the fact that the 'no adjustment' variant produces a more feminine population. This is because the female CDRs are significantly lower than those of males, perhaps partly because female deaths were less well registered, and the population is closed to (predominantly male) immigration. A higher proportion of females, especially in more recent decades, produces marginally higher overall life expectation, and, given indirect standardization, somewhat lower total fertility. Moreover, whereas the 1981 census enumerated 6.9 million people, the variant produces a population of only 6.4 million. The difference is presumably largely attributable to immigrants and their descendants.

To conclude, it is clear that our main results are reasonably robust to these different assumptions. In reality Berar's population would have departed from them in different ways which sometimes may have been offsetting. However Table 5 provides a useful backcloth against which to interpret the main results. It should be noted that we have compared decadal averages. This hides the fact that annual variation in both life expectation and total fertility is highly correlated between all the runs in Table 5. This is because the principal determinant of change in all variants are the adjusted series of vital rates.

Intercensal Analysis

We have made two comparisons of the main simulation results with indications from the censuses. The first pertains to the age structure of the population. In the simulation the initial age distribution was selected with reference to the 1881 census. But subsequently the projected age structure evolves independently. Therefore we can use the age data from the decennial censuses to check how well our adjusted series determine the evolution of the age structure after 1881. Several indices of age structure could be used for comparison. Here we employ a crude measure of fertility, the child/woman ratio (CWR) i.e. the ratio of the population aged 0 – 4 to the female population aged 15 – 44. The results of the comparison are shown in Fig. 4. The correspondence is certainly close, especially if one bears in mind the problems associated with census CWRs. Fig. 4 leaves no real doubt that the adjusted series, particularly the CBRs, do indeed embody the main demographic trends in Berar after 1881.

The second comparison is more ambitious. The decennial census age – sex distributions were subjected to a full intercensal analysis. Briefly, the following steps were involved. For each intercensal decade the level of male and female early age mortality was fixed as the mean of the adjusted IMRs for the ten constituent years of the decade (see Appendix). With levels of early age mortality so determined, and again taking a West model life table (level 5) as standard, the beta parameter in the logit system was used to generate life tables embodying a wide range of relationships between adult and early age mortality. The survival rates implied by these life tables were then used to project the census age distribution at the start of each decade forward ten years. Comparison of the cumulated projected populations above given ages with the cumulated populations actually enumerated at the end of each decade gives a series of adult mortality estimates, each with a value of beta. The level of intercensal mortality was fixed by the mean of the first nine values. Having isolated sex specific intercensal life tables the average CBR and CDR holding in each decade were estimated using both forward and reverse procedures. Again, indirect standardization gives estimates of the average decadal level of total fertility. The exact technique employed has recently been used to produce intercensal estimates for India and its main states.[29]

This analysis is not entirely independent of the main simulation since both use the adjusted IMRs to fix the level of early age mortality. But without some such information intercensal analysis is limited to providing estimates of life expectation from age five.[30] Moreover we should stress that it is only infant mortality that the two procedures have been constrained to share: the principal determinant of the intercensal results are Berar's successive census age distributions.

Table 6 shows considerable overall agreement between the two sets of estimates, both as regards levels of demographic parameters and their trends. The figures for female life expectation show particularly close agreement. The sole exception is for 1901 – 10 when the intercensal analysis implies somewhat lighter mortality. The male comparisons are a little less satisfactory; the intercensal estimate for 1901 – 10 implies significantly lighter mortality, and this is also true for 1951 – 60 and 1961 – 70. A plausible explanation for the better overall correspondence of the female figures is that intercensal estimates for females are less affected by migration.

An interesting feature of Table 6 is the higher female than male life expectation of the intercensal analysis up to and including 1941 – 50. This provides limited support to the previous indications of overall

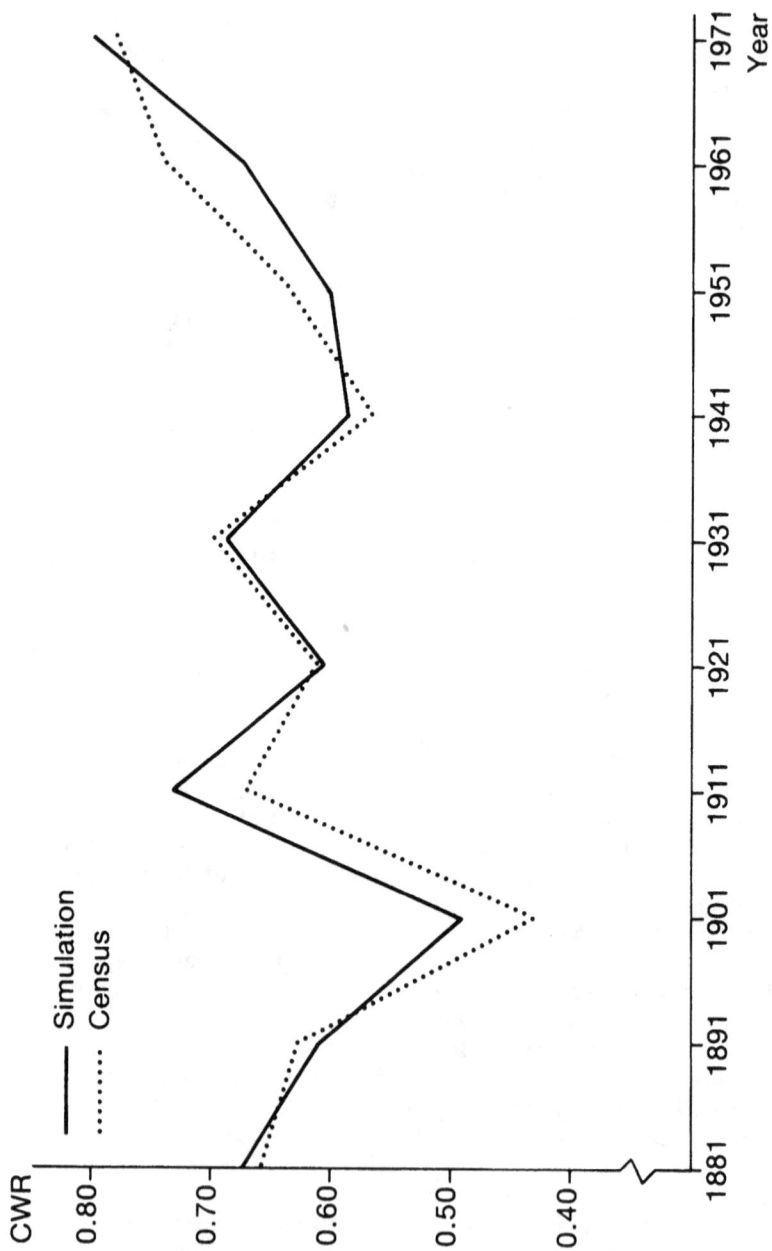

Fig.4 Comparison of Child/Woman Ratios from the Census and the Main Simulation Run, 1881 – 1971

Table 6. Comparison of Demographic Estimates: Vital Registration/Simulation Analysis and Intercensal Analysis.

| Decade | Life Expectation | | | | Crude Birth Rate (CBR) | | Crude Death Rate (CDR) | | Total Fertility Rate (TFR) | |
| | male | | female | | | | | | | |
	VR/ Simulation	Intercensal	VR/ Simulation	Intercensal	VR/ Simulation	Intercensal	VR/ Simulation	Intercensal	VR/ Simulation	Intercensal
1881 – 1890	29.49	32.25	30.14	32.70	39.4	40.3	34.4	32.2	5.10	4.93
1891 – 1900	23.78	21.71	24.96	24.71	38.3	37.4	43.6	42.4	4.78	4.56
1901 – 1910	26.36	30.29	27.56	31.27	47.1	42.8	38.9	32.4	5.65	5.20
1911 – 1920	24.00	25.38	26.24	26.95	45.6	42.4	45.5	41.8	6.02	5.58
1921 – 1930	28.55	29.82	30.74	29.96	44.1	44.5	33.7	33.3	5.79	5.93
1931 – 1940	28.99	27.81	30.22	30.49	40.7	39.7	33.7	35.1	5.12	5.01
1941 – 1950	30.14	30.42	31.24	32.38	38.6	38.1	32.3	33.3	4.75	4.90
1951 – 1960	38.30	44.16	40.72	41.24	38.4	40.4	23.0	21.3	4.75	5.37
1961 – 1970	45.32	51.10	49.32	50.69	41.1	38.7	17.2	16.4	5.66	5.43
1971 – 1980	54.64	n.a.	60.44	n.a.	28.4	n.a.	10.2	n.a.	4.04	n.a.

Note: (1) In each case the intercensal estimates given are the mean of the forward and reverse survival figures.

lighter female mortality in Berar. The reversal of this position in the intercensal estimates for 1951 – 70 could well reflect bias introduced by male immigration. This explanation would also help account for the large gap between the simulation and intercensal male life expectation estimates for the same period.

Estimates of CBR and CDR levels and trends are also reasonably consistent between the two analyses (see Table 6). Again the most obvious discrepancy pertains to 1901 – 10. The higher life expectation at birth of the intercensal analysis obviously implies a lower CDR for this decade; it also produces a lower CBR, whether forward or reverse survival is employed. In comparing simulation and intercensal estimates for these early decades it should be noted that they produce the same trends: the CBR evidently rose from 1891 – 1900 to 1901 – 10, and then fell slightly to 1911 – 20; the CDR fell from 1891 – 1900 to 1901 – 10, before rising sharply in 1911 – 20. But there remains a discrepancy of CBR and CDR *level*, especially for 1901 – 10.

Considering total fertility Table 6 suggests a reasonable degree of accord. Both analyses show that for most of the century about five live births per woman was the norm. In general the simulation figures are slightly higher and probably to be preferred. This is because the intercensal estimates are likely to be influenced by the over-representation of women in the prime reproductive years.

Turning to the discrepancies for 1901 – 10 immigration may be part of the explanation. A significant net inflow would, *ceteris paribus*, bias intercensal estimates of life expectation upwards and bias downwards estimates of both vital rates. A more insidious possibility relates to changes in census coverage. These might influence the results of both analyses. For example, if the terrible mortality of 1900 adversely affected the level of census enumeration in 1901 then registration CBRs and CDRs for 1891 – 1910 would be biased upwards. It is certainly our view that any defects in the adjusted series are as likely to derive from denominator problems than from difficulties with the numerator. In an intercensal analysis a relative undercount in 1901 (or relative overcount in 1911) would produce an overestimation of life expectation for 1901 – 10. Again both vital rates for this decade would be biased downwards. The deviations between the estimates in Table 6 could be thought consistent with such a scenario. Undoubtedly many of the 1901 census staff were previously engaged in famine relief work. But there is little other evidence to suggest a particularly poor count in 1901 (or better count in 1911). We have already noted that the 1901 census count agrees fairly well with the 1891 population brought forward and adjusted for net migration. Also, recovery from the famine in 1900 appears to have been rapid, following a good autumn crop. Certainly by the start of 1901 relief administrations were no longer required. The Census Commissioner for Berar was of the opinion that the preliminary enumeration was better conducted and the census agency more efficient so that 'the margin of error was smaller in 1901 than in any of the previous censuses'.[31]

Table 7. Estimates of Net Decadal Migration, Main Simulation Run.

Decade	Size of Net Annual Flow		Average Annual Net Migration Rate
	males	females	
1881 – 1890	+5,176	+4,016	+3.2
1891 – 1900	+2,843	+907	+0.2
1901 – 1910	+5,157	+1,955	+2.3
1911 – 1920	+3,804	–1,379	+0.5
1921 – 1930	+4,364	–1,229	+0.9
1931 – 1940	–3,699	–4,512	–2.4
1941 – 1950	–1,718	–3,661	–1.4
1951 – 1960	+13,491	+3,607	+3.7
1961 – 1970	–175	–6,622	–1.5
1971 – 1980	+6,579	+812	+0.9

Notes:
(1) The migration rate is expressed per thousand population per year. We have derived it from the figures in Table 2.

(2) The estimated net annual migration flows derive from the comparisons of projected and enumerated population totals made in the main simulation run. We must stress the approximate nature of these figures.

It is perhaps appropriate to examine the indications from the main simulation regarding the direction and volume of net migration. The figures in Table 7 emerge as residuals after accounting for the component of intercensal population change implied by the adjusted vital rates. Thus they must be interpreted with considerable caution since they reflect errors due to variation in both registration and census coverage. Nevertheless we can certainly ascertain some broad features. It seems likely that the immigration of the last half of the nineteenth century continued for several decades in this century. Table 7 also suggests that males formed the majority of immigrants. Indeed in half of the decades female emigration is implied.[32] In most periods the annual rate and volume of net migration is really very low. In relation to the discrepancies for 1901 – 10 there is some suggestion of an increase in immigration during that decade; alternatively the figures in Table 7 could themselves merely reflect relatively poor census coverage in 1901 (or improved coverage in 1911). For both 1931 – 40 and 1941 – 50 a net loss of both sexes is implied. Lastly, the large swings in net migration implied for the three most recent decades appear on the face of things a little suspect.[33]

To conclude, while admittedly not totally independent, this intercensal analysis nevertheless provides considerable support for the main simulation results. Clearly we should be especially cautious regarding the decade 1901 – 10. But in general, trends and levels of life expectancy (especially for females) and total fertility show fair agreement. And the intercensal CBRs and CDRs do much to confirm the basic validity of the adjusted series of vital rates. Fertility in Berar does not appear to have exceeded moderate levels, and both analyses indicate that in most periods females may have outlived males. This section also illustrates some of the limitations of an intercensal approach. Table 6 contains no intercensal estimates for 1971 – 80 simply because appropriate data for 1981 are not yet available, yet registration figures are produced regularly each year. Further, intercensal estimates are ten year averages. One naturally tends to interpret changes in such figures as shifts in average levels of fertility and mortality. But annual figures derived from registration can reveal that it may be more appropriate to interpret such changes merely as outcomes of the occurrence (or absence) of extreme years within a given decade, rather than reflecting fundamental shifts in underlying levels of fertility and mortality.

Comparison with Other Research

Lastly in this section we inquire how the present results compare with other research. We know of no other demographic study specifically focused on Berar. But given the province's location and predominantly Marathi-speaking population, the present estimates compare favourably with indications of other work. And the general features of Berar's demographic history fit reasonably well with what is known about the demographic development of India.

As previously intimated, Berar's broad decadal pattern of population growth (see Table 1) was shared by the country as a whole. Most regions had negative or near zero growth during 1891 – 1900 and

1911 – 1920, and comparatively fast growth during 1881 – 1890 and 1901 – 1910. The rapid growth of the post-Independence era has been almost universal. Our estimates of average life expectation at birth for decades before 1940 (see Table 6) may seem very low. But in fact they are slightly higher than estimates for all-India provided by Kingsley Davis and later scholars. Interestingly there are occasional references to the comparative longevity of Berar's population in census reports. The Census Commissioners attributed it to the area's relative wealth and advancement.[34]

In our view it is highly significant that Berar lies to the south of the Satpura hills since this assigns it demographically as part of south India. Two features of the province's demography that otherwise might seem rather surprising — namely its moderate levels of fertility and comparatively favourable female mortality — are in fact broadly consistent with south Indian demographic characteristics. Attitudes towards the sexes are well illustrated by the following quotation from the 1910 Akola Gazetteer: 'A son is valued far more highly than a daughter, and perhaps female children are slightly neglected, but on the whole children of both sexes are regarded with great affection.'[35]

Several surveys in the 1950s in the nearby districts of Kolaba, Nasik, Poona and Satara also found only modest levels of fertility. In addition indirect estimates for Maharashtra for recent decades using newer data sources and advanced techniques are broadly similar to our present estimates for Berar. For example, a recent report puts total fertility in Maharashtra in 1961 – 70 at 5.3 live births and male and female life expectations at 49.1 and 49.7 years respectively.[36]

In summary, this section has demonstrated that our vital registration and simulation results are reasonably robust to our principal assumptions, and that basically they agree fairly well with intercensal results. Further, there is nothing obviously incongruous or surprising about our present estimates; they accord reasonably well with other work.

COMMENTARY ON RESULTS

Heavy mortality dominated every aspect of the historical demography of Berar, including its patterns of marriage and fertility. Fig. 1 shows that the period 1881 – 1920 witnessed repeated major mortality crises. In those forty years the annual CDR exceeded 50 deaths per thousand population on four occasions, and the death rate was higher than the birth rate in twelve separate years. The worst years were probably the 1890s when 'calamity begat calamity with unexampled rapidity, culminating in the famine of 1900'.[37] In that single decade the CDR exceeded the CBR five times, and the net effect was a 5 per cent population loss over 1891 – 1900 in spite of continued immigration.

The simulation results allow us to address such facts from a different angle. Thus twice during the 1890s life expectation at birth dropped into the range 15 – 20 years. For example this happened in the famine of 1897, chronicled at the time as resulting from 'high prices rather than . . . scarcity of food.'[38] According to the present estimates life expectation in 1897 fell to only about 17 – 18 years for both men and women (see Appendix).

However, in an *extremely* bad year — such as the great famine of 1900 or the influenza epidemic of 1918 — period life expectation fell to less than ten years.[39] Interestingly, both of these events were double disasters. In July at the height of the famine of 1900, just over 20 per cent of the entire population of Berar was engaged on official relief works.[40] Perhaps not surprisingly then, this famine was accompanied by a major outbreak of cholera. The 1918 influenza epidemic occurred in circumstances where reserve grain stocks were already seriously depleted, partly due to exportation, and prices had already reached famine levels.[41] Interestingly, 1918 is the only year where the data suggest heavier female than male mortality; and the recorded infant mortality rate was about 400 per thousand (see Appendix). In both these great crises epidemic disease and food shortage interacted synergistically at the population level, and it is extremely difficult to discern the independent effect of either. Yet it is worth noting that the level of mortality appears to have recovered faster immediately after 1900 (and 1897) than it did after 1918.

The case of healthy years with no famine or epidemic is also worth considering. According to the Berar Census Commissioner, 1898 was such a time: 'A year of prosperity . . . Rainfall fair . . . Prices fell considerably . . . Public health excellent; no epidemics'.[42] The present estimates put life expectation at birth in 1898 at around 36 – 38 years, and during 1881 – 1920 it exceeded 33 years on nine separate occasions (see Appendix).

Berar's moderate level of fertility was sufficient for rates of natural increase to be positive in most decades, provided there was no extreme crisis. The negative and near zero growth of 1891 – 1900 and 1911 – 20 resulted chiefly from the great mortality peaks of 1900 and 1918. But 1881 – 1890 and 1901 – 1910 were free of very great crisis; consequently rates of natural increase were quite respectable and population growth was further boosted by immigration. The particularly high indicated annual growth rate of 1.8 per cent for 1867 – 1881 certainly reflects immigration, and possibly improved census coverage too. But official records suggest that Berar was free of extreme crisis during this period, so natural increase may well have made a significant contribution.

The moderate rates of population growth between 1921 and 1950 must surely be seen as resulting mainly from the disappearance of major mortality peaks (although 1930, 1931, and 1938 were still years of considerable crisis). This basic point is eloquently made by Fig. 1. Berar's rapid population growth of the post-Independence era occurred on top of earlier gains in the control of both famine and epidemic. Given the synergistic relationship of these two phenomena, improvements in the control of one should also have aided control of the other. This is not the place to document fully these health gains. But in brief, the possibility of very major famine fell after 1900. For example, lean years during the 1920s saw the regular import into the region of wheat from Punjab and even Australia. Mass preventive health measures before 1946 were much less effective than those implemented afterwards. Thus the major killers of malaria and tuberculosis were probably little affected; indeed the latter, especially prevalent in cotton districts, may have increased with greater urbanization and communication. But it is hard to believe that health measures taken before 1946 had no impact. They included: (i) against cholera — inoculation, well disinfection, and provision of protected water supplies during fairs (ii) against smallpox — vaccination and considerable revaccination, and (iii) against plague — inoculation and drives to kill rats.[43]

The 1920s were fairly prosperous. There were good agricultural conditions in most years, and a favourable world price of cotton until 1929 – 30. Table 2 shows that Berar's rate of natural increase in that decade exceeded one per cent per annum; there was also immigration. Circumstances changed during the 1930s and 1940s. Population growth rates were lower, and there was net emigration (see Table 7). Returns from the 1951 census indicate that many of these emigrants were non-agriculturalists. They left to help fuel the growing industrial expansion of Bombay.[44]

Fig. 3 indicates that the mortality levels of the 1920s, 1930s and early 1940s were broadly comparable to those of the 1880s. In each of these periods average life expectation was about 30 years (see Table 5). But as we have intimated, the basis of these similar levels was probably significantly different; some diseases (e.g. tuberculosis) may have increased, while other causes of death (e.g. famine) were reduced. Nevertheless, so far as the first seventy years of our simulation are concerned, there is some suggestion that it is the decades of extreme crisis that represent the exception.

Fig. 3 allows us to locate the start of the major downward trend in Berar's mortality during the mid-1940s. In 1946 DDT spraying began, and paludrine became available for the first time. In the late 1940s there was a rapid increase in anti-malaria units, and in areas where they functioned hospital attendance is reported to have dropped by 60 – 75 per cent within a few years.[45] Our present estimates suggest that life expectation at birth increased by about eight years between 1948 and 1952 (see Appendix). This is not as rapid as in Sri Lanka. But it is sufficient to suggest that dramatic improvement at that time may have been common in the subcontinent. Of course, an equally important event for Berar's subsequent mortality was the final transference of political power in 1947. Since then gains in mortality have been continual. According to the present estimates male and female life expectation during 1971 – 80 were about 55 and 60 years respectively; and at the end of the decade the annual figure for both sexes combined may have exceeded 60 years.[46]

Perhaps our most significant conclusion regarding fertility in the province is that it rarely exceeded moderate levels. Only for brief periods early this century did the average TFR exceed six — and then only slightly. In six of the ten decades under review the TFR was around, or less than, five live births per woman (see Table 5). We consider these results further evidence that Western Europe was not the only pre-transitional region characterized by modest levels of fertility.

Fig. 2 shows that annual birth rate fluctuation was generally rather limited. Excluding years after 1974, the TFR fell below four live births only three times — in 1898, 1900 and 1901. These were all immediate post-famine years. In contrast, while fertility fell in 1919 following the influenza epidemic, it did not do so to anywhere near the same degree. Part of the explanation probably relates to the migration of men in search of work during times of famine. Such migration did not occur in 1918.

Fig. 3 shows a general inverse correlation between birth and death rate variation continuing until around 1945. Since this is also found in the TFR and life expectation estimates, and since the indicated net migration flows are generally relatively small, we can probably discount the proposition that this is simply an age structure effect brought about, for example, by periods of immigration in which young adults were preponderant. Instead, conditions of heavy mortality and morbidity, with their attendant social and economic disruption, would be expected to exert downward pressure on birth rates. In addition to the separation of spouses due to distress migration, likely mechanisms probably included reductions in coital frequency and delays in the onset of cohabitation.

But other factors must have operated to have kept the average level of total fertility at only about five live births. It is unlikely that birth control played any significant role. In the 1920s it was apparently strongly disapproved of in the region, and virtually unknown in rural areas (although a few methods were sold through newspaper advertisements in larger towns).[47] Almost certainly patterns of breast-feeding played a major fertility-limiting role. For example, the 1910 Akola Gazetteer states that 'A child is generally suckled for a year, and often, if there is no other claimant, for two or three years, and sometimes longer still'.[48]

Another factor that certainly depressed the overall level of the province's fertility was widowhood. The statistics in Table 1 show that until comparatively recently the betrothal of very young children was usual. Widow remarriage was undoubtedly possible, particularly among agricultural castes. But it is apparent that often it did not occur; after all, it can lead to difficulties in matters such as inheritance and descent. The result was a high level of widowhood. Averaging across the four censuses from 1901 to 1931, about 6 per cent of Berar's women aged 20 – 29 were classified as widows. For women aged 30 – 39 and 40 – 49 the figures are 18 and 41 per cent respectively. Clearly these statistics imply a major loss of fertility. In 1901 the proportions of women reported as widows in each age group substantially exceeded these average figures, whereas in 1911 the reported proportions were less than these averages.[49] Circumstances during 1901 – 1910 were described by a contemporary source as being of 'monotonous prosperity'.[50] What seems to have happened is that favourable conditions enabled above-average widow remarriage, and hence a period of unusually high average fertility. Clearly in such a population a Malthusian 'preventive check' could operate through variation in the propensity to remarry. Such a rationale may help account for the comparatively high fertility we have estimated for the first three decades of this century. Yet, to reiterate, an average of about five live births per woman was sufficient to produce natural increase in most decades despite heavy mortality.

In Berar, as in the country as a whole, the birth rate seems to have undergone a long-run decline from the high levels prevailing at the start of the century. The slower population growth of the 1930s and 1940s certainly owed something to a reduction in CBR at that time (see Table 6). The simulation results suggest that most of this modest CBR reduction stemmed from a fall in the level of total fertility; a residual element may reflect age structural change following the smaller cohorts produced by the events of 1918 – 20.

Fig. 3 shows that the birth rate rose during the late 1950s and early 1960s. Interestingly, the indicated rise in total fertility between 1951 – 60 and 1961 – 70 is 19 per cent, compared with a rise in the crude birth rate of only 7 per cent. The difference arises because mortality improvements after the mid-1940s reduced the proportion of the population in the prime reproductive years. A reduction in widowhood probably contributed to the pre-decline fertility rise. Lastly, Fig. 3 shows that the start of sustained CBR decline dates from around 1965. This said, it may be more appropriate to locate the onset of demographic transition in the mid-1940s. For it was then that the inverse mould of Berar's traditional demographic regime was well and truly broken (see Fig. 3).[51]

CONCLUSIONS

In this paper we have tried to show that vital registration in Berar over 1881 – 1980 was generally of a high standard. The province had a longstanding reputation for reasonable registration. Local arrangements for recording births and deaths, and checking the system, appear to have been impressive. While obviously there are gaps and defects, the corpus of statistics we have assembled are both internally consistent and plausible given other information. Implied rates of natural increase from registration are in close agreement with population growth rates from the censuses. Intercensal analysis gives similar figures to the registered birth and death rates. In addition the intercensal estimates of life expectation and total fertility are in good accord with the results of the main simulation. Further, we have shown that the present results are not critically dependent upon the assumptions and procedures employed — although no doubt these could be improved.

Perhaps it is natural to ask why registration became so well established in Berar? Did it reflect the province's comparatively advanced level of socio-economic development and its provision of the important crop of cotton? Was the region's administration especially efficient? These considerations are probably relevant. But in our opinion the initial question is somewhat misplaced. The Annual Indian Sanitary Reports suggest that there are quite a few districts in India where registration became well established from soon after its inception. For example, this was true of parts of Punjab and Central Provinces. Certainly in the latter region there are plenty of promising districts for parallel research.[52] Careful exploitation of vital registration data is probably the most promising avenue for increasing our understanding of India's population past, and developing the subject of Indian historical demography. Moreover, the fact that reasonable registration operated in the past has obvious implications as regards the future development of vital registration in India.

However, even so far as Berar is concerned, the present work clearly constitutes only a first step. The statistics forwarded here can provide a framework for further research on many subjects. There is no shortage of supplementary data, particularly as regards mortality. Other topics might include changes in the province's cause of death structure, seasonal and urban-rural differentials, developments in health policy, and interrelations between wage, price and demographic time series. Surely a full understanding of contemporary demographic change must involve both time-series data and a historical perspective. When both are employed the onset of transition may often be detected much earlier than either cross-sectional survey or census data suggest. Thus in Fig. 3 it is the mid-1940s that mark the end of the traditional pattern of demographic variation in Berar.

Finally, research such as this can provide contrasts for the study of demographic behaviour in other world regions. In the first fifty years analysed here Berar's demography was dominated by heavy mortality and periodic extreme crisis — circumstances often different from those uncovered by historical demographers working on Europe. Interestingly, levels of fertility prevailing in both Western Europe and South India appear to have been broadly similar. Yet moderate fertility in both was attained in different ways. It seems likely that future research on Indian historical demography will find mechanisms of adaptation — such as alterations in widow remarriage rates — that were also specific to the region's past demographic circumstances.

NOTES TO CHAPTER 6

1 Census of India, 1891, Volume VI, *Berar or the Hyderabad Assigned Districts*, Office of the Superintendent of Government Printing, Calcutta, 1892, p. (i).
2 See for example, P. N. Mari Bhat, S. Preston and T. Dyson, *Vital Rates in India, 1961 – 1981*, National Academy Press, Washington, D.C., 1984; and S. B. Mukherjee, *The Age Distribution of the Indian Population*, East-West Center, Honolulu, 1976.
3 Our description of Berar is drawn mainly from census reports; see especially Census of India, 1901, Volume VIII, *Berar*, Part I, Report, Pioneer Press, Allahabad, 1902, pp. 1 – 5; and Census of India, 1931, Volume XII, *Central Provinces and Berar*, Part I — Report, Government Printing, Central Provinces, Nagpur, 1933, pp. 13 – 22. We have also used the relevant District Gazetteers.
4 Census of India, 1881, *Report on the Census of Berar, 1881*, printed at the Education Society's Press, Byculla, Bombay, 1882, pp. 34 – 5.
5 The original six districts were named Amraoti, Akola, Ellichpur, Buldana, Wun and Basim. Until 1903 the 'population under registration' in Berar covered slightly over 98 per cent of the province's population, but excluded the rugged, hilly Melghat *taluk* in Ellichpur.
6 *Fifteenth Annual Report of the Sanitary Commissioner with the Government of India for 1878*, Office of the Superintendent of Government Printing, Calcutta, 1880, p. 65.

7   For these quotations see *Fifteenth Annual Report of the Sanitary Commissioner with the Government of India for 1878*, cited in note 6, p. 64; and the *Twentieth Annual Report of the Sanitary Commissioner with the Government of India for 1883*, Office of the Superintendent of Government Printing, Calcutta, 1884, p. 107.

8   For more on the problems with the migration tables, and also the quotations cited, see Census of India, 1891, cited in note 1, pp. xiv – xv.

9   See Census of India, 1901, cited in note 3, pp. 32 – 4.

10 See *Annual Report of the Sanitary Commissioner with the Government of India for 1895*, Office of the Superintendent of Government Printing, Calcutta, 1896, p. 96.

11 This quotation and most of the details in this paragraph are taken from Census of India, 1901, cited in note 3, p. 33.

12 See Census of India, 1931, cited in note 3, pp. 138 – 9; and Census of India, 1951, Volume VII, *Madhya Pradesh*, Part 1 – A, Report, Government Printing, Madhya Pradesh, Nagpur, 1953, pp. 366 – 70. See also note 46 below.

13 A list of all data sources is given in the notes to Table 2. A few additional points should be made: (i) prior to 1903 slight adjustments were made to denominators to allow for Melghat's exclusion (see note 5); (ii) although our CBRs and CDRs for 1941 – 5 and 1947 are derived from average figures for 1941 – 5 and 1943 – 7, the availability of rates for 1946 and 1948 permits us to 'solve' separately for 1941 – 2, 1943 – 5 and 1947; (iii) Akola was excluded in weighting district CDRs for 1952 because the published figure (11.4) was obviously faulty; and (iv) although for years from 1957 onwards total numbers of vital events in each district are published, when combined with the published district population totals they do not give the published official CBRs and CDRs. Often the discrepancies are large; clearly they do not arise simply because the denominators employed have been adjusted for intercensal growth. One possibility is that the official rates relate to a subset of registration areas within each district. Whatever the cause, the inconsistency led us to adopt the straightforward procedure of simply using the published official figures.

14 To quote Benjamin Franklin, Sanitary Commissioner with the Government of India in 1902: '. . . in 1900, the year before the census was taken, the number of births recorded in Berar was 89,302, while in 1902 the number was 154,954; in 1902 the death rate of infants, calculated on the census figure was 620.1 per 1000 among males and 523.3 among females, whereas the corresponding figures, calculated upon the numbers born during the year, were 203.8 and 182.9', see *Annual Report of the Sanitary Commissioner with the Government of India for 1902*, Office of the Superintendent of Government Printing, Calcutta, 1903, pp. 59 – 60.

15 Some additional points relating to the infant mortality series are as follows: (i) for the separation factor used here to compute IMRs see G. W. Barclay, *Techniques of Population Analysis*, John Wiley and Sons, New York, 1958, p. 140; (ii) data to calculate IMRs for 1881 and 1882 was not

published, so estimates were obtained using the following linear regressions relating sex-specific IMRs to CDRs for years 1883 – 1911: IMR(m)=0.104+3.521.(CDRm), and IMR(f)=0.072+4.019.(CDRf). The correlation coefficients are 0.894 and 0.897 respectively; (iii) Akola's IDR (53.36) was excluded from the weighting for 1952 (see note 13); and (iv) due to considerations of data availability we had to use IDRs for 1946, 1957, 1976, 1977 and 1980; at times of increasing size of annual birth cohorts computed IDRs tend to be slightly lower than IMRs. So where we have used IDRs they may marginally understate the levels of infant mortality prevailing.

16 The IMR of 198 for 1947 also results from linear interpolation between rates for 1946 and 1948.

17 Unfortunately it did not prove feasible to apply 'growth balance' methods to the distribution of deaths by age in Berar to get an independent check on the level of death registration. The procedure was attempted using census data of 1911, 1921 and 1931. But the available registration tabulations centring on these years allow comparison of only eight sets of partial birth and death rates. When graphed these deviate markedly from linearity, so the slope (i.e. correction factor for the level of death reporting) is highly dependent upon the inclusion or exclusion of particular points. Probable reasons for the method's failure here include (i) very poor age reporting, both of the living and the dead, (ii) migration-effects on the age structure and (iii) deviation of the population from a stable or quasi-stable state.

18 For this argument, and the corollary that India actually experienced a decline in its rate of population growth between 1961 – 70 and 1971 – 80, see for example, T. Dyson, 'The Preliminary Demography of the 1981 Census', *Economic and Political Weekly*, Volume XVI, Number 33, August, 1981.

19 For the first quotation in this paragraph see, Census of India, 1921, Volume XI, *Central Provinces and Berar*, Part I, Report, Government Press, Nagpur, 1923, p. 6. For the second quotation see, Census of India, 1901, cited in note 3, p. 31.

20 These broad conclusions on age errors are not dependent upon the particular choice of model used for comparison.

21 The 1881 census showed 234,129 males and 201,574 females (19.5 per cent of the total population) born outside Berar. Noting that the overall population sex ratio was 1.071 (see Table 1) the 1881 census report remarks: 'Deducting the immigrants there are 105 males to 100 females'. It also states that 'Immigration, chiefly of an agricultural nature, affects the age-returns between the ages of 20 and 40', see Census of India, 1881, cited in note 4 p. 98 and p. 100. The 1901 census report for Central Provinces refers to 'a large temporary movement to Berar exactly at the time when the census takes place, and there is no means of estimating what proportion of the total return should be assigned to this special influx', see Census of India, 1901, *Central Provinces*, Part I, Report, printed at the Secretariat Press, Nagpur, 1902, p. 131. On the prominent role of female labour in the region's agricultural operations see, for example, A. E.

Nelson (ed.), *Buldana District*, printed at the Baptist Mission Press, Calcutta, 1910.

22 The reported 1881 age distribution has 37.8 per cent aged under 15 and 15.4 per cent aged 45+. Accordingly the three parameter model selected (shown in Table 3) has 38 per cent under 15, 16 per cent 45+, and a growth rate of 0.5 per cent per annum. For the model population tables see N. Carrier and J. Hobcraft, *Demographic Estimation for Developing Societies*, published by the Population Investigation Committee, London, 1971. We stress that neither the main simulation results nor our conclusions regarding deviations in the 1881 data are seriously affected either by use of a stable model, or by selection of a particular model within any reasonable range.

23 See the age-splitting coefficients in Carrier and Hobcraft cited in note 22. Note that there is three months displacement between the census totals and the total population figures of the projection.

24 For the logit life table system see for example, W. Brass, 'On the Scale of Mortality' in *Biological Aspects of Demography*, (Symposia of the Society for the Study of Human Biology, Vol. X), London: Taylor and Francis, 1971; see also Carrier and Hobcraft cited in note 22.

25 For the West model, and also an example of its use on 1911 census data for India, see A. J. Coale, P. Demeny and B. Vaughan, *Regional Model Life Tables and Stable Populations*, Second Edition, Academic Press, London 1983. I am indebted to Barbara Vaughan for access to single year versions of the West model up to age one hundred. Mukherjee cited in note 2 also employs the West.

26 A sex ratio at birth (m/f) of 1.05 was assumed throughout.

27 For this model see B. Zaba, 'Use of the Relational Gompertz Model in Analysing Fertility Data Collected in Retrospective Surveys', Centre for Population Studies Working Paper No. 8, London School of Hygiene and Tropical Medicine, 1981.

28 For use of the South pattern on recent Indian data see Bhat *et al.* cited in note 2. On the doubt that the South pattern prevailed in earlier decades see chapter 4 of the present volume, and P. N. Mari Bhat, 'Age Patterns of Mortality and Estimates of Birth and Death Rates in India', paper presented to the New Delhi Workshop of the Panel on India, of the Committee on Population and Demography, National Academy of Sciences, Washington, 1979. See also the references cited in note 25.

29 See Bhat *et al.* cited in note 2, especially pp. 106–22. Also on forward and reverse survival see United Nations, *Manual IV — Methods of Estimating Basic Demographic Measures from Incomplete Data*, Population Studies No. 42, New York, 1967. The intercensal analysis used the same model fertility distribution as the main simulation, see note 27.

30 See United Nations cited in note 29.

31 See Census of India, 1901, cited in note 3, p. 6. See pp. 31–2 of the same publication for a description of the rapid improvement of conditions in late 1900. Some suggestion that the intercensal analysis may be mainly responsible for the discrepancy for the 1901–10 decade comes from the summary age data in Table 4. The sizeable expansion of the population

aged 45+ in 1911 could account for the apparent deviations of the intercensal estimates.

32 This result could be consistent with, though not necessarily indicative of, a greater tendency to underregister female deaths.

33 They might be indicative of relatively poor census coverage in 1971. The indications are that the 1971 count deteriorated especially for females. In this context the relatively high overall 1971 census sex ratio of 1.057 in Table 1 is interesting; so too is the larger implied net female annual emigration for 1961 – 70 in Table 7; see also note 18.

34 See K. Davis, *The Population of India and Pakistan*, Princeton University Press, Princeton, New Jersey, 1951, pp. 33 – 7; also Mukherjee cited in note 2, pp. 220 – 33. On the similar population growth paths of the former British districts of Gujarat, Deccan, Karnatak, and Konkan see M. B. McAlpin, *Subject to Famine*, Princeton University Press, Princeton, New Jersey, 1983, p. 52. On the relatively high life expectation in the Maratha Plain division (of which Berar formed a major part) and the apparent fact that females outlived males, see for example, Census of India, 1931, cited in note 12, pp. 119 – 25.

35 See C. Brown (ed.), *Akola District*, printed at the Baptist Mission Press, Calcutta, 1910, p. 142.

36 On the importance of the Satpura hills and the south Indian demographic regime see T. Dyson and M. Moore, 'On Kinship Structure, Female Autonomy and Demographic Behavior in India', *Population and Development Review*, Volume 9, No. 1, March 1983; see also T. Dyson, 'India's Regional Demography', *World Health Statistics Quarterly*, Volume 27, No. 2, 1984. On the surveys see V. Sovani and K. Dandekar, *Fertility Survey of Nasik, Kolaba and Satara (North) Districts*, Gokhale Institute of Politics and Economics, Publication No. 31, Poona 1955, and V. M. Dandekar and K. Dandekar, *Survey of Fertility and Mortality in Poona District*, Gokhale Institute of Politics, Publication No. 27, Poona, 1953. But for a study of Nagpur district that found higher fertility see E. Driver, *Differential Fertility in Central India*, Princeton University Press, Princeton, New Jersey, 1963. On the estimates for Maharashtra see Bhat *et al.* cited in note 2.

37 See Census of India, 1921, Volume XI, *Central Provinces and Berar*, Part I — Report, Government Press, Nagpur, 1923, p. 4.

38 See Census of India, 1901, cited in note 3, p. 30. This is just one of many 'modern' observations to be found in these early census reports.

39 Our estimates of life expectation for 1918 are encouragingly close to those derived by Mills using different estimation procedures; see chapter 8 of the present volume.

40 See Census of India, 1901, cited in note 3, p. 31.

41 See Census of India, 1921, cited in note 37, p. 5.

42 See Census of India, 1901, cited in note 3, p. 29.

43 Plague seems to have lost much of its virulence after about 1920. For a fuller documentation of health measures see especially, Census of India, 1951, cited in note 12, pp. 41 – 7.

44 See Census of India, 1951, cited in note 12, pp. 27 – 8.

45 See Census of India, 1951, cited in note 12, p. 42.
46 Recall that for years after 1940 the sex differential in mortality is assumed rather than empirically-based. Our procedure of adding one point to gain the male CDR, and subtracting one point to gain the female CDR, may exaggerate any female mortality advantage of recent years. While the male CDR exceeded that of females by two points on average over 1881 – 1940, the registration data suggests that such male mortality excess was particularly great when the overall mortality level was particularly high (i.e. during decades 1891 – 1900 and 1911 – 20). Hence a two point CDR differential may be too large for contemporary conditions. Also, some of the most recent estimates of life expectation in the Appendix may well be biased upwards if, as some believe, registration coverage deteriorated in the early 1970s as *panchayats* played a greater role in the registration system (K. Srikantan, personal communication). Registration of infant deaths may have deteriorated somewhat earlier.
47 See Census of India, 1931, cited in note 12, p. 25.
48 See Brown (ed.) cited in note 35, p. 73.
49 In 1901 the corresponding figures are 8, 22 and 48 per cent. In 1911 it is not possible to isolate data for Berar alone by these age groups. But for Central Provinces and Berar (combined) in 1911, the figures are 4, 15 and 38 per cent.
50 See S. V. Fitzgerald and A. E. Nelson (eds.), *Amraoti District*, Caxton Works Press, Bombay, 1911, p. 149.
51 Note from Table 1 that female marriage patterns may have begun to change in the period immediately before 1941. It is clear that the origins of demographic transition, as it relates to mortality, fertility and marriage, are located before 1951 in this population.
52 They include Nagpur, Bhandara, Wardha, Chanda, Balaghat, Jabalpur, Saugor, Mandla, Hoshangabad, Nimar, Betul, Chhindwara, Raipur and Bilaspur. For profitable use of registration data for some other areas see McAlpin, cited in note 34. We suspect it might be possible, with considerable work, to produce long-run demographic time series for as many as fifty Indian districts.

APPENDIX TO CHAPTER 6

Annual Demographic Measures for Berar, 1881–1980

Year	Population (000's)	Adjusted CBR	Adjusted CDR	Total Fertility TFR	Infant Mortality Rate male	Infant Mortality Rate female	Life Expectation male	Life Expectation female
1881	2,673	39.9	29.1	5.18	210	185	32.8	34.1
1882	2,701	41.7	29.1	5.42	210	186	33.0	34.2
1883	2,735	39.7	54.3	5.15	296	285	18.6	17.9
1884	2,695	40.4	24.1	5.24	194	186	37.5	38.0
1885	2,739	41.7	33.1	5.41	217	203	29.7	30.9
1886	2,763	35.9	35.3	4.66	232	219	27.8	28.2
1887	2,764	38.5	43.1	4.98	226	211	23.8	23.8
1888	2,752	39.1	23.4	5.05	180	169	37.8	38.8
1889	2,795	37.2	39.9	4.79	244	227	24.7	25.4
1890	2,787	39.6	33.0	5.09	227	208	29.1	30.1
1891	2,897	42.8	40.7	5.51	241	225	24.7	25.2
1892	2,904	39.7	28.9	5.10	202	181	32.5	34.1
1893	2,935	39.1	32.7	5.01	206	195	29.7	31.0
1894	2,954	33.3	42.0	4.22	249	229	23.0	24.2
1895	2,928	37.2	49.8	4.66	269	255	19.3	19.9
1896	2,891	38.2	43.7	4.74	224	204	22.4	23.9
1897	2,875	39.7	52.6	4.88	313	306	17.0	18.6
1898	2,837	31.3	23.4	3.81	179	166	36.0	37.9
1899	2,860	50.3	39.8	6.13	272	251	24.4	25.7
1900	2,890	31.4	82.4	3.77	416	413	8.7	9.2
1901	2,754	30.8	27.7	3.63	198	182	31.8	32.7
1902	2,763	41.4	32.5	4.86	297	266	27.4	28.8

1903	2,787	47.2	40.9	5.55	278	253	23.7	24.9
1904	2,805	53.6	36.1	6.34	215	198	28.6	29.6
1905	2,854	51.6	40.4	6.18	276	249	26.0	26.8
1906	2,886	50.4	51.9	6.06	265	239	20.7	21.0
1907	2,881	49.1	47.5	5.91	263	243	22.5	22.7
1908	2,886	49.3	33.8	5.97	236	205	30.1	31.5
1909	2,931	49.8	32.5	6.09	227	185	30.7	33.5
1910	2,981	47.5	46.0	5.85	293	248	22.2	24.0
1911	3,057	50.1	36.7	6.29	239	197	27.5	30.2
1912	3,098	49.1	48.6	6.24	331	274	20.3	23.1
1913	3,100	49.4	30.6	6.37	247	204	31.3	34.9
1914	3,158	51.2	40.6	6.70	308	251	24.6	27.5
1915	3,191	47.8	34.1	6.35	250	211	29.2	31.5
1916	3,235	43.0	47.3	5.79	281	238	21.2	22.6
1917	3,221	45.4	38.1	6.19	248	211	25.8	28.0
1918	3,244	40.0	111.3	5.45	429	373	6.3	5.9
1919	3,013	36.8	38.0	4.98	283	245	23.5	25.6
1920	3,010	43.4	29.6	5.88	236	191	30.2	33.1
1921	3,075	41.2	38.0	5.65	271	223	24.5	26.8
1922	3,085	38.3	31.0	5.19	254	211	29.0	31.5
1923	3,107	48.7	31.8	6.56	221	185	30.1	32.1
1924	3,160	44.3	37.7	5.91	279	226	25.4	28.0
1925	3,181	45.6	30.3	6.02	237	196	31.3	33.5
1926	3,229	46.1	35.8	6.02	280	229	27.3	29.0
1927	3,262	44.1	30.4	5.69	231	189	31.4	33.5
1928	3,307	45.0	28.7	5.75	243	196	32.5	35.4
1929	3,361	44.3	33.2	5.61	256	211	29.2	31.3

Year	Population (000's)	Adjusted CBR	Adjusted CDR	Total Fertility TFR	Infant Mortality Rate male	Infant Mortality Rate female	Life Expectation male	Life Expectation female
1930	3,398	43.7	40.1	5.48	284	232	24.6	26.2
1931	3,442	45.9	43.5	5.79	319	267	22.8	23.5
1932	3,450	44.9	24.8	5.67	195	163	36.8	38.8
1933	3,519	43.6	28.8	5.53	229	192	33.0	35.0
1934	3,571	41.2	32.5	5.26	283	244	29.3	30.9
1935	3,603	43.9	35.6	5.62	248	216	28.0	28.6
1936	3,633	38.4	38.0	4.92	266	228	25.8	26.6
1937	3,634	36.1	31.3	4.64	222	192	30.2	31.2
1938	3,651	39.8	43.0	5.09	284	249	22.5	23.1
1939	3,640	36.2	30.3	4.61	213	186	30.7	32.1
1940	3,661	36.7	29.6	4.65	228	197	30.9	32.4
1941	3,605	41.2	28.9	5.21	210	210	32.1	33.6
1942	3,649	41.2	28.9	5.19	208	208	32.5	34.0
1943	3,694	36.8	36.2	4.61	206	206	27.5	28.2
1944	3,697	36.8	36.2	4.56	204	204	27.3	28.0
1945	3,699	36.8	36.2	4.53	202	202	27.3	27.9
1946	3,702	40.0	28.2	4.89	200	200	32.7	34.2
1947	3,745	36.8	36.2	4.48	198	198	27.4	28.1
1948	3,747	36.8	36.5	4.44	196	196	27.2	27.9
1949	3,749	41.8	29.2	5.03	165	165	32.7	34.0
1950	3,796	37.6	26.5	4.52	160	160	34.8	36.5
1951	3,784	37.1	27.6	4.47	151	151	34.0	35.6
1952	3,820	42.6	26.3	5.16	123	123	36.0	37.7
1953	3,882	41.4	25.4	5.05	145	145	36.3	38.3
1954	3,945	40.1	24.5	4.93	145	145	37.0	39.1
1955	4,006	38.9	23.6	4.81	145	145	37.6	39.9

1956	4,067	37.7	22.7	4.69	145	145	38.2	40.7
1957	4,128	36.4	21.9	4.55	158	158	38.6	41.3
1958	4,188	34.5	23.1	4.33	164	164	37.1	39.5
1959	4,236	36.0	18.3	4.53	115	115	42.8	46.0
1960	4,311	39.2	16.4	4.98	103	103	45.5	49.2
1961	4,580	39.8	20.9	5.22	119	119	40.6	43.6
1962	4,667	39.9	19.4	5.29	127	127	42.0	45.5
1963	4,763	45.7	19.4	6.14	116	116	42.7	46.2
1964	4,888	43.2	17.9	5.88	113	113	44.6	48.5
1965	5,011	45.6	15.8	6.29	96	96	47.4	51.8
1966	5,160	42.2	18.9	5.90	108	108	43.6	47.3
1967	5,280	38.8	17.0	5.46	113	113	45.3	49.5
1968	5,395	41.4	14.3	5.86	95	95	48.9	53.7
1969	5,541	37.5	15.3	5.33	81	81	47.7	52.0
1970	5,664	36.9	13.3	5.26	73	73	50.3	55.1
1971	5,729	37.4	11.5	5.40	73	73	52.7	58.3
1972	5,878	32.8	11.8	4.74	73	73	52.1	57.4
1973	6,000	28.8	13.3	4.16	79	79	49.5	54.4
1974	6,093	26.3	10.2	3.79	59	59	54.2	60.0
1975	6,192	30.7	10.2	4.40	63	63	54.4	60.2
1976	6,319	28.7	9.8	4.11	59	59	55.1	61.0
1977	6,438	25.8	10.9	3.67	69	69	53.0	58.7
1978	6,534	24.4	7.9	3.43	51	51	58.4	65.1
1979	6,641	25.6	9.4	3.54	61	61	55.9	62.1
1980	6,749	23.4	6.8	3.18	44	44	61.0	68.3

Notes: (1) In every census year the population size is pro-rated to correspond to the census total. (2) As elsewhere, crude birth and death rates are per thousand population. Total fertility is expressed per woman. The infant mortality rates are per thousand live births.

7

POPULATION DYNAMICS OF FAMINE IN NINETEENTH CENTURY PUNJAB, 1896 – 7 AND 1899 – 1900

Deborah Guz

In the closing years of the nineteenth century, parts of the Punjab were affected by two famines which, in their turn, were each to be called 'the worst of the century'.[1] The first, in 1896 – 7 was a general one which prevailed over much of India, in the North West Provinces, Oudh, Bengal, Madras, the Central Provinces, Berar and Bombay, as well as the Punjab. The more severe famine in 1899 – 1900 was much less widespread, occurring in the Central Provinces, Berar, Ajmer, Bombay and the Punjab. While other districts of the Punjab suffered from scarcity of varying degrees, distress in Hissar district was reported to be by far the worst in both cases, its intensity matching that of the most acutely suffering areas of India.[2] Both famines were precipitated by drought and both were preceded by years of bad harvests. The two crises cannot be studied separately. While the durations of food shortage were distinct, their demographic impacts spread over many years and the effects of the two famines overlapped.

This paper will examine the famines in Hissar. First the events of the famines will be explored, and then the mechanisms of their effects and the adequacy of the government's attempts to deal with them will be discussed.

The basic sources for this study are the Punjab Famine Reports of 1896 – 7 and 1899 – 1900, and the annual Sanitary Reports which include vital registration statistics. The demographic analysis will rely mainly on registration data. While it is appreciated that these data are probably deficient due to underreporting and lateness of reporting, it is assumed here that the types and levels of deficiency are constant before, during and after the famines.[3] It is therefore presumed valid to use the unadjusted data for purposes of comparison and identifying trends and patterns.

In the examination of births and deaths absolute numbers of events are used more often than rates. This is because figures for population totals and age distributions exist only for the census years of 1891 and

1901. It is difficult to make any estimate of the population in intercensal years, because while much migration to seek employment and food was reported for both famines, there are no data on its magnitude. Where rates are used, they are based on the 1891 population for the years 1891 – 1900 and on the 1901 population for subsequent years.

THE FAMINES IN HISSAR

Hissar was one of the seven districts of the Delhi Division of what was formerly the southern Punjab, and is now Haryana. An area of flat plains, it had four towns and sixty-four villages in 1891, with a population of 776,006, about 84 per cent of which was rural.

Hissar has two rainy seasons, the main one being the summer monsoon lasting from July to September, and two harvests a year, the main *kharif* harvest of October providing 70 per cent of the normal annual crop, and the secondary *rabi* harvest of March and April.[4] Both harvests are dependent on the summer monsoon, for the maturing of the kharif, and the sowing of both crops. The rabi crop also requires winter rains in December and January for the completion of sowing and the maintenance of the planted crop.

The area experiences great seasonal and annual variations in temperature and rainfall, and consequently variation in annual harvests, mitigated partly by the extension of irrigation. Normally Hissar was a net exporter of foodgrains, and wheat was the staple crop of the province.

The agricultural year in the Punjab runs from October to September. Fig. 1 presents data on harvests and prices for the period of the famines. The harvests of 1892 – 5 in Hissar were good, and their average acreage will be used as an indicator of normal yield. The following year had very poor kharif and rabi harvests, 30 per cent and 46 per cent of normal respectively. However, despite these severe failures there was no acute scarcity owing to the stocks built up over the previous good years. In 1896 the monsoon arrived late, and by August there was almost no rain. Crops already in the ground dried out and sowings were reduced. Consequently the kharif of 1896 was even worse than that of the previous year, yielding only 25 per cent of normal acreage. Pasture and fodder crops for cattle also failed.

By now stocks were exhausted necessitating foodgrain imports. Prices shot up, those of all foodgrains converging, to the highest levels ever recorded. The government refused to intervene to regulate prices. It was the 'policy of British Government to let grain pass freely from one place to another, trusting that the interest of the grain dealers will always lead them to send it to the place where it is dearest, that is to say,

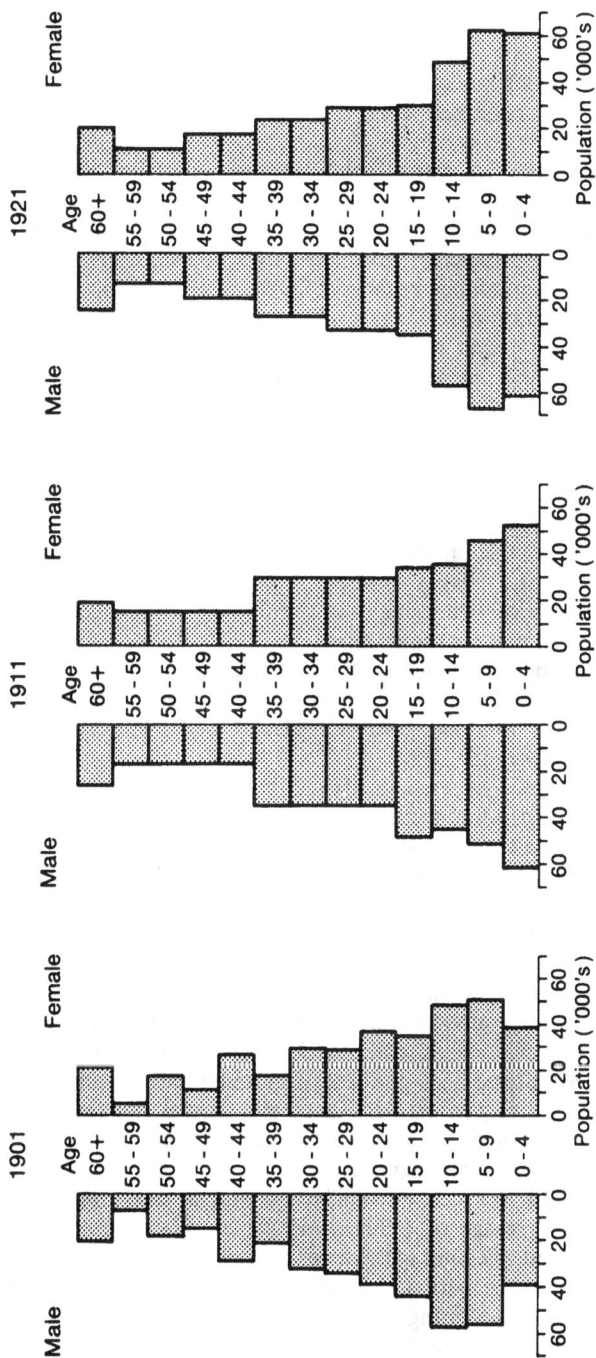

Fig.3 Census Population Pyramids, 1901, 1911, 1921

to the place at which it is most needed.'[5] The highest price of wheat was reached in December and after that the wheat price continued to fluctuate at a high level.

By November famine was officially recognized and relief measures were instituted. The major part of famine relief was public works, with attendant camps to house workers, which provided employment to those who had insufficient resources to buy food, and there were also poor-houses and gratuitous relief for those unable to work.

The rains failed again in January 1897, although, with the exception of Delhi Division, the Punjab received adequate supplies of winter rain and consequently a reasonable rabi harvest. The rabi in Hissar, however, was again very poor. Prices fell a little because of the availability of food imports from adjacent areas within Punjab, but the numbers on relief continued to rise until the maximum in July, and there were no signs of the easing of distress. June and July were the worst months of all, with intense heat and dry water tanks, and over 10 per cent of the population was on relief. Although there are no figures for migration, most villages were partly deserted by this stage of the famine, and much wandering was observed, with a few deaths occurring on the roadside from thirst.

Cattle died due to the dearth of fodder, even though government forests were opened for free grazing. An estimated 92 per cent of plough and well cattle, alive in April 1895, had died or been transported from Hissar by October 1897.

The monsoon of 1897 arrived late in Hissar, but it eventually broke on 12 July, causing an immediate decline in the numbers on relief due to the demand for agricultural labour, boosted by government loans to enable farmers to take full advantage of sowing conditions. The kharif crop of 1897 was extremely good with an increase of 391 per cent on that of the previous year.

The famine was over. Hissar's Deputy Commissioner noted that patience and resignation had been prevalent during the famine and there had been no increase in violent crime, or grain riots.[6] He also observed that village menials, while forming 25.1 per cent of the district's population, constituted 46.3 per cent of those on relief.[7] According to this official, suffering might have been still greater but for the help some people received from others in adjacent non-famine tracts, connected by ties of caste and marriage.[8]

Harvests in 1897 – 8 were good in Hissar with the total crop being 94 per cent of the average of 1892 – 5. However, the poor harvests of 1898 – 9 followed, yielding only 25 per cent of the normal crop. Since stocks had only been partially replenished during 1897 – 8, scarcity began to be felt in the spring of 1899. Although the monsoon of 1899 arrived with adequate rainfall in June, it was very scanty in July, and by August there was total drought. The consequent failure of the kharif was complete, producing only 9 per cent of the normal crop.

Due to lack of rain there was almost no grass in Hissar and water was scarce. Many cattle died, or were killed for meat, as their owners were unable to feed them. This temporary abundance of cheap meat mitigated the effects of grain shortage for some people, but the dominant Hindu population did not eat meat, and this benefit was far outweighed by the massive loss of milch and plough cattle. An estimated 43 per cent of the animals were lost in the famine.

The presence of wandering immigrants from neighbouring Indian states provided an early warning of impending disaster, and famine was declared in September. Famine relief measures were implemented and the numbers on relief rose progressively to a maximum of 161,561, over one-fifth of Hissar's population, on 3 March 1900.

Prices began to rise in August, reaching their highest level in November. However, the rise was much less than in 1896 – 7, as the later famine was less widespread (see Fig. 1). From November prices dropped slightly and stabilized for the rest of the famine.

Due to the monsoon failure the rabi sowings were only one quarter of the previous year's. The further failure of the winter rains assured a poor harvest and the rabi of 1900 was only 13 per cent of normal. Nevertheless, irrigated areas of Hissar, and other areas of the Punjab, had reasonable harvests and so a nearby source of food, easily transported by rail, became available. Furthermore, the numbers on relief during the rabi dropped because alternative employment was afforded by harvesting crops in the irrigated tracts of Hissar.

After the rabi harvest numbers on relief rose again until 14 July 1900 when they amounted to 111,573. On this day the late rains finally arrived, and from the end of July, Hissar received sufficient rain. People began to leave relief works to sow kharif crops, using government loans for buying seed and equipment. The large relief works were finally closed on 31 August. Other forms of relief were terminated in the middle of October.

During the famine there had been an increase in petty theft in Hissar district, but none in serious crime.[9] Officials noted the courage and patience with which people had borne their suffering, and the way people helped each other.[10] That this famine had a greater impact than the earlier one is illustrated by the fact that landowners showed a greater tendency to seek relief in 1899 – 1900. The Deputy Commissioner of Hissar observed, in December 1900 that many 'formerly well to do, but . . . reduced in circumstances by the former scarcity, have now been ruined.'[11]

DEMOGRAPHIC IMPACT OF THE FAMINES

Fig. 1 presents quarterly births and deaths for 1893 – 1903, as well as harvest output and wheat prices, all on the same time scale, to illustrate the temporal response of births and deaths to the famines.

Mortality

The years 1893 and 1894 did not appear to suffer any mortality crisis and therefore the mortality in these years will be used as an indicator of normal mortality in Hissar. Using mortality as an indicator of the severity of the crisis it appears that the famine of 1899 – 1900 was about twice as bad as the earlier famine. It is immediately seen from Fig. 1 that the number of deaths shot up not only during the famines, but that there was a lag of mortality behind food shortage, and deaths continued to increase to their highest levels immediately after the food shortage had ended. Clearly, most of the mortality increase occurred in the second calendar year of each famine, as Table 1 confirms. In both cases the peak number of deaths actually occurred in October, the month when good harvests arrived breaking the famine, and the number of deaths continued to remain very high throughout the last quarter of the year. In 1897 there was an increase of 75 per cent on normal, with an excess of 15,214 deaths.[12] In 1900 the number of deaths was almost four times normal, the excess being 54,862. It is not very surprising that there was only a relatively small increase in deaths in the first calendar year, 28 per cent in the first famine, and 14 per cent in the second, since severe famine only set in during the last part of those years.

The mortality experience of the post-famine years varied substantially in the two cases. While, after the former less severe famine, mortality declined immediately to an almost normal level in 1898, with an index value of 107 (index = 100 for normal mortality), it had as high an index value as 171 in 1901, which only gradually declined to 135 by 1904 (see Table 1). Unfortunately, it is very difficult to disentangle the effects of famine on the mortality of 1903 and 1904 which were very unhealthy years in the whole Punjab, both in areas which had and had not experienced scarcity, with the highest mortality ever yet recorded. The death rate in Hissar was in fact ten and fourteen points respectively below the provincial rates in these two heavy mortality years. It would therefore be unwarranted to attribute the high mortality of these years to the famine of 1899 – 1900. However, the mortality of 1901 and 1902 cannot be dissociated from this famine with deaths in 1901 almost as high as in 1897. It is clear that the much more severe famine of

Table 1. Total Deaths in Hissar, 1893 – 1903

| | | Number of Deaths | |
	Total	Excess	Index*
Year			
1893	19233	– 703	96
1894	20639	703	104
1895	21339	1403	107
1896	25541	5605	128
1897	35150	15214	176
1898	21501	1565	107
1899	22726	2790	114
1900	74798	54862	375
1901	34159	14223	171
1902	30950	11014	155
1903	29786	9850	149

*Index 100 is average for 1893 and 1894.

Source: Report on the Sanitary Administration of the Punjab (various years).

1899 – 1900 had mortality consequences long after it had terminated. In both famines the period of food shortage was not identical to the period of resultant mortality. The fatal results of the famines appear to have worked through an initial starvation phase and a later epidemic phase.[13] This is particularly well illustrated by the two mortality peaks of the later famine (see Fig. 1). To investigate the working of these phases it is necessary to look at the causes of death over time.

Cause of Death

Great care must be taken in interpreting cause of death data since the cause of death was not always diagnosed correctly,[14] and the chaukidars (village watchmen) who kept the records often did not bother to probe to find the exact cause of death.[15] Moreover, the data are likely to be particularly error prone in a mortality crisis. Officials were often sent to check the returns and found much misreporting. For example, on checking deaths in the Hissar tahsil (administrative subdivision of a district) it was found that only 82 out of 187 cholera deaths were

correctly reported between 1 April and 12 May 1900, while the actual
number of 90 fever deaths in the same period was reported as 194.[16]
Although the forms for death returns had a heading for deaths from
starvation it was found impossible to distinguish between 'deaths from
starvation and deaths accelerated by privation'.[17] 'Typical starvation
deaths show other identifiable symptoms at the final stages'.[18]
Consequently, very few deaths were reported in the starvation
category.

Fig. 2 and Table 2 present cause of death data for the worst mortality
years. As in normal years, the bulk of deaths were attributed to fevers,
but deaths increased in all categories, especially cholera and diarrhoea
and dysentery. Fevers form a very general category, usually dominated
by malaria, but also including influenza, measles and typhoid, among
other diseases. During the famines malaria was absent due to the failure
of the rains. So, according to the Punjab Government, most fever
deaths in the famine period were caused directly by the famine. It was
claimed that the high mortality in Hissar was due to 'the prevalence of
some fatal types of fever other than malarial fevers, aggravated by the
debilitating effects of want of food'.[19] Findings of officials suggest that
these types of fever were predominantly Malta and enteric fever. Other
fevers observed during the famine of 1899 – 1900 included pneumonia
and measles. The extremely cold winter of that year, combined with
crowding in camps and people's general weakness, brought on
conditions such as these.

The fever deaths which accounted for the highest quarterly mortality
of the famines, in October to December 1900, however, were largely
due to malaria outbreaks caused by the coming of the rains. 'When
famine is due to drought malaria is not usually rampant at the same
time, but is often deadly on a particularly large scale when the rains
finally come'.[20]

Fever deaths returned to pre-famine levels in 1898 and 1899, but,
though declining sharply, they were still double the normal level in
1901 and not much less in 1902. The worst mortality due to famine
appears to have resulted from malaria epidemics which sprang up after
the famines, and continued to attack for some time. The Famine
Reports completely failed even to mention these most serious after-
effects of the famines, not appreciating that the mortality phase of a
famine may lag behind and be longer than the food shortage stage.

According to Ackroyd diarrhoea is 'an almost universal manifestation of famine'.[21] The synergistic relationship between diarrhoeal
disease and malnutrition is well known. The increased malnutrition
caused by famine weakens the body's resistance to diarrhoeal infection
while the infection reduces appetite and capacity to absorb food, and
increases the body's metabolic demands. In general, lack of food

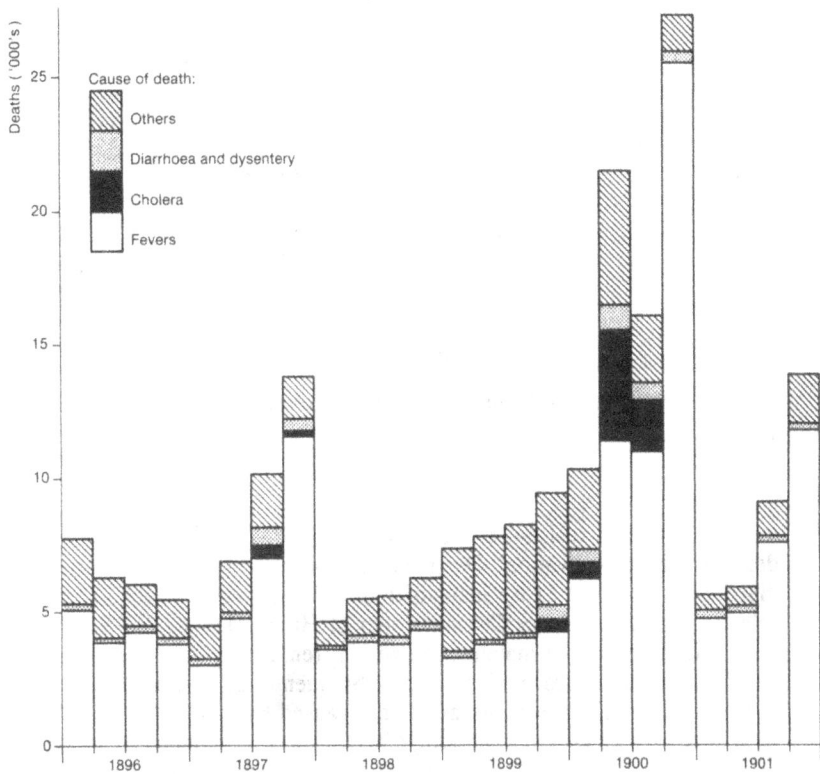

Fig.2 Quarterly Deaths by Cause, 1896–1901.

Table 2. Deaths by Cause, 1895 – 1902

	Cholera	Smallpox	Dysentery & Diarrhoea	Fevers	Others	Total
Year						
Normal*	25	136	408	14580	4783	19936
1895	0	1182	433	14694	5030	21339
1896	0	2821	703	16944	5073	25541
1897	538	626	1571	26555	5860	35150
1898	0	73	523	15538	5367	21501
1899	308	140	868	15399	6011	22726
1900	6399	1301	2823	54324	9951	74798
1901	4	69	440	29040	4606	34159
1902	0	47	372	24014	6517	30950

*Normal is the average for 1893 and 1894.

Source: Report on the Sanitary Administration of the Punjab (various years).

lowers the body's resistance to disease and for this reason the cause of death is rarely starvation. Death is precipitated by infection, often diarrhoeal, encouraged by malnutrition. Officials were aware of this relationship. The Deputy Commissioner of Hissar claimed that deaths were indirectly due to malnutrition which 'renders the constitution an easy prey to any disease which may subsequently be contracted'.[22]

Many of the diarrhoeal diseases were caused by eating indigestible food such as grasses, bark and jungle berries, and other material which only by a 'slight stretch of the imagination [might] be declared unfit for human food'.[23]

Apart from those diseases classified under dysentery and diarrhoea, diarrhoeal diseases also include enteric fever and cholera. Although cholera was not a major cause of death in Hissar every year, in years when epidemics occurred the winter was usually free of the disease. As Fig. 2 shows, significant deaths due to cholera occurred in the summer of 1897. In 1899, however, cholera broke out in the winter, in December in relief camps, and again in March, continuing through the famine and peaking in April. In this month there were 1,735 deaths against only 188 in the corresponding month of 1892 when there was a great cholera epidemic. The epidemic faded out at the end of the summer with only 49 deaths in the rest of 1900. The epidemic was believed to have been brought to Hissar by migrants who had left Hissar for the North West Provinces at the beginning of the famine, but returned on the opening of relief works. In the camps these migrants came into contact with large concentrations of people and the disease was easily transmitted, especially through communal water supplies. The lowering of host resistance due to famine and crowding in relief camps are thought to be common causes of cholera.[24]

Smallpox deaths rose substantially in 1896 and 1900 (see Table 2). However, they were relatively few compared to deaths from other major causes. This might have been a far more significant cause of death in 1900 had there not been immediate vaccinating campaigns wherever signs of the disease were found.

In summary, increased mortality owing to the famines was caused by the principal diseases that killed in normal years, the main one being malaria.[25] However, during the food shortage period it appears that gastro-enteric diseases were dominant, and many of the resulting deaths were subsumed in the category of fever mortality. The other interesting feature of cause of death is the cholera outbreaks, which due to misclassification, probably contributed to the reported 'fever' deaths of the famine years.

Sex and Age Differentials in Mortality

The sex ratio of the enumerated population of Hissar was 114.9 males for every 100 females in 1891. This ratio is typical of northern India of the time, and Visaria has shown that it was mainly a result of very high female mortality relative to male (usually males have higher mortality), although differential enumeration was partly responsible.[26] It would therefore be expected that females had higher death rates than males in normal years.

Table 3 presents the annual ratio of male to female death rates. Prior to the famine years the ratio was close to unity, which suggests that female deaths were probably underregistered relative to male deaths. Nevertheless, assuming that differential registration by sex was constant throughout the period, it is possible to identify changes in differential mortality.

During both famines the ratio of male to female death rates dropped in favour of males and the differential persisted for one year after the famine. Furthermore, although the ratio of male to female infant mortality rates shows the usual biological advantage of females in non-famine years, it dropped to almost unity during the famines (see Table 3). Both ratios fell more sharply in the earlier famine than in the later one.

Table 3. Ratio of Male to Female Death Rates, 1893 – 1902.

Year	Ratio (Male/Female) All Ages*	Infants +
1893	0.97	1.08
1894	1.00	1.12
1895	1.00	1.07
1896	1.00	1.13
1897	0.95	1.00
1898	0.95	1.13
1899	1.00	1.06
1900	0.97	1.03
1901	0.97	1.30
1902	1.02	1.12

* (Registered Male Deaths/Number of Males in 1891)/
(Registered Female Deaths/Number of Females in 1891).

+(Registered Male Deaths/Registered Male Births)/
(Registered Female Deaths/Registered Female Births).

Source: Report on the Sanitary Administration of the Punjab (various years).

The movement of the sex differential in mortality in favour of men is an unusual finding as most studies of famines, including nineteenth century famines in south and western India, find that women are relatively protected during famines.[27] However, it is consistent with cultural practices in north India which are known to favour males in the allocation of resources in normal times.[28] When household access to food and care falls below a critical level it seems likely that females would suffer relatively more and take longer to recover than males. It is possible that the sex differential in death rates was smaller in the second famine because its greater severity allowed a lesser degree of protection of males, and because a larger proportion of weaker females had already succumbed to the earlier famine leaving a relatively strong group of survivors compared with males.

Table 4a presents the annual infant mortality rate, calculated as infant deaths per thousand births in each calendar year. It rose very sharply in the famine years, to 269 in 1897 and a staggering 481 in 1900,

Table 4. Deaths by Age, 1895 – 1902

4a. Infant Mortality Rate (deaths per 1,000 live births)

	Year								
Normal*	1895	1896	1897	1898	1899	1900	1901	1902
174	183	218	269	177	194	481	262	243

4b. Age Distribution of Deaths

Age	Normal*	1895	1896	1897	1898	1899	1900	1901	1902
0 – 1	6052	6988	7671	7071	5920	7296	9191	6126	8241
1 – 4	3677	4760	5580	8993	4777	3581	14600	5201	3208
5 – 9	1027	1024	1461	2597	1522	1030	6155	2776	1704
10 – 19	968	945	1121	2251	1147	1054	7231	2827	2315
20 – 29	1151	1154	1259	1843	1296	1334	5300	2726	2874
30 – 39	1177	1016	1134	1637	1163	1211	5557	2553	2469
40 – 49	1218	1016	1283	1810	1178	1349	6019	2887	2784
50 – 59	1234	1163	1463	2150	1190	1395	6346	2865	2574
60 +	3435	3273	4569	6798	3308	4242	14399	6198	4781

*Normal is the average for 1893 and 1894.
Source: Report on the Sanitary Administration of the Punjab (various years).

increases of 55 per cent and 176 per cent respectively on the normal rate. Although breast-feeding infants might be expected to be protected from a shortage of food, the Famine Report of 1900 observes 'mothers milk drying up on account of insufficient and proper nourishment'.[29] Mothers were unable to replace or supplement their low nutrition milk with cows milk because of the serious losses of milch cattle due to the fodder famine.

Infants were not the only age group to suffer increases in mortality during the famine. Two main conclusions emerge from Table 4b, which presents the annual age distribution of deaths. The first is that although adults aged 20 – 49 appeared to escape fairly lightly in the earlier famine, all age groups experienced enormous increases in mortality in the second famine, with deaths more than tripling in all age groups between 1899 and 1900. The second is that the groups with the highest excess number of deaths were young children (1 – 4) and the elderly (60 +). Excess deaths would have been much higher amongst young children in 1900, if the group had not declined in size because of the low birth rates and high death rates of the previous five years. It appears, therefore, that the normal age differentials in mortality persisted during the crises, and that the young and the old were most vulnerable to death, as in normal times.[30]

Despite their sharp increases in mortality rates infants' share of total deaths declined dramatically in the two heaviest famine mortality years. In normal years infant deaths accounted for almost one-third of all deaths but their share fell to 20 per cent in 1897 and 12 per cent in 1900. These massive drops were due to the decline in the number of births in these years. Consequently, total deaths were much lower than they would have been without a decline in births, and therefore the level of mortality should be viewed with caution as a single absolute indicator of the severity of famines.

Fertility

Although attention is usually focused on the mortality effects of famine, fertility is also substantially altered. Table 5 shows that the crude birth rate maintained a normal level of about 45 per thousand during the first year of both famines and plunged sharply in the second year, falling as low as 25 in 1900. Recovery was faster in the first famine, the crude birth rate in 1898 almost reaching its 1896 level and climbing still further in 1899. In the second famine the crude birth rate rose to only 32 in 1901, and had only fully recovered in 1902. Annual figures, however, obscure the relationship of the changing birth rate to the events of the famines. Quarterly data are much more revealing.

Table 5. Crude Birth, Death and Natural Increase Rates, 1893 – 1902.

	Crude Birth Rate per 1,000	Crude Death Rate per 1,000	Crude Rate of Natural Increase per 1,000
Year			
1893	42	25	17
1894	48	27	21
1895	49	28	21
1896	45	33	12
1897	34	45	– 11
1898	43	28	15
1899	48	29	19
1900	25	96	– 71
1901	32	44	– 12
1902	43	40	3

Source: Report on the Sanitary Administration of the Punjab (various years).

Fig. 1 shows the graph of quarterly births superimposed on a shaded area giving the range between the highest and lowest number of quarterly births of the years 1891 – 5. These include years of very low births, 1891 and 1892, as well as the year of the highest number of births of the decade, 1895. The marked seasonal swings of the pre-famine years are maintained throughout the period examined. Most peaks are in the fourth quarter of the year. Assuming that foetal deaths are evenly distributed over time, conceptions usually peak in the first quarter.

The time path of conceptions can be inferred from births nine months ahead in time. Changes in the pattern of births can be taken to be a reasonable representation of changes in the pattern of conceptions nine months previously, although distortions may occur due to changing levels of foetal wastage, and migration of women.

The pattern of conceptions seems to mirror the progress of the famines. The number of conceptions began to drop off markedly as scarcity intensified in the second quarters of 1896 and 1899, and continued to decline, falling below the lowest levels of 1891 – 5. As soon as the scarcity was over conceptions increased dramatically, shooting up beyond the highest levels of 1891 – 5 in the fourth quarters of 1897 and 1900, and then declining sharply to reach the upper normal range in the first quarters of 1898 and 1901, after which normal levels were maintained.

The small downturns in births right at the beginning of the famines, in the final quarters of 1896 and 1899 when a peak would normally have been expected, could not have been the result of the depressing effect of famines on conceptions. Although conceptions may have fallen off nine months earlier, possibly as an immediate response to the initial scarcity, this may be mainly due to increases in foetal wastage due to acute malnutrition, or emigration of pregnant women which would affect the birth rate much sooner than the fall off in conceptions.

The Famine Report of 1899 – 1900 suggests that the cause of these changes in fertility is 'that famine interfered with the productiveness of the people'.[31] The Sanitary Commissioner also suggests that the low birth rates during the famine years may be a consequence of migration out of the district, although the extent of this is unknown. Furthermore, the Sanitary Commissioner perceptively states that in the 'second year after a famine the birth rate is always much higher, the cause of this probably being greater vigour in the organs of reproduction after a period of rest.'[32]

There are several ways in which famine may interfere with 'productiveness'. The physiological effects of low nutritional status, acute malnutrition and increased stress are important factors contributing to lowered fertility. These probably include an increase in the incidence of amenorrhoea and reductions in coital frequency and fecundity which would reduce the conception rate, and an increase in foetal wastage which would further affect the birth rate. Famine may also encourage behavioural changes which lower the total exposure to risk of conception in the population, in particular the postponement of marriage and child-bearing until better times. Another factor contributing to loss of exposure is the temporary separation of spouses when the husband migrates in search of food and employment. However, this reason was probably not predominant in Hissar as officials reported that whole families usually migrated together in the search for work and food. On the other hand some of the decline in the number of births may have been due to extensive net emigration of women of child-bearing age, with or without their husbands; their births may simply have taken place elsewhere. Finally, some of the decline in births results directly from the elevated mortality of women of child-bearing age during the famines.

The sharp rise in conceptions immediately after the famines also has several explanations. Total exposure to the risk of conception would have increased, partly because there were fewer already pregnant women in the population, and partly because of an increase in the proportion of women living with spouses, due to the occurrence of marriages which had been postponed and the reuniting of spouses who had been separated. Overall fecundity may also have increased as health and nutritional status improved and women whose infants had died, curtailing breast-feeding, resumed ovulation earlier than otherwise. Alteration of sexual behaviour probably also occurred as couples relaxed attempts to postpone child-bearing or tried to replace a dead child. Finally, returning migrants would have increased the total population, and consequently the number of births, even if there had been no change in the actual birth rate.

Probably several, if not all of the above reasons operated together to produce the changing pattern of births. Moreover, it must be remembered that because the second crisis followed so soon after the first, there must have been some overlapping of the effects of each on the birth rate. For example, the dramatic drop in the birth rate from 1899 to 1900 was partly due to the fact that conceptions were very high after the first famine and thus fewer women were exposed to risk of pregnancy because they were already pregnant or lactating, as well as the independent depressing effect on conceptions of the second famine.

Population Growth

Table 5 shows the immense impact of the famines on the crude rate of natural increase, which was negative in 1897, 1900 and 1901, its lowest value being − 71 per thousand in 1900.

Census figures provide more reliable estimates of growth in the intercensal years because population totals exist only for the census years and vital registration was probably more deficient than the censuses. Between 1881 and 1891 there had been a 15.4 per cent increase in the enumerated population of Hissar.[33] Although this was probably an exaggeration of the true growth because census coverage probably improved between 1881 and 1891, it is still likely that there was substantial population growth.[34] However, between 1891 and 1901 population growth was completely checked with an increase of only 0.8 per cent in the enumerated population, which may even be an overestimate of true growth due to improved census coverage. It is likely that migration played little part in checking this growth since the economic and cultural system encouraged people to stay in the locality of their birth.[35] Most migration during the famines would have been to nearby districts of the Punjab which were unaffected by famine. The fact that the Punjab census of 1901 showed that 98 per cent of Punjab residents who were born in Hissar were living in Hissar, and that, as in 1891, 81 per cent of those living in Hissar were born there suggests that migration indeed had little overall impact on population growth.

The decade after the famines, 1901 – 11, had a low growth rate of only 2.9 per cent, but it was still markedly greater than that of 1891 – 1901. The low growth rate was partly due to the famines of the 1890s which left the population more susceptible to epidemics due to its weakened physical condition and social disruption. The effect of the famines is even greater when the probable growth of the population between 1891 and 1896 is considered. A conservative estimate of the growth rate in this period is 0.9 per cent per annum, which was the average rate of growth over the decades 1881 – 91 and 1901 – 11. This gives an 1896 population of 810,729 persons. The 1901 census population was 781,717 persons. Thus, there was probably a decline of at least 4 per cent in population between 1896 and 1901. If the population had continued to grow at 0.9 per cent per annum for the rest of the decade, the 1901 population would have been 847,007, 8 per cent larger than it actually was. Thus a crude estimate of the loss due to the famines is 65,290 persons, excluding any effects after 1901.

The mortality crises affected the age structure of the population as well as its size. Fig. 3 shows that the population pyramid for the 1901 census population was severely undercut in the 0 – 4 age group due to heavy child and infant mortality and the reduction in births. Following this age group through ten years, there are still signs that this group was 'too small' relative to the age groups adjacent to it. By 1921 the group was aged 20 – 24. Unfortunately, because the census figures for the 20 – 24 age group are aggregated with the 25 – 29 year olds, it is not certain how large this group was. However, the fact that the 0 – 4 age group of 1921 was smaller than the 5 – 9 age group suggests some deficiency in the prime child-bearing group.

DISCUSSION

As has been shown, both famines took a year to build up. The harvests of 1895 – 6 and 1898 – 9, the pre-famine years, were very similar, at around one quarter of the normal harvest. The failure in 1899 – 1900 was even greater than that of 1896 – 7. Nevertheless prices rose less in the later famine. The Punjab as a whole was a net exporter of foodgrains in every year of famine and therefore, although prices rose more in 1897 because of higher demand throughout India, the problem of the famine was not that of food availability. Furthermore, although food prices rose sharply in the first months of the famines they stabilized in the first quarter of the second year and, though fluctuating, tended to fall slowly throughout the rest of the famines while deaths were rising (see Fig. 1).

High prices are a boon to those who continue to produce or hold stocks during a famine. They also have little adverse effect on

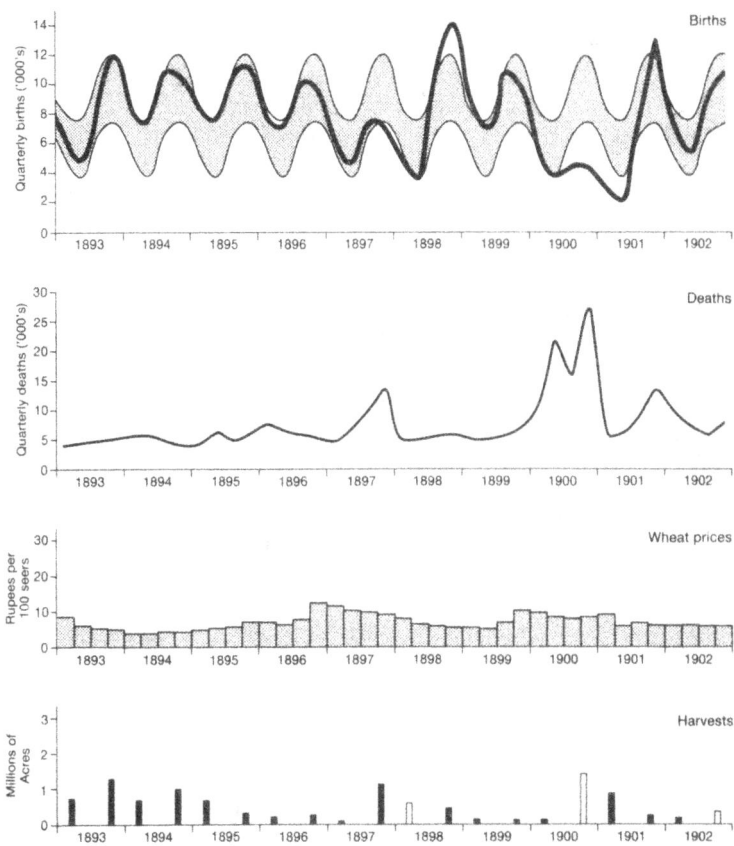

Fig.1 Births, Deaths, Wheat Prices and Harvests, 1893–1903.

agricultural labourers who remain in employment and are paid in food. They are only harmful to those not in productive agriculture. Clearly then, price movements do not really indicate the direction or level of mortality changes. The higher prices of the lighter mortality famine, especially, suggest that famine was not imposed by the market. Indeed the market seems to have responded reasonably favourably by increasing the food supply through imports.

People starve because they cannot command food. This command does not only depend on prices and conditions of supply. Theft and looting, for example, can be used to acquire food. However, both Famine Reports note that there was no great increase in crime. Most important, therefore, in a person's capacity to command food are the conditions of demand. Without purchasing power an individual cannot compete to buy food at any price. As well as causing food shortage, crop failure creates unemployment. Without productive employment there is no source of income, whether in money or in kind, for either the agricultural labourers or the landowners, although landowners are protected for longer than landless labourers. Hissar was unusual in the Punjab because 'the tenant element is of great importance in its social and agricultural economy. The cultivation . . . is mainly carried out by a moving population and not by strong proprietary bodies'.[36] Landless labourers were unlikely to have stocks of food or other assets to tide them over crises, particularly because real wages had been declining for twenty years.[37] Thus, the crop failures immediately deprived most of the agricultural workforce of employment and ultimately pushed even some landowners outside the market, denying them access to food. This is one reason why the famine of 1899 – 1900 was so much worse than that of 1896 – 7. Despite the lower prices and greater imports more people lost food or cash entitlements because of the greater local crop failure. As the Executive Engineer of the Punjab reported 'the famine was attributable rather to the want on the part of people of means of purchasing than to the deficient supply, for, owing to the facilities afforded in the way of communications, the import of grain was easily arranged for.'[38]

The famine of 1896 – 7 provided the first opportunity to employ and test the Indian Famine Code.[39] This code, of which each province had its own substantially similar version, set out the procedures by which government should deal with famine. On observing imminent famine the Code requires that public test works and poor-houses be set up, and that the number seeking employment or relief from these be used as a test of the presence and degree of famine. The public test works were deliberately designed to involve such unpleasant work at so low a wage that only the really desperate, with no alternative subsistence opportunities, would come to them. Once the existence of famine has been established the Code stipulates the setting up of relief works to provide employment and gives detailed directions for the administration of work camps. Instructions are also given concerning suspension of land revenue demands, the opening of public forests for cattle grazing and loans for the purchase of seed and equipment for the next harvest.

Despite all the instructions of the Famine Code, very severe mortality crises resulted from the famines. The main failing of the government was, as Alamgir put it, that it had a 'wait and see' policy.[40] Although, as McAlpin shows,[41] the government's policies of improvement of the economic infrastructure, especially the development of the railways and irrigation, greatly reduced the incidence of famine, its *laissez-faire* principles deterred it from pursuing more direct preventive measures on observing early warning signals of possible impending crisis. It only stepped in once excess mortality and severe social disruption had occurred.

Whereas the most common definition of famine today is the widespread shortage of food accompanied by excess deaths, the official understanding of famine in the 1890s was 'the term applicable to the conditions under which people in considerable numbers accept employment at relief work rates of wages.'[42] On the one hand this shows an understanding of the dislocation effect of famine on agricultural labour causing a loss of earning capacity, be it in terms of a money wage or direct subsistence food, and the need to provide sufferers with purchasing power. On the other hand it led to a preoccupation of the administration with the running and cost of public works, with a consequent neglect of the direct health and mortality effects of the famines. Furthermore, although government relief undoubtedly saved many lives, constituting the only source of food left to the indigent, the conditions under which it was given were very tough, and also inefficient.

Inexperienced and unqualified officials assessed the eligibility of applicants and many in need were turned away. Such was the emphasis on deterring 'opportunists' that 'stone breaking' was recommended as test work as 'only those who are in dire distress will undertake such work'.[43] Those accepted for relief works were obliged to attend places of work at some distance from their homes or receive reduced wages to prove that they were really in need, live in crowded camps, work extremely hard and receive a wage that was often below survival level. Relief was administered with the Victorian principle of 'self-help' in mind, and the main worry of officials appeared to be that people should not become 'demoralized' by receiving unearned relief, rather than that they might die. The stated object of relief was to 'maintain that feeling of self-help so essential to the well-being of a race'.[44] Despite the fact that many relief works actually netted a loss, implying that it would have been cheaper to give relief without work, only those incapable of work were allowed gratuitous relief. There was no appreciation of the fact that energy demands of hard labour would cause great harm to acutely malnourished people. Children over the age of ten had to work, while younger and very old dependants were given free allowances but were obliged to appear daily at the works. The report of one investigator, suggesting that high child mortality was due to the exposure of children to fierce heat on the works while their working parents were unable to attend to them, was totally rejected and denied.[45] While the special needs of new mothers were recognized, the concession made to them was that they were granted the maximum wage plus a child's wage with added milk for only one week, after which they were required to resume work under normal conditions.

Wages were laid down in terms of the cost of fixed quantities of grain by the Famine Code. However, the Code allowed a 25 per cent deviation from these, and for most of the famine periods, wages were substantially below those recommended. In view of this, the assertion that 'it only required reasonable exertion . . . to ensure . . . a supply of cash sufficient to procure an ample quantity of simple food'[46] has a hollow ring.

According to Bhatia, conditions of relief were even more stringent in 1899 – 1900 than in 1896 – 7.[47] The strict and inclement attitude of the relief administration probably accounted, in part, for the greater mortality of the later famine. The other major reason for this was simply that it came so soon after the first. The people had had no time to regain their health or economic position after the first crisis. The government exacerbated the situation by collecting the arrears of revenue for 1896 – 7, depriving the people of the necessary resources for recovery and rehabilitation. When famine reappeared its impact was harder and more widespread, reaching the richer as well as the poorer classes. Consequently, recovery was much slower after the second famine.

CONCLUSION

Famine is a very complex phenomenon. Apparently food shortage was not the cause of the Hissar famines of 1896 – 7 and 1899 – 1900, although both were precipitated by drought. It appears that crop failures induced the famines by eliminating the purchasing power of labourers, artisans, and small landholders. This happened because there were no alternative employment opportunities outside agriculture. This was recognized by British officials in India after the famines. The Deputy Commissioner of Hissar stressed that future famine preventive measures should take the form of industrial development.[48]

Although there were many failings in the government's handling of the situation its analysis was very perceptive. While their harshness in administering relief must be decried, it should be remembered that identification of the needy is a difficult task. Mortality cannot be used as an identifier of individuals since deaths are final and, as Seaman and Holt point out, selection by low body weight can only be effected once starvation is well under way.[49] Test works, therefore, did play a role in ensuring that relief was given only to those in great need rather than wasted on everybody. However, they also excluded many of the most vulnerable.

Fertility and mortality provide clear indicators of famine for retrospective analysis. Although the level of mortality is most relevant, it being part of the very definition of famine, fertility is clearly extremely sensitive; the pattern of births falling off, followed by a short rise, and then returning to normal levels, is indicative of a morbidity/ mortality crisis of the famine type.

Finally, the temporal boundaries of famine are not easy to define. Although Seaman and Holt write that famine 'may appear with frightening suddenness'[50] both the famines examined here developed slowly. More importantly, the fertility, and particularly the mortality effects of the famines extended long after the capacity to command food was restored. Concern and relief measures cannot be relaxed as they were in Hissar, as soon as normal diet is resumed.

NOTES TO CHAPTER 7

1   See B. M. Bhatia, *Famines in India*, (London: Asia Publishing House, 1963), p. 239.
2   The crude death rates for Hissar were greater than the rates for the whole Punjab province by about 50 per cent in 1897 (45 per thousand compared with 31 per thousand) and by about 100 per cent in 1900 (98 per thousand compared with 48 per thousand).
3   The view of officials at the time was that the completeness of registration had not been affected during the famines, because at no time did the famines reach the stage at which the village headmen and watchmen, responsible for keeping records, abandoned their villages, and the omissions due to wandering were balanced by greater accuracy in the famine relief camps. See, *Punjab Census, 1901*, Report I, pp. 41 – 2.
4   The *kharif* and *rabi* are, respectively, the names of the autumn and spring harvests.
5   See *Report on the Famine in the Punjab in 1896 – 97*, (Lahore: Punjab Government Press, 1898), p. 34.
6   Ibid., App. 1, p. 3.
7   Ibid., App. 1, p. 9.
8   Ibid., p. 75.

9 See *The Punjab Famine of 1899 – 1900*, (Lahore: Punjab Government Press, 1901), Vol. 1, p. 35.
10 Ibid., Vol. 1, p. 35.
11 Ibid., Vol. 1, p. 36.
12 Excess deaths are the difference from normal deaths, that is, the average deaths for 1893 and 1894.
13 See A. K. Sen, *Poverty and Famines*, (Oxford: Clarendon Press, 1981), p. 203.
14 See K. Davis, *The Population of India and Pakistan* (Princeton: Princeton University Press, 1951), p. 42.
15 See Famine Report, cited in note 5, p. 70.
16 See Famine Report, cited in note 9, Vol. 2, App. 18, p. 171.
17 Ibid., Vol. 2, App. 9, p. 76.
18 See Sen, cited in note 13, p. 203.
19 See Famine Report, cited in note 9, Vol. 1, p. 28.
20 See J. Mayer, 'Coping with famine' in *Foreign Affairs*, 53, no. 1 (October 1974), p. 101.
21 See W. R. Ackroyd, *The Conquest of Famine* (London: Chatto and Windus, 1974), p. 18.
22 See Famine Report, cited in note 5, p. 70.
23 See Famine Report, cited in note 9, Vol. 2, App. 19, p. 166.
24 See B. S. Drasar, A. M. Tomkins and R. G. Feachem, 'Diarrhoeal diseases', in R. Chambers, R. Longhurst and A. Pacey (eds.), *Seasonal Dimensions to Rural Poverty*, (London: Frances Pinter Ltd., 1981), p. 106.
25 Malaria was also a major killer in the south India famine of 1876 – 8, see R. Lardinois, 'Famine, epidemics and mortality in South India: A reappraisal of the demographic crisis of 1876 – 1878', *Economic and Political Weekly*, 20, No. 11 (March 1985), p. 456.
26 See P. Visaria, 'The sex ratio of the population of India and Pakistan and regional variation during 1901 – 1961', in A. Bose (ed.), *Pattern of Population Change in India, 1951 – 61* (New York: Allied Publishers, 1967).
27 See Lardinois, cited in note 25, p. 460; M. B. McAlpin, *Subject to Famine: Food Crises and Economic Change in Western India, 1860 – 1920*, (Princeton: Princeton University Press, 1983) pp. 56 – 67; and S. Cotts-Watkins and J. Menken, 'Famines in historical perspective', *Population and Development Review* 11, no. 4 (December 1985), pp. 655 – 6.
28 See T. Dyson and M. Moore, 'On Kinship Structure, Female Autonomy, and Demographic Behaviour in India', *Population and Development Review* 9, No. 1 (March 1983). They argue that differences in female autonomy between northern and southern cultural areas of India affect the demographic situation of women. It is interesting to note that the famines in the 1970s in Bangladesh, which lies adjacent to their northern India region, accentuated the female disadvantage in mortality amongst children, (see A. K. M. A. Chowdury and L. C. Chen, 'The dynamics of contemporary famine', *Mexico International Population Conference*, Vol.

1 (Liege: International Union for the Scientific Study of Population, 1977), pp. 415 – 16), whilst their southern region includes western and southern India where the reverse occurred in famines of the nineteenth century, see Lardinois, cited in note 25, and McAlpin, cited in note 27.

29 See Famine Report, cited in note 9, Vol. 2, App. 18, p. 178.

30 See Lardinois, cited in note 25, p. 460, McAlpin, cited in note 27, pp. 59 – 62, and Chowdury and Chen, cited in note 28, p. 415.

31 See Famine Report, cited in note 9, Vol. 1, p. 29.

32 *Report on the Sanitary Administration of the Punjab for the Year 1900*, (Lahore: The 'Civil and Military Gazette' Press, 1901), p. 1.

33 The boundaries of Hissar were changed in 1889. The rate of growth between 1881 and 1891 was calculated on the basis of the population living within the boundaries pertaining in 1891 in both years.

34 See Davis, cited in note 14, p. 26.

35 Ibid., pp. 107 – 8.

36 See *Punjab Census, 1901*, Report I, p. 51.

37 See M. Alamgir, *Famine in South Asia: Political Economy of Mass Starvation*, (Cambridge: Oelgeschlager, Gunn & Hain, 1980), pp. 74 – 5.

38 See Famine Report, cited in note 9, Vol. 3, App. 23, p. 15.

39 For history of the Famine Code, see Alamgir, cited in note 37, ch. 3.

40 Ibid., p. 83.

41 See McAlpin, cited in note 27, Chs. 6 and 7.

42 See Famine Report, cited in note 5, p. 2.

43 See Famine Report, cited in note 9, Vol. 3, App. 23, p. 8.

44 Ibid., Vol. 3, App. 23, p. 1.

45 Ibid., Vol. 2, App. 23, p. 172.

46 Ibid., Vol. 3, App. 23, p. 15.

47 Bhatia, cited in note 1, p. 253.

48 See Famine Report, cited in note 5, App. 1, p. 3.

49 J. Seaman and J. Holt, 'Markets and famines in the Third World', *Disasters*, 4, no. 3 (1980), p. 296.

50 Ibid., p. 284.

8

INFLUENZA IN INDIA DURING
1918 – 19

Ian D. Mills

Hirsch has identified ninety-four influenza epidemics between 1175 and 1875 of which some fifteen were of pandemic proportions.[1] Since 1875 there have been further pandemics in 1889 – 90, 1918 – 19, 1957 – 58, 1968 – 70 and 1977.[2]

What makes the 1918 – 19 experience of particular interest is not simply its existence as one of a series, but the fact that it is considered to 'rank in respect not only of absolute but even of relative mortality not lower than third and perhaps even second upon the roll of great pestilences. No epidemic of smallpox or cholera, not even the typhus periods of the earlier nineteenth century, can vie with the influenza of 1918 – 19 as agents of destruction.'[3] Collier[4] suggests that the 'Plague of Justinian', which, lasting for 50 years around A.D. 542, supposedly slew 100 million, and the Black Death of 1347 – 50 with a toll of 62 million, are the only pandemics comparable in recorded history. Jordan,[5] writing in the 1920s, and using only the available uncorrected data, estimated that global deaths during the influenza pandemic totalled over 21.5 million, resulting from over one billion cases (more than half the world's population), in a total time period of less than two years. As will be seen later, this estimate of mortality is likely to prove a severe underestimate.

While the severity of this visitation of '. . . the last of the Great Plagues',[6] compared to the usually comparatively benign behaviour of influenza, makes it of interest, the Indian experience is deserving of special attention for several reasons. Firstly, studies surveying the global effect of the pandemic suggest that '. . . no part of the world suffered as severely as did India during the latter half of 1918.'[7] The 1921 Indian Census Report[8] gives, as a conservative estimate, between

This chapter is reprinted, with permission of Sage Publications India Pvt. Ltd., from *Indian Economic and Social History Review*, Vol. 23, No. 1 (1986), pp. 1 – 40; © Indian Economic and Social History Association, New Delhi.

twelve and thirteen million deaths for India as a whole, in a period of between three and four months. This exceeds by nearly two million the total estimated deaths from plague over the entire period 1898 – 1918, and is more than twice the death rate attributable to the famines of 1897 – 1901. India thus represents possibly the hardest hit country in the most virulent outbreak of influenza in recorded history.

Secondly, because of this sheer volume of morbidity and mortality, the demographic consequences of the pandemic should be easier to pick out against the general background of ill health in India at the beginning of the twentieth century.

Thirdly, the 1918 – 19 influenza pandemic was the last large-scale, high-mortality epidemic to occur in India,[9] and thus the effects on the population structure may be visible for some period, uncomplicated by the repercussions of later outbreaks of the same or other diseases.

Lastly, but by no means of least importance, the high mortality consequent upon this particular epidemic may allow the uncovering of important clues regarding the dissemination of influenza in developing countries, where the morbidity data necessary for the study of the more general, less virulent outbreaks are lacking.

This study will be extensively based on the use of vital registration data. The usefulness of this data in India tends to be played down, and emphasis is placed on data collected during the long history of the Indian census. However, while it is undeniable that the registration data are incomplete, and that the cause of death classification used is rudimentary, it can be argued that such deficiencies are outweighed by the possibilities for greater sensitivity and detail in analysis, compared to that possible with census material when dealing with a short period of time.

One constraint imposed by the use of vital registration data is that the registration system was in operation only in those areas directly under British administration, covering some seventy-five per cent of the population. This necessitates the extrapolation of results to the national level, with the attendant problems of representativeness. However, for greater specificity, much of the detailed analysis here is concentrated upon Bombay Presidency, and Bombay City.

The absence of reliable annual population totals makes the computation of rates problematical, and thus much of the data used are presented in terms of numbers of events. Where rates are used, they are based either on the 1911 census population, or, where considered necessary, on the estimated mid-1918 population, calculated on the basis of a continuation of the 1901 – 11 growth rate.

The Appendix gives details of the calculation of correction factors for death registration data. Given the uncertainty inherent in the derivation of such factors for Indian data, any results corrected on this basis are always accompanied by the corresponding results based on the uncorrected figures.

The discussion will briefly consider the genesis and dissemination of the 1918 – 19 influenza outbreak on the world scale, before focusing on the Indian case. Interest will then concentrate on deriving an estimate of the overall level of Indian influenza deaths, and an examination of the spatial pattern of mortality. The study then moves on to consider the specific cause of death during the pandemic, and differential mortality by age and sex. The repercussions on fertility subsequent to the enhanced mortality then comes under scrutiny, before, finally consideration is given to the question of whether the pandemic had a socioeconomic class-specific element.

ORIGIN AND SPREAD

The 1918 – 19 pandemic swept the world in two waves (with a third wave apparent in some areas, i.e. England and Wales).[10] The major spread of the disease seems to have radiated from northern France in April 1918, reaching North Africa in May, and India and China in June.[11] Crosby asserts that the pandemic rounded the globe in only four months.

Superficially, the mode of entrance of the disease into India seems clear. The report of the Sanitary Commissioner for India for 1918[12] states that a troop transport ship arrived at Bombay on 29 May, and that shortly after arrival, a few cases of influenza (diagnosed at the time as sandfly fever) were found on board. Unfortunately, forty-eight hours (a period no longer than the incubation period of the disease) elapsed before the cases developed, and no cases occurred on the ship while it was at sea. It is thus unclear exactly when the sufferers acquired the infection. Phipson[13] describes exactly the same series of events as occurring in Karachi, with a troop transport arriving on 20 June. So, the question posed is whether the epidemic was introduced to India from outside, or whether there were existing endemic foci of infection. Several facts point to the former as being the more likely.

Despite the occurrence of a disease '. . . resembling influenza . . .' in Thana district of Bombay Presidency in March 1918, and the existence of influenza cases in various jails in the Presidency during 1917, the disease did not become epidemic until June 1918.[14] Influenza maintains its power to arise in epidemic form because of its ability to undergo change in antigenic character, thus 'sidestepping' any immunity conferred from previous attacks. The normal pattern is of a gradual 'drift' in antigenic character over a period of years, with periodic major 'shifts' '. . . so great that pre-existing immunity has no apparent influence on infection or disease',[15] and so epidemic or pandemic conditions occur as, after a major change '. . . the entire population of the world constitutes a virgin soil for the mutant strain.'[16] Whether such a change in antigenic character can be expected to occur in only one place, or in many places simultaneously, is a question which will be returned to in discussion of the second wave. However, the conformity of the first wave of the pandemic with natural sequence, both chronological and geographical, with Bombay City being attacked after the United Kingdom, Southern Europe and Egypt, and before the seaports of Karachi, Colombo, Rangoon, Singapore and Shanghai,[17] points to the likelihood of the spread of the disease from a single area of mutation.

The level of detail regarding the first wave is necessarily sketchy as at this time the disease was widespread, but not especially virulent.[18] Detailed study thus requires morbidity data which, in general, are not available for India at this time. However, the Sanitary Commissioner's report[19] suggests that the first wave did radiate from Bombay City, the principal port of entry for military and passenger traffic, thus further strengthening the argument for infection from outside.

The final piece of evidence is supplied by Phipson,[20] using data gathered on the incidence of infection among employees of the various firms and other employers in Bombay City. He shows that the first cases among the civilian population occurred on 10 June among the Indian ranks of the City Police, several of the sufferers being employed at the docks. After this, the next groups attacked were: employees of W. & A. Graham's Shipping Firm (15 June), The Government Dockyard (16 June) and the Bombay Port Trust (17 June), after which the disease became general in the city. While not conclusive, it is difficult to resist Phipson's suggestion that '. . . the origin of this epidemic was in some way connected with docks and shipping.'[21]

Working from the diagnosis of the appearance of the disease amongst troops, the Sanitary Commissioner[22] suggests that the first wave then spread across the whole of India by August, aided by the movements of the troops themselves, the postal peons of the Railway Postal Service, and panic migration of sick people, by railway, from infected areas.

All of these points seem to fall in line with the concept of the first wave originating at a single point, and spreading around the world, covering India in its turn, as also appeared to occur in the 1889 – 90 influenza pandemic,[23] and was more clearly mapped in the 1957 – 8 pandemic.[24]

The spread of the second wave, however, had a rather different character, on the world scale at least. In the last week of August, a new, far more virulent form of influenza broke out simultaneously in three port cities thousands of miles apart: Freetown (Sierra Leone), Brest

(France) and Boston (Massachusetts).[25] Crosby considers the possibilities that this was a result of a single mutation of the influenza virus, which then travelled at unprecedented speed to the other two ports, or that it was due to three simultaneous mutations of the virus. He categorizes the first of these hypotheses as 'improbable' and the second as 'highly improbable'.[26] However, some support for the latter proposition is supplied by the case of cholera in Bangladesh,[27] where, in 1982, the 'classical' strain of cholera supplanted the 'El Tor' strain which had become dominant in 1973. The important point for this argument is that '. . . Classical cholera suddenly reappeared simultaneously in different areas [of Bangladesh], striking victims who had no apparent contact.'[28]

Another explanation (though from a hypothesis which possibly also merits the appelation 'highly improbable') comes from Hoyle and Wickramasinghe who argue that the pattern of disease during influenza epidemics,[29] including the 1918 – 19 pandemic,[30] is only explicable if infective material drifts down on to the planet's surface after the planet has passed through the 'bacterial debris' in the tails of comets. They argue that the speed and pattern of spread of influenza is both too rapid and too erratic to be caused by person to person transmission. Senn,[31] though, using the same data, disagrees on purely statistical grounds.

In India, the second wave, again, began in Bombay Presidency, and was well established by the month of September.[32] Fig. 1 gives an impression of the direction and rate of spread of the epidemic through British India, showing the death rate from causes classified as fevers and respiratory diseases, in excess of the average for the five years preceding the pandemic, by month. This measure is used here as a proxy for influenza mortality, since influenza was not classified in its own right, and deaths were usually placed under these two heads. This measure removes any effects of fluctuations in mortality due to other epidemic diseases such as smallpox, cholera and plague, which are classified separately, but is open to disturbance by fluctuations in mortality from malaria, which is generally classified under 'fevers'. This disturbance may have been only small in 1918 as this was not an exceptional year for malaria.[33]

Using the peak of influenza mortality as a measure of timing, it can be seen that the general direction of spread is from west to east, with an October peak in Bombay Presidency, November in the centre and north, and December in Bengal. It is interesting that Burma and Assam have mortality peaks earlier than Bengal. This may be due to the second epidemic wave being introduced into Rangoon by shipping,[34] thus short-circuiting the cross-country path of transmission.

The precise point from which the second wave began its journey through India was, the Sanitary Commissioner for India suggests,[35]

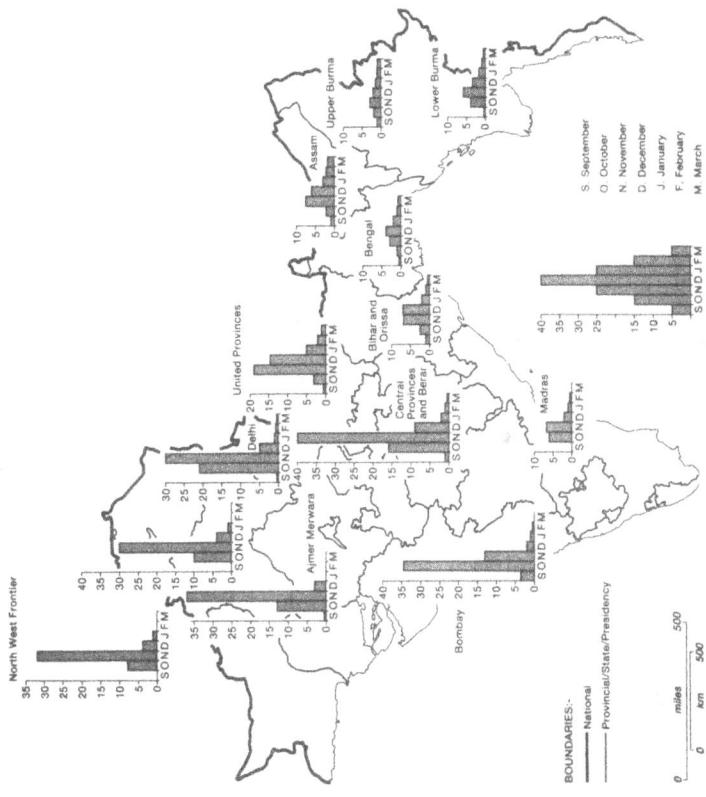

Fig. 1 Monthly Excess Mortality due to Fevers and Respiratory Diseases: Major Areas of British India: September 1918 – March 1919

Source: *Reports of the Sanitary Commissioner with the Government of India,* 1913–19
Note: rates are based on 1911 census population.

Poona district in the Deccan region of Bombay Presidency. This further complicates the question of the international spread of the second wave as Poona district is some 100 miles inland from Bombay City, the nearest port. Confirmation of this point of origin can be attempted utilizing weekly mortality data for towns of over 20,000 population in Bombay Presidency.[36] Unfortunately, except for Bombay City, the data series does not begin until the week ending 7 October, the week of peak mortality in Bombay City. This week also shows a peak for Poona, and Sholapur (which lies in the district adjoining Poona to the south-east), but there is no way of ascertaining the mortality in the weeks prior to this, thus leaving open the question of origin. These data do, however, show a clear movement of the wave from south to north in the Presidency, with the districts in Sind having mortality peaks a full three weeks later than Bombay City.

THE LEVEL OF MORTALITY

The Indian influenza mortality figure, quoted above, of between twelve and thirteen million deaths is based on the use of unadjusted vital registration data, extrapolated to national coverage.[37] This, however, appears to be a substantial underestimate. Davis has calculated a correction factor for registered death rates, on the basis of estimating the intercensal number of births (using reverse survivorship), subtracting the intercensal growth rate, and comparing the resultant estimated death rate with that obtained from the vital registration data.[38] Applying this correction to the death rate for the epidemic years, and the average of the surrounding years, Davis calculated that excess deaths due to the influenza pandemic amounted to twenty million in the Indian subcontinent.[39]

This estimate can be checked by utilizing the 'growth balance method'. Working with the Indian registration data for 1911 (in order to avoid the problems inherent in estimating intercensal population totals by age), a correction factor of 1.7 is found (see Appendix) and a total influenza mortality for 1918 – 19 of seventeen million deaths. Given the uncertainty characterizing both methods, it could be argued that these two estimates are reasonably compatible. However, they can be brought into closer correspondence. Davis uses as an average mortality level, the average of the rates for 1913 – 17 and 1920 – 24. His own calculations, though, suggest that the level of mortality in 1920 – 24 was considerably lower than that prevailing in 1913 – 17.[40] This would tend to bias downwards his 'average' level of mortality, and thus increase the excess during the pandemic years. Reworking Davis' exercise, using only 1913 – 17 as the 'average', results in a total influenza mortality of 17.4 million.

The same line of argument can be employed with regard to a check used by Davis based on the intercensal rate of growth.[41] He contrasts the 1911 – 20 population growth with that expected on the basis of the 1901 – 10 and 1921 – 30 average growth rate and assumes the differences to be attributable to the influenza pandemic, there being no other outstanding catastrophe in the decade 1911 – 20. Thus, the average 1901 – 10/1921 – 30 growth rate was 8.35 per cent per decade, giving an 'expected growth' for 1911 – 20 some 22.6 million above that actually occurring. However, again due to the mortality decline shown after 1920, this growth rate can be argued to be too high. The 1921 Census Report[42] suggests that the rate of population growth for 1911 – 17 was generally a continuation of that found for 1901 – 11, that is at 6.8 per cent per decade. Using this as an indicator of the level of 'expected growth' for 1911 – 20 gives an excess mortality of 18.5 million.

It may be then that Davis' estimate is slightly too high. However, the important point is the demonstration that the figures based on uncorrected registration data are substantially understated and that, with some 17 – 18 million deaths in India alone, Jordan's estimate of pandemic mortality for the whole world of 21.5 million must also be far too low.

While it may be accepted that the above calculations result in a reasonable estimate of the all-India level of influenza mortality, it is clear from Fig. 1 that not all areas of India suffered to the same extent, with the mortality rate being particularly high in the west, north-west and central regions. Bearing in mind the above demonstration of the incompleteness of vital registration data, the first consideration must be whether this is an artefact of differential registration coverage. Using the growth balance method once more, it can be argued that this is not the case.

Although a gradient of registration coverage does appear to exist, with Assam vital registration data being less than 50 per cent complete, and Bombay Presidency around 65 per cent complete,[43] this is not sufficient to explain the pattern. Firstly, not all low influenza mortality areas have particularly bad registration of vital events. For example, Madras Presidency data appears to be as complete as that for Bombay Presidency. Secondly, the level of completeness of death registration in Assam would need to be five or six times worse than in Bombay for the influenza mortality rates to be comparable, and this, even allowing for considerable error in the method, does not seem to be the case.

An alternative explanation is thus required. Gill suggests that '. . . the amplitude of the diurnal range of temperature possesses a special significance from the point of view of the transmission of influenza.'[44] Gill shows that the level of mortality in different areas of India does indeed bear some relationship to the average daily range of temperature in November, the peak month for mortality in India as a whole. In particular, he stresses the importance of the 25°F Isogram which not only divides the high and low mortality areas of India, but also '. . . serves to divide the strictly tropical from the sub-tropical part of India.'[45]

It might be asked, however, why climate should have such an effect on *transmission* of the disease in India, as suggested by Gill, when the existence of the disease in such climatically different areas as the U.S.A., Brazil, India, South Africa and New Zealand at the same time suggests that climate had little part to play on the world scale.[46] The U.K. Ministry of Health report also argues that weather conditions do not rank among the primary factors explaining pandemic prevalences.[47] In addition, in the influenza pandemic of 1889 – 90, both Bombay *and* Calcutta were particularly hard hit,[48] cutting across Gill's temperature range division.

Instead, it can be argued that what Gill's statement really reflects is a relationship between diurnal temperature range and the propensity to develop pneumonic complications of influenza, rather than influenza itself. Information on the prevalence of influenza among the general population is not available in India, as only mortality, and not morbidity data were compiled. However, appropriate figures do exist for jail populations for some provinces for 1918 (see Table 1). It is arguable that jail populations are not representative of the population as a whole, being (i) more likely to contract influenza due to high transmission rates in a crowded environment, (ii) less likely to die from the disease because of the presence of medical personnel, and (iii) having a quite different sex and age structure. The main point, however, can be made from *relative* levels. It can be seen from Table 1 that, while the ordering is not identical, those provinces with high influenza mortality in the general population also tend to have high jail influenza mortality, whether using the whole jail population, or the number of influenza cases as the denominator. There is a clear dichotomy, represented by the line across the Table. In contrast, there is no obvious division among the figures shown for incidence rates, which, in addition, display far less variability than the mortality figures, varying by only 1.6 times compared to four times for general influenza mortality, and seven times for jail case mortality. This suggests that the prevalence of influenza was fairly constant across India, and that what varied was mortality.

A further possible explanation of the pattern is that the virus decreased in virulence over time, though not in infectivity, as it spread from the west to the east of the subcontinent. This idea has however been discounted as a factor in the spread of the pandemic in the U.S.A.

Table 1. Influenza Mortality Rates, Incidence Rates and Case Mortality Rates: Province and Jail Populations, India 1918

Province	Province Influenza Mortality per 1000	Jail Influenza Mortality per 1000	Jail Influenza Incidence Rate per 1000	Jail Influenza Case Mortality per 1000
Central Provinces	67.6	34.8	457.5	76.1
Bombay Presidency	54.3	36.0	348.0	103.4
United Provinces	47.2	20.9	296.7	70.4
Punjab	46.0	38.9	334.7	116.2
North West Frontier	44.4	28.6	311.1	91.8
Assam	26.1	5.9	351.1	16.7
Lower Burma	16.2	6.4	278.6	22.9
Madras Presidency	15.8	10.9	318.7	34.3

Sources: Proceedings of the Department of Education: Sanitary — Part A, 1918; and Annual Report of the Sanitary Commissioner with the Government of India, 1918.

as the decline in virulence would be too slow for a few weeks to make much difference.[49] Also, the relationship between diurnal temperature and influenza mortality can be seen within Bombay Presidency (see Fig.2) with the coastal areas displaying markedly lower mortality levels. The spread from Poona district (the suggested origin of the second wave, and a high mortality area) to the coast could only have taken days.

The relationship found by Gill does, then, seem to correspond to the observed spatial variation in influenza mortality, both at the national level, and at the local level within Bombay Presidency, although his interpretation of the correspondence is questionable. Accepting that it

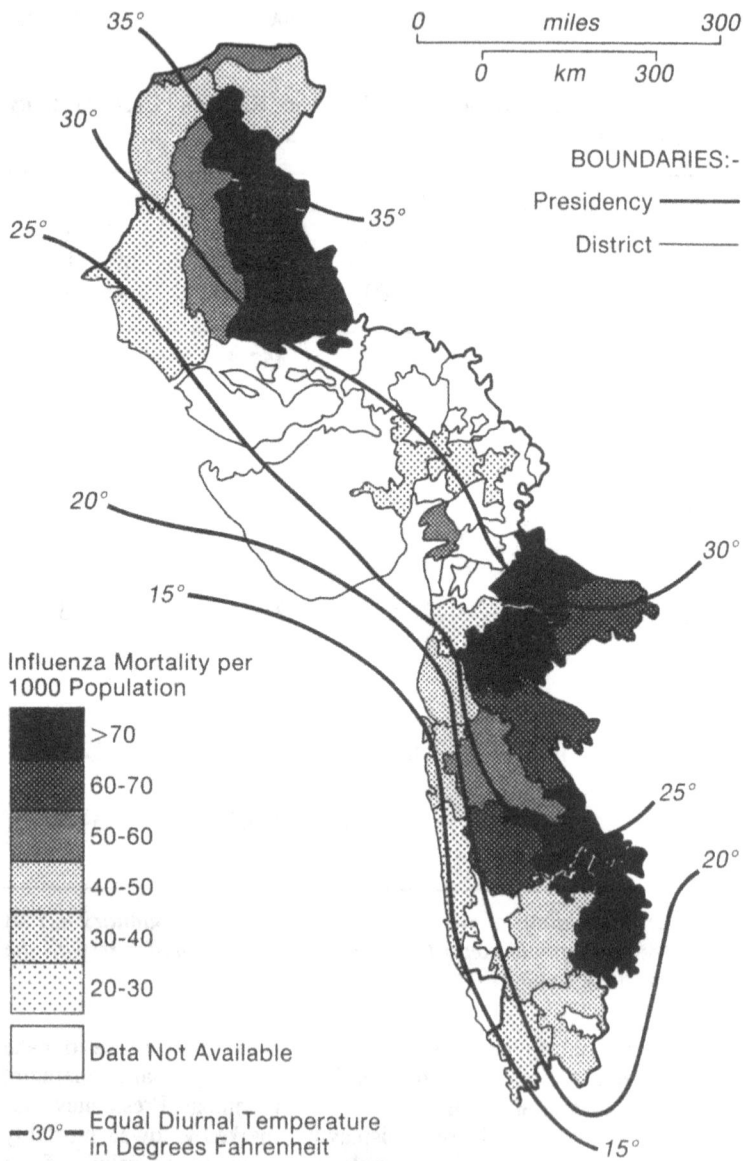

Fig.2 Influenza Death Rate: Districts in Bombay Presidency, 1918, and Mean Diurnal Range of Temperature, October 1918

Sources: Govt. of India, Met. Dept. *Monthly Weather Review,* Aug.–Dec. 1900; *Annual Report, Sanitary Commissioner, Bombay Presidency,* 1918

does in fact refer to influenza mortality, rather than transmission, an understanding of the causal mechanism involved is desirable. To approach this requires some study of the precise cause of death.

CAUSE OF DEATH

The particular facet of the 1918 – 19 pandemic which made it one of the most virulent of any disease in recorded history was the tendency for sufferers to succumb to pneumonia. Crosby[50] surveys the various theories proposed over the years to explain this enhanced virulence. One of the more sophisticated suggestions was a 'symbiosis' theory. Shope[51] found evidence in pigs that the influenza virus could combine with Pfeiffer's bacilli to cause a severe fever with pneumonic complications. He was unable to show the same effect in man, but he argued that this was the mechanism through which the 1918 – 19 pandemic gained its extraordinary virulence. Unfortunately, while Pfeiffer's bacillus was frequently found in the lungs of victims, there were also cases where other bacteria were responsible for the onset of pneumonia.[52] Crosby suggests that, rather than working in symbiosis with a bacteria, the 1918 – 19 mutation of the influenza virus acted more as a 'pathfinder' for secondary infection. It '. . . mowed away the respiratory system's first line of defence . . . [and] provided an environment of opportunity for scavenger bacteria.'[53] It may well be, then, that the relationship discussed above between climatic factors and mortality during the pandemic works through the susceptibility of people to infection by bacteria, the secondary agents of infection, varying under different climatic conditions. In particular, the eastern provinces, with their lower humidity, and less violent fluctuations in temperature, might present less favourable conditions for the action of bacterial infection.[54]

While it is clear from this discussion that the primary cause of death would be expected to be respiratory infection, Phipson and Jordan[55] both suggest that '. . . the disease fights in part under its own flag and in part treacherously under other flags.'[56] It is thus of interest to look at the cause of death data, shown for Bombay Presidency in Figure 3 and Table 2. The most noticeable point is the predominance of 'Fevers' as the cause of death during the peak pandemic months, forming ninety-two per cent of all deaths in October 1918, and being some thirty times higher than for non-pandemic months. The massive scale of the mortality can be gauged from the fact that the mortality from fevers alone in the month of October is equal to the average *annual* mortality from *all* causes over the previous five years. This does not necessarily bear any strict relationship to the clinical cause of death. It can be seen

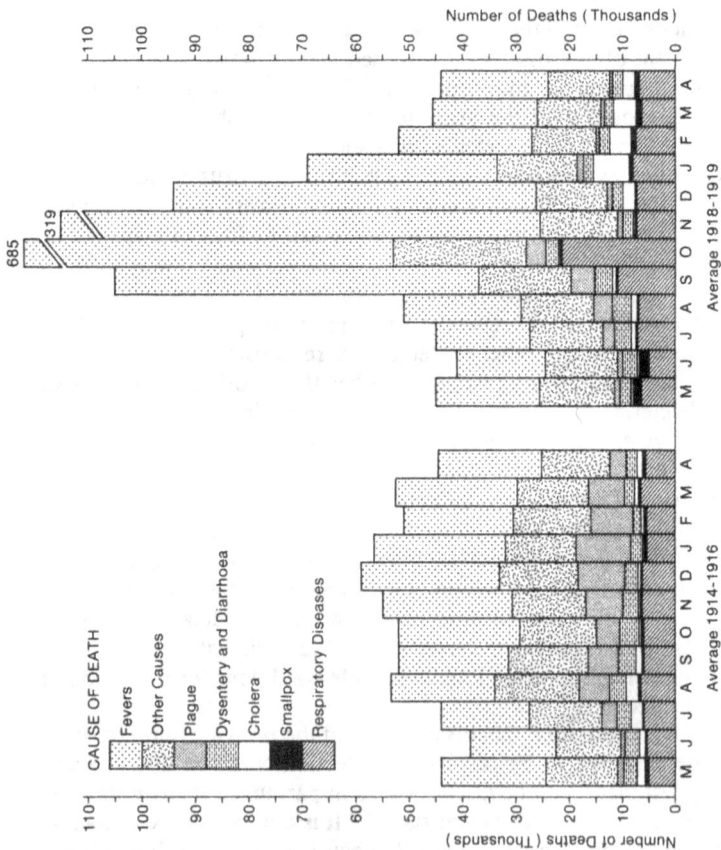

Fig.3 Monthly Deaths by Cause, Bombay Presidency: May 1918–April 1919, and Average 1914–16

Source: *Bombay Government Gazette* – Part II, 1914–19

Table 2. Monthly Deaths by Cause, Bombay Presidency, May 1918 – April 1919

Month	Fevers	Respiratory Disease	Smallpox	Cholera	Dysentery & Diarrhoea	Plague	Other Causes	Total
1918								
May	19,580	6,583	1,133	367	2,166	1,239	13,720	44,788
June	16,784	6,069	568	629	2,689	902	13,541	41,182
July	17,344	6,971	331	1,101	3,489	1,742	13,911	44,892
August	19,669	6,609	153	1,608	3,788	3,122	13,887	50,859
September	68,398	11,079	102	864	3,173	4,429	17,360	105,408
October	631,412	21,470	39	560	2,213	3,857	24,847	684,518
November	293,296	7,801	27	205	1,780	1,227	14,421	318,935
December	67,749	7,530	106	1,824	2,440	913	13,366	93,945
1919								
January	35,126	8,282	336	6,853	2,243	1,054	14,794	68,668
February	25,054	7,391	544	4,469	1,928	684	11,832	51,898
March	21,538	6,830	762	1,429	1,782	689	11,593	45,213
April	19,960	6,809	781	2,413	1,962	582	11,380	43,999

Source: Bombay Government Gazette — Part II, 1918 – 19.

that in non-pandemic months fevers also comprise a large proportion of total deaths, and the 1921 Census Report[57] suggests that this is in reality a 'catch-all' category, only slightly more specific than the 'other causes' category. Bombay Presidency, however, appears to be one of the more exacting areas as regards classification. In non-pandemic years, only around forty per cent of deaths are classified as fevers, compared to sixty per cent for all registration India, and up to eighty per cent in the worst areas (i.e. Coorg and North West Frontier Province).[58]

Assuming that the rise in deaths due to respiratory diseases and fevers represent influenza mortality, it is of interest to look at the pattern in the other categories. Smallpox, dysentery and diarrhoea, and cholera all decreased in prevalence during the major epidemic months of September, October and November. This may simply be a recurrence of the usual seasonal pattern suggested by the average experience from 1914 – 16, shown in Fig. 3. Two possible alternative explanations also suggest themselves. Firstly, it may be that influenza intervened as the ultimate cause of death in cases where people were already suffering from one of these diseases. Or it is possible that the stress placed on the vital registration system by the pandemic, with, in some cases, registration being suspended, and the figures reconstructed later,[59] led to a general assumption that death was due to influenza. It might be noted though, that plague deaths rise in September and October, before falling to a low level in the latter stages of the pandemic. This fits with none of the above hypotheses. It may, however, be another example of mis-diagnosis. The prevalence of respiratory complications, and the unfamiliarity of registration staff with influenza, may have led to cases being categorized as pneumonic plague,[60] as also happened in the U.S.A..[61] On the other hand it may simply have been a resurgence of the disease following epidemic plague conditions at the end of 1917 and the beginning of 1918.

The final category, 'other causes', also shows a significant increase in September and October. Some clues as to the nature of this increase can be gained from data for Bombay City, where this category is broken down into its component parts.[62] Of the subcategories showing any significant deviation during the weeks of maximum mortality in Bombay City (week ending 21 September to week ending 19 October),[63] by far the largest effect is shown by 'diseases of the respiratory system', rising from a base level of less than 300 deaths per week to 2,693 deaths in week ending 5 October. As this category represents over seventy per cent of deaths from 'other causes' at this time, it suggests that, for Bombay City at least, excess deaths under the 'other causes' heading are also largely due to influenza.

Other subcategories exhibiting peaks in phase with the influenza mortality are: diseases of the digestive system, diseases of the nervous system, old age, debility and anaemia, and premature births. This last subcategory is also of particular interest as we shall see below.

AGE AND SEX SPECIFIC MORTALITY

In influenza epidemics since 1918 – 19, as in those before, the common conclusion is that '. . . influenza . . . extinguishes the life of those who are aged or have chronic disease.'[64] Data for England and Wales show that, since 1953, over seventy-five per cent of those dying in any year from influenza have been aged over 55.[65] In marked contrast to this general pattern, Fig. 4 shows the age distribution of 1,000 excess deaths in Bombay Presidency (defined here as the excess of 1918 over the mean of 1913 – 17 for all causes, as age-specific data are not differentiated by cause) for males and females. The concentration of deaths in the age range 20 – 40 is a spectacular departure from the common influenza pattern. Here, only twenty per cent of excess deaths occur to those over the age of 50, while forty-two per cent of deaths are in the age range 20 – 40.

Another feature of note is that infants appear to escape relatively lightly, having excess mortality considerably lower than that for children aged 1 – 4. This is a surprising feature in a society where the normally high infant mortality rate suggests that infants have a particularly precarious grasp on life.

To dispose of the obvious suspicion that these effects are due to patterns of age misstatement or omissions, Fig. 4 also shows the average age pattern of mortality for 1913 – 17 in Bombay Presidency. This displays a more 'normal' mortality pattern, with peaks for the very young and the very old, and only a slight rise in mortality for women in the main child-bearing ages. In addition, the same data are presented for influenza and pneumonia deaths in the U.S.A. in 1918. While there will clearly be differences in age structure between the two countries which will affect the comparison, the similarity of the pattern is striking (see Fig. 4).

Why this particular pandemic should have departed so radically from the usual influenza age pattern of mortality is a mystery. However, several suggestions have emerged. One of these is that the older age group had immunity conferred upon them from the last influenza pandemic, in 1889 – 90, and from intervening influenza prevalence. Several points can be proposed against this argument. Firstly, as mentioned earlier, influenza retains its power to arise in epidemic form

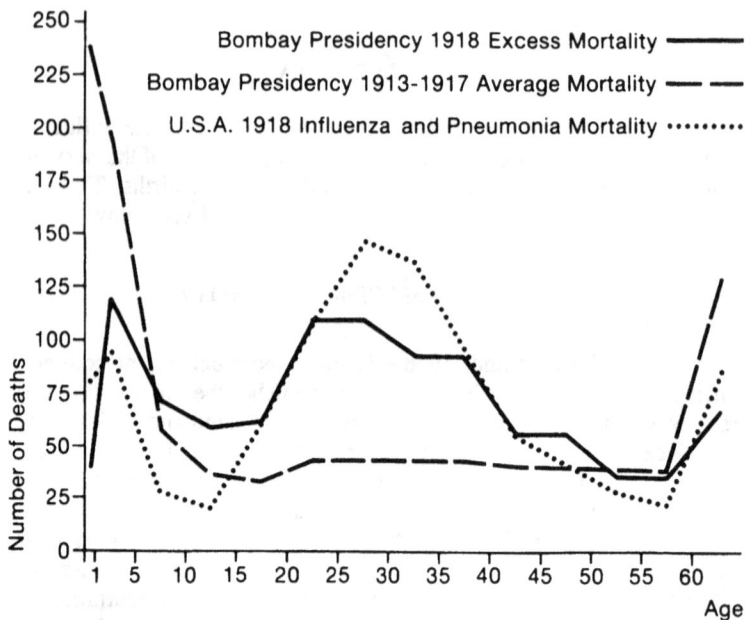

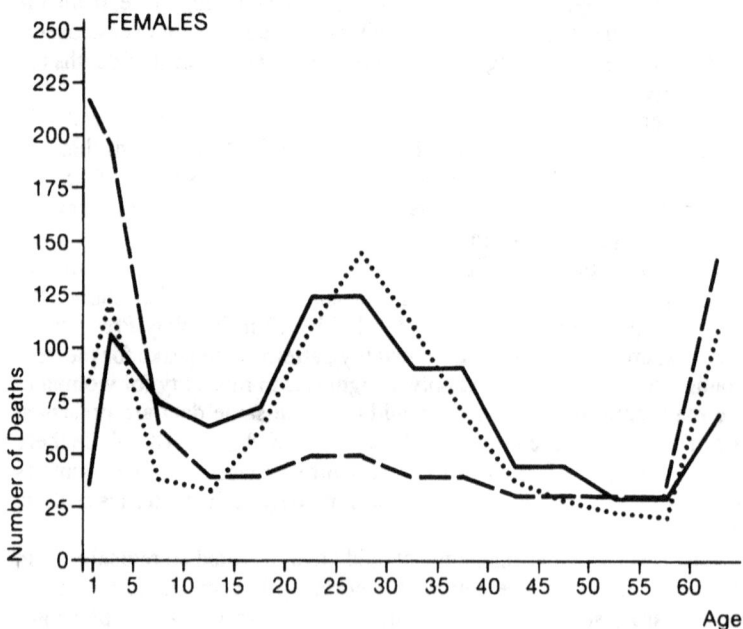

Fig.4 Distribution by Age of 1,000 Excess Deaths, Bombay
Presidency 1918; 1,000 Deaths (all causes) Bombay
Presidency, Average 1913–17; and 1,000 Influenza and
Pneumonia Deaths, U.S.A. 1918

Sources: *Annual Reports, Sanitary Commissioner, Bombay Presidency,*
1913–18; and Crosby, W.: *Epidemic and Peace, 1918.* p.211

due to the ability of the virus to mutate. Thus '. . . the degree and extent of . . . acquired immunity is slight, transient, variable and incomplete.'[66] Secondly, with the last epidemic occurring some 28 years previously, it would be logical to expect those aged 30 and over to exhibit immunity, and not those under. However, as Fig. 4 shows, those aged 30 – 40 were particularly hard hit, while the 5 – 15 age range escaped lightly. Gill suggests that this may be due to young people being attacked by a mild form of influenza, before or at the beginning of the main pandemic, caused by a quantum of infection insufficient to give rise to the disease in adults. This would be expected to lead to a relatively greater degree of protection in the 5 – 15 age group.[67] Unfortunately, the circumstances which would give rise to such a chain of events are as inexplicable as the puzzle they purport to solve.

A further set of explanations revolve around the fact that the pandemic occurred at the end of a World War. The grouping together of young and middle-aged adults in, for example, the armed forces or munitions factories, may have allowed the disease an unprecedented opportunity to fasten upon these age groups. Linked to this argument is the idea that adolescents and adults were suffering from the debilitating influences of war, i.e. from strain and exposure.[68] While conditions of this nature could be expected to increase both transmission rates (as the disease is spread by air-borne droplets), and susceptibility to the disease, the fact that the pandemic overran populations far removed from the war[69], with the same effects, means that this can only be a partial explanation.

A more purely biological hypothesis is proposed by Burnet and Clark,[70] and summarized by Crosby.[71] They argue that the mutated 1918 – 19 virus was particularly virulent, and in the absence of any resistance in the general population, was able to permeate rapidly the entire respiratory tract of people of all ages. The particular age incidence of mortality is, then, a function of the way the body's defence mechanisms change with age. They argue that, in a person of any age, the response to infection is inflammation of the infected area, by which means a quantity of blood, fluid, antibodies and white blood cells infuses the affected tissue. In a child, the inflammation process enables it to respond to widespread infection; the diseases of childhood. By adolescence, this stage is past, and the body generally suffers localized injuries, such as wounds, broken bones, etc. For this reason, the young adult is able to produce intense localized inflammation, to deal with localized injury. Thus, with the sudden large-scale invasion of the mutated influenza virus, '. . . the intense local inflammation becomes intense general inflammation. The inflammation . . . is so massive that a springtide of fluids overwhelms the lungs.' The young adults' bodies

'. . . reacted so vigorously to the threat of influenza that the reaction drowned them.'[72]

With the ageing of the body, the ability to summon up such massive reaction fades, and thus the mortality level declines, until the physical degeneration of old age once again enhances the risk of death.

Table 3. Sex Ratio of Registered Death Rates: Bombay Presidency, 1916 – 18 (male deaths per female death).

	Age Group				
	0 – 1	1 – 4	5 – 19	20 – 39	40 +
Average:					
1916 – 17	1.045	1.035	0.795	0.918	1.122
1918	1.050	1.040	0.753	0.805	1.057
1918 as % of 1916 – 17	100.5	100.5	94.7	87.7	94.2

Sources: Annual Reports, Sanitary Commissioner, Bombay Presidency, 1916 – 18.

As well as being strongly selective by age, the pandemic also displayed a propensity to attack women more severely than men. Table 3 shows the sex ratio of age-specific death rates (based on the 1911 population totals) for Bombay Presidency. It is interesting that, in the childhood ages (0 – 4) there is no change in the sex ratio of deaths during the pandemic year, possibly because this age range was not particularly hard hit. At the older ages, however, there is evidence that the female death rate increased to a higher level than the male rate during the pandemic year. The effect is marked in the age range where mortality was especially concentrated, 20 – 40 years. Here, female mortality deteriorates, relative to males, by some twelve per cent.

The particular virulence of the disease for women of reproductive age was noted at the time in India, the explanation offered being that '. . . in addition to the ordinary tasks of the house, on them fell the duty of nursing the others even when themselves ill.'[73] The logic of this is hard to refute, given the patriarchal nature of Indian society and the consequent low status of women. The causation, however, goes rather deeper than this. One element might be that women were more susceptible to the disease. Jordan[74] suggests that, in the U.S.A., the case incidence was slightly higher for women. Unfortunately, this cannot be demonstrated for India due to the lack of general morbidity data, and the jail population of women, for whom data does exist, was too small to be enlightening.

Even with equal susceptibility for both sexes, a mortality differential could still be expected, with pregnancy acting as an intervening variable. Previously healthy pregnant women have been found to be particularly at risk during influenza epidemics,[75] with the last trimester of pregnancy being especially hazardous.[76] In several studies, termination of pregnancy by premature delivery or spontaneous abortion whilst suffering from influenza, during the 1918 – 19 pandemic, appears to have almost guaranteed death.[77] In this context, the pattern found above in the analysis of cause of death for Bombay City takes on new significance. Deaths due to premature birth (referring to the mothers rather than the children) in Bombay City trebled during the peak mortality weeks.[78] While the exact level of the deaths is uninstructive, due to most influenza deaths, as mentioned earlier, being classified under fevers or respiratory diseases, the exact correspondence of the peaks of mortality does provide a strong indicator that pregnancy and death from influenza were linked.

Table 4. Monthly Still Births, Bombay City, 1918, as Percentage of Average Monthly Still Births, 1916 – 17.

Jan.	Feb.	Mar.	Apr.	May	June	July	Aug.	Sep.	Oct.	Nov.	Dec.
113.7	103.2	94.7	102.6	116.9	100.4	111.9	86.2	140.5	161.1	107.3	115.1

Source: Administration Report of the Municipal Commissioner for the City of Bombay, 1916 – 18

An indirect piece of evidence supporting this is displayed by the effect of the pandemic upon the viability of the foetus, rather than the mother. Table 4 shows monthly still births in Bombay City as a percentage of average still births in the period preceding the pandemic. While all but two months show an increase in still births in 1918 (possibly linked to an increasing number of total births consequent upon the continuing rapid growth of Bombay City),[79] September and October show an average fifty per cent increase in the incidence of still births, coincident with the two peak influenza months in Bombay City. In the absence of any other reported health problem which could lead to this phenomenon, it can be claimed as a corollary of the extreme effects of influenza upon pregnant women.

THE EFFECT UPON FERTILITY

The preceding section introduced three of a series of mechanisms which appear to have caused a significant effect upon the fertility of Bombay Presidency, and indeed the whole of India. Table 5 shows the crude birth rate, crude death rate, and resultant crude rate of natural increase for Bombay Presidency and India, in the years surrounding the pandemic. The picture for Bombay Presidency is a little confused with regard to the effect of the influenza pandemic because of epidemic plague during 1917, which results in a negative crude rate of natural increase for this year as well as 1918 and 1919. The set of figures for registration India, though, show the impact of the pandemic more clearly, with excess deaths only in the two pandemic years. Both sets of data show the gradual recovery of pre-pandemic levels of natural increase, the 1913 – 1915 level being regained by about 1922 – 23.

Fig. 5 shows the monthly births for 1918, 1919 and 1920 indexed against the average for the corresponding month in 1914 – 17 to remove the residual effect of any seasonality of births. The most outstanding feature here is the decline in births in mid – 1919 to less than one half the average for 1914 – 17. This, it can be argued, is likely to be the result of decreased coital frequency during the period of the pandemic, some nine months previously.

That an effect of this magnitude is plausible can be seen by a consideration of the likely influenza attack rate, and the consequent level of morbidity. In the absence of data for the civilian population, recourse will be made once more to data for the jail population. Assuming that the Bombay Presidency jail case mortality is an acceptable approximation for the general population, around 10.3 per cent of those contracting the disease died. (The validity of this assumption is a little doubtful. On the one hand, the jail figure may be too low, as the jail incidence rate might be inflated by the high transmission rate in such a closed environment. However, on the other hand, data on jail incidence rates are based only on those hospitalized with a disease.[80] Those reporting to the surgery on a daily basis would be excluded. This would tend to bias the jail case mortality upwards. It is to be hoped that these two effects are largely self-cancelling, thus improving the quality of the estimate.) So, with a case mortality of 10.3 per cent the estimated 1,062,852 influenza deaths in Bombay Presidency[81] will have resulted from some 10.3 million cases. With an estimated mid-1918 population of 20.5 million,[82] it can be seen that

Table 5. Crude Birth Rate, Crude Death Rate and Crude Rate of Natural Increase, Bombay Presidency and Registration India, 1913 – 24.

	1913	1914	1915	1916	1917	1918	1919	1920	1921	1922	1923	1924
Bombay Presidency (rates per 1,000)												
CBR	35.0	37.4	37.1	36.0	35.7	31.6	27.9	30.3	32.6	32.8	35.6	35.6
CDR	25.1	29.5	27.3	33.3	40.8	88.1	32.1	28.7	26.0	23.6	25.9	27.6
CRNI	9.9	7.9	9.8	2.7	-5.1	-56.5	-4.2	1.6	6.6	8.8	9.7	8.0
Registration India (rates per 1,000)												
CBR	39.4	39.6	37.8	37.1	39.3	35.4	30.2	33.0	32.2	31.9	35.1	34.4
CDR	28.7	30.0	29.9	29.1	32.7	62.5	35.9	30.8	30.6	24.0	25.0	28.5
CRNI	10.7	9.6	7.9	8.0	6.6	-27.1	-5.7	2.2	1.6	5.8	10.1	5.9

Source: Statistical Abstract for British India: Vol. 3, 1921 – 25.

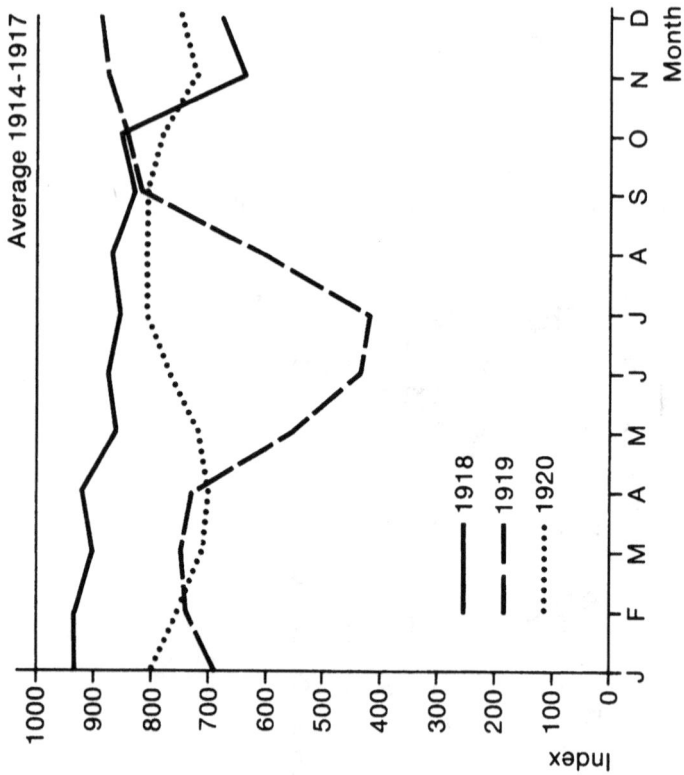

Fig.5 Bombay Presidency Births: 1918, 1919, 1920, indexed against Average Births, 1914–17

Source: *Bombay Government Gazette* – Part II. 1914–1921.

around one half of the population suffered from influenza during the pandemic. Clearly, the use of uncorrected registration data will make this an underestimate. Using a correction factor of 1.5,[83] approximately 75 per cent of the Presidency population are found to have suffered. Additional to this, couples may well have avoided sleeping together during the pandemic in order to reduce the chances of infection.

With such an effect, a peak of births would be expected to follow, consequent upon the resumption of sexual relations. This is clearly seen in the last few months of 1919, where births reach a level higher than that for any month in 1920, and get back to within ten per cent of the 1914 – 17 average. That this recovery of births did not exceed the average figure can be seen as a result of the mortality effect of the pandemic, as opposed to the morbidity effect of reduced coital frequency. As explained previously, women of reproductive age were particularly at risk of death, both because of the pure age effect (which, of course, affected both sexes), and also because of the complications attendant upon contracting the disease while pregnant.

On the basis of the uncorrected vital registration figures, 344,430 excess deaths occurred to women aged 15 – 49 in 1918 in Bombay Presidency.[84] This amounts to 6.76 per cent of the female population of reproductive age, or 9.39 per cent if the death registration data are corrected by a factor of 1.39.[85] This straightforward reduction in the number of women exposed to risk plays its part not only in limiting the level which births can regain, but also in the precipitous drop in the number of births during the second wave of the pandemic. The enhanced risk of mortality for women in the later stages of pregnancy could be expected to contribute to the shortfall of births in November and December 1918. Adding to this effect would be the previously noted propensity for the number of still births to rise.

This does, however, highlight one curious facet of the data, in that there appears to be no effect on the number of births in October, the peak month for influenza mortality, when in excess of half a million people died from the disease in the Presidency. This suggests that the data are incorrect in some manner. The pattern discussed above, though, would seem too logically consistent to simply be the product of a totally defective vital registration system. One possible explanation is that there is some kind of lag in the data (with births tabulated by date of registration, rather than date of occurrence), such that births recorded for October in fact refer to a previous month, possibly September, thus shifting all of the reported totals back one month. This would locate the 1918 nadir in October, a position more consistent with expectation.

Unfortunately, the same effect applied to 1919 results in the shortfall of births attributed to reduced coital frequency being located at too early a date. While it could be argued that the first wave of influenza also resulted in reduced coital frequency, and thus led to the shortfall of births, it is more likely that an effect of this magnitude is linked to the second, more virulent and more prolonged wave. It is likely, then, that the errors in the data are of a more complex nature. More sophisticated analysis of fertility is unfortunately not possible. Data on births by age and parity are not available for India before 1959.[86]

This discussion should not be taken to suggest that no conclusions can be drawn from the data, defective though they may be. The pattern in 1919, and the continuation of a low number of births throughout 1920 testify to an effect over and above that which could be expected from a simple disruption of registration during the pandemic.

In the search for support for a fertility reduction consequent upon the influenza mortality, the effect upon marriage can be studied. This can arise in two ways. Firstly, marriages will be dissolved where one or both partners die as a result of the pandemic, and secondly, marriage ceremonies may be postponed, either because of illness, or because the death of a near relative makes it inappropriate to marry at that time. Of course, the death of one of the proposed partners may lead to 'postponement' until the surviving partner finds a replacement.

Pool,[87] in a study of the pandemic effect on the New Zealand Maoris, suggests a method for calculating the proportion of marriages dissolved by death during the pandemic:
Proportion of marriages dissolved =
$$(q_{male} \times q_{female}) + (p_m \times q_f) + (p_f \times q_m)$$
where: q = probability of a spouse not surviving the pandemic.
p = probability of a spouse surviving the pandemic.
Assuming that, in Bombay Presidency, women marry men eight years older than themselves, and that the probability of dying is the same irrespective of marital status, and working with the number of excess deaths in 1918,[88] and the estimated mid-1918 population,[89] it is estimated that 13.2 per cent of marriages involving women aged 20 – 29, and 12.4 per cent of those involving women aged 30 – 39, were dissolved by the death of one or both partners from influenza. Using the correction factors calculated in the Appendix, these become 19.1 per cent and 18.0 per cent. Clearly, the break-up of such a large proportion of marriages can be expected to exert a downward pressure on fertility.

Some corroborative evidence can also be gleaned from the census material. Table 6 details the proportions widowed in successive census years around the pandemic. For both sexes, and for all ages 15 – 49, the proportion widowed rises between 1911 and 1921. The trend is then for a fall again by 1931. For males, the pattern reverts almost exactly to that for 1911, while for females, at ages 35 – 39 and 45 – 49, the proportion widowed is actually higher in 1931. This may reflect the

Table 6. Proportions Widowed, Bombay Presidency, 1911, 1921 and 1931.

Age Group	Male 1911	1921	1931	Female 1911	1921	1931
15 – 19	.012	.016	.012	.037	.044	.030
20 – 24	.025	.033	.020	.062	.069	.047
25 – 29	.038	.056	.037	.100	.111	.097
30 – 34	.055	.080	.050	.169	.188	.151
35 – 39	.072	.099	.080	.254	.273	.285
40 – 44	.105	.132	.105	.398	.403	.375
45 – 49	.133	.161	.155	.491	.499	.540

Sources: Census of India — Bombay Presidency: 1911, 1921, 1931.

lack of opportunity, especially for older women, for widow remarriage. However, the pattern does indeed point to a substantial rise in the incidence of widowhood and widowerhood prior to 1921.

Table 7. Marriages of Europeans and Indian Christians of Part-European Descent, Bombay City, 1913 – 23.

Year:	1913	1914	1915	1916	1917	1918	1919	1920	1921	1922	1923
Number:	944	941	788	840	669	636	1012	1227	1275	1034	854

Source: Ecclesiastical Returns — Bombay City, 1913 – 23.

The postponement of marriage is rather harder to demonstrate. While, since the end of the nineteenth century, the Municipal Corporation of the City of Bombay could '. . . in their discretion provide either wholly or partly for . . . the registration of marriages',[90] the lack of published data suggests that this prerogative was not exercised. Evidence of a rather unsatisfactory nature can be gained from the ecclesiastical records of Bombay City. This is unsatisfactory because it refers only to Europeans or Indian Christians of part

European descent, who comprised less than five per cent of the population of Bombay City, and therefore less than one quarter of one per cent of the population of the Presidency. In addition, they can by no means be considered representative of the population as a whole. Nevertheless, as shown in Table 7, 1918 saw considerably fewer marriages in this group than in the surrounding years, although there were also very few in 1917, another year of high mortality. The table shows a marriage 'boom' in the years following the pandemic.

Table 8. Proportions Single by Age, Bombay Presidency, 1911, 1921 and 1931.

Age Group	Male			Female		
	1911	1921	1931	1911	1921	1931
5 – 9	–	–	–	.835	.860	.776
10 – 14	.852	.865	.864	.455	.512	.569
15 – 19	.630	.645	.549	.116	.128	.109
20 – 24	.356	.376	.351	.035	.045	.044
25 – 29	.173	.187	.140	.021	.028	.022
30 – 34	.092	.100	.086	.018	.022	.018
35 – 39	.057	.060	.050	–	–	–

Sources: Census of India — Bombay Presidency: 1911, 1921, 1931.

Again, census material allows for some measure of support for this pattern, and generalization to the wider population. In Table 8, the proportion single by age rises from 1911 to 1921, and then declines again by 1931 (with the exception of females aged 10 – 14). This appears to confirm the suggestion that marriages were postponed from the pandemic period. In fact, on the basis of Table 7, the census data possibly understate the rise in proportions single as, by 1921, the number of marriages, in that group at least, had been above average for two years, in the post-pandemic marriage boom.

It seems valid to conclude that, as suggested by the vital registration data, there was a pronounced effect on fertility, brought about by mortality, acting through heightened maternal mortality, and the dissolution of marriages; and morbidity, acting through coital frequency, increased still births, and the postponement of marriages. In sum, the death of five per cent of the population (seven and a half per cent if corrected), and the illness of at least fifty per cent, from influenza in 1918 led to a decline in births of around thirty per cent in 1919 in Bombay Presidency.[91]

Such sudden age selective effects as described above can be expected to leave their mark upon the population distribution. The population pyramid for the population under registration in Bombay Presidency for 1921 bears witness to the major consequences of the pandemic. The 0 – 4 age group is severely undercut, as would be expected from the preceding discussion, and the middle age groups, especially 20 – 29 years, show a distinct reduction compared to 1911. It was hoped that these effects could be followed over time as they worked their way through the population pyramid. However, in the 1931 distribution, little trace remains of the occurrence, only thirteen years earlier, of the worst epidemic in recorded Indian history. This is possibly a consequence of age misstatement, and age shifting in particular, combined at older ages with attrition due to the normal high level of Indian mortality.

MORTALITY AMONG POPULATION SUB-GROUPS

In India, Klein proposes, 'death was class orientated, although in many communities different social groups had similar sanitary practices and exposure to disease.'[92] This comment refers to Indian mortality in general, but it is no less true when referring specifically to influenza mortality. The ordering of communities in Table 9 is '. . . in general terms, the order in which one would place [them] as regards general enlightenment, education and approximation to Western methods of life.'[93] This ordering can thus be taken as a rough classification of social and economic class.

It is particularly striking that low caste Hindu influenza mortality is higher than mortality from all causes for any other group. Also, while mortality from all causes for low caste Hindus is 5.5 times higher than for Europeans, influenza mortality is 7.5 times greater. This raises the question of whether the observed differences are due to different rates of transmission of the disease among different races and castes, or whether the differential is rooted in varying levels of mortality, once infected.

Once again, unfortunately, the argument founders for want of statistical evidence. However, recourse can be made to some indirect indicators. Data for the army in India are presented separately for British and Indian troops, and show that British troops had an influenza incidence rate of 219.5 per 1,000 in 1918, whereas for Indian troops it

Table 9. Mortality by Race, Religion and Caste Group: Influenza and
All Causes, Bombay City, 1918.

| | Mortality per 1,000 population | |
	Influenza	All Causes
Europeans	8.3	29.1
Parsees	9.0	29.5
Eurasians	11.9	42.0
Jews	14.8	40.2
Indian Christians	18.4	53.7
Caste Hindus	18.9	53.3
Muslims	19.2	61.2
Low Caste Hindus	61.6	162.7

Sources: Influenza mortality — Phipson cited in note 13 p. 517. All
causes mortality — *Admin. Report of Municipal Commissioner*,
Bombay, 1918.

was only 136.8 per 1,000.[94] It should be noted that these rates, in
common with those for jail populations, are computed on the basis of
the numbers admitted to hospital, and may therefore say more about the
differential in levels of care for Indian and British troops than about any
racial differences in the propensity to contract influenza. The main
point, though, is that these figures do *not* argue that Indians are more
prone to fall prey to influenza than Europeans. The difference must
therefore, as with the geographical differences noted above, be a
function of case mortality.

This hypothesis is supported by the Army data. Despite a lower
reported incidence of influenza, Indian troops' death rate from
influenza in 1918 was 15.23 per 1,000 compared to 8.81 per 1,000 for
British troops.[95] This difference cannot be explained by climatic
variation, as the geographical differences were, since there is no
particular pattern of spatial concentration of either Indian or European
troops in the high and low mortality areas, and so different factors must
be in operation at the micro level.

As mentioned earlier, the virulence of the 1918 – 19 influenza virus
was due to its propensity to bring pneumonic complications in train. It
appears that Indian troops suffered considerably more from pneumonia,
even in non-pandemic years, than British troops, the respective
mortality rates from this cause for 1917 being 5 per 1,000 compared to

0.36 per 1,000. This may be a function of the differential level of care inferred from the influenza admission rates given above. Among the general population, the Sanitary Commissioner for Bombay suggested that '. . . the divergence in the mortality of nursed and unnursed cases [is] very apparent . . . I have been told unofficially that it is about eight fold.'[96] Thus, one component of the mortality differential may be the level of access to medical treatment among different classes, and the opportunity available for rest and recuperation.

Relief work was undertaken in the pandemic period by switching medical staff from plague and vaccination operations to influenza work, and by opening roadside and travelling dispensaries, and temporary hospitals.[97] Such efforts were, unsurprisingly, concentrated in the urban areas, and were constrained by the fact that medical staff were as liable to contract influenza as anyone else, indeed, possibly more so due to their continual contact with influenza victims. These special measures were further undermined as '. . . a certain number of medical practitioners . . . [took] the opportunity to double their fees.'[98] Such action would be likely to concentrate medical attention among the wealthier urban sections of the population.

A second possible explanation may lie in the nature of the infection itself. It was proposed above that the 1918 – 19 influenza virus paved the way for bacterial invasion leading to pneumonic complications. In this light, it is interesting that '. . . malnutrition associated with low intake of nitrogen results in definite impairment of immune responses and a corresponding increase in susceptibility to bacterial diseases.'[99] More specifically, a link has been found between malnutrition and bacterial pneumonia.[100] It is to be expected that those at the lower end of the social spectrum would be more prone to malnutrition and thus, by this reckoning, to pneumonic complications. However, the argument can be taken further.

In 1918, the south-west monsoon (generally occurring in June and July) failed in several parts of India, and consequently the crops failed. The areas affected were scattered parts of Gujarat, Bombay, Deccan, Berar, Rajputana, the southern part of Central Provinces, Orissa and United Provinces. Conditions were so severe in Central Provinces, and United Provinces that famine was declared.[101]

The correspondence of these areas with those suffering the most severe influenza mortality (as shown in Fig. 1) is remarkable. It would seem logical to expect the poorest sections of the population to be hardest hit by such a crop failure, given their lack of resources to fall back on.[102] The Bombay Health Officer's Report for the third quarter of 1918 states that '. . . there has been a large influx, especially of poorer people, into the city . . . from districts affected with scarcity and dearness of food',[103] and a further report mentions '. . . thousands of refugees from famine stricken areas in a weakened and destitute condition.'[104] Such reports of distress migration into Bombay City attest to the condition of the poor in the rural areas of Bombay Presidency, and strengthen the argument that this was a factor, not only in the interclass mortality differentials, but also possibly in the geographic distribution of mortality.

Mitra,[105] in surveying the plethora of epidemics and famines to which India has fallen victim, comments upon the fact that the same areas appear regularly upon the roll of those suffering most severely. In this case at least, a reason for such a confluence of misery can be posited.

In addition to the failure of the crops affecting influenza mortality through the mechanism of malnutrition, the influenza pandemic in its turn affected agricultural production in the most severely stricken regions. In Bombay Presidency the severe second wave came at the time of harvest of the early crop, and sowing of the late crop.[106] With morbidity estimated to be in excess of fifty per cent of the general population, and with the concentration of severe attacks in the most productive age range, 20 – 40, the effect on agricultural production was extreme. The effects of rain failure and a work-force incapacitated by illness combined to result in a nineteen per cent decrease in the area under food crops in 1918 compared with 1917, and a fifteen per cent decrease in the area under non-food crops. Staple food prices rose by 100 per cent as a result of this reduction of area, coupled with failure of growth and the scanty outcome, and famine or scarcity was declared over the greater part of the Presidency.[107]

Thus, it would appear that the famine and the pandemic, in the Indian context, formed a set of mutually exacerbating catastrophes. While the synergistic effects of malnutrition and infection are well recorded at the individual level, this suggests that such relationships, though brought about by somewhat different mechanisms, also occur at the societal level. Whether such interlinkages exist for other crises is a topic worthy of further research.

CONCLUSION

The 1918 – 19 influenza pandemic is unique in terms of the sheer scale of mortality caused. Rivers became clogged with corpses when insufficient firewood was available for the cremation of Hindus.[108] With such a concentration of deaths, the effects can be clearly mapped out despite the inadequacies of the data. It offers a unique opportunity for the study of demographic crisis in India.

The influenza virus of 1918 – 19 has been shown to have given rise to a disease marked by the usual high infectivity of influenza, but with a virulence in the second wave unprecedented in outbreaks of the disease reported before or since.

The level of mortality is graphically illustrated by the calculation of a period life table for 1918. If the pandemic year level of mortality were general, expectation of life at birth, based on corrected vital registration data, for Bombay Presidency would be around six years. Even on the basis of uncorrected data, this rises to only eleven years.

The pandemic was a highly concentrated phenomenon, with the severe second wave sweeping a given area in a period of only two to three months. In India as a whole, the second wave lasted a matter of only four months, and yet accounted for the lives of around seventeen to eighteen million people in that brief period.

Those hardest hit by the outbreak tended to be people in the prime years, 20 – 40, with women suffering disproportionately more. This age and sex selective effect exacerbated the subsequent effect on fertility which would be expected under crisis conditions, resulting in a reduction of births in 1919 of around thirty per cent. In addition, the greatest mortality was experienced by those social classes which normally had the weakest grip on life, with malnutrition acting as an intervening variable in the contraction of usually fatal complicating disease.

The role of malnutrition, in relation to the existence of famine in the north, west and centre of India may also help explain not only the geographical distribution of mortality within India (providing an alternative to the pre-existing hypothesis based on climatic differences), but also India's position as the country with the highest recorded mortality during the pandemic.

APPENDIX TO CHAPTER 7

Calculation of Correction Factors for Indian Death Registration Data, and Derivation of Estimated Total Influenza Mortality

The technique used here to adjust for underregistration of deaths in the vital registration system is the 'growth balance' method, in particular the variant procedure proposed by Brass.[109] The problems involved in applying this method to historical Indian registration data will be briefly illustrated using male deaths for registration India, 1911, as an example. Table A1 gives both the raw data required (i.e. numbers of persons and deaths by age) and a summary of the necessary computations. The calculated partial birth and death rates are denoted by ny/py and dy/py respectively. It is apparent from Table A1 that, due to the available age groupings, there are only seven sets of partial vital

Table A1. Growth Balance Method Applied to Data for Registration India, Males, 1911.

Age Group	Number (000's)	Deaths (000's)	Age Point	n_y	P_y	d_y	$\dfrac{n_y}{P_y}$	$\dfrac{d_y}{P_y}$
0 – 4	16,032.0	1,586.2	5	3,324.9	104,536.9	2,339.9	0.0318	0.0223
5 – 9	17,217.1	274.4	10	3,172.7	87,319.9	2,059.4	0.0363	0.0236
10 – 14	14,509.7	180.4	15	2,485.7	72,810.2	1,879.1	0.0341	0.0258
15 – 19	10,347.1	152.5	20	2,038.9	62,463.1	1,726.5	0.0326	0.0276
20 – 29	19,175.9	301.1	30	1,838.6	43,287.1	1,425.5	0.0425	0.0329
30 – 39	17,595.6	351.4	40	1,496.7	25,691.5	1,074.1	0.0583	0.0418
40 – 49	12,338.1	310.1	50	983.5	13,353.4	764.0	0.0737	0.0572
50 – 59	7,332.9	304.0						
60+	6,020.5	460.1		f (estimated) = 1.75				

Source: Annual Report, Sanitary Commissioner, India, 1911.

rates with which to work. Moreover the calculated partial birth and death rates in Table A1 also deviate substantially from linearity. This is especially true for age points 5, 10, and 15, which form a cluster. Also out of line is the set of partial rates for age point 50. This leaves only three points (15, 20 and 30) on which to base an estimate of the level of death registration coverage. The omission of the oldest age point seems justifiable, as curvature of points at higher ages is a common occurrence, probably due to age misstatement in the census and at registration of death. Also Brass suggests that a cluster of points at younger ages can be omitted, since such a pattern is often a distortion arising from a combination of fertility change and age errors.[110] Consequently the correction factor (slope of the line) for underregistration of deaths calculated in Table A1 (f = 1.75) is computed solely on the basis of a straight line fitted through the partial birth and death rates for age points 15, 20 and 30.

Table A2. Correction Factors for Death Registration, India and Selected Provinces, 1911.

| Area | Correction Factors | | | Registration Completeness |
	Male	Female	Both Sexes	
Registration India	1.75	1.65	1.70	59%
Bombay Presidency	1.58	1.39	1.49	67%
Madras Presidency	1.45	1.63	1.54	65%
Assam	2.48	2.02	2.25	44%

Calculated from data in: *Annual Report, Sanitary Commissioner*, 1911.

Clearly, such a correction factor does not provide a robust estimate of the true number of deaths, since death registration data for the whole human age range are being 'corrected' on the basis of information gained only from the prime adult ages. Further problems arise when applying the method to subnational units since the method's assumption of population stability (by no means definitely fulfilled for registration India) is brought further into doubt by inter-regional migration. However, the various correction factors calculated, which are utilized in the text, are given in Table A2.

Table A3. Excess Deaths due to Fevers and Respiratory Diseases, 1918 – 19, over Average for 1913 – 17, Provinces under Vital Registration.

Ajmer Merwara	26,572	Delhi	24,681
Assam	158,087	Lower Burma	98,692
Bengal	540,195	Madras Presidency	630,370
Bihar and Orissa	743,995	North West Frontier Province	90,672
Bombay Presidency	1,062,852	Punjab	889,900
Central Provinces	941,076	United Provinces	2,211,737
Coorg	123	Upper Burma	43,176

Sources: Annual Reports, Sanitary Commissioners, (various years).

Excess deaths, June 1918 to May 1919, from fevers and respiratory diseases for the various provinces with vital registration in British India, are shown in Table A3. The total is 7,462,088 for registration India. The population covered by the registration area is 75.33 per cent of the 1911 census population. So, extrapolating to national coverage, on the assumption that the average mortality in the registration area is representative of the whole country, gives 9,905,865 deaths. Correcting this with a factor of 1.7 (see Table A2) results in an estimated national influenza mortality of 16,839,970. This amounts to almost 5.5 per cent of the total population.

The assumption that the registration India mortality level is appropriate for all areas may lead to an underestimate. Of those areas without vital registration coverage, Baluchistan, Rajputana, Kashmir, Central India, and the western part of Hyderabad all lie in the north, west and central parts of India which were all characterized by a high influenza mortality rate (see Fig. 1). Only Mysore, the eastern part of Hyderabad, and the small native states of Cochin and Travancore represent the lower influenza mortality area.

Also possibly biasing the estimate downwards is the assumption that the 1911 level of registration completeness adequately represents the situation in 1918 – 19. In fact, vital registration was disrupted by the pandemic, and figures were reconstructed later, probably leading to an increased level of omission. This, of course, will affect both this estimate, and that proposed by Davis, to the same extent.

NOTES TO CHAPTER 8

This paper is based upon a thesis undertaken as part of the M.Sc. in Demography at the London School of Economics.

1 McNeill, W. H.: *Plagues and People*. Blackwell. 1976. p. 356.
2 Beveridge, W. I. B.: 'Where did 'Red Flu' Come From?' *New Scientist* Vol. 77 no. 1095. 1978. p. 791.
3 Ministry of Health, U.K.: 'Report on the Pandemic of Influenza, 1918 – 19'. *Reports on Health and Medical Subjects*. No. 4. HMSO 1920. p. 182.
4 Collier, R.: *The Plague of the Spanish Lady — The Influenza Pandemic of 1918 – 19*. Macmillan. 1974. p. 306.
5 Jordan, E. O.: *Epidemic Influenza: A Survey*. American Medical Association. 1927. p. 229.
6 Stuart-Harris, C. H. & Schild, G. C.: *Influenza: The Virus and the Disease*. Edward Arnold. 1976. p. vi.
7 Ministry of Health, U.K., op. cit. p. 383, and Jordan, op. cit. p. 222.
8 *Census of India — 1921*. Volume 1 — India. Part 1 — Report. p. 14.
9 Davis, K.: *The Population of India and Pakistan*. Princeton University Press. 1951. p. 34.
10 Ministry of Health, U.K., op. cit. part 1.
11 Crosby, A. W.: *Epidemic and Peace. 1918*. Greenwood Press. 1976. pp. 25 – 8.
12 *Annual Report of the Sanitary Commissioner with the Government of India — 1918*. Government of India. 1920. p. 59.
13 Phipson, E. S.: 'The Pandemic of Influenza in India in the Year 1918.' *The Indian Medical Gazette*. Vol. 58. 1923. p. 511.
14 Ibid. p. 511.
15 Fox, J. P., Hall, C. E. & Elveback, L. R.: *Epidemiology — Man and Disease*. Macmillan. 1970. p. 52.
16 Ibid. p. 215.
17 Phipson, op. cit. p. 511.
18 *Census of India — 1921*. Vol. 1 (1). p. 12.
19 *Annual Report, Sanitary Commissioner, India 1918*. p. 61.
20 Phipson, op. cit. p. 512.
21 Ibid. p. 512.
22 *Annual Report, Sanitary Commissioner, India, 1918*. p. 60.
23 Phipson, op. cit. p. 510.
24 Fox et al. op. cit. p. 216.
25 Crosby, op. cit. p. 37.
26 Ibid. p. 37.
27 International Centre for Diarrhoeal Disease Research, Bangladesh.: *Glimpse — ICDDR, B Newsletter*. Vol. 5. No. 1. 1983. pp. 2 – 3.
28 Ibid. p. 2.
29 Hoyle, F. & Wickramasinghe, C.: 'Influenza from Space?' *New Scientist*. Vol. 79. No. 1122. 1978. pp. 946 – 8.
30 Hoyle, F. & Wickramasinghe, C.: 'Does Epidemic Disease Come from Space?' *New Scientist*. Vol. 76. No. 1078. 1977. p. 403.

31 Senn, S.J.: 'Can You Really Catch Cold from a Comet?' *New Scientist*. Vol. 92. No. 1276. 1981. pp. 244 – 6.
32 *Annual Report, Sanitary Commissioner, India 1918*. p. 61.
33 Ibid. p. 55.
34 Government of India: *Proceedings of the Department of Education — Sanitary*. Part A. March 1919. Proc. No. 29.
35 *Annual Report, Sanitary Commissioner, India 1918*. p. 61.
36 *Bombay Government Gazette — Supplement*. 7/9/1918 — 21/12/1918.
37 *Census of India — 1921*. 1 (1). p. 14.
38 Davis, op. cit. p. 36.
39 Ibid. p. 237.
40 Ibid. p. 37.
41 Ibid. p. 237.
42 *Census of India — 1921*. 1 (1). p. 16.
43 See Appendix for details.
44 Gill, C.A.: *The Genesis of Epidemics*. Bailliere, Tindall & Cox., 1928. p. 258.
45 Ibid. p. 261.
46 Jordan, op. cit. p. 480.
47 Ministry of Health, U.K., op. cit. p. 160.
48 *Procs. Dept. of Ed. — Sanitary*. Part A. Oct. 1918. Proc. no. 7.
49 Crosby, op. cit. p. 64.
50 Ibid. pp. 215 – 20.
51 Shope, R.E.: 'Influenza: History, Epidemiology and Speculation.' *Public Health Reports*. Vol. 73. 1958. p. 176.
52 Crosby, op. cit. p. 219.
53 Ibid. p. 220.
54 Burnet, F. M. & Clark, E.: *Influenza — A Survey of the Last 50 Years in the Light of Modern Work on the Virus of Epidemic Influenza*. Macmillan. 1942. pp. 64 & 84 – 5. And Fox *et al.* op. cit. p. 97.
55 Jordan, op. cit. p. 13. and Phipson, op. cit. p. 514.
56 Phipson, op. cit. p. 514.
57 *Census of India — 1921*. 1 (1). p. 15.
58 Calculated from data in: *Annual Report, Sanitary Commissioner, India 1915*. p. xix.
59 *Census of India — 1921*. 1 (1). p. 13.
60 *Procs. Dept. of Ed. — Sanitary*. Part A. Nov. 1918. Proc. no. 17.
61 Crosby, op. cit. p. 9.
62 *Bombay Government Gazette — Supplement*. Aug. – Dec. 1918.
63 Phipson, op. cit. p. 518.
64 Stuart-Harris & Schild, op. cit. p. 115.
65 Ibid. p. 117.
66 Ministry of Health, U.K., op. cit. p. xiv.
67 Gill, op. cit. p. 247.
68 Ministry of Health, U.K., op. cit. p. xv.
69 Crosby, op. cit. p. 230.
70 Burnet & Clark, op. cit. pp. 90 – 9.
71 Crosby, pp. 221 – 2.

72 Ibid. p. 222.
73 *Census of India — 1921.* 1 (1). p. 13.
74 Jordan, op. cit. p. 200.
75 Stuart-Harris & Schild, op. cit. p. 99.
76 Jordan, op. cit. p. 272.
77 For example, see: Beveridge, W. I. B.: *Influenza — The Last Great Plague.* Heinemann. 1977. pp. 14 – 15.
78 *Bombay Government Gazette — Supplement.* Aug. – Dec. 1918.
79 *Bombay Executive Health Officer's Quarterly Report.* 3rd Quarter, 1918. p. 1.
80 *Procs. Dept. of Ed. — Sanitary.* Part A. March 1919. Proc. no. 26.
81 See Appendix.
82 Assuming that the 1901 – 11 rate of growth continued to mid-1918.
83 See Appendix.
84 Here, excess deaths are calculated on the basis of the 1918 deaths from all causes compared to the average of 1913 – 17 deaths from all causes. This change in definition is necessary because age-specific data is not broken down by cause. The data are from: *Annual Reports, Sanitary Commissioner, Bombay Presidency.* 1913 – 18.
85 See Appendix.
86 *Vital Statistics of India. 1959.* Government of India. p. iii.
87 Pool, D.I.: 'The Effects of the 1918 Pandemic of Influenza on the Maori Population of New Zealand.' *Bulletin of the History of Medicine.* Vol. 47. No. 3. 1973. p. 278.
88 See note 84.
89 See note 82.
90 Michael, L. W.: *The History of the Municipal Corporation of the City of Bombay.* Union Press. Bombay. 1902. p. 36.
91 Calculated as the difference between births in 1919, and average births for 1914 – 17.
92 Klein, I.: 'Death in India, 1871 – 1921.' *Journal of Asian Studies.* Vol. 32. No. 4. 1973. p. 643.
93 Phipson, op. cit. p. 519.
94 *Annual Report, Sanitary Commissioner, India 1918.* pp. 5, 31.
95 Ibid. pp. 5, 31.
96 *Procs. Dept. of Ed. — Sanitary.* Part A. Nov. 1918. Proc. no. 17.
97 Ibid, Procs. no. 6 – 17.
98 Ibid, Proc. no. 15.
99 Fox *et al.*, op. cit. pp. 77.
100 Messih, G. A., Mullah, T. & Tajeldin, H.: *Epidemiology — Principles and Application to Infectious Diseases.* All-Hurriyah Printing House. 1976.
101 Srivasta, H. S.: *The History of Indian Famines and the Development of Famine Policy: 1858 – 1918.* Sri Ram Mehra & Co., Agra. 1968. pp. 319 – 20.
102 Guz, D.: *Famine in the Punjab: A Case Study of the Famines of 1896 – 97 and 1899 – 1900.* Unpublished M.Sc Dissertation. London School of Economics. 1982. p. 31. See also chapter 7 of the present volume.

103 *Bombay Executive Health Officer's Quarterly Report.* 3rd Quarter, 1918.
     p. 5.
104 *Administration Report of the Municipal Commissioner for the City of
     Bombay.* 1918. p. 3.
105 Mitra, A.: *India's Population: Aspects of Quality and Control.* (2 Vols.)
     Family Planning Foundation of India. 1978. p. 784.
106 *Bombay Season and Crop Report.* 1918 – 19. p. 1.
107 Ibid. p. 8.
108 *Procs. Dept. of Ed. — Sanitary.* Part A. March 1919. Proc. no. 26. and
     ibid. Part B. Jan. 1919. Proc. no. 23.
109 Brass, W.: *Indirect Methods of Estimating Mortality: Illustrated by
     Application to Middle East and North African Data.* Mimeo. pp. 12 – 15.
110 Ibid. p. 13.

9

CHOLERA MORTALITY IN BRITISH INDIA, 1817 – 1947

David Arnold

It has never been in serious dispute that cholera was a major cause of death in India during the nineteenth century and for a large part of the twentieth. Current scholarship places cholera alongside malaria, smallpox, plague and influenza as one of the principal epidemics behind India's past high mortality rates. Nineteenth-century British observers, reacting in part to Europe's own vulnerability to the disease, put cholera in the front rank, and it almost invariably appeared first in official health reports and mortality statistics. Controversy, therefore, surrounds not the importance of the disease as a factor in high mortality levels in India, but the reason why a disease, so widespread and well entrenched in the region, began to decline in the early twentieth century and, after a partial resurgence in the 1940s, continued to diminish in the post-Independence decades.

The controversy is not without contemporary relevance. Cholera, unlike smallpox, an epidemic disease with which it shared certain common characteristics, has not been eradicated, and continues from time to time to reach epidemic proportions, especially in Bangladesh and West Bengal. Immunization, long seen as a vital control measure, is now regarded with such medical scepticism that the Government of India has recently decided to abandon compulsory inoculation for pilgrims attending religious fairs and festivals, a policy that has been followed for almost fifty years.[1] Should one conclude from this that inoculation (and possibly other forms of medical intervention) had little part in cholera's decline? Did other factors — such as the relative absence of famine after about 1908 (the Bengal famine of 1943 apart) or a change in the bacteriological nature of the disease — play a more influential role? Were there social and economic changes that helped diminish cholera's importance as a cause of mortality in India?

These kinds of issues are not, of course, confined to cholera or to India, but figure in the wider discussion about the relationship between epidemic disease and demographic change. There has been a sustained, and as yet inconclusive, debate about the relevance of medicine, improving living standards and epidemiological shifts to the demography of eighteenth and nineteenth-century Europe, and of such colonial and ex-colonial territories as Sri Lanka in more recent times. Razzell has argued forcefully that medical intervention in the form of smallpox inoculation was sufficiently widespread and effective in eighteenth-century England to have a decisive impact on mortality rates and population growth.[2] But perhaps the weight of scholarly opinion, exemplified by McKeown in a series of articles, favours the view that medicine in the main had little influence on mortality before at least the mid-nineteenth century, and that either the dwindling virulence of such diseases as scarlet fever or, more probably, improvements in living conditions, diet and food availability were responsible.[3] For Third World countries, however, the opposité argument is often made. Modern medical technology — from mass inoculation to DDT-spraying and cheap drugs — has, it is argued, made possible the eradication or containment of disease (and hence brought about a demographic revolution) without any corresponding social and economic transformation.[4] But here, too, there has been dissent, particularly over the extent to which control measures have been effective and how far economic and political variables have been critical.[5]

One of the first needs is for disaggregation. While there may be factors, such as economic growth or sanitary improvements, which affect a wide spectrum of diseases, it is important to bear in mind that each disease has its own characteristics, its own relationship to the human environment. The factors that influenced the decline in cholera may not be identical with those responsible for the fall in plague or smallpox mortality.[6] All-India aggregations can conceal considerable and significant regional and social variations, and one way of trying to establish the underlying trends in cholera mortality in India, and the reasons behind them, is to examine local patterns and to compare them with the broader picture. For the purposes of this essay, the Madras Presidency in southern India and the United Provinces (U.P.), now Uttar Pradesh and until 1901 the North-Western Provinces, in northern India, which together accounted for about 30 per cent of cholera mortality in British India,[7] will be taken up for more detailed consideration. By looking, too, at the period from the early nineteenth century up to the middle of the twentieth, it is possible to suggest some of the long-term trends that emerge from nearly 150 years of cholera in India.

LONG-TERM TRENDS

Any attempt to identify the long-term variability of Indian cholera mortality is hampered by the absence of a consistent statistical record before the mid-1860s or 1870s and by the dubious reliability of the data thereafter. In rural areas of British India the initial collection of mortality and cause of death information was made by the village watchman (*chaukidar* in northern India). Illiterate (and so unable to keep a written record) and without the medical training to make valid diagnoses, the chaukidars were required to report vital data to the nearest police station over a period that varied from a week to as much as a month. In such circumstances it is not surprising that an estimated 22 per cent of deaths in UP went unrecorded during the 1920s.[8] For want of better diagnosis, many deaths were attributed to 'fever' or entered under 'other causes'. There is little doubt that many cholera deaths were omitted and that other causes of death crept into the 'cholera' category. The strongest evidence for the latter was the inclusion in times of famine of many cases of 'famine diarrhoea', the symptoms of which bore a superficial resemblance to cholera.[9] The consequent inflation of the cholera statistics may have somewhat exaggerated the apparent correlation between famine mortality and cholera epidemics. Famines, too, were periods of extreme administrative and social disruption and made the accurate reporting of the number and causes of death more than ever problematic. On the other hand, it was maintained that cholera, because of the violence of its seizures, the characteristic 'rice-water stools' of its victims, and the rapidity with which death followed in some half of cases, was one of the few diseases villagers could reliably identify. Checks on the accuracy of cause of death data suggested that this was generally the case.[10]

Reservations about statistical reliability aside, the available record suggests that there was a general decline in cholera mortality in British India between 1900 and 1940, and that this trend was resumed and strengthened in the post-Independence decades (see Table 1). Of the 24.3 million deaths from cholera recorded for the period between 1865 and 1950, 59 per cent (14.3 million) fell in the 46 year period up to 1910. The downward trend was, however, interrupted by the decade of the 1940s, which witnessed the Quit India movement and the Second World War, the Bengal famine and Partition, all of which were directly or indirectly conducive to a resurgence in cholera mortality.

Table 2 suggests a possible periodization. The last quarter of the nineteenth century was a period of high cholera mortality throughout India. The peak in fact came in 1900 when 805,698 cholera deaths were recorded, equivalent to a cholera death rate of 3.70 per thousand of the population. Thereafter, over the next quarter-century, cholera mortality

Table 1. Cholera Mortality in India: Decennial Averages, 1865 – 1960.

Period	Decennial Average
1865 – 1870 (6 years)	146,998
1871 – 1880	218,033
1881 – 1890	301,040
1891 – 1900	444,923
1901 – 1910	374,298
1911 – 1920	350,631
1921 – 1930	243,467
1931 – 1940	144,147
1941 – 1950	214,512
1951 – 1960	53,023

Note: (1) The figures exclude Burma, but include Pakistan from 1947 to 1960, except for East Bengal (Bangladesh) for 1946 – 9. Before 1948 India's princely states are also excluded.

Sources: H. W. Bellew, *The History of Cholera in India from 1862 to 1881* (London, Trubner, 1885): 684; *Annual Report of the Sanitary Commissioner with the Government of India, 1899* (Calcutta, Superintendent of Government Printing, 1900): 131; R. Pollitzer, *Cholera* (Geneva, World Health Organization, 1959): 58.

became more variable and showed some tendency to fall. From 1925 to 1947 the downward trend was clear, with less than half the rate of mortality of the previous period. The most dramatic decline came, however, after Independence in 1947, and was further accelerated after 1964 as the less fatal 'El Tor' strain of cholera displaced the 'classic' form over most of India. By that stage cholera mortality was barely 0.1 per cent of what it had been in the late nineteenth century.[11]

For the period before 1865 cholera statistics are so fragmentary and impressionistic that few firm conclusions can be drawn from them. The most consistent data relate to soldiers and prisoners, but they were such markedly atypical social groups (whose crowded and insanitary conditions made them exceptionally subject to a disease of bad sanitation and infected water supplies) that it would be rash to apply mortality rates among them to the population at large.[12] However, without expecting much statistical exactitude, one can identify certain characteristics about cholera in the pre-registration period.

Table 2. Cholera Mortality in India, 1874 – 1968.

Period	Average Annual Cholera Mortality Rate	Expressed as a % of the 1874 – 1899 figure
1874 – 1899	1.68	–
1900 – 1924	1.58	94
1925 – 1947	0.74	44
1948 – 1963	0.17	10
1963 – 1968	0.0017	0.1

Notes: (1) Here and in Tables 3 and 4 the mortality rate is cholera deaths per thousand population per year.
(2) The figures are for British India for the period 1874 – 1947, and for India and Pakistan combined for 1948 – 1968.

Sources: L. Rogers, *The Incidence and Spread of Cholera in India: Forecasting and Control of Epidemics* (Calcutta, Thacker, Spink & Company, 1928): 28; J. B. Shrivastav, 'Prevention and Control of Cholera', in Dhiman Barua and William Burrows (eds.), *Cholera* (Philadelphia, Saunders, 1974): 420.

Although cholera undoubtedly existed in India long before the start of the nineteenth century and was certainly present late in the eighteenth,[13] the cholera epidemic which began in Bengal in 1817 and swept through much of India in the course of the following four years, was so rapid in its progress and so destructive of human life, that it has often been seen as virtually the birth of a new disease.[14] Estimates of the epidemic's mortality vary considerably, and generally rest upon no sound statistical base. In 1831 the French physician Moreau de Jonnès, alarmed by the inroads cholera was already making into western Europe, compared the disease to the Black Death, and reckoned on the basis mainly of information from Bengal during the height of the epidemic, that cholera had caused roughly 18 million deaths in British India since 1817.[15] Others, elaborating on Jonnès, suggested that cholera had been the cause of 50 million deaths world-wide since 1817, four-fifths of them in India.[16] Given a population of perhaps 160 million in India at the time,[17] this would have been a devastating scale of mortality. The death toll was undoubtedly very heavy, but, to judge by the limited social and economic disruption that resulted, and by the statistics available, the loss of life cannot have been anywhere near as great as Jonnès and his contemporaries estimated.

Data collected by Jameson for the Bengal Medical Board in 1820 showed that the epidemic had been particularly severe in those areas of Bengal that were later identified as the main cholera endemic zone of eastern India. Jessore district alone was said to have lost 10,000 lives to cholera in two months of 1817. In Sylhet one person in every 29 died (equivalent to a death rate of about 33 per thousand); in Nadia 13 in every thousand persons perished; in the city of Dhaka (Dacca) the figure was 31 per thousand. These were rates considerably above those found in Lower Bengal during most of the late nineteenth century epidemics. But Jameson also noted that towns and districts higher up the Ganges valley suffered rather less than those closer to Calcutta.[18] Reports from Bombay and Ahmadabad suggest that mortality in western India was relatively low. Among the estimated 210,000 inhabitants of Bombay island, for instance, there were 24,227 cases of cholera reported, but only 1,450 deaths in the critical period from August 1818 to August 1819. This is a surprisingly low tally considering the fifty per cent mortality usually associated with the disease.[19] In the Madras Presidency, where the main force of the epidemic was felt between July 1818 and September 1819, district figures varied widely from as little as 3,009 deaths in Nellore (equal to about 7 per thousand of the population) to as much as 13,478 (24 per thousand) for Tirunelveli, and 15,000 (14 per thousand) for Cuddapah.[20] Taking the eight districts for which figures are available, the average cholera mortality rate in Madras appears to have been around 12 per thousand, roughly what it was at the height of the 1875 – 8 epidemic and famine. It would seem likely, therefore, that the extreme severity of the epidemic in Lower Bengal was not (as Jonnès assumed) repeated over India as a whole, nor did it remain at such catastrophic heights for more than a few months.

The exceptional mortality caused by the 1817 – 21 epidemic is emphasized by the absence of famine as a contributory cause. In subsequent decades, however, cholera epidemics frequently occurred alongside periods of drought and famine. In the Madras Presidency, for example, cholera and starvation together accounted for the death of an estimated two million people during the 'Gunter famine' of 1833. More than 200,000 cholera deaths were reported in the province during the famine year of 1866. The epidemic which raged in northern India in 1861 inflicted further suffering on a region already subject to famine.[21]

Before discussing the connection between cholera and famine in more detail, it is worth reflecting further on the possibility that the cholera that affected India in 1817 – 21 was a 'virgin soil epidemic', or at least represented the emergence of a new and more virulent strain of the disease. The way in which 'El Tor' cholera, originating in Indonesia, spread throughout most of South Asia in 1964 – 5 and displaced the 'classic' form of the disease,[22] suggests the ease and speed with which such a transformation could occur. It is tempting, too, to go a stage further and suggest that the declining mortality from cholera was a consequence of the long-term decline in the virulence of the new strain between the 1820s and the 1960s, and thus that human intervention played very little part. It is more likely, however, that a lack of human immunity to cholera, or to this form of the disease, accounted for the exceptional scale of mortality in 1817 – 21, but that thereafter a certain level of 'herd immunity' existed and prevented epidemic mortality from reaching such heights again. Moreover, given favourable circumstances, as in Bengal in 1943, cholera remained as lethal as it had been in the middle and late nineteenth century. While bacteriological change cannot be entirely discounted, it seems unlikely that it would solely or substantially explain the overall decline in cholera mortality between 1900 and 1960.

FAMINE AND IRRIGATION

If one of the striking characteristics of the 1817 – 21 epidemic was the absence of famine, for much of the nineteenth century and the early years of the twentieth major epidemics often coincided with years of drought and hunger. The relationship between famine and nutritional deficiency on the one hand and epidemic disease and mortality on the other is a complex one, and precise correlations have proved difficult to establish.[23] Scholars working on South Asia have perhaps been rather too eager to equate cholera deaths occurring during periods of famine with famine mortality as such.[24] They are partly driven to this by the absence or paucity of figures for starvation deaths in the official records. In truth, cholera in many cases must have been simply the immediate cause of death for individuals already fatally weakened by hunger, exhaustion and despair. Moreover, as already indicated, a large number of fatalities attributed to cholera were actually caused by 'famine diarrhoea'. But it would be a mistake to see cholera mortality and famine deaths as identical or interchangeable, and thus conclude that the decline in cholera merely followed from the dwindling incidence or severity of famine in India after about 1908.[25]

One of the best-documented illustrations of the relationship between cholera and famine comes from the Madras Presidency in the 1870s. From a low point of 840 reported deaths in 1873 and 313 in 1874, the provincial total rose sharply in 1875 to 94,546 with the start of a new epidemic cycle. In 1876 mortality reached 148,193 and it was during

this year that famine conditions became acute in the dry, interior
districts of Bellary, Kurnool and Cuddapah (known collectively as the
'Ceded Districts'). The epidemic peaked in 1877 at 357,430 deaths (a
rate of 12.24 per thousand of the population) before falling back to
47,167 in 1878 and returning to a new low of 613 in 1880. The onset of
the epidemic in 1875 preceded the famine and was most pronounced in
Thanjavur and other parts of southern Tamil Nadu not in the Ceded
Districts. But during 1876 and the early months of 1877 famine and
cholera coalesced. In 1877 the ten principal famine districts had a
cholera mortality rate of 18 per thousand, while the five in which
famine developed later averaged 11.1. In the remaining six 'non-
famine' districts the rate was 4.6 per thousand.[26] But just as the
epidemic had begun before the famine, so it faded away before the
famine was over and long before the population had begun to recover
from its effects.

Although dry conditions were normally inimical to the survival of the
cholera vibrio, certain aspects of the famine situation and of the human
response to it helped favour this fatal conjuncture. As W. R. Cornish,
the Madras Sanitary Commissioner, noted in his 1877 report:

> The unnatural life of the people in famine times, and the resort to unusual
> kinds of food, undoubtedly tend to disorder the digestive organs; at the same
> time, the wandering propensities of the people, their neglect of ordinary
> cleanliness, the crowding of people on relief-works and in centres of relief,
> or in towns where food is to be had, all tend to the aggravation of the
> intensity of cholera epidemics. As a consequence of drought . . . the water
> for domestic use becomes scarce, and the sources of supply are liable to be
> fouled in every conceivable way. The usual surface wells and tanks have
> dried up, and the sources that are available are so much polluted that even
> persons who are particular about the quality of their water are unable to
> procure a wholesome supply.[27]

But Cornish also argued that what happened during famine was an
accentuation of the conditions that favoured cholera at other times. 'All
the normal insanitary conditions of native rural life', he wrote, 'viz.,
bad feeding, bad housing, bad conservancy, and bad water were
intensified by the famine distress.' While the exceptional nature of the
famine undoubtedly increased the risk of infection and the resultant
mortality, 'it must be borne in view that cholera epidemics pursue their
own course quite independent of the accident of famine'.[28]

The intricacy of the famine-cholera connection and the strength of
Cornish's general argument can be illustrated by looking at the
incidence of the disease in two different districts of the Madras
Presidency, Thanjavur and Kurnool, between the mid-1860s and late

Table 3. Cholera Mortality in Kurnool and Thanjavur Districts of Madras, 1866 – 1939.

Period	Kurnool Average Annual Cholera Deaths	Kurnool Average Annual Cholera Death Rate	Cholera Deaths as a % of All Deaths	Thanjavur Average Annual Cholera Deaths	Thanjavur Average Annual Cholera Death Rate	Cholera Deaths as a % of All Deaths
1866 – 1870	2,174	2.9	10.8	6,195	3.8	16.9
1871 – 1880	2,514	2.7	5.3	4,405	2.3	7.3
1881 – 1890	130	0.2	0.7	7,174	3.4	12.7
1891 – 1900	1,557	2.0	6.7	8,980	4.0	15.2
1901 – 1910	1,571	1.8	6.1	5,533	2.5	9.0
1911 – 1920	1,472	1.6	4.3	5,297	2.3	8.1
1921 – 1930	1,125	1.2	4.0	4,509	1.9	7.4
1931 – 1939	358	0.4	1.2	2,107	0.9	3.6

Sources: Annual Reports of the Sanitary Commissioner for Madras, 1866 – 1920; Annual Reports of the Director of Public Health, Madras, 1921 – 1939.

1930s (see Table 3). Kurnool was one of the poorest, driest and most famine-prone districts in the Madras Presidency. It was estimated to have lost nearly a third of its one million inhabitants in the famine of 1876 – 8, and it was hard hit by other years of drought and dearth including 1866, 1891 – 2, 1896 – 7, 1900, and 1921 – 2, in each of which relief works were opened.[29] Thanjavur, by contrast, was one of the most agriculturally productive districts. It enjoyed a virtual immunity from famine, drawing water for its irrigated ricelands from channels fed by the River Cauvery. Famine, however, was not without its effects: in 1866 and especially in 1876 – 7 thousands of villagers from drought-stricken areas flocked into Thanjavur in search of food and relief.[30] This was one factor in the high incidence of cholera in the district during those years. But in Thanjavur cholera was endemic; in Kurnool it occurred only periodically, often in association with famine, and in many years was absent altogether. In Kurnool the annual cholera mortality sank below a thousand deaths in fifty-three of the seventy-four years represented in Table 3, and in 12 years no cholera deaths were recorded at all. In contrast in Thanjavur during 1866 – 1939 there were only 13 years with fewer than 1,000 fatal cases, and none in which mortality sank to zero. Over the period from 1881 to 1925, Thanjavur had the highest average annual cholera mortality rate per thousand inhabitants of any district in the province (2.9); Kurnool stood sixteenth with 1.3.[31]

Like similar irrigated areas in the province (such as the Kistna-Godavari delta further north) and elsewhere in India (notably the lower Ganges valley), Thanjavur owed its high cholera mortality to an abundance rather than a scarcity of water. The irrigation channels and distributaries that transected the Cauvery delta were also used to provide water for drinking, washing and cooking. Through defecation along the banks or in the dry channels ('elongated latrines' as they were once described) before the 'freshes' arrived, or by washing contaminated clothing and vessels, the water-borne vibrio was readily transmitted downstream from one village to another. The high density of rural settlement in such irrigated areas and the exclusion of the labouring classes (like the Harijans of Thanjavur) from high-caste wells and tanks, further facilitated this process.[32] In the drier, upland *taluks* of Thanjavur the incidence of cholera was normally significantly lower than in the irrigated areas.[33] But even in dry districts, like Coimbatore or Cuddapah, the highest incidence of cholera often lay along the course of a river or canal, and the seasonal fluctuations in the disease were linked to the principal monsoon months when the heavy rain washed faeces and other infected material into wells and streams. In general, however, the reliance upon wells and tanks in the dry areas reduced the risk of contamination or restricted its impact when it did occur.[34] The exception was in times of drought and famine when, as the quotation from Cornish indicated, such sources quickly became infected and helped spread the disease.

Other factors, too, contributed to the prevalence of cholera in Thanjavur and along India's eastern littoral. The cyclones that periodically swept in from the Bay of Bengal brought flooding and the contamination of water supplies in their wake. One of the most devastating of the late nineteenth century epidemics in Bengal, that of 1876, had its origin in this sequence of events, as did lesser epidemics in Nellore and Thanjavur on the Madras coast.[35] Flooding by rain-swollen rivers could have a similar effect.[36] Social and cultural variables were important as well. The migrant labourers who helped transplant and harvest the rice crop in Thanjavur and Kistna were often identified with local epidemics: their mobility, their use of open channels for drinking water, and their tendency to flee once cholera broke out among them, made the labourers a significant link in the epidemiological chain.[37] So, too, were the pilgrims who visited the major temples and festivals at Chidambaram, Kumbakonam, Srirangam and Thanjavur and carried cholera with them.[38] Famines, therefore, represented but one extreme illustration of the ways in which infected water supplies, human mobility, and the problems of rural health, sanitation and poverty in general combined together to produce high levels of cholera mortality in India.

PILGRIMAGE

In British perceptions Hindu festivals and pilgrimages were among the principal agencies by which cholera was spread. To some extent this was a Western response to the 'Indianness' of the disease, part of an attempt to explain the etiology of cholera in terms of India's cultural, social or climatic peculiarities.[39] But during the late nineteenth and early twentieth centuries an enormous body of evidence was accumulated to show that there were real epidemiological connections between cholera and Hindu fairs (*melas*) and pilgrimage places.

In some respects pilgrims resembled the famine poor and played a comparable part in epidemics. Mobile, often poorly fed, clothed and housed, congregating in lodging houses, *dharmsalas* and open camps at the principal sacred sites of Hindu India, the pilgrims provided a suitable human vector for the disease, infecting not only other pilgrims but also villages and towns *en route*. In addition, the direction and timing of the pilgrim traffic were often peculiarly favourable to the dissemination of epidemic cholera. It was early on observed that the peaks of cholera mortality occur in various parts of India at different times. Across northern India, for example, the disease is most prevalent in Bengal between October and January and again in March and April. In Bihar, Orissa and eastern U.P. the main cholera season falls between April and August, while further west in Punjab June to August are the most dangerous months.[40] These annual cycles bear a complex relationship to temperature, rainfall and humidity;[41] but they can also be influenced or accentuated by human activity. In much of U.P., for example, the main cholera season corresponded to the period of marriage festivities and the movement of pilgrims between the main fairs of the province. The Magh mela held annually at Allahabad in eastern U.P. in January and February was attended by large numbers of pilgrims from the cholera endemic areas of Bengal and Bihar. Many pilgrims then continued further west to Brindaban, Ayodhya, Hardwar and Badrinath, each of which in turn could become a centre from which cholera was disseminated. As Banerjea pointed out, 116 fairs and festivals were held in U.P. in March and April alone, attracting some three million people at a time of year that was climatically suited to cholera epidemicity.[42]

Even more dangerous from an epidemiological viewpoint than the annual pilgrim traffic were the Kumbh melas held at Allahabad and Hardwar every twelve years and the intervening Ardh Kumbh melas. As many as three million pilgrims at a time participated in these festivals, living in crowded and insanitary lodgings or encampments, bathing *en masse* in the sacred Ganges and sipping its holy water — conditions that were almost ideal for cholera transmission. When they left the mela, the pilgrims carried cholera with them, infecting tanks and wells, towns and villages over a vast area. In 1867, to take one of the best-documented cases, only nineteen people suffering from cholera were detected at the Hardwar Kumbh mela among possibly three million people. But with the dispersal of the pilgrims after the main bathing day, cholera was spread across northern India along the myriad pilgrim routes. A total of 117,181 deaths were recorded in the course of this epidemic.[43]

If one adds up the total number of cholera deaths in U.P. during the Kumbh and Ardh Kumbh years between 1877 and 1950 the annual average amounts to 68,941 compared with 43,106 (a third fewer) for the non-mela years.[44] The figures are to some extent misleading. Some epidemics, falling in mela years, were not the direct result of the festivals, and the Allahabad and Hardwar melas (although the largest) were not the only such gatherings to have an effect on cholera mortality. But there is ample justification for Pollitzer's assertion that there was a 'close association' between the Kumbh melas and cholera epidemicity and that they had a 'dismal influence' on mortality in neighbouring provinces as well.[45]

If one looks, however, at the distribution of cholera mortality in the long-term in U.P. the influence of the Hardwar and Allahabad melas is less pronounced. Saharanpur (the district in which Hardwar is located) formed part of a belt of districts along the western and southern margins of U.P. with comparatively low cholera mortality levels for the period 1877 to 1948 as a whole. The highest levels were to be found in eastern U.P. (with Sultanpur the worst afflicted district with an average cholera death rate of 2.30 deaths per thousand inhabitants) and along the Nepalese border.[46] This distribution cannot be explained by pilgrimages and fairs alone, though they were certainly a factor. The eastern districts also suffered rather less from famine during the period than those further west. One likely explanation is that cholera was either endemic in the area or was repeatedly imported by pilgrims and other travellers from Bengal and Bihar and by pilgrims, traders and coolies from across the border with Nepal, where there was a constant reservoir of infection.[47] Within eastern U.P. itself, such important religious centres as Banaras and Allahabad, as well as many smaller sacred places and festival sites, aided in the transmission and dissemination of the disease, with pilgrims, for example, returning from Banaras, bringing cholera to Gorakhpur and Basti.[48] Conditions within these districts were also conducive to cholera. Gorakhpur, for instance, included parts of the swampy Terai, where surface water was as easily contaminated as in the irrigated lands of Bengal or Thanjavur.[49] Pilgrimage, like famine, was one among a number of influences which shaped the distribution of cholera mortality in this and other provinces.

SANITATION AND MEDICINE

We return, then, to the basic issue. Why did cholera mortality decline after 1900, and how far was human intervention and activity responsible? Certainly the absence of famine after about 1908 (or the greater effectiveness of relief measures in reducing its impact) was significant in reducing cholera mortality from the high levels of the late nineteenth century. But it would not appear to explain why that mortality continued to fall fairly consistently in subsequent decades. It might perhaps be argued that the first half of the twentieth century witnessed significant economic or social changes. But it seems unlikely that the economic conditions of the bulk of the Indian population improved after 1900, and more probable that they actually deteriorated.[50] It seems improbable, too, that there were social or cultural changes that had a substantial effect upon the incidence of cholera during this relatively short period. Indeed, to take the pilgrimage phenomenon just described, this was a factor that remained fairly constant throughout the period from the mid-nineteenth to the mid-twentieth centuries, and may even have expanded in scale as the advent of rail and later motor transport encouraged and facilitated mass pilgrimage. It would seem to be necessary to look elsewhere, therefore, for an explanation for cholera's falling mortality.

It is generally accepted that in Britain the cholera epidemics of the 1830s, 1840s and 1860s were a vital stimulus to sanitary reform and the institution of public health measures, which in turn helped to eliminate the threat of cholera by the late nineteenth century. The provision of clean drinking water (even before Koch had identified the cholera vibrio in the 1880s) and the efficient disposal of sewage were the key elements in this sanitary programme. To what extent and to what effect did India follow in Britain's footsteps?

Although the desirability of sanitary improvements began to be discussed in medical circles in India as early as the 1850s and was acknowledged in the appointment of provincial sanitary commissioners in the following decade, there were enormous practical and political obstacles in the way of sanitary reform. Not until the late 1860s and 1870s did provincial governments begin to collect the vital statistics on which an effective understanding of India's health problems could be based. Controversy over the nature of the disease and the mode of its transmission inhibited the development of a concerted cholera control policy before the 1890s. The financial and political interest of the colonial regime in the extraction of wealth from India made it equally disinclined to make major investments in Indian public health. It was feared, too, (and with some justification in the light of popular opposition to vaccination and anti-plague measures) that Western medical and sanitary intervention, particularly in the case of cholera involving pilgrims and Hindu temples and festivals, would arouse a degree of hostility that was politically undesirable and, in sanitary terms, counter-productive.[51] Not until the early decades of the twentieth century did a more constructive attitude emerge. The campaigns against smallpox and plague revealed a growing, if still reluctant, public acceptance of Western medical and sanitary measures, and there was increasing confidence among medical experts in India that cholera could be eliminated if sufficient funds were made available for the purpose.[52] The expansion of local self-government and the allocation of public health to elected Indian ministers under the Government of India Act of 1919 gave further impetus to cholera control measures. The pace of this development should not, however, be exaggerated. Financial constraints remained, and the municipalization of public health, which had been of such importance in nineteenth-century Britain with its wealthy industrial and commercial cities, was often an unsatisfactory solution when applied to small and impoverished pilgrimage towns like Hardwar, Puri or Pandharpur. The case of cholera in Britain had been resolvable partly because it was an urban problem, especially acute in big cities. In India the problem was largely rural and small-town, and the difficulties of protecting countless wells and water courses appeared, even in 1947, almost insuperable.[53]

None the less, it is likely that sanitary and medical intervention played a significant, perhaps even a decisive, part in the decline in cholera mortality during the first half of the twentieth century. Improvements in cholera therapy as such made little contribution. Sir Leonard Rogers, who pioneered the treatment of cholera patients with solutions of hypertonic and alkaline salts to replace the massive loss of body fluid that occurred during a cholera attack, reckoned that this technique reduced mortality by between a quarter and a third.[54] But it was not a treatment that could be applied on a mass scale and, initially at least, it was too unpopular to be widely used.[55] During the Bengal famine of 1943, when admittedly hunger and exhaustion also had a negative effect, cholera patients were dying in hospital at the rate of 42 per hundred, not much below the mortality rate of fifty per cent normally ascribed to the disease.[56]

Better methods of prevention and interception, rather than improved therapy, provided the crucial development. By the 1920s it had become possible, through the accumulation of fifty years of statistical data, and the researches of men like Rogers, King, Russell and Sundararajan,[57] to anticipate when a major epidemic might occur and the most likely points of origin. The towns and districts in which cholera had proved endemic were singled out for special attention. In the United Provinces, for example, a new cholera scheme, first introduced in eastern U.P. in 1913 and later extended to other areas, provided additional funds and staff for the disinfection of wells and the instruction of village officers in basic principles of hygiene and sanitation. In 1925 the scheme was further elaborated by giving the chaukidars special postcards to be despatched to the nearest health officer as soon as a case of cholera was detected. Between 1913 and 1919, U.P.'s Sanitary Commissioner claimed, the scheme had saved 40,000 lives that would otherwise have been lost to the disease.[58] During the 1930s mobile dispensaries toured the remoter parts of districts or were despatched to outbreak areas. It was through these that many anti-cholera inoculations were administered.[59] Other provisions were directed principally at the pilgrims. The main festival sites were provided with piped water and latrines, and special medical staff kept watch at the melas for cholera suspects. From the early 1920s close surveillance was also kept over pilgrims entering U.P. through the main rail links with eastern India.[60] In this way the likelihood of epidemics occurring or developing on a serious scale was significantly reduced, as the record of the Kumbh melas began to show. Selective intervention against a targeted group like the pilgrims did not remove basic problems of rural under-nutrition and impure water supplies, but it did help to break the links in the epidemiological chain, to contain cholera even while not eliminating it entirely.[61] When these control measures weakened or broke down, as happened in parts of eastern and northern India between 1940 and 1948 as a result of the multiple crisis of the Second World War, the Bengal famine and Partition, cholera rapidly recovered much of its former destructiveness.

The role of cholera inoculation is not easy to evaluate. Although Haffkine experimented with an anti-cholera serum in India in 1893 – 5 and was pleased with the results,[62] the Government of India remained doubtful about its utility, more than for political than for medical reasons. It believed that any attempt at compulsory inoculation, whether among famine-sufferers or pilgrims, would provoke a religious outcry. This negative attitude persisted as late as 1930.[63] By that date, however, voluntary inoculation was beginning to be practised on a significant scale. The pressure for compulsory inoculation of pilgrims was also increasing,

partly as a result of initiatives from Indian doctors and politicians, and
was first adopted at Pandharpur in 1936. By the mid-1940s compulsory
inoculation was widely enforced. In 1945, 3.4 million cholera
inoculations were performed in U.P. alone, many of them on pilgrims
attending the Ardh Kumbh mela. In British India as a whole the number
of inoculations rose from 3.7 million in 1931 to 10.8 million in 1938: it
doubled during the war years and reached 28.8 million in 1944.[64]

Rogers argued that cholera inoculation, and especially the compulsory inoculation of pilgrims, a policy with which he had been closely
associated since the mid-1920s, was largely responsible for the
dramatic fall in cholera mortality in India.[65] This claim might be viewed
with some scepticism, especially in the light of recent doubts about the
effectiveness of cholera vaccines.[66] Certainly, the adoption of mass
immunization in the late 1930s and 1940s came only at a time when
cholera mortality was already showing a downward trend. It may, of
course, have helped to sustain and strengthen that downturn, especially
after Independence. Again, the massive increase in inoculations during
the Second World War did not prevent a resurgence in cholera
mortality: in 1943 there were nearly half a million cholera deaths in
India, the highest figure since the end of the previous war. Mass
inoculations were often carried out only when an epidemic was already
in being rather than in anticipation of it, though this, too, might prevent
it from gaining even greater proportions. But the recent evidence that
cholera vaccines might be successful in only about 55 per cent of cases
(33 per cent in cases of children) and confer protection for no more than
3 to 6 months does not necessarily invalidate the argument that they
reduced the risk of an epidemic during the short period of a festival or
mela. Taken alongside other medical and sanitary measures, inoculation probably did help limit the incidence of the kinds of 'explosive'
epidemics that had occurred before 1920, and thus contributed to the
overall decline in cholera mortality by 1947.

CHOLERA IN THE TOWNS AND CITIES

Another way of assessing the impact of medical and sanitary
intervention (as well as furnishing further evidence of the variation in
the incidence of cholera mortality) is by looking at the urban context.
One would expect Western medicine and sanitation to have their
greatest effect in urban areas since these were the places where the
colonial presence was generally strongest.

During the second half of the nineteenth century India's largest and
most European cities followed British precedents by installing piped
water and sewerage systems for at least their more affluent wards and

suburbs. In the case of Calcutta and Madras, two of the most populous of India's colonial cities, these measures had an immediate and dramatic effect on cholera mortality. Calcutta, inside Bengal's cholera endemicity zone, suffered severely from the disease in the first half of the nineteenth century, with between 2,500 and 7,000 deaths each year between 1841 and 1865. But in 1865 a sewerage network was inaugurated, followed in 1869 by piped water. Although Calcutta continued to grow in population, the number of cholera deaths exceeded 3,000 in only one year (1895) between 1870 and 1900. Thereafter, however, mortality remained stubbornly high, rising above the 3,000 mark on four further occasions between 1900 and 1950 and falling below 1,000 in only seven years.[67]

In Madras, too, the introduction of piped water from the Red Hills in 1872 brought about a significant reduction in cholera mortality. In the 15 years before 1872 deaths from cholera averaged 1,447 annually, while in the 15 years from 1872 to 1886 the figure was 699, despite the mortality occasioned by the famine and epidemic of 1875 – 8.[68] Although cholera continued to affect the city from time to time, control measures could be fairly promptly and effectively applied, as in 1927 when nearly 100,000 inoculations were performed in two months to avert an expected epidemic.[69] As can be seen from Table 4, cholera mortality in the city of Madras between 1881 and 1939 remained consistently below the average rates for the province as a whole and even for its urban population (with the exception of the quinquennium 1901 – 5).

In the biggest cities outbreaks of cholera could be swiftly reported and promptly dealt with. Hospitals and other medical facilities were concentrated there, and, especially in a provincial capital like Madras, there existed the administrative capacity and the political incentive to react speedily and effectively. By the 1920s and 1930s many large European employers of Indian labour, such as the textile mills, railways and steamship companies, were quick to vaccinate or inoculate their workers when an epidemic threatened: they showed noticeably less interest in other aspects of their workers' health and material well-being.[70]

In the smaller towns, however, or even in the second rank of India's cities, cholera was often (relative to the size of the population) more prevalent than in the largest urban centres. Sometimes this was because piped water reached only a section of the population while others continued to use contaminated sources; or there was no piped water supply at all. As late as 1935, 51 towns with a population of over 30,000 in British India were still without a proper water supply. Of the 1,131 towns below 30,000 inhabitants, only 149 had piped water.[71] Even in substantial towns like Madurai and Thanjavur, which had been

Table 4. Urban Cholera Mortality Rates in the Madras Presidency, 1876 – 1939.

Period	Madras Presidency	Madras Urban	Madras City	Madurai Town	Thanjavur Town
1876 – 1880	3.88	3.48	4.32	n.a.	n.a.
1881 – 1885	1.40	3.06	1.00	6.18	3.82
1886 – 1890	1.46	2.90	0.90	1.40	5.24
1891 – 1895	1.74	2.52	1.30	8.44	13.26
1896 – 1900	2.11	2.74	0.74	5.76	8.66
1901 – 1905	0.94	1.38	1.98	4.10	2.68
1906 – 1910	2.40	2.68	1.02	14.66	3.66
1911 – 1915	1.42	1.64	1.14	9.34	4.02
1916 – 1920	1.60	1.54	0.52	4.12	1.40
1921 – 1925	0.72	0.94	0.18	3.84	2.10
1926 – 1930	0.80	0.94	0.52	2.63	2.70
1931 – 1935	0.42	0.40	0.16	1.81	0.38
1936 – 1939	0.40	0.43	0.10	0.26	0.31

Sources: Annual Reports of the Sanitary Commissioner for Madras, 1876 – 1920; Annual Reports of the Director of Public Health, Madras, 1921 – 1939.

provided with piped water in the 1890s, cholera mortality (while fluctuating considerably) remained generally much higher than in the provincial capital (see Table 4). In smaller towns, such as Dharmapuri, Palni, Bodinayakanur and Pollachi in western Tamil Nadu, cholera deaths in the early 1920s remained as high as 3.0 to 4.6 per thousand inhabitants.[72] Although municipalities in general had substantially more to spend on public health than district boards,[73] such small towns could find little money to pay for expensive water, sewerage and drainage schemes, and government grants were not always forthcoming or adequate. In consequence, the fall in mortality rates from cholera was often more laggardly there than in the big cities or even many rural areas.

CONCLUSIONS

That upwards of two million cholera deaths occurred in British India during the last decade of colonial rule is indicative of the extent to which the disease remained a significant cause of mortality and shows the frailty of the sanitary and medical measures thus far deployed against it. None the less, viewed in the longer term, a significant decline in cholera mortality had begun to occur and was one factor in the wider reduction in Indian death rates during the first half of the twentieth century.[74]

There are two general lines of argument to this chapter. The first is that any understanding of the nature of disease mortality and its changes during this period needs to take into account the character of the disease itself, the manner of its occurrence, and the multiplicity of factors that have a bearing upon its incidence and distribution. This is not merely a matter of reciting bacteriological or climatic determinants. The nature of social organization, cultural practices and political structures also play an important, if at times elusive, contributory part.[75]

It follows from this that the reasons for the decline in the occurrence or fatality of a disease are likely to be diverse and complex. Bacteriological change, although helping to explain the high levels of mortality at the start of the period, and the supplanting of 'classic' by 'El Tor' cholera in the 1960s, does not, in itself, seem an adequate explanation. More evidently important was the declining incidence or severity of famine between about 1908 and 1943. But even this does not account for more▸ than part of the story. It seems reasonable to conclude, therefore, that sanitary and medical intervention, effected first in the very restricted context of the major cities (and military camps) and gradually extended to the countryside and smaller urban centres by the 1920s and 1930s, was also an important factor. Improved sanitation, piped water, medical surveillance at fairs and festivals, inoculation — each in itself might be partial and imperfect and leave the basic problems of urban and rural poverty and ill-health unresolved. But they began the task of breaking the links in the epidemiological chain, a task taken up with greater vigour in the decades after Independence in 1947.

NOTES TO CHAPTER 9

1 'Writing off cholera too soon', *Economic and Political Weekly*, 11 January 1986: 50 – 1. See also 'Jab gibe', *New Internationalist*, June 1985: 3.

2 P. E. Razzell, ' "An Interpretation of the Modern Rise of Population in Europe" — a Critique', *Population Studies* 28, No. 1 (March 1974): 5 – 17; and his *The Conquest of Smallpox: The Impact of Inoculation on Smallpox Mortality in Eighteenth Century Britain* (Firle, Caliban Books, 1977).

3 Thomas McKeown and R. G. Brown, 'Medical Evidence Related to English Population Changes in the Eighteenth Century', *Population Studies* 9, No. 2 (November 1955): 119 – 41; Thomas McKeown and

R. G. Record, 'Reasons for the Decline of Mortality in England and Wales During the Nineteenth Century', ibid., 16, No. 2 (November 1962): 94 – 122. In a recent essay, McKeown is more sceptical about the role of declining disease virulence: McKeown, 'Food, Infection, and Population', in Robert I. Rotberg and Theodore K. Rabb (eds.), *Hunger and History: The Impact of Changing Food Production and Consumption Patterns on Society* (Cambridge, Cambridge University Press, 1985): 29 – 49.

4 Kingsley Davis, 'The Amazing Decline of Mortality in Underdeveloped Areas', *American Economic Review* 46, No. 2 (May 1956): 305 – 18; R. H. Gray, 'The Decline of Mortality in Ceylon and the Demographic Effects of Malaria Control', *Population Studies* 28, No. 2 (July 1974): 205 – 29; R. H. Cassen, *India: Population, Economy, Society* (London, Macmillan, 1978); 78 – 92.

5 See for example P. Krishnan, 'Mortality Decline in India, 1951 – 1961: Development vs. Public Health Program Hypothesis', *Social Science and Medicine* 9 (1975): 475 – 9.

6 Though there does appear to be a common trend: see Kingsley Davis, *The Population of India and Pakistan* (Princeton, Princeton University Press, 1950): 46.

7 The distribution of cholera deaths between provinces remained fairly consistent between 1910 and 1950: see R. Pollitzer, *Cholera* (Geneva, World Health Organization, 1959): 82.

8 *Census of India, 1951, volume II: Uttar Pradesh. Part IA Report* (Allahabad: Superintendent of Printing and Stationery, 1953): 72 – 3, 467 f.

9 *Review of the Madras Famine, 1876 – 1878* (Madras, Government Press, 1881): 118.

10 *Annual Report of the Director of Public Health of the United Provinces, 1928* (Allahabad, Government Press, 1929): 17 (this series hereafter cited as *ARUP, 1928* etc.); *ARUP, 1936*: 10; but for a contrary impression, see *ARUP, 1920*: 11 – 12.

11 Despite considerable fluctuations, cholera also accounted for a falling share of the overall mortality: see Davis, *Population of India and Pakistan*: 46.

12 But see Leela Visaria and Pravin Visaria, 'Population (1757 – 1947)', in Dharma Kumar (ed.), *The Cambridge Economic History of India, volume 2, c. 1757 – c. 1970* (Cambridge, Cambridge University Press, 1983): 473 – 9.

13 John MacPherson, *Annals of Cholera: From the earliest period to the year 1817* (London, Ranken, 1872).

14 See for example Aidan Cockburn, *The Evolution and Eradication of Infectious Diseases* (Baltimore, Johns Hopkins Press, 1963): 175.

15 A. Moreau de Jonnès, *Rapport au Conseil Supérior de Santé sur le Choléra-Morbus Pestilentiel* (Paris, Cosson, 1831): 84.

16 Anon., 'The Asiatic Cholera', *Fraser's Magazine* 19, no. 4 (December 1831): 614; Augustin Fabre and Fortuné Chailan, *Histoire du Choléra-Morbus Asiatique* (Marseille, Olive, 1835): 10.

17 Visaria and Visaria, 'Population (1757 – 1947)': 466 give various estimates.

18 James Jameson, *Report on the Epidemick Cholera Morbus* (Calcutta, Government Gazette Press, 1820): 166 – 84.

19 Secretary, Bombay Medical Board, to Chief Secretary, Bombay, 13 September 1819, Bombay Public Proceedings, 29 September 1819, India Office Records, London (hereafter IOR).

20 W. Scot, *Report on the Epidemic Cholera* (Madras, Asylum Press, 1824): 43, 46 – 7, 49; F. R. Hemingway, *Madras District Gazetteers: Trichinopoly* (Madras, Government Press, 1907): 196; Collector, Salem, to Board of Revenue (BoR), Madras, 8 September 1819, Madras BoR Procs, 16 September 1819; Collector, Cuddapah, to BoR, 20 September 1819, BoR Procs, 30 September 1819; Magistrate, Guntur, to Secretary, Judicial, 30 September 1819, Madras Judicial Procs, 8 November 1819; Magistrate, Tirunelveli, to Chief Secretary, 14 August 1819, Madras Judicial Procs, 26 Nov. 1819: IOR.

21 *Report on the Census of the Madras Presidency, 1871* (Madras, Government Press, 1874): 2; W. R. Cornish, *Report on Cholera in Southern India, 1869* (Madras, Government Gazette Press, 1870): 27; *Report of the Commissioners Appointed to Inquire into the Cholera Epidemic of 1861 in Northern India* (Calcutta, n.p., 1862): 64, 70 – 1, 85 – 7.

22 For 'El Tor' cholera and its impact on India, see Barua and Burrows (eds.), *Cholera*, cited in the sources to Table 2.

23 For discussion of the issue, see W. H. Foege, 'Famine, Infections and Epidemics', in G. Blix, Y. Hofvander and B. Vahlquist (eds.), *Famine: A Symposium Dealing with Nutrition and Relief Operations in Times of Disaster* (Uppsala, Almquist and Wiksell, 1971): 64 – 73; I. H. Rosenberg, W. B. Greenough, J. Lindenbaum and R. S. Gordon, 'Nutritional Studies in Cholera: The Influence of Nutritional Status on Susceptibility to Infection', in *Proceedings of the Cholera Research Symposium, January 24 – 29, 1965, Honolulu, Hawaii* (Washington, D.C., U.S. Department of Health, Education, and Welfare, 1965): 68 – 72; Frederik B. Bang, 'The Role of Disease in the Ecology of Famine', *Ecology of Food and Nutrition* 7, No. 1 (June, 1978): 1 – 15. See, too, the various contributions to Rotberg and Rabb (eds.), *Hunger and History*; also Pollitzer, *Cholera*: 747.

24 Roland Lardinois, 'Une Conjoncture de Crise Démographique en Inde du Sud au XIX⁰ Siècle: La Famine de 1876 – 1878', *Population* 2 (1982): 377 – 9; Michelle B. McAlpin, *Subject to Famine: Food Crises and Economic Change in Western India, 1860 – 1920* (Princeton, Princeton University Press, 1983), chapter 3; A. K. Sen, 'Famine Mortality: A Study of the Bengal Famine of 1943', in E. J. Hobsbawm *et al.* (eds.), *Peasants in History* (Calcutta, Oxford University Press, 1980): 204, 216.

25 For a convenient summary of the major famines, see Visaria and Visaria, 'Population (1757 – 1947)': 528 – 31.

26 *Review of the Madras Famine, 1876 – 1878*: 125, see also Lardinois, 'Une Conjoncture': 377 – 9.

27 *Annual Report of the Sanitary Commissioner for Madras, 1877* (Madras, Government Press, 1878): xxv (this series, variously titled, hereafter *ARM, 1877,* etc.)
28 *Review of the Madras Famine, 1876 – 1878:* 126.
29 *Census of India, 1881: Madras, Vol. 1: Report* (Madras, Government Press, 1883): 26; *A Statistical Atlas of the Madras Presidency* (Madras, Government Press, 1936): 286f.
30 F. R. Hemingway, *Madras District Gazetteer: Tanjore* (Madras, Government Press, 1906): 147 – 9; *Statistical Atlas:* 752f.
31 *ARM, 1926,* map facing p. 18.
32 Satya Swaroop, 'Epidemiology of Cholera in the Madras Presidency', *Indian Journal of Medical Research* 34, No. 2 (April 1951): 185 – 96; *ARM, 1884:* 15 – 16; *ARM, 1924:* 13; *ARM, 1928:* 16; *ARM, 1947:* 10. For the general distribution of cholera in relation to the main river systems of eastern India, see Satya Swaroop, 'Endemicity of Cholera in India', *Indian Journal of Medical Research* 39, No. 2 (April 1951): 143; Pollitzer, *Cholera:* 52 – 3; cf. Davis, *Population of India and Pakistan:* 48.
33 In the quinquennia 1898 – 1902, 1908 – 12, 1921 – 5 and 1926 – 30, the average annual cholera mortality rate in the dry taluk of Pattukottai was 1.4 deaths per thousand inhabitants. Over the same period it was 3.8, 4.0 and 5.3 respectively for the irrigated taluks of Mannargudi, Mayavaram and Kumbakonam. Calculated from: *Madras District Gazetteers: Statistical Appendix for Tanjore District,* Addison & Co., 1905): 5; *Statistical Appendix for Tanjore District* (Madras, Government Press, 1915): 15; K. N. Krishnaswami Ayyar, *Statistical Appendix for Tanjore District* (Madras, Government Press, 1933): 17 – 18.
34 *ARM, 1893:* 73 – 8; *ARM, 1899:* 41; *ARM, 1921:* 13; *ARM, 1923:* 14.
35 H. W. Bellew, *Cholera in India, 1862 to 1881* (Calcutta, Bengal Secretariat Press, 1884): 106, 109 – 15; Hemingway, *Tanjore:* 150; *ARM, 1927:* 17.
36 For example at Tiruchirapalli in 1924: *ARM, 1924:* 1. In Bengal, however, cholera was less common during the rainy months when water was abundant, than in drier months when villagers relied upon the dwindling volume of water in tanks and channels: Leonard Rogers, *The Incidence and Spread of Cholera in India: Forecasting and Control of Epidemics* (Calcutta, Thacker, Spink & Co., 1928): 148 – 9; R. M. Glasse, 'Cultural Aspects of the Transmission of Cholera', in *Proceedings of the Cholera Research Symposium:* 337.
37 Swaroop, 'Epidemiology of Cholera': 193; *ARM, 1927:* 16; *ARM, 1933:* 13 – 14. The relationship between migrant labour and cholera was also found among groundnut harvesters in the drier districts of Tamil Nadu: *ARM, 1925:* 19; *ARM, 1948:* 16.
38 Swaroop, 'Epidemiology of Cholera': 193 – 4; Hemingway, *Tanjore:* 154.
39 David Arnold, 'Cholera and Colonialism in British India', *Past and Present,* No. 113 (November 1986).

40   Pollitzer, *Cholera*: 55; *Annual Report of the Sanitary Commissioner for the North-Western Provinces, 1869* (Allahabad, Government Press, 1870): 7 – 8 (this series hereafter *ARNWP, 1869*, etc.); *ARNWP, 1878*: 12.
41   Rogers, *The Incidence and Spread of Cholera*; S. N. Rastogi, B. G. Prasad and J. K. Bhatnagar, 'A Study of Epidemiology of Cholera in Uttar Pradesh: A Study in Retrospect', *Indian Journal of Medical Research* 55, No. 8 (August, 1967): 844 – 50; Pollitzer, *Cholera*: 827 – 35.
42   A. C. Banerjea, 'Note on Cholera in the United Provinces', *Indian Journal of Medical Research* 39, No. 1 (January 1951): 22; R. B. Lal, 'Fairs and Festivals in India', *Indian Medical Gazette*, 72 (February 1937): 96 – 101.
43   *Report on the Cholera Epidemic of 1867 in Northern India* (Calcutta, Superintendent of Government Printing, 1868).
44   Banerjea, 'Note on Cholera': 20, 31. Data from *Annual Reports*, 1877 – 1950.
45   Pollitzer, *Cholera*: 79, 883.
46   Banerjea, 'Note on Cholera': 25.
47   *ARUP, 1927*: 28 – 9; *ARUP, 1930*: 40; *Gorakhpur: Supplementary Notes and Statistics* (Allahabad, Government Press, 1921): 17.
48   *ARNWP, 1887*: 7A – 10A; *ARUP, 1924*: 29.
49   *ARNWP, 1887*: 7A – 10A; H. R. Nevill, *Gorakhpur: A Gazetteer* (Allahabad, Government Press, 1909): 36.
50   See Shri Gopal Tiwari, *Economic Prosperity of the United Provinces* (Bombay, Asia Publishing House, 1951); but for the argument that the agrarian economy was improving before 1920 and thus reduced the likelihood of high famine (and epidemic) mortality, see McAlpin, *Subject to Famine*.
51   Arnold, 'Cholera and Colonialism'.
52   *ARM, 1923*: 13; *ARM, 1928*: 16.
53   *ARM, 1947*: 10.
54   Leonard Rogers, 'Thirty Years' Research on the Control of Cholera Epidemics', *British Medical Journal* 2 (July – December 1957): 1193.
55   *ARM, 1918*: 11.
56   K. S. Fitch, *A Medical History of the Bengal Famine, 1943 – 44* (Calcutta, Government Press, 1947): 12. As late as 1959, of the approximately 100,000 cholera cases reported in India, 47,000 proved fatal: Indian Council of Medical Research, *Proceedings of Seminar on Immunity and Immunoprophylaxis in Cholera* (New Delhi, ICMR, 1971), foreword.
57   Rogers, *The Incidence and Spread of Cholera: ARM, 1893*: 73 – 8; A. J. H. Russell and E. R. Sundararajan, *The Epidemiology of Cholera in India* (Calcutta, Thacker, Spink & Co., 1928).
58   *ARUP, 1913*: 9; *ARUP, 1919*: 13; *ARUP, 1925*: 11.
59   *ARUP, 1934*: 20; *ARUP, 1938*: 12.
60   *ARUP, 1929*: 12; *ARUP, 1930*: 21A.
61   In this there was a parallel with the earlier targeting of an even smaller social group, British soldiers in India, among whom the cholera rate was

dramatically reduced between the 1860s and 1890s mainly as a result of improved sanitary and medical measures.

62 W. M. Haffkine, *Anti-Cholera Inoculation* (Calcutta, Thacker, Spink & Co., 1895).

63 Arnold, 'Cholera and Colonialism'.

64 Central Advisory Board of Health, *Report of the Sub-Committee to Examine the Possibility of Introducing a System of Compulsory Inoculation of Pilgrims Against Cholera (1939)* (Simla, Government of India Press, 1940); Rogers, 'Thirty Years' Research': 1195.

65 Rogers, 'Thirty Years' Research': 1195.

66 See the references cited in note 1, and for other appraisals of the effectiveness of cholera vaccines in India, see R. Adiseshan, C. G. Pandit and K. V. Venkatraman, 'Statistical Evaluation of Anti-Cholera Inoculation as a Personal Prophylactic Against Cholera', *Indian Journal of Medical Research* 35, No. 3 (July 1947): 131 – 52; C. Chandra Sekhar, 'Statistical Assessment of the Efficacy of Anti-Cholera Inoculation', ibid., 35, No. 3 (July 1947): 153 – 70; B. Cvjetanovic, 'Earlier Field Studies of the Effectiveness of Cholera Vaccines', *Proceedings of the Cholera Research Symposium*: 355 – 61; D. Barua, 'Cholera Vaccination as a Tool for Cholera Control', *Bulletin de la Société de Pathologie Exotique* 64 (September – October 1971): 652 – 9.

67 Sanitary Commissioner to the Government of India, to Secretary, Government of India, 13 June 1871, India Sanitary Procs, No. 2, 1 July 1871, IOR; Pollitzer, *Cholera*: 94.

68 *ARM, 1884*: 92.

69 *ARM, 1927*: 21.

70 Dipesh Chakrabarty, 'Conditions for Knowledge of Working-Class Conditions: Employers, Government and the Jute Workers of Calcutta, 1890 – 1940', in Ranajit Guha (ed.), *Subaltern Studies II* (Delhi, Oxford University Press, 1983): 273 – 5.

71 Davis, *Population of India and Pakistan*: 50.

72 *ARM, 1926*; 57.

73 *ARUP, 1947*: 8 – 9. While UP's municipalities spent 36 per cent of their Rs. 47,305,224 budget on public health, district boards spent only 3 per cent of their Rs. 30,242,195.

74 Davis, *Population of India and Pakistan*: 33.

75 For further discussion of this multiplicity and interdependency, see Bireswar Banerjee and Jayatri Hazra, *Geoecology of Cholera in West Bengal: A Study in Medical Geography* (Calcutta, Hazra, 1974).

10

ON THE COMPARATIVE HISTORICAL PERSPECTIVE: INDIA, EUROPE, THE FAR EAST

Nigel Crook

Historical demography, or the art of reconstructing population history from incomplete or fragmentary data, using the tools of statistical analysis specifically designed for this purpose, is of comparatively recent origin. The pioneering studies used European data. They started modestly, meticulously working through parish records from a handful of villages to reconstruct the dynamics of population change. As techniques of analysis became more sophisticated (in response to the urgent need to understand more fully the contemporary populations of the developing countries), and as data processing equipment developed too, researchers became more ambitious. In 1981 the results were published of the first comprehensive attempt to reconstruct a country's demographic past from the evidence of hundreds of village records subjected to demographic analytical techniques.[1]

Such an approach to population history offers a perspective and a degree of rigour (though, of course, the techniques themselves are subject to a degree of healthy controversy). It can illuminate, elucidate, or sometimes confuse the impressions we have gained from the more patchy, less quantitative, or less demographically critical, historical studies that have a long tradition of scholarship. These latter studies have not been restricted to Europe. Malthus himself raked together an assortment of observations on demographic experience in the Far East and (some would argue) drew some rather hasty conclusions about high fertility and overpopulation. An excellent summary of what can be gleaned from historical population counts is given in McEvedy and Jones' *Atlas of World Population History*: the focus is on size of populations and on rates of growth.[2] But estimates of fertility and mortality in the history of oriental populations, using techniques of demographic analysis, are recent and still rare. Nevertheless, a small range of studies has now been completed for China, Japan, Taiwan, the Philippines and Indonesia. At the same time, less demographically

285

rigorous studies with a focus on critical events, famines and epidemics, are now coming forth in profusion for these regions. Does any common pattern, do any themes emerge? How does our current understanding of India's demography and its component events compare or conflict with our view of other demographic experience in the east, and further, with the picture we have reconstructed from the pre-transition period in western Europe?

What is interesting is that while the European patterns were being elucidated, some speculation was being hazarded (perhaps unwisely) about the populations that lived further east. This temptation was partly due to the demographic work done on the central Asian republics: maybe what was true of central Asia was true of all Asia? Hajnal's work on European marriage patterns was consolidated and expanded by Coale and fellow researchers at Princeton.[3] What emerged was that eastern Europe and central Asia in the late nineteenth century were distinguished by a pattern of early and almost universal marriage, which, on the whole, also gave rise to high rates of total fertility (given the limited control of fertility within marriage). Broadly speaking, the further east, the higher the fertility, in the era before the onset of the demographic transition. The moderate pre-transition level of fertility that held in most countries of western Europe, and gave rise to birth rates in the region of forty per thousand, were thought probably to be unique in the world. Far Eastern societies were known to marry young (i.e. with women being in their teens) and believed to practise no contraception. Under such circumstances it was likely that total fertility would reach a level of at least seven, with birth rates of fifty per thousand. We can now say confidently, I believe, that this view would display serious cultural insensitivity: that the oriental experience can now be shown to have been as diverse as the European.

The most striking exception to the 'universal oriental' view is that of Japan. Hanley and Yamamura have shown convincingly that a selection of villages they studied experienced quite large swings in fertility levels over time, the main regulatory mechanism being the proportions married.[4] In extreme cases up to twenty per cent of the female population remained single by the age of fifty; and birth rates as low as twenty-six per thousand were recorded in the nineteenth century. It is not possible to generalize from this evidence. Japan is also a diverse country. But sufficient contrary evidence from these first villages has emerged to challenge the universality of a Far Eastern marriage pattern. A later study by Morris and Smith revealed a further remarkable fertility-reducing phenomenon in an outcaste Japanese village: a high incidence of marital dissolution through divorce (dissolving forty per cent of marriages in the mid-nineteenth century).[5] Furthermore, analysis of marital fertility in the Japanese villages studied by Hanley and Yamamura indicated considerable length of inter-birth intervals (around four years).

While Japanese evidence of this kind is a clear exception to assumed Far Eastern high fertility, much controversy has surrounded a more extensive set of studies from the Chinese mainland. Coale and colleagues at Princeton reanalysed a collection of survey data from the late 1920s subjecting them to demographic techniques (mainly devised by Brass) to allow for possible underreporting of births. The level of fertility that emerges is in the region of five births per woman, again quite modest, and giving rise to birth rates around forty per thousand.[6] Wolf has challenged these reconstructions, and his own survey data, collected from elderly women post-Revolution, suggest that higher rates may have prevailed for women first married in the 1920s;[7] the discrepancy mainly relates to the later years of child-bearing, and, as Wolf points out, could be larger than his *raw* data indicate. If this were so, total fertility of around seven is likely. On the other hand, respondents aged fifty-five and over who have survived the turmoils of the twentieth century in China may have been exceptionally tough and selectively fertile. The controversy is probably past solution. Wolf and Coale discuss further evidence from vital registration data in Taiwan for the same period. If the Taiwanese registers are complete, the age-pattern and level of fertility are remarkably close to those of the Princeton reconstructions for the Chinese mainland, with the exception of the 15 – 19 age group. The contrast with pre-transitional English *marital* fertility is striking, the latter being about forty per cent higher at ages 20 – 44.

It is with this less universalistic picture of the Far East emerging that the studies of historical India may be compared. Dyson's work on Berar emphasizes an important conclusion: pre-transitional fertility levels were not always high.[8] Indeed, once again, birth rates in the region of forty per thousand are indicated, and this is clear from a variety of consistency checks against the demographic theoretic model. As with the Chinese case, the mechanism subduing fertility is not solely marriage behaviour: fertility within marriage is also relatively low. Dyson is careful not to generalize unduly. Berar displays cultural characteristics more akin to those of southern India than to the north. We are certainly not in a position to claim that high oriental fertility is a universal myth, but we can safely claim it is not a universal truth. Indeed there is sufficient counter-evidence to indicate at least a wide range of experience, perhaps as diverse as that which Hajnal and Coale showed to characterize Europe.

So far we have only discussed statistical demography. Can we go beyond, towards explanation? As we mentioned above, the Far Eastern data indicate prolonged birth intervals with a pattern not suggestive of conscious fertility control. Such characteristics of marital fertility can most readily be associated with breast-feeding behaviour. Other factors that may influence birth intervals include disease and severe undernutrition: the effect of the latter is still subject to debate. The quantitative importance of breast-feeding in prolonging inter-birth intervals is, however, well established. It might be observed in this connection that relatively long birth intervals are found in contemporary populations in the Indian subcontinent in rural areas where conscious fertility control is reported or thought to be insignificant. Studies in Bangladesh and in Bihar have indicated this, though the proximate determinant responsible has only been suggested as breast-feeding in each case.[9]

What has by now been established by these historical studies is that fertility swings and fluctuations were common. These can be related more often to the recovery from crisis (wherein disease or separation may have physically depressed fertility) than to longer-term planning decisions. The latter, however, cannot be ruled out, and in the possibly exceptional case of Japan it is clearly shown that families regarded children as economic goods whose presence might hinder or help the family's economic circumstances, upward mobility being easier for children of smaller families.[10] All this sounds very modern. It has not yet been established, as far as I know, that marriage or child-bearing were delayed deliberately when economic crisis loomed, as is now fairly well documented for the period of the post-Revolutionary Chinese famine,[11] and as was originally documented under less severe scarcity conditions in the pioneering study of Devonian villages in England.[12]

Pasternak documents changing incidence of uxorilocal marriage dependant on changing labour demand requirements in rural China: the theory is ingenious; the regulatory mechanism is more immediate than in the case of fertility choice where the labour supply is being determined some fifteen years in advance.[13] As in the case of Europe, the immediate pressure on the family budget is the most convincing reason for conscious marital or fertility decisions. In the absence of modern birth control techniques, and under normative pressures for early marriage, regulation is unlikely to be exact. But to assume it non-existent is, to my mind, inconsistent with what we know about decision-making in peasant societies. To put the point as conservatively as possible, there is enough evidence of conscious fertility choice in pre-modern Asian societies to question the view that the well-documented fluctuating fertility rates were caused by exogenous factors such as the biological effects of starvation. Historical oriental fertility was neither universally high, or universally static; nor, I suspect, was it universally uncontrolled.

Historical oriental *mortality* is less easily diagnosed. This is largely due to the nature of mortality itself, complicated as it is by being both age and sex-specific, and with an immense variety of proximate causes (registered, if recorded at all, as categories of disease) in the pre-transition era. It is clear that the experience of large short-term fluctuations, that is periodic crises, was the general rule of the mortality regime, exactly as it was in Europe. Death rates might double or more in the course of a year (i.e. the difference between peaks and troughs is often 100 per cent, and this can be true of infant as well as total mortality). The yearly fluctuations documented in the current volume by Dyson for Berar are paralleled by data for nineteenth century Japan and the Philippines, eighteenth-century England and France.[14] The crises are both epidemics and famines, and as we are becoming increasingly aware, the two interrelate. It would require longer series of data and clear criteria of analysis for a meaningful comparison to be made between populations in respect of the relative severity or frequency of such crises. It has sometimes been argued that pre-modern populations increased until a mortality crisis annulled the accumulated growth: hence over the long-run population growth was zero. But the examination of any series of death statistics indicates short-run fluctuations of considerable amplitude, underlying which there is a level or trend of mortality which arguably reflects the endemnicity of disease and the average state of undernourishment that would afflict three-quarters of the population (in historical Asia as in historical Europe, and as in much of Asia today). Unless one understands the latter phenomenon, one understands little: the really major crises, like the Tempo famine or the influenza pandemic are, in comparison, relatively rare. It is clear from census data that oriental populations were capable of growth spurts up to sustained rates of one per cent per annum lasting a quarter of a century or more: we have evidence from India, Burma, Japan; in the cases of Indonesia and the Philippines the growth could have been well over one per cent. What we need to know is whether, during these periods, the base-line level of mortality was falling (perhaps to re-establish a relatively low level previously attained, just as in eighteenth-century England mortality gradually declined back to the levels achieved in the early seventeenth century); or whether the amplitude or frequency of the short-run crises were becoming less. *A priori* the latter seems unlikely as short-run crises are most often related to harvest failure, to combat the effects of which one needs at least good storage and distribution (with or without enhanced surpluses) none of which was present in Asia until the twentieth century (or a little earlier in Japan). Indeed, sharp short-run fluctuations seem to have persisted in England throughout the seventeenth and early eighteenth centuries. A third explanation of periods of increased population growth could be a secular rise in fertility (as in England of the eighteenth century). I will delay comment on this possibility until the conclusion of this chapter, but enough has already been said on fertility to indicate my views on its plausibility.

The recurring crisis that stands out both alone and as being implicated in other mortality crises is that of famine. In the modern world it is the only mortality crisis that regularly haunts the land, as in areas of Africa, or is of too recent memory for comfort, as in areas of South Asia. Presumably for this reason it has attracted much recent attention in demographic study. The view that famine is often a social rather than an ecological phenomenon has a sound intellectual history. It has sometimes not been appreciated that the implications of that view were clear to the authorities in the colonial era: that is that the problem was not so much deficient stocks of food as insufficient effective demand among local populations to purchase it. A. K. Sen has drawn attention to the inadequate understanding of the colonial authorities of British India in 1943.[15] Guz, however, in the current volume, shows clearly that the solution proposed by the authorities to the crisis in northern India in the 1890s was essentially correct, namely, to create effective demand by establishing public works programmes; and the author of the current chapter has been impressed by evidence of the same understanding in the case of the south-west India crisis in the 1870s.[16] In both cases the contemporary debate was not about what to do, but how to reduce the cost of doing it. In the process too heavy work for the half-starved beneficiaries and inadequate remuneration often resulted (as can still be documented in such projects today). The detailed demographic impact is subject to considerable controversy. The *proportional* increase in mortality is sometimes not clearly age-selective, despite the presupposition that the youngest and eldest would suffer relative neglect to a greater extent than they normally do. Nor, similarly, it seems are women more likely to be exceptionally disadvantaged. The evidence is mounting that male mortality often increases most, perhaps due to greater stress being put on the male bread-winner migrating to public works, nearby towns, or wild food resources in search of sustenance for the family.[17] One thing we can see more clearly, however, from the historical data, is that subdued fertility was experienced during a famine crisis and that this was subsequently compensated for in a surge of post-crisis conceptions and consequent births. The same pattern is documented by Kane during the late 1950s famine in China,[18] and by Owen during the devastating typhoon of the 1840s in the Philippines.[19] These demographic relationships are exactly as those now familiar to us from the study of historical Europe.

By the turn of the nineteenth century (during which most of the demographic accounts in this volume begin) a degree of epidemiological homogeneity had been attained.[20] Most diseases are known to most places (within the Eurasian world) and an extreme crisis like the Black Death would seem unlikely to occur again. Indeed it takes a disease of self-transformation (or mutation) to bring quite the same devastation, as notably in the influenza pandemic of 1918 discussed by Mills in the present volume. Less devastating epidemics will none the less recur, and cholera in particular ripped periodically through parts of Asia and Europe where its endemnicity was not adequately established. Epidemics kill adults as well as children; endemic disease usually kills children and immunizes the survivors so that adults escape (among the exceptions to this rule being tuberculosis which may lie dormant in the human until later adulthood). It may only be recently therefore that the familiar lifetable mortality pattern, derived from the experience of late nineteenth century Europe, was established:[21] previously, high levels of infant and child mortality may have coexisted with a wide range of adult mortality, a phenomenon that probably persists into the nineteenth century in Asia (and is demonstrated by the rise in specifically adult mortality, proportionally more than child mortality, during the influenza pandemic in England, as in India). At the same time enhanced natural increase (whether due to fertility rise or mortality decline or both) shifts the demographic importance of mortality from the old to the young (by rejuvenating the age structure). Taking these scenarios into consideration, there is quite wide scope theoretically for variation in crude death rates in different countries *before* the onset of economic development or the rise of modern medicine (indeed a true range from 30 to 45 per thousand for the sustained, or average, crude death rate is plausible in different countries or at different times, although the onus is still on the demographers who come up with such contrasts to convince us that their reconstruction from registration or census data has been sound).

By the last quarter of the twentieth century the homogeneity of the modern world takes on another form. The urban environment had always been a stimulant to disease transmission and a focal point for its spread throughout the rural population. Urban mortality generally surpassed rural, and there is some demographic evidence from Japan parallel to that from England and Wales;[22] again, however, I suspect some considerable variety within countries to have existed. The cleansing of urban environments in the west dates roughly from the mid-nineteenth century cholera outbreaks: the politics of the public health process resulted in much dragging of the feet of reform. The cleansing of Asian cities under colonial rule was bound to follow, and sanitary officials were vocal from Calcutta to Shanghai;[23] the infrastructural improvements that followed in the metropolitan cities at least (where the European administration lived) must have indirectly benefited wider populations than the élites. At the same time, medical interventions proceeded more rapidly through the colonies than is sometimes appreciated: smallpox inoculation and vaccination (which some authorities believe to have made a serious dent in European mortality)[24] were practised in a serious fashion in the Far East by the early nineteenth century.[25] It seems clear therefore that prior to the dramatic declines in mortality that all of Asia experienced after the second World War, there is reason to believe that some areas had sustained reduction in death rates from high to moderate levels. It is also clear that the reverse process could take place (as we noted above happened in England); or that a plateau might be reached due to the increase in a particular endemic disease inhibiting further decline. Malaria, for instance, began to establish itself more securely in Java in the mid-nineteenth century (and perhaps thereby delayed or reduced the more rapid demographic growth experienced later); malaria may also have sustained the mortality plateau achieved in Burma in the early twentieth century (after a period of more rapid demographic growth).[26]

If in a broad sense we can refer to an increasing epidemiological homogeneity, we are none the less masking the process of demographic change by this regional or national aggregation. Disease has always had both social and environmental determinants. The assumption of diffusion is usually no better than hypothesis. How much more vulnerable was the smallholder or unskilled labourer than the rest is not studied by demographers (the historical data do not usually allow it; nor, for that matter, do contemporary data for much of Asia; nor will they ever, unless demographers clamour for such study to begin). In the more specialist study of famine some social differentials have been detected. A classic case in Europe is the potato famine in Scotland, which largely occurred because landowners moved tenant farmers from potential pastures for sheep to marginal areas by the coast, thus encouraging the introduction of a productive but vulnerable monoculture. In Asia, in the Bengal famine of 1943, destitution occurred primarily among landless labour and certain traders whose prosperity depends directly on the effective demand of the rural poor — evidence of the importance of the economic 'multiplier' in spreading a famine through society. The study of fertility decline is subject to the same ambiguity. The 'diffusionists' have an easy time due to the paucity of socially (but not of regionally) undifferentiated data; everything looks like diffusion on a map. The 'structuralists', who argue that objective conditions bearing on fertility may differ for different classes at different points in time, have a hard time finding data to test their hypothesis. It has to be admitted that our understanding of these demographic data that we are now unearthing on a wider scale than ever before, is extremely shallow.

It may well appear from the foregoing that there is no straight-forward demographic pattern or demographic evolution over time that will characterize the pre-modern era in the Asian world. There are strands of similarity, that is all. Nor is there any good single explanatory model, economic or biological, that will help us understand the longer term progression of fertility and mortality in these populations of the eastern world. Neither of these conclusions is surprising. Each coincides with our experience of the western world. The immense pre-transitional variety of Europe, the local variations, the diverse century-long experiences, are being redis-covered, with the growth of sophisticated analysis, in Asia too. Previously we might have guessed this diversity to be the case, now we can be confident it is so. This is a rather weak position on which to conclude. But the honest historian has to admit that however well we may have progressed in demographic reconstructions, and however bright the future may look for painstaking archival inquiry and shrewd statistical work, our understanding of what underlies these demographic manifestations through time is very poor. It is here that the most serious intellectual challenges lie.

We used to think we could draw a model of demographic evolution in Europe as follows. Over the long pre-modern era death rates and birth rates fluctuated rapidly around a mean value that was approximately the same for both, the difference being less than five per thousand, and the levels approximately forty per thousand. During the transition death rates fell precipitously and birth rates followed on a similar course. Within half a century a regime of low birth and death rates was established, again each at similar levels. The diagram traditionally drawn is familiar and easily visualized. It was also assumed that this experience, thought to characterize Europe, would be imitated in Asia, though the evidence of an incipient decline in the birth rates was slow to appear; the latter is now, of course, almost universal (and evident in the huge populations of China, India, and Indonesia). It was also assumed that the pre-transitional birth rate in Asia must have been higher than in western Europe due to the 'universal' practice of early marriage. The logical corollary of that assumption, that needed to hold good if the demographic model were universal, would be that death rates were also higher in the pre-transition period. A priori, given the range of diseases still rampant in most of Asia, this was not difficult to believe.

We should no longer draw this model of demographic evolution. Our reconstructions of the long-term progression in demographic rates in Europe, particularly in England, prior to the nineteenth century, have indicated how misleading the model is. Prior to the transition death rates were indeed fluctuating rapidly, but they were also rising and falling in a secular fashion in long swings that might last fifty or a hundred years (between maximum and minimum). Similarly, birth rates were subject to long swings between highest and lowest points. It is true of course that neither birth rates nor death rates ever fell as low as even twice the level of post-transition era rates; but it is clearly wrong to think of long-term equilibrium at rates of approximately forty per thousand. To all intents and purposes (that is assuming that 'long-term' means a century rather than a millenium) there was no such equilibrium. We should redraw part of the notorious diagram.

At present we cannot prove that the general pattern of the old model will not apply to Asia either. But we can show that the second rather weak hypothesis that the equilibrium in pre-modern Asia (if an equilibrium existed) was established at a higher fertility level than in historical Europe is false. This far we have progressed in our knowledge without doubt. I would be prepared to proceed further than this. From the evidence considered in this volume from India, and the evidence surveyed in this chapter from other oriental countries, I would advance the hypothesis that the old model does not hold well for Asia either. I suggest that, as in Europe, there were both short-term fluctuations and substantial long-term swings (lasting fifty to one hundred years) in both fertility and mortality over the centuries preceding the current demographic transition. We will have to await more substantial demographic reconstructions to see whether this hypothesis holds.

However, as asserted above, the reconstruction of the demographic evolution and consequent revision of the demographic model, are only the first stages in our advancement of the scientific study of population. We are already making further steps in understanding the underlying causes, both biological and social, of short-term fluctuations in fertility and mortality. These latter fluctuations are understood moderately well by exploring the implications of household economics (a simple, if extreme, example being of how crisis may lead to the neglect of infants already born and the postponement of further births). What we are less able to explain are those interrelating forces, interactions between family, class, and nation, that gives rise to the long-term demographic trends. Such an explanation would not only be of historical interest. For we would do well to know whether long-term swings are likely to recur in populations that have passed through the demographic transition in the West, or in populations that are soon to complete such a transition in the East.

NOTES TO CHAPTER 10

1 E. A. Wrigley and R. S. Schofield, *The Population History of England 1541 – 1871*, Edward Arnold: London, 1981.

2 C. McEvedy and R. Jones, *Atlas of World Population History*, Penguin: Harmondsworth, Middlesex, 1978.

3 J. Hajnal, 'European Marriage Patterns in Perspective' in D. V. Glass and D. E. C. Eversely (eds.), *Population in History*, Edward Arnold: London, 1965; A. J. Coale, 'The Decline of Fertility in Europe from the French Revolution to World War II' in S. Behrman *et al.* (eds.), *Fertility and Family Planning: A World View*, University of Michigan Press: Ann Arbor, 1964; and A. J. Coale and S. C. Watkins (eds.), *The Decline of Fertility in Europe*, Princeton University Press: Princeton, New Jersey, 1986.

4 S. B. Hanley and K. Yamamura, *Economic and Demographic Change in Pre-industrial Japan, 1600 – 1968*, Princeton University Press: Princeton, New Jersey, 1977.

5 D. Morris and T. C. Smith, 'Fertility and Mortality in an Outcaste Village in Japan, 1750 – 1869', in S. B. Hanley and A. P. Wolf (eds.), *Family and Population in East Asian History*, Stanford University Press: Stanford, California, 1985.

6 G. W. Barclay, A. J. Coale, M. A. Stoto, and T. J. Trussell, 'A Reassessment of the Demography of Traditional Rural China', *Population Index*, 42 (Oct. 1976).

7 The protagonists in this debate come to grips with eloquence in the collection of essays cited in note 5 above, edited by S. B. Hanley and A. P. Wolf.

8 T. Dyson, 'The Historical Demography of Berar 1881 – 1980', chapter 6 in this volume.

9 K. Srinivasan and T. Kanitkar, 'The Contrasting Demography of Bihar and Rajasthan: findings from recent sample surveys', in T. Dyson and N. Crook (eds.), *India's Demography: Essays on the Contemporary Population*, South Asian Publishers: New Delhi, 1984; L. C. Chen *et al.*, 'A Prospective Study of Birth Interval Dynamics in Rural Bangladesh', *Population Studies*, 28:2 (July 1974).

10 See Hanley and Yamamura, cited in note 4 above.

11 P. Kane, 'Famine in China 1959 – 61: Demographic and Social Implications', paper presented at a Conference of the International Union for the Scientific Study of Population, held in Tokyo, 1984.

12 E. A. Wrigley, *Population and History*, Weidenfeld and Nicolson: London, 1969.

13 B. Pasternak, 'On the Causes and Demographic Consequences of Uxorilocal Marriage in China' in S. B. Hanley and A. P. Wolf (eds.), op. cit. in note 5 above.

14 See for example Y. Sasaki, 'Urban Migration and Fertility in Tokugawa Japan: the City of Takayama, 1773 – 1871' in S. B. Hanley and A. P. Wolf (eds.), op. cit. in note 5 above; N. G. Owen, 'Measuring Mortality

in Nineteenth Century Philippines' in N. G. Owen (ed.), *Death, Disease, and Famine in South East Asia* (forthcoming); E. A. Wrigley and R. S. Schofield op cit. in note 1 above; J. Meuvret, 'Demographic Crisis in France from the Sixteenth to the Eighteenth Century' in D. V. Glass and D. E. C. Eversely, op. cit. in note 3 above.

15 A. K. Sen, *Poverty and Famines: An Essay on Entitlement and Deprivation*, Oxford University Press: Oxford, 1981.

16 See the correspondence recorded in the British parliamentary papers: 'The Famine in South-West India', *House of Commons Accounts and Papers*, 1877:17.

17 See further the discussion in M. B. McAlpin, *Subject to Famine: Food Crises and Economic Change in Western India 1860 – 1920*, Princeton University Press: Princeton, New Jersey, 1983.

18 P. Kane, op. cit. in note 11 above.

19 N. G. Owen, op. cit. in note 14 above.

20 For an elaboration of this view see W. H. McNeill, *Plagues and Peoples*, Penguin: Harmondsworth, Middlesex, 1979.

21 This point is especially congruent with Mari Bhat's observations in chapter 4 of this volume.

22 For example in Y. Sasaki, op. cit. in note 14 above.

23 For these two specific examples see the British parliamentary papers, 'Annual Report of Sanitary Commission for Bengal', *House of Commons Accounts and Papers*, 1877:17; and the Shanghai Municipal Reports of the Public Health Department for various years in the 1930s.

24 See A. Mercer, 'Smallpox and Epidemiological-demographic Change in Europe — the Role of Vaccination', *Population Studies*, 1985:39.

25 See McNeill, op. cit. in note 20 above.

26 On Java see P. Boomgaard, 'Morbidity and Mortality in Java, 1820 – 1880: Changing Patterns of Disease and Death' in N. G. Owen (ed.) op. cit. in note 14 above; on Burma see J. Richell, 'Determinants of Demographic Change in Colonial Burma', Ph.D. thesis in preparation, School of Oriental and African Studies, University of London.

For Product Safety Concerns and Information please contact our EU
representative GPSR@taylorandfrancis.com
Taylor & Francis Verlag GmbH, Kaufingerstraße 24, 80331 München, Germany